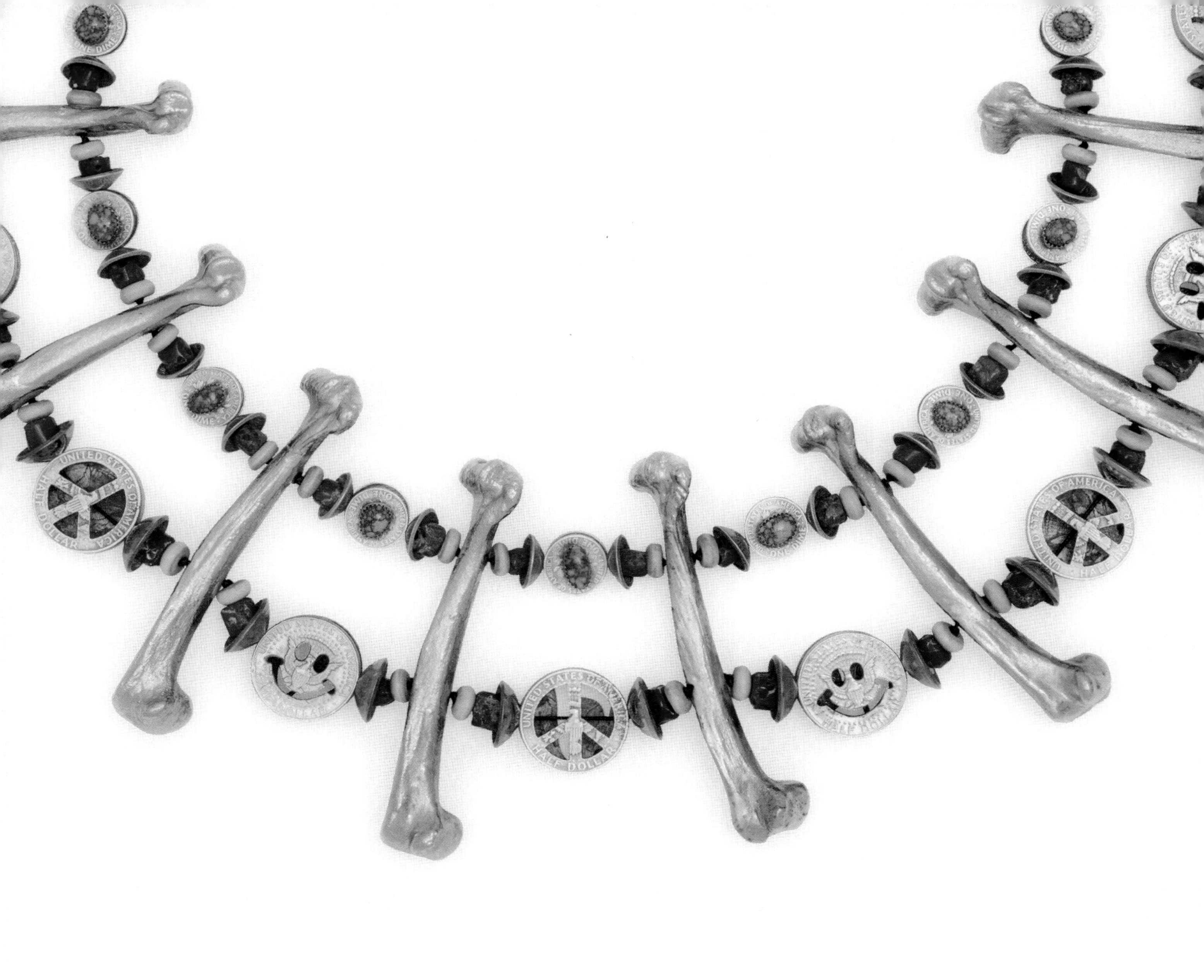
UNITED STATES OF AMERICA
HALF DOLLAR
ONE DIME

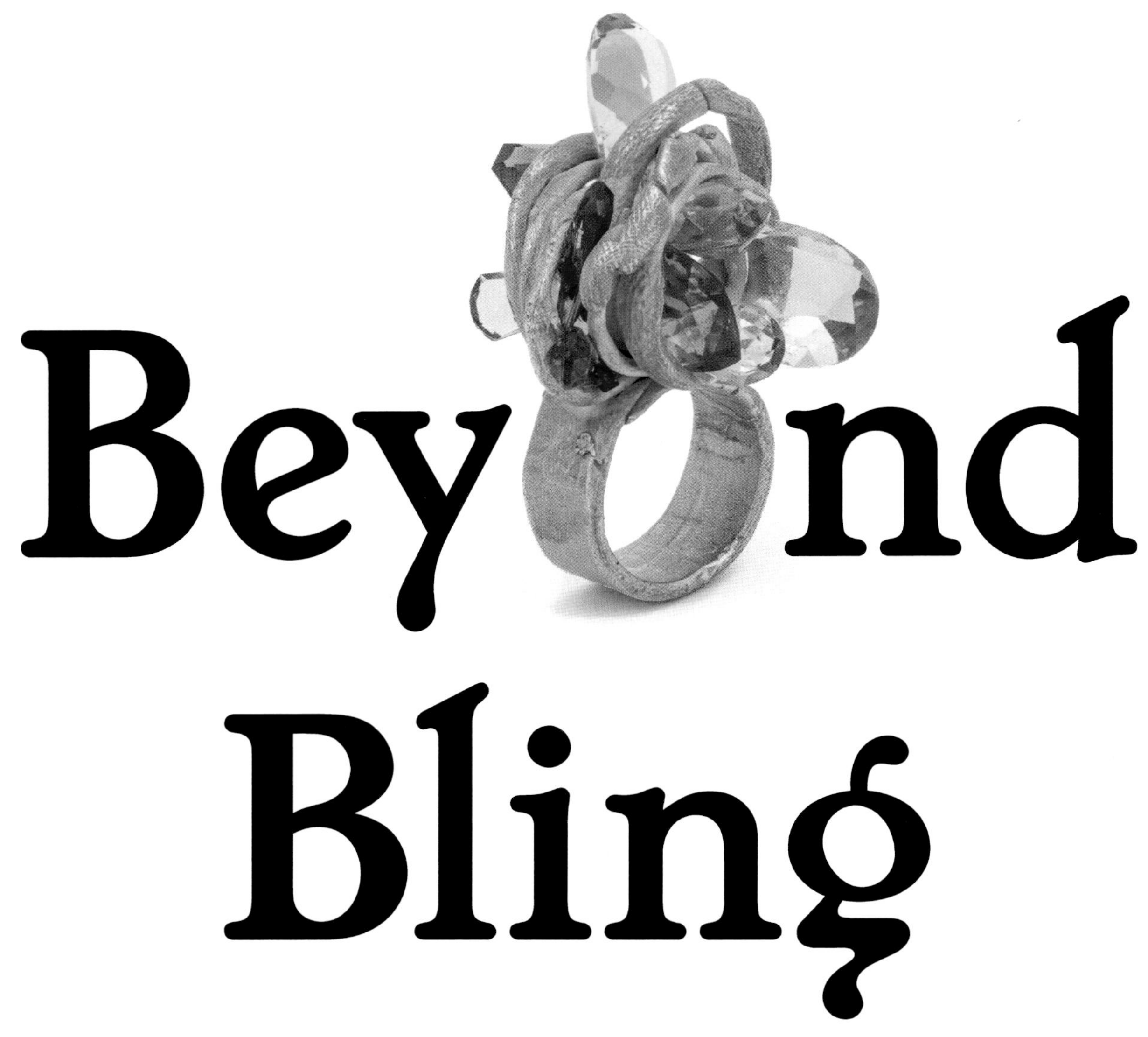

Beyond Bling

Rosie Chambers Mills & Bobbye Tigerman

Contemporary Jewelry from the Lois Boardman Collection

With essays by

Helen W. Drutt English • Blake Gopnik • Benjamin Lignel
Rosie Chambers Mills • Bobbye Tigerman

Los Angeles County Museum of Art
DelMonico Books • Prestel Munich, London, New York

Contents

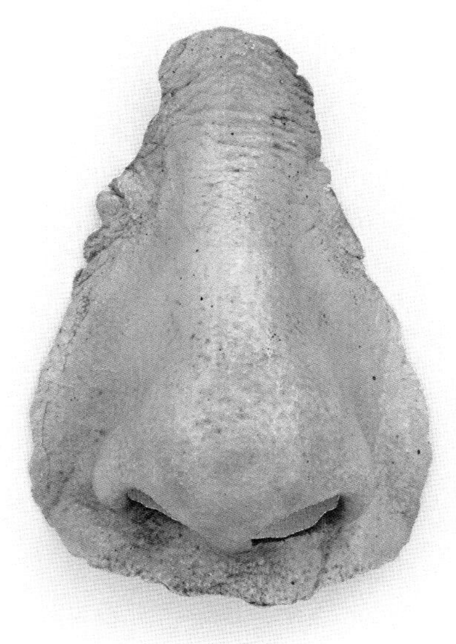

Foreword

Michael Govan

CEO and Wallis Annenberg Director
Los Angeles County Museum of Art

It gives me great pleasure to present *Beyond Bling: Contemporary Jewelry from the Lois Boardman Collection* at the Los Angeles County Museum of Art (LACMA). Lois and Bob Boardman have been staunch advocates of LACMA for decades, as both donors of important works of art and longtime supporters of the museum, and I am thrilled to acknowledge them and their unprecedented gift of contemporary studio jewelry. Distinguished by great depth, breadth, and quality, it represents the full spectrum of independent jewelry making in the late twentieth and early twenty-first centuries, and in one stroke vaults LACMA's jewelry collection to the top ranks in the country.

The Boardman collection comprises more than three hundred objects made primarily by jewelers from the United States, Europe, Australia, and New Zealand, and is the product of over three decades of judicious collecting. It follows the rise of the studio jewelry movement from the late 1960s to the present, a movement distinguished by individual practice, an emphasis on innovation, a critical engagement with craftsmanship, and an ability to convey complex ideas. As such, it perfectly complements LACMA's rich holdings of international studio ceramics, glass, and turned wood. It also resonates with countless other objects, both ancient and contemporary, in the museum's broader encyclopedic collection.

The extensive nature of the Boardman collection will allow us to exhibit it in a variety of ways, whether as thematic displays, as in this first installation, or in focused overviews of individual artists. The concentration of pieces made by jewelers working in proximity, particularly in California, the Pacific Northwest, Germany, Switzerland, the Netherlands, and Italy, enables us to show how communities of jewelry artists developed and contributed to the larger movement. And just as Lois and Bob had hoped, their donation has already spurred several other collectors to gift significant jewelry to the museum, further reinforcing LACMA's important new role as a leader in this exciting field.

I am deeply grateful to the many individuals and organizations that helped us realize this project—most especially to Lois and Bob, who additionally contributed to the care, research, and interpretation of the collection. I wish to also thank the Pasadena Art Alliance, the Society of North American Goldsmiths (SNAG), the Rotasa Foundation, Typecraft, the John and Robyn Horn Foundation, and LACMA's Decorative Arts and Design Council for their generous support of the exhibition and this publication.

Finally, I would like to commend curators Rosie Chambers Mills and Bobbye Tigerman for their illuminating research and thoughtful approach to integrating the collection with the museum's wider holdings. Most of all, I am delighted to share this wonderful new resource with LACMA's local and international audiences, who will benefit from its richness for years to come.

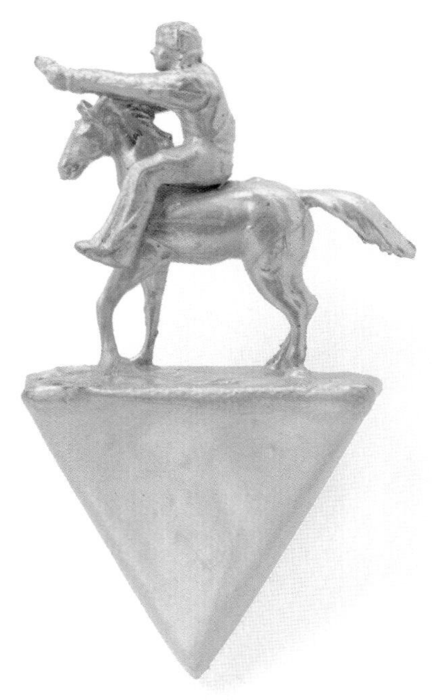

Vaughn Stubbs, *Horse and Rider* brooch, 1987

Introduction

Rosie Chambers Mills & Bobbye Tigerman

When collector Lois Boardman wore her gold nosepiece by German jeweler Gerd Rothmann to the supermarket, fellow customers averted their gaze. It was too strange and, she supposed, may have appeared to be a prosthetic (fig. 1). Of course, the piece is not a false appendage; it was made using an impression of Boardman's real nose taken with the help of her dear friend and ceramist Ralph Bacerra. Rothmann's "body prints" are intended to give the wearer the feeling of something bespoke, something so special they identify with it completely.[1] While Rothmann certainly achieved this for Boardman, the chosen body part clearly had a powerful impact on viewers as well. Although unsuspecting shoppers probably could not recall the golden nose worn by sixteenth-century astronomer and nobleman Tycho Brahe (who lost his own nose in a duel),[2] nor surviving examples in metal and ivory worn by other disfigured aristocrats from the period,[3] their first encounter with Boardman's *Die Goldene Nase* of 1988 probably was informed by having seen such medical prostheses, albeit of the more modern and modest variety.

Much has changed since Boardman mailed an impression of her nose to Munich for Rothmann to work into something extraordinary, however. We might expect a different reaction from people in the supermarket today, not least because the concept of bling has become so widely diffused within American culture. When confronted with *Die Goldene Nase* now, it is the removable gold dentistry—pioneered by Eddie Plein, popularized by hip-hop culture, celebrated in the 2005 hit single "Grillz" by Nelly, and currently sported by socialites and singers alike—that comes most readily to mind (fig. 2).[4] Both are glorious celebrations of precious materials customized to the individual and placed unconventionally on the body to draw attention to the wearer.

The Boardman nosepiece also can be seen as a droll and literal play on the difficult to translate German idiom "to earn a golden nose," which means "to make a fortune."[5] "Bling" entered the *Oxford English Dictionary* in 2003 with this definition: "(A piece of) ostentatious jewellery." Used adjectivally, it means "ostentatious, flashy; designating flamboyant jewellery or dress. Also: that glorifies conspicuous consumption; materialistic." It is designated as slang, with a reference to its origins in the language of rap and hip-hop. The etymology of "bling" is "probably imitative (compare e.g. ping, ting)" and may represent "the visual effect of light being reflected off precious stones or metals."[6] Shortened from its original form "bling-bling," as in the 1999 song "Bling Bling" by BG (Baby Gangsta) of Cash Money Millionaires, "bling" has become more widely used for jewelry in general. The gold nose (like many other pieces in the Boardman collection) certainly fits the description, yet it is not limited by it. Likewise, the necessarily succinct dictionary definition belies the complexity of contemporary attitudes toward bling.

FIG. 1
Lois Boardman wearing Gerd Rothmann's *Die Goldene Nase* nosepiece (1988, see p. 220) in front of LACMA's Lynda and Stewart Resnick Exhibition Pavilion

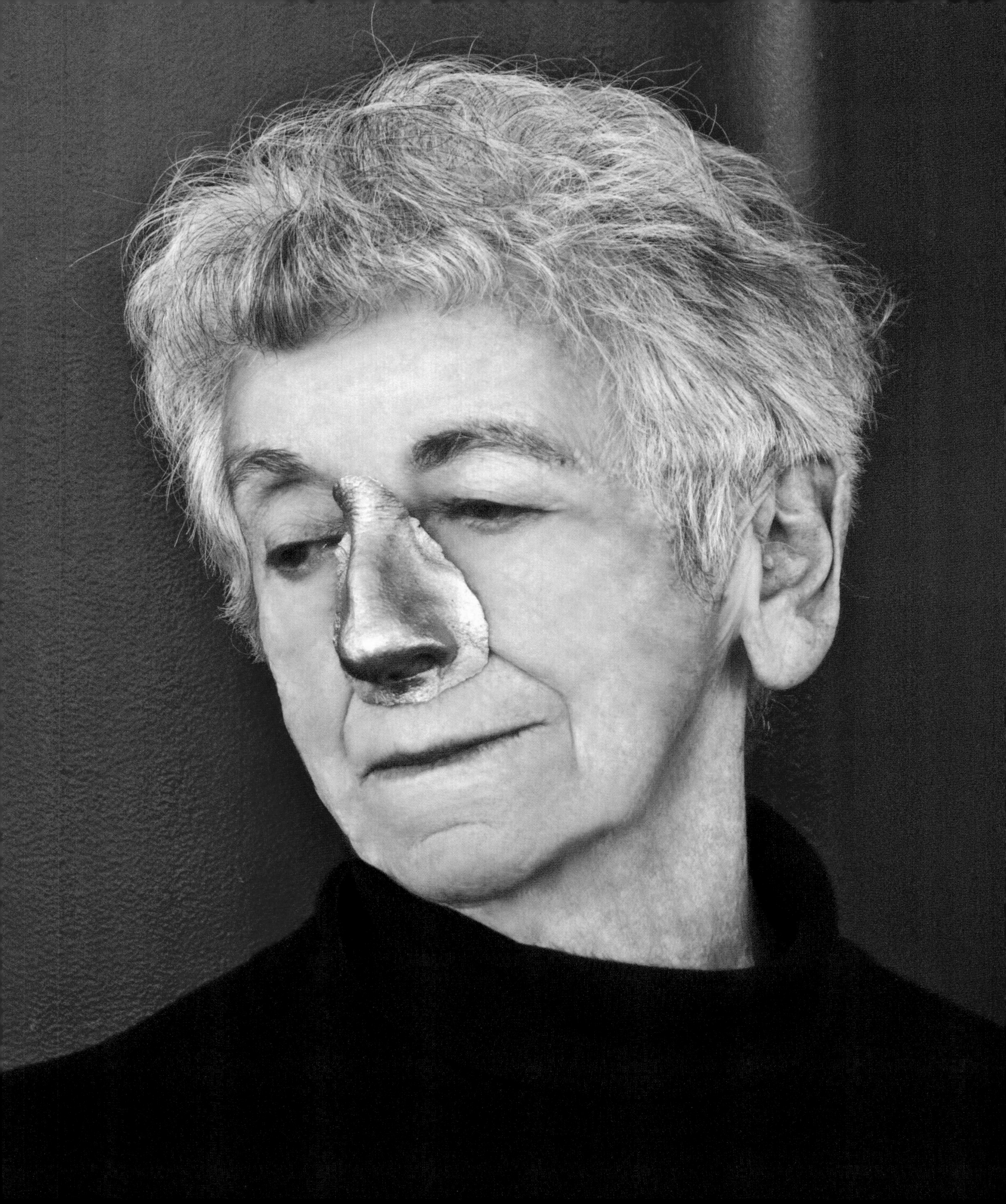

The entry of the word into the mainstream lexicon might have established what it denotes, but bling's connotations (positive as well as pejorative) continue to shift, thereby eliciting greater self-awareness in the wearing and witnessing of all jewelry and adornment. Anthropologist Susan Falls sees the exaggeration or emphasis that distinguishes bling from conventional jewelry as intended to provoke debate. By interviewing people most directly targeted by conventional diamond marketing in the United States (mostly white, middle-class Americans), she has demonstrated how their various experiences and perceptions of bling—from social climbing to social confidence—have enabled them to articulate their own attitudes about diamond jewelry. For example, one informant used bling to express why she so disliked one particular, conventional jewelry form: "With the whole rap thing and ghetto fab and hip-hop, it's different... they are playing with images and being self-conscious about it.... There's a difference between bling and tennis bracelets: tennis bracelets are oppressive and stupid, bling is more ironic and witty."[7]

In 2009 Krista Thompson placed bling and the visual culture of hip-hop within a broader historical aesthetic of surface and "shine" in the Western art tradition, demonstrating its continuity in the work of contemporary artists such as Kehinde Wiley and Luis Gispert.[8] Her 2015 book, *Shine: The Visual Economy of Light in African Diasporic Aesthetic Practice*, also identifies the dazzle of reflective materials like bling as part of an aesthetic shared by dispersed communities with African heritage around the world. Thompson has shown how bling can be read as an artistic expression of both Euro-American and sub-Saharan visual traditions. Bling thus has broadened perceptions of jewelry and shown how it participates in the visual economies of the art world; it has become something that helps us think and communicate about, as well as through, jewelry.

The advent of bling (however you understand it), along with the emergence of body ornament as a subject of scholarly consideration, has opened minds to the cultural and artistic significance of jewelry. The Boardman collection, which has been generously donated to the Los Angeles County Museum of Art (LACMA), was assembled precisely to provoke and promote conversation: to prompt the question, "*what* are you wearing?" (not "*who* are you wearing?" as the red-carpet refrain goes). In a city legendary for its glamour and glitz, this collection encourages discussions about how all jewelry communicates powerful messages besides the wearer's wealth and status. Increasingly, museums are becoming public spaces where we can understand ourselves more clearly through expanding and enriching our experiences. LACMA has gladly accepted Boardman's incitement to debate (in our post-bling world) what jewelry means to all of us beyond the conventional boundaries of adornment.

The collection comprises more than three hundred objects representing independent jewelry making in the late twentieth and early twenty-first centuries and reflects the movement's full chronological, geographical, and typological scope. The issue of what to call this jewelry is well documented and the list of names used to describe it long—various commentators have proposed "art jewelry," "auteur jewelry," "contemporary jewelry," "the new jewelry," "research jewelry," "studio jewelry," and so on.[9] We generally use the phrase *contemporary studio jewelry* because it conveys, in the most precise way, the essence of the collection: all of the works have been made in the contemporary period (since the late 1960s) and the majority by independent jewelers working in a studio environment, though we employ other phrases when their specific meanings are more fitting.

Contemporary studio jewelry emerged in the 1960s and 70s in several places simultaneously in the world—most notably in the Netherlands, Germany, Britain, and the United States—and the various concerns of its makers represent this diversity of geography. The objects in this collection also exemplify many of the movement's central precepts, namely a critical examination of the values of the conventional jewelry industry, the use of nontraditional materials and techniques, explorations of the work's relationship to the body, the expression of personal or political messages, and the potential to shock and delight.

This extraordinary collection was gathered by a longtime admirer, and advocate of, contemporary art and design in general and jewelry in particular. Born in Chicago, Lois Myer was studying in Lausanne, Switzerland, when she met her future husband, Bob Boardman, a fellow American studying abroad who was then enrolled in medical school. The couple settled in Southern California by 1959. Always avidly interested in the arts, Boardman studied ceramics with Bacerra at the Chouinard Art Institute (now CalArts). She began working at the avant-garde Pasadena Art Museum (PAM) in 1964, organizing exhibition-related and independent programming. In 1969 she joined the Pasadena Art Alliance, initially founded to support PAM and now an independent volunteer group supporting

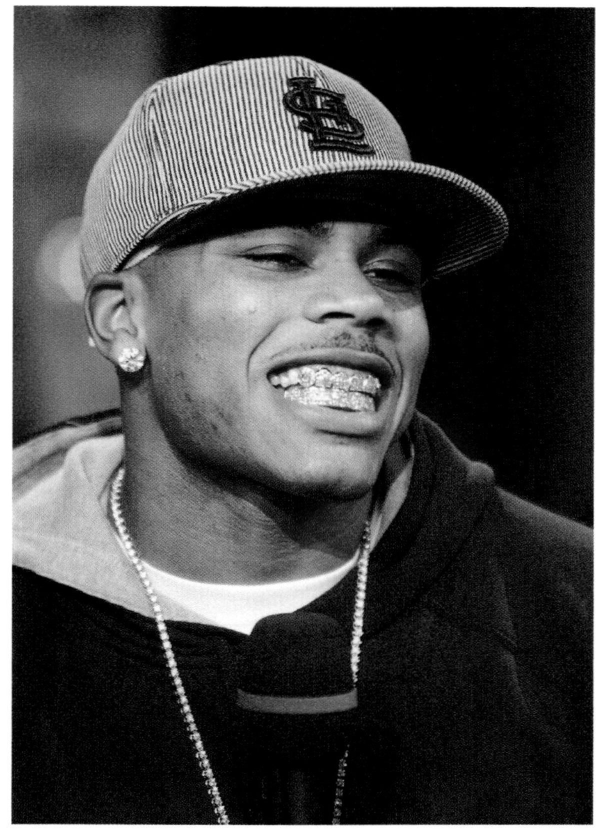

FIG. 2
Rap star Nelly appearing onstage during MTV's *Total Request Live* wearing "grillz" encrusted with yellow diamonds on his teeth, 2005

contemporary art throughout Southern California. She has served both as an active member and on its board for more than forty-five years.[10]

From 1978 to 1985, Boardman served as director of California Design, an independent nonprofit organization (at one time affiliated with PAM) that curated exhibitions and produced publications about design in California. Eudorah M. Moore, a passionate advocate for craft and design and Lois's great friend, was curator of the 1962 display and dramatically raised its profile by widening eligibility to all California designers and craftspeople (previously it had been limited to Los Angeles County), expanding press coverage, and publishing a beautifully illustrated catalogue. As a result, the triennial *California Design* exhibitions became a crucial vehicle for designers and craftspeople to show their work. Boardman served on the board and was instrumental to the operation during this time. When Moore resigned from California Design in 1978 to become crafts coordinator for the National Endowment for the Arts (NEA), Boardman assumed the role of director.[11]

In 1980 Moore invited Boardman to participate in the NEA-sponsored National Crafts Planning Project, the mission of which was "to study the needs of America's craftspeople with a plan of action and resolutions to advance the field."[12] At a project meeting at Black Mountain College in North Carolina, Boardman met the indomitable craft collector and gallerist Helen Drutt (now Helen W. Drutt English), initiating a decades-long friendship. Drutt and Boardman carried on an extended dialogue over several years about contemporary jewelry, discussing the merits and virtues of each piece through phone conversations and faxes and, later, through email

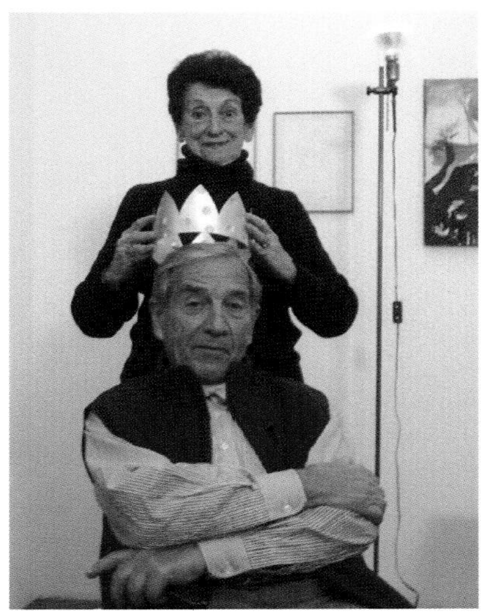

FIG. 3
Lois Boardman crowning Bob Boardman in Gerd Rothmann's Munich studio during Schmuck jewelry fair, 2012, from the series They Came to Visit Me and Crowned Themselves

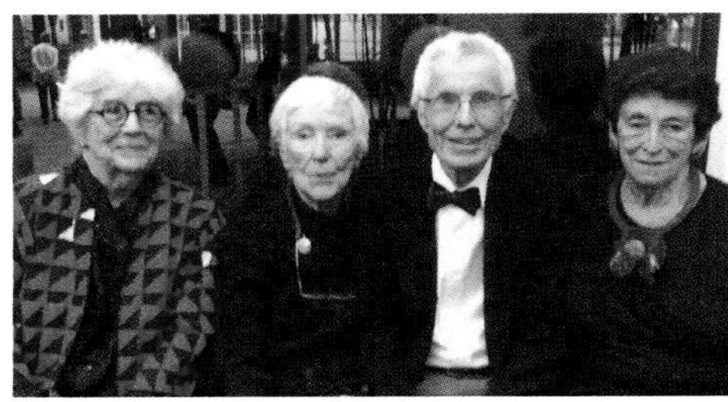

FIG. 4
Gere Kavanaugh, Eudorah Moore, Bernard Kester, and Lois Boardman at the opening of the exhibition *California Design, 1930–1965: Living in a Modern Way* at the Los Angeles County Museum of Art, October 1, 2011. Lois is wearing Robert Baines's *Neckpiece No. 26*, 2010 (see p. 209)

messages. Boardman also traveled frequently to Schmuck (fig. 3), the annual jewelry fair in Munich, and when Drutt closed her gallery in 2003, Boardman continued her collecting through a wider circle of dealers. The arc of Boardman's development as a collector is traced by Drutt herself in this volume in the essay "Between Friends," a tribute of deep respect and friendship.

Built in Los Angeles, the collection has a distinctly Western point of view, a fact that both lends it a unique character and serves as the impetus for two of the essays in this catalogue. The collection is especially strong in work by West Coast jewelers, with such prominent figures as Arline Fisch, Helen Shirk (fig. 5), and Nancy Worden represented by several works. Bobbye Tigerman uses this as an opportunity to write a history of postwar studio jewelry on the West Coast, revealing how several jewelry centers developed independently yet in concert with international developments in the field. Lois Boardman increasingly mitigated her great geographic distance from makers and galleries by using online resources to learn about and locate work. Inspired by the internet's important role in the formation of this collection, Benjamin Lignel (editor of the website and online magazine *Art Jewelry Forum*) explores the multitude of ways that new media has transformed the jewelry field, particularly its production, dissemination, consumption, and reception.

All of the essays emerge from issues raised by the collection itself, but they speak to larger concerns of the field as well. The son of a contemporary studio jeweler, art critic Blake Gopnik laments the rise of luxury-brand exhibitions and makes a passionate and compelling appeal for more thought-provoking jewelry in contemporary art museums. Rosie Chambers Mills considers the further benefits of including this material within the broader framework of encyclopedic museums. By borrowing principles and aesthetics that date back to their origins in cabinets of curiosities, Mills shows how museums can deepen existing knowledge and generate new insights by comparing visual similarities across diverse categories.

In the past decade, several museums have been fortunate to receive major private collections of contemporary studio jewelry as gifts, including the Dallas Museum of Art; the Metropolitan Museum of Art; the Museum of Arts and Design, New York; the Museum of Fine Arts, Boston; the Museum of Fine Arts, Houston; and the Rijksmuseum, Amsterdam; among others. Lois and Bob Boardman's unprecedented gift to LACMA is a gift to all of Los Angeles, providing the city and region with an unparalleled cultural resource. The collection will be the first of its kind to enter a museum on the West Coast, and its rich treasures will spark new conversations across LACMA's diverse holdings.

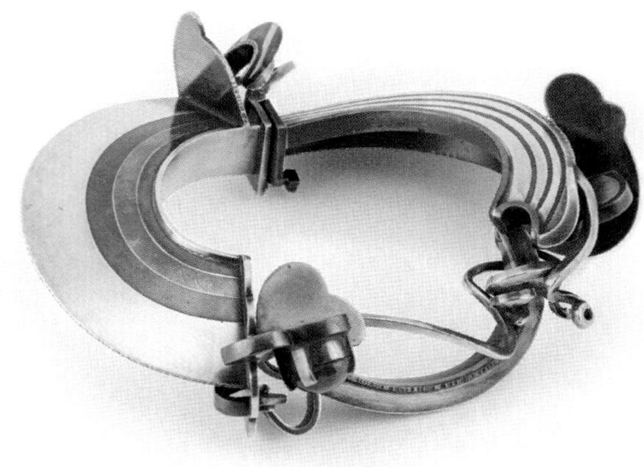

FIG. 5
Helen Shirk, *Bracelet with Agate*, 1975

Notes

1. See Gerd Rothmann, *Werkverzeichnis: Catalog Raisonné* (Stuttgart: Arnoldsche, 2009), 384–86.

2. Exhumation in 2010 confirmed Brahe habitually wore a brass, rather than a gold, nose. See National Museum Prague, "Research of the Tomb and Remains of Tycho Brahe," http://muzeum3000.nm.cz/national-museum-news/research-of-the-tomb-and-remains-of-tycho-brahe, posted November 2, 2013.

3. See Mary-Ann Ochota, "Beddingham Nose," in *Britain's Secret Treasures: Extraordinary Finds Uncovered by Members of the Public* (London: Headline Publishing Group, 2013), 65–66.

4. Regie Ossie and Gabriel Tolliver, *Bling: The Hip-Hop Jewelry Book* (New York: Bloomsbury Publishing, 2006), 84–103; *Encyclopedia of African American Popular Culture*, vol. 1, ed. Jessie Carney Smith (Santa Barbara, CA: Greenwood, 2010), 169–71.

5. Rothmann, *Werkverzeichnis*, 262.

6. See Oxford English Dictionary online, http://www.oed.com/view/Entry/257508?rskey=29tU9J&result=1&isAdvanced=false#eid, accessed February 23, 2016.

7. Susan Falls, *Clarity, Cut, and Culture: The Many Meanings of Diamonds* (New York: New York University Press, 2014), 129–57, esp. 144.

8. Krista Thompson, "The Sound of Light: Reflections on Art History in the Visual Culture of Hip-Hop," *Art Bulletin* 91, no. 4 (December 2009): 481–505.

9. Liesbeth den Besten, *On Jewellery: A Compendium of International Contemporary Art Jewellery* (Stuttgart: Arnoldsche Art Publishers, 2011), 6–15.

10. "Pasadena Art Museum: Lois Boardman," interview by Joanne L. Ratner, Oral History Program, University of California, Los Angeles, 1990.

11. Eudorah M. Moore served as curator and Gere Kavanaugh and Bernard Kester as both installation designers and exhibitors for the *California Design* exhibitions held at the Pasadena Art Museum and Pacific Design Center between 1962 and 1976 (see fig. 4).

12. John McLean (National Crafts Planning Project, National Endowment for the Arts, and National Assembly of State Arts Agencies), *A Report on the Project and Congress: July 1, 1980, through August 15, 1981* (Washington, DC: National Endowment for the Arts and National Assembly of State Arts Agencies, 1981), 3.

Selected Works

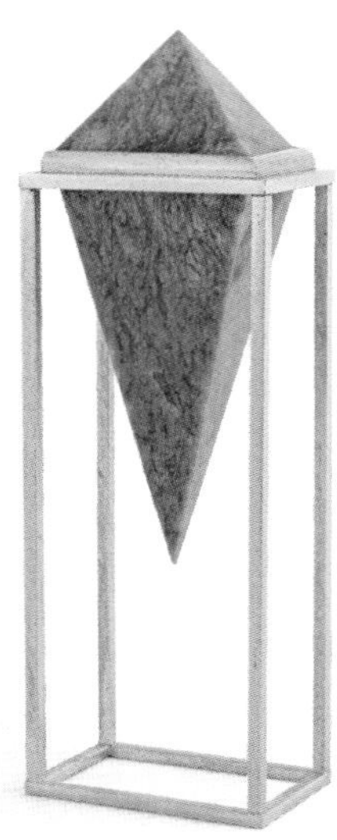

For complete object information,
please see "Checklist of the Collection" on page 208

All works are credited Los Angeles County Museum of Art,
gift of Lois and Bob Boardman

Philip Sajet, *Damocles* ring, designed 1987, made 2008

Lois Boardman wearing Nancy Worden's *Gilding the Past* necklace (2001, see p. 223) and Rena Koopman's earrings (1990, see p. 215) in front of Michael Heizer's *Levitated Mass* (2012) at the Los Angeles County Museum of Art

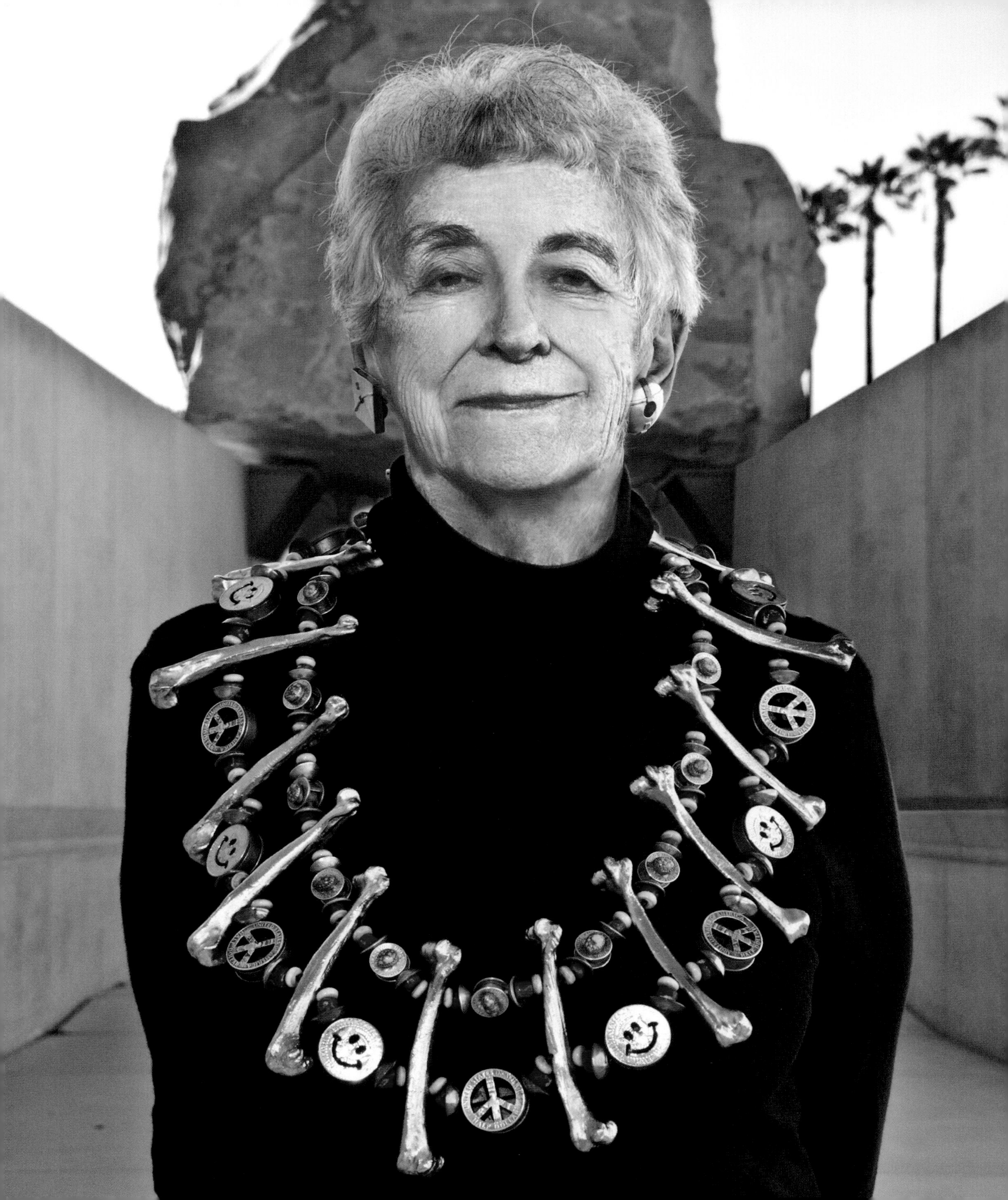

Vicki Ambery-Smith

(b. 1955, England)

***Tuscan* ring, 1988**
Silver, varicolored gold
1⅜ × ⅞ × ¾ in.

***Renaissance Farmhouse* brooch, 1989**
Silver, varicolored gold, emerald
¹¹⁄₁₆ × 2½ × ⅜ in.

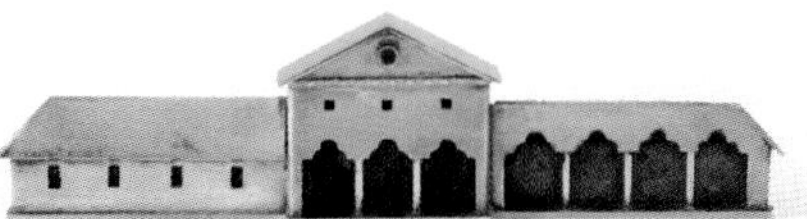

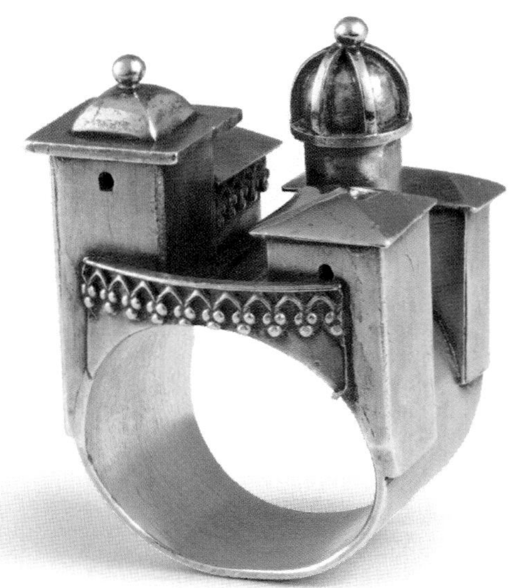

Klaus Arck

(b. 1956, Germany)

Brooch, 1986
Painted balsa, plastic filament, felt, stainless steel
1¼ × 6¾ × 1⅛ in.

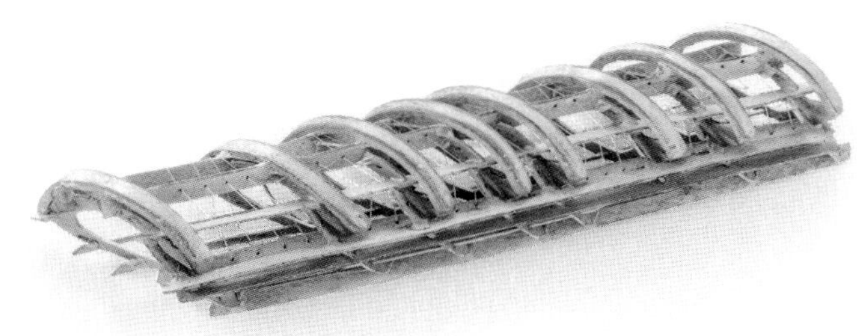

Giampaolo Babetto

(b. 1947, Italy)

***Cerchio Triangolo* necklace, 1983**
Gold, alkyd resin
5⅝ × 5⅝ × ⅛ in.

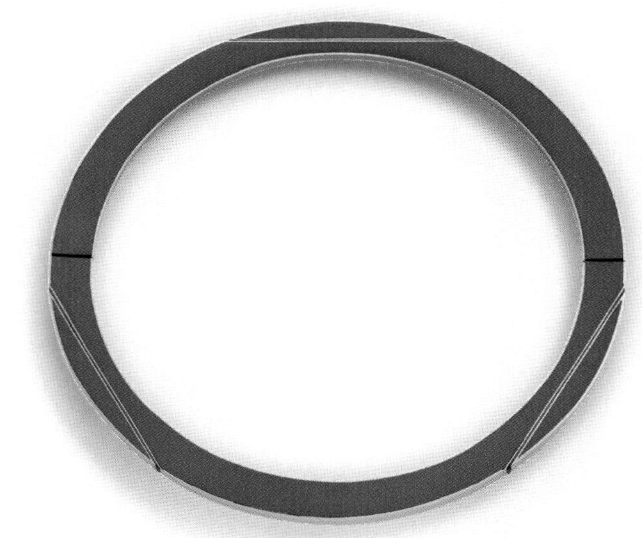

Robert Baines

(b. 1949, Australia)

***Brooch No. 122*, 1999**
From the series Bloodier than Black, 1998–present
Silver
6¾ × 5¾ × 2 in.

***Neckpiece No. 26*, 2010**
From the series Redder than Green, 2009–present
Powder-coated silver, gilded silver, styrene plastic
10½ × 7 × 3¼ in.

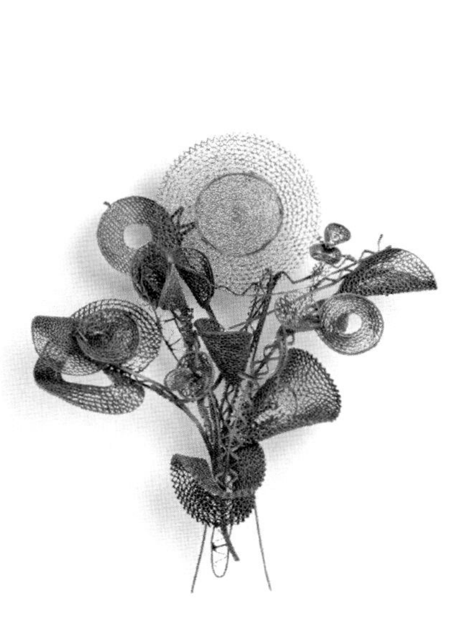

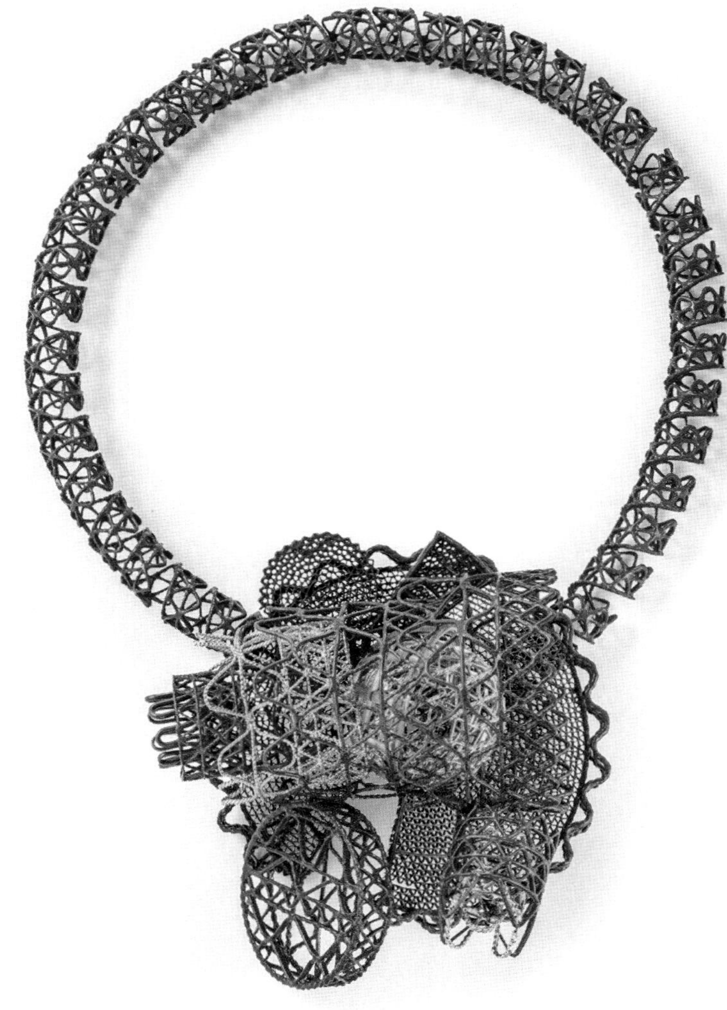

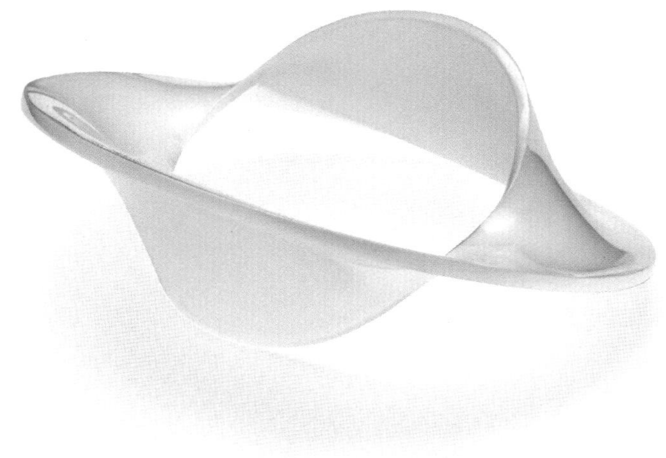

Gijs Bakker

(b. 1942, Netherlands)

***Circle in Circle* bracelet, designed 1967, this example made 1989**
PMMA
2⅝ × 4¾ × 4¾ in.

***Dew Drop* necklace, 1982**
PVC, print
19½ × 21⅝ × 1⁄16 in.

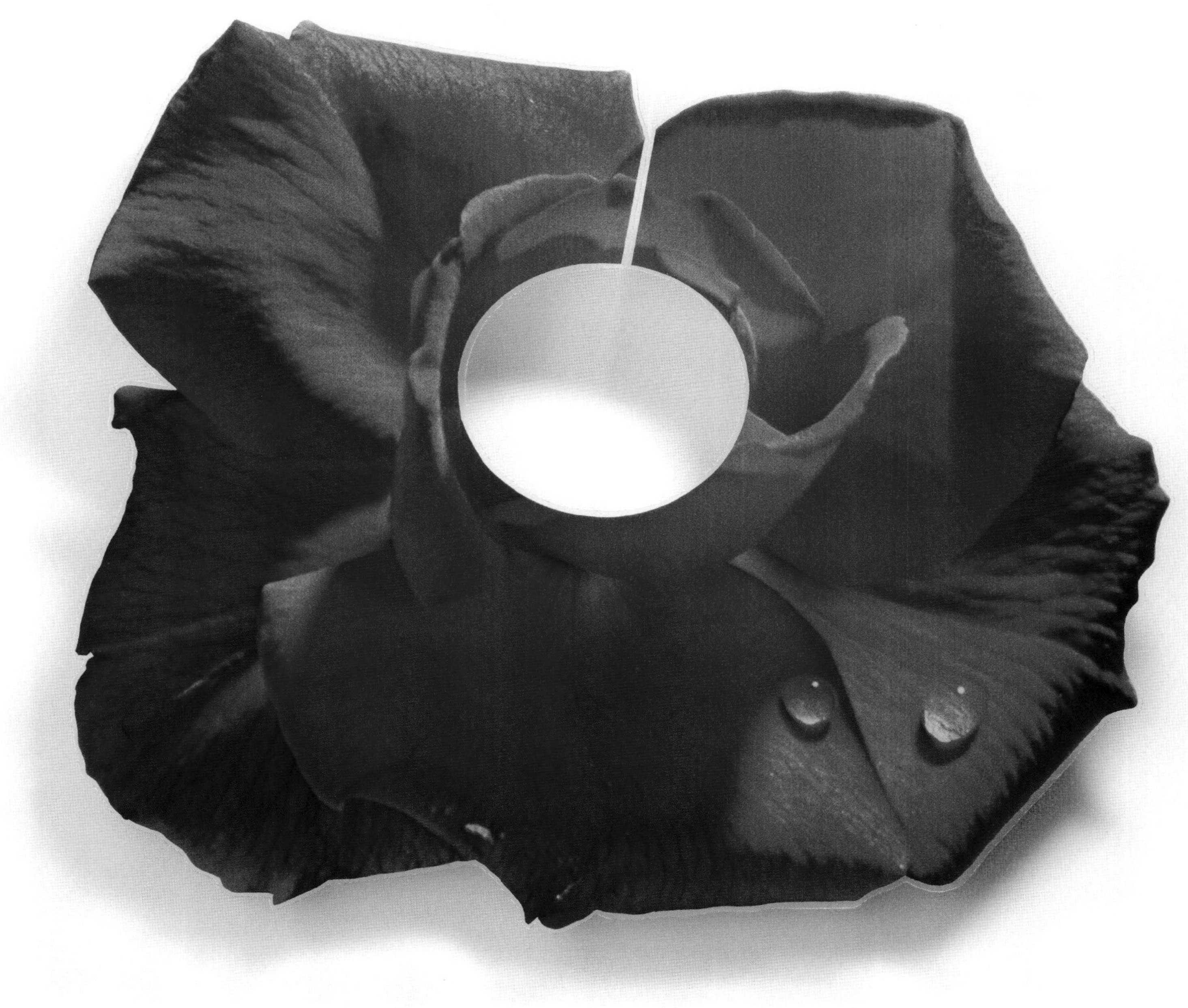

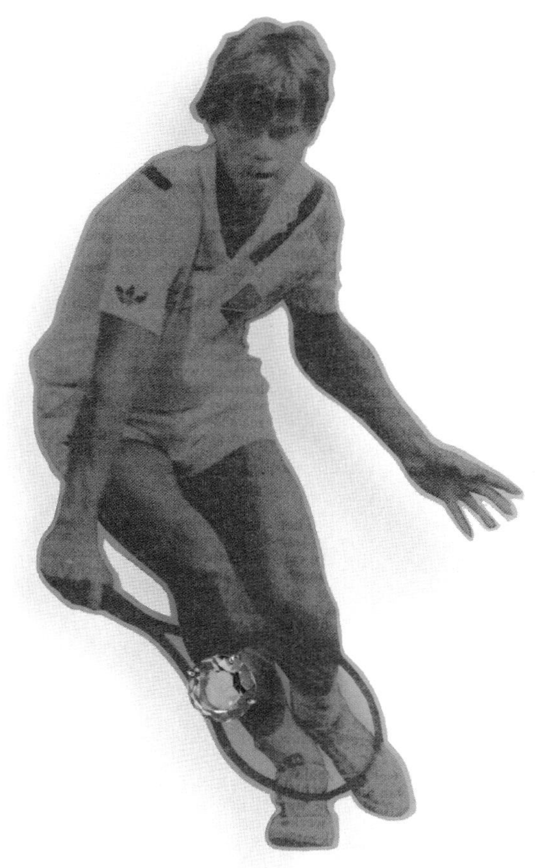

Gijs Bakker

(continued)

***Edberg* brooch, 1985**
From the series Sports Figures, 1985–91
PVC, newspaper, citrine, gold
6 ½ × 3 ¾ × ⅜ in.

***The Cry* brooch, 2010**
Number 1 from an edition of 5
Silver, diamonds
3 ⅞ × 2 ½ × ½ in.

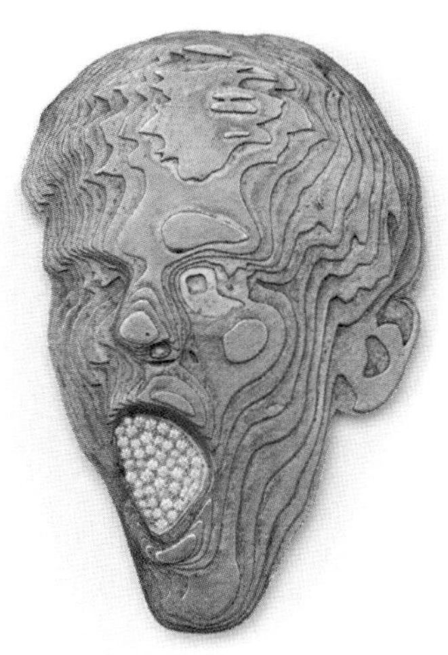

Ralph Bakker

(b. 1958, Germany, active Netherlands)

Necklace, designed 2001, made 2007
Niello on silver, silver, gold
8¾ × 8¾ × ⅛ in.

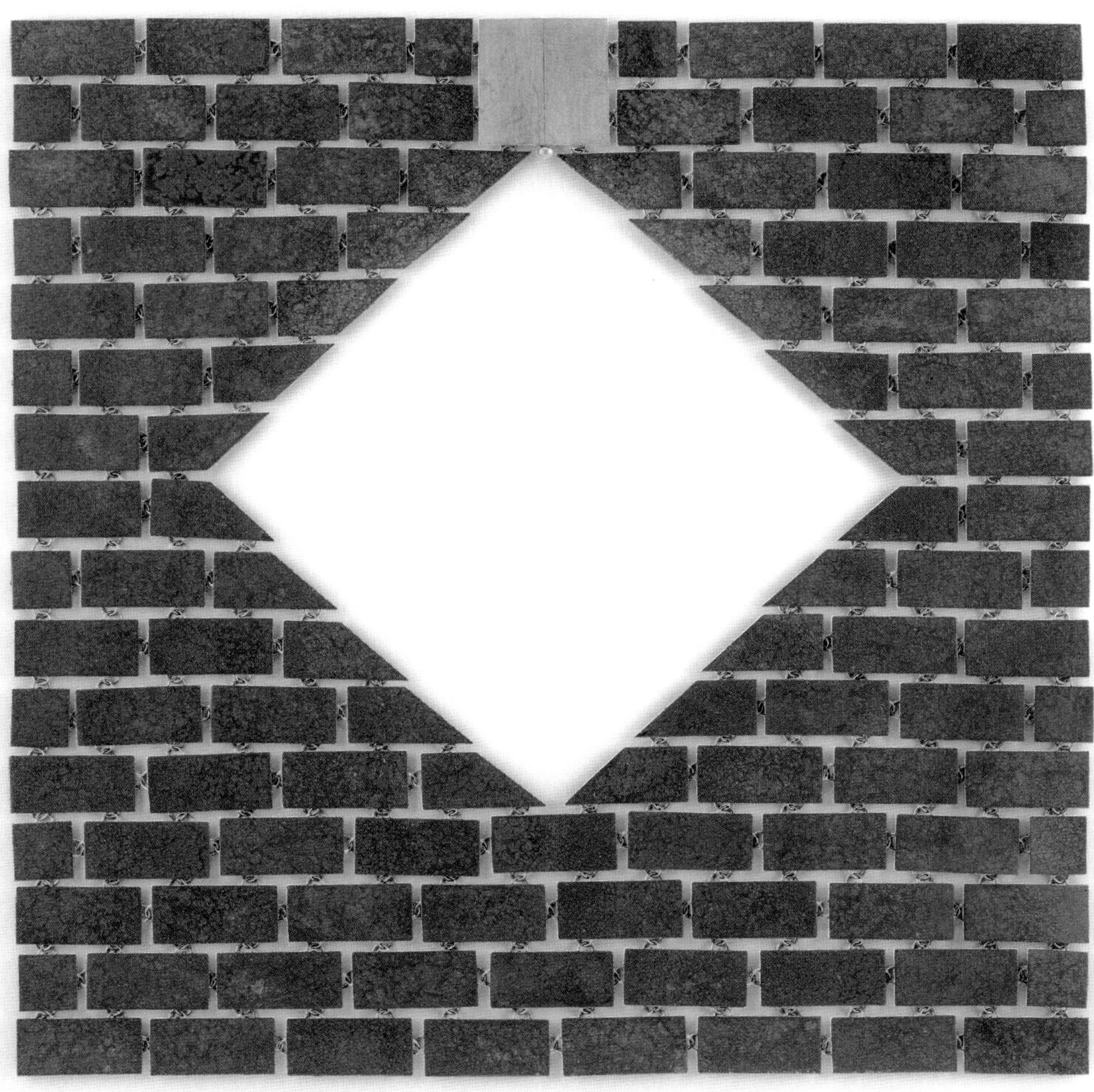

Michael Becker

(b. 1958, Germany)

***6×5×8* brooch, 1990**
Gold, synthetic spinel
⅜ × 3¾ × ½ in.

Brooch, 1999
Gold
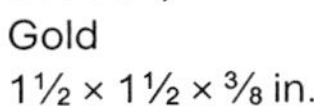
1½ × 1½ × ⅜ in.

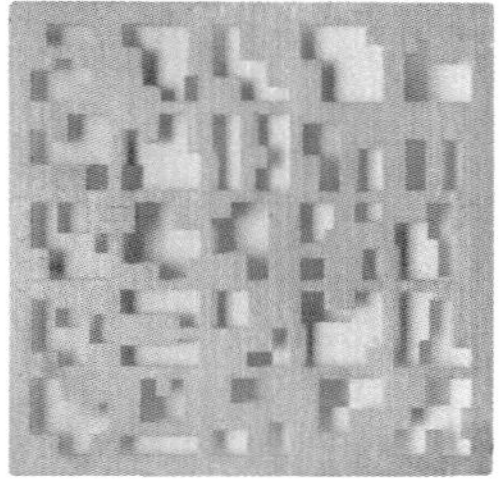

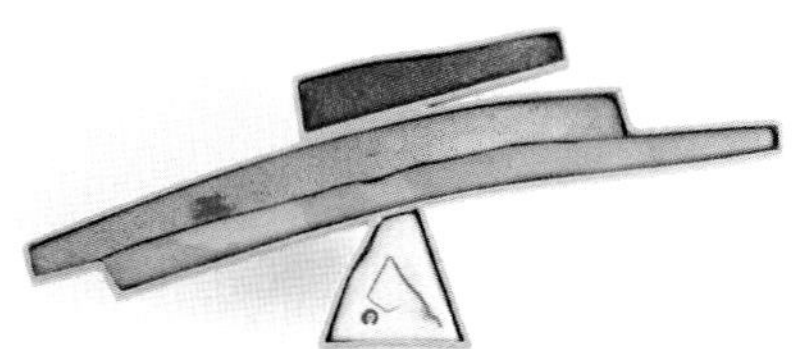

Jamie Bennett

(b. 1948, United States, active New York)

***Coloratura II* brooch, 1984**
Number 2 of 23 in the series
Coloratura, 1984–85
Enamel on copper, silver
1½ × 3¾ × ¼ in.

***Petrossa Neckpiece 4*, 1990**
Number 4 of 5 in the series
Petrossa, 1989–90
Enamel on copper, gold
13⅛ × 6¼ × ½ in.

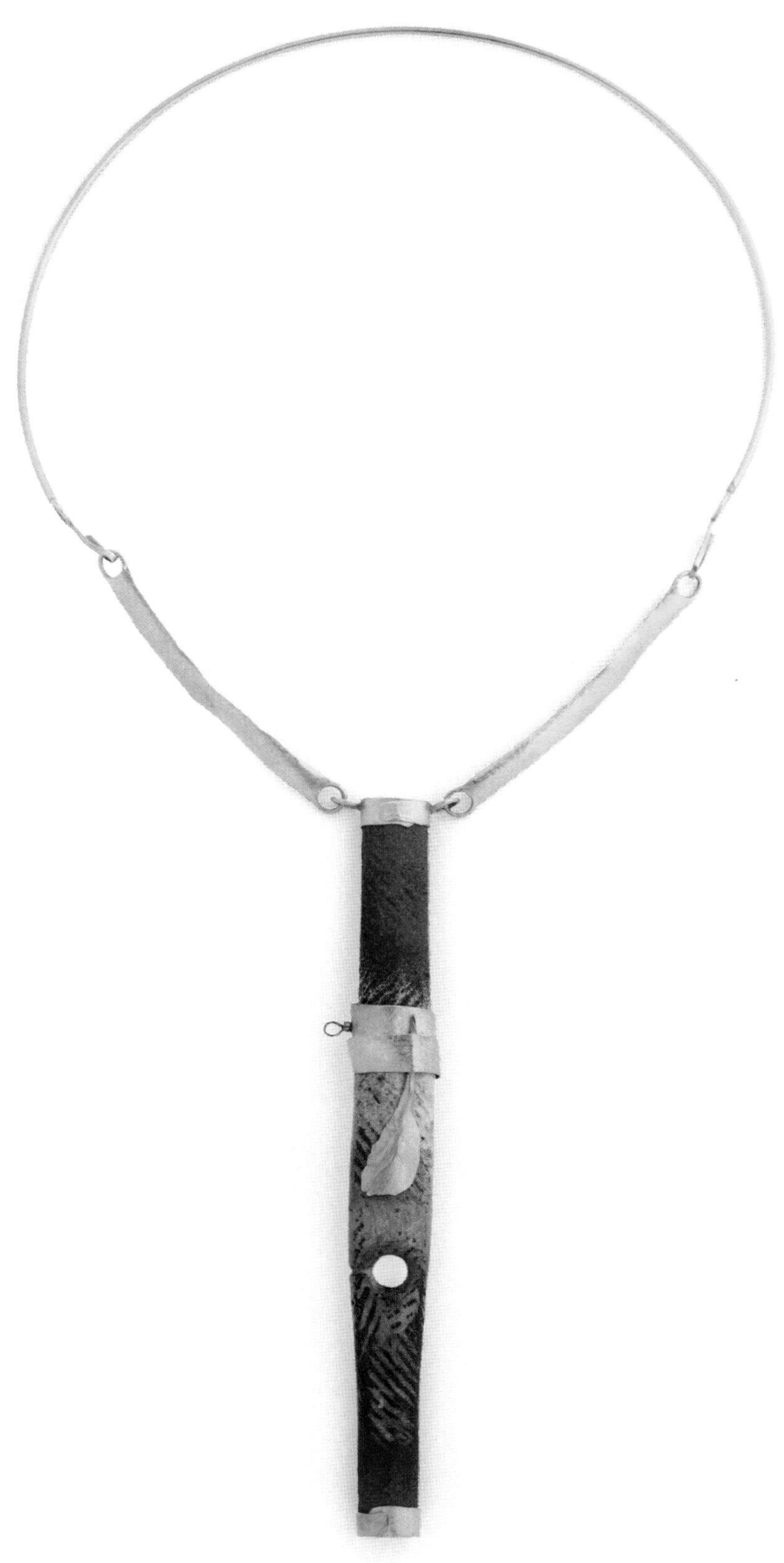

David Bielander

(b. 1968, Switzerland, active Germany)

***Dung Beetle* brooch, 2007**
From an edition of 50
Stainless-steel teaspoon, gold
2¾ × 1⅞ × 1 in.

***Koi* bracelet, 2013**
Leather, thumbtacks, silver
5¼ × 5 × 4½ in.

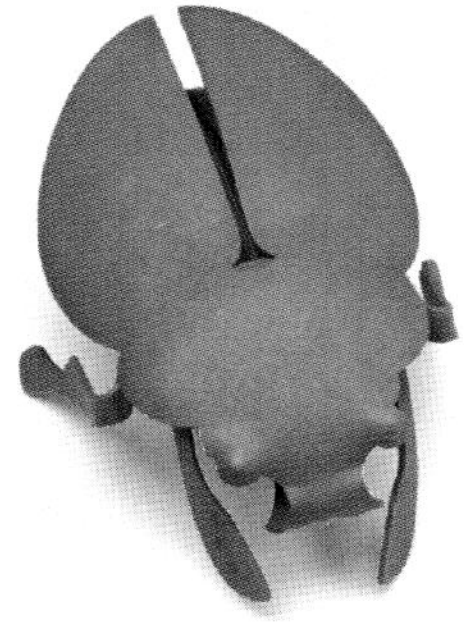

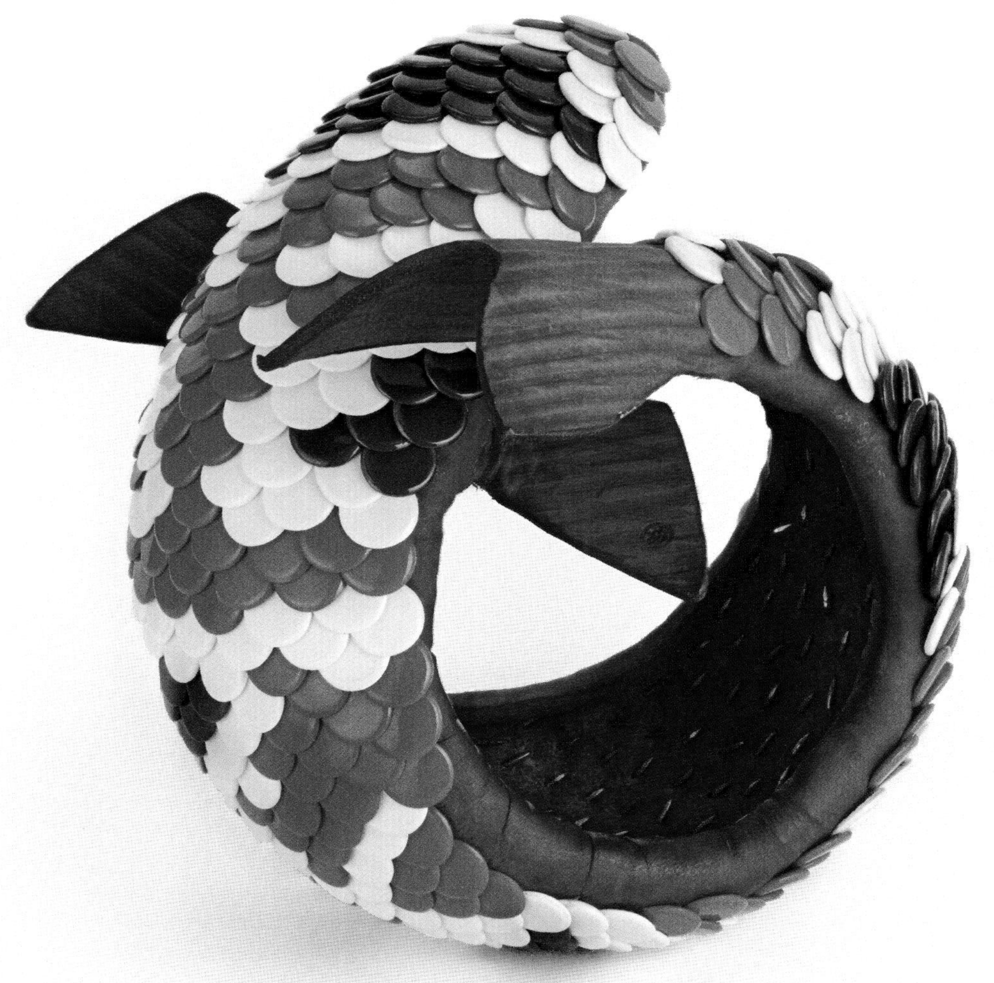

Manfred Bischoff

(1947–2015, Germany, active Italy)

***Physikalisches Modellbild* brooch, 1987**
Silver with gilding, coral
3 1/16 × 3 1/4 × 5/8 in.

Ring, 1993
Gold, mirror, coral
1 3/4 × 1 1/2 × 1 1/4 in.

***Zoological* brooch, 1998**
Gold
3 5/8 × 2 3/4 × 1 1/4 in.

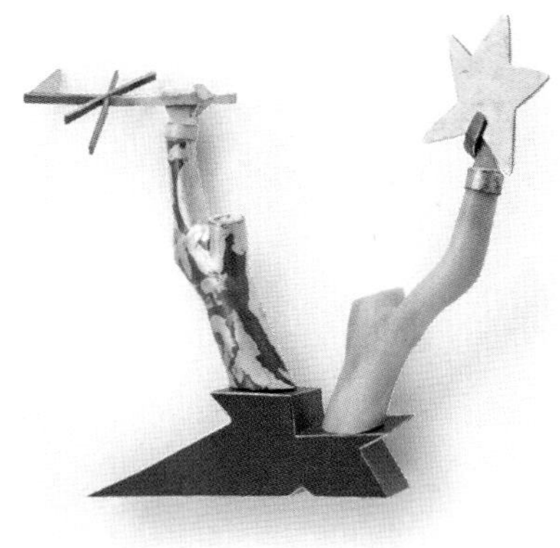

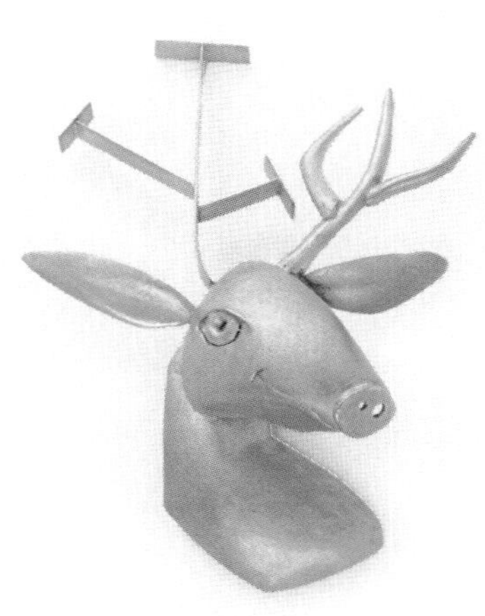

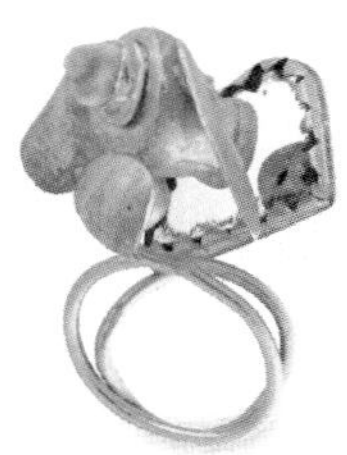

Manfred Bischoff

(continued)

***Night Visitors* ring, 1998**
Gold, coral
1¼ × 1½ × 1 in.

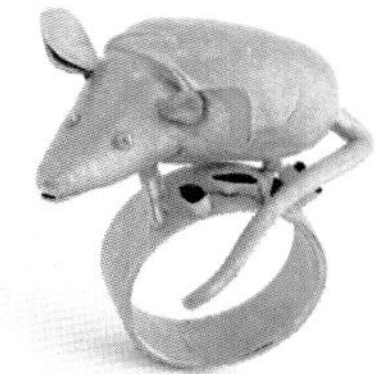

***Night Visitors* drawing, 1998**
Ink and graphite on board
11½ × 8¼ in.
Photographed with ring

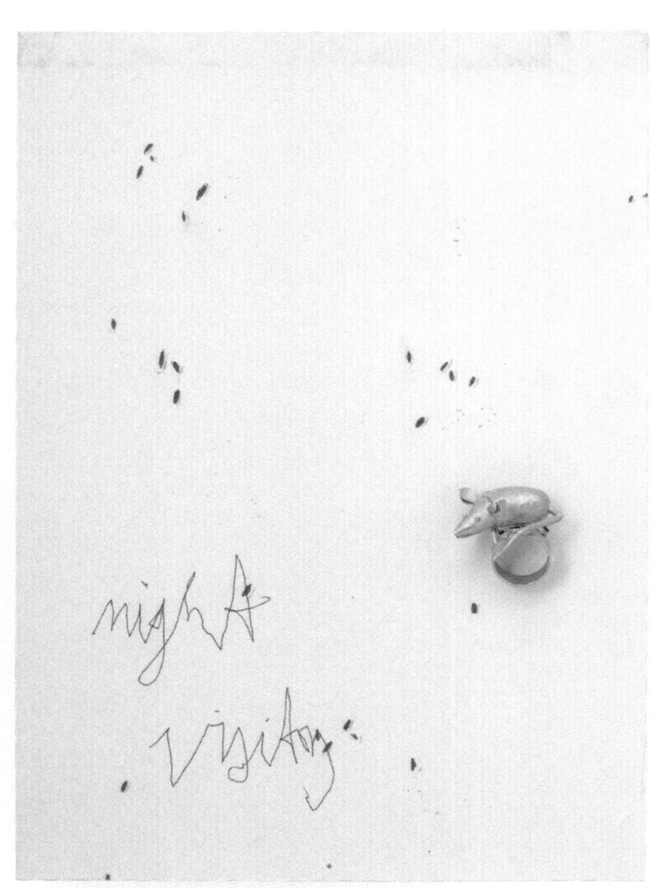

***Pomme de Terre–Pathètique–Tragique* brooch, 2002**
Gold, coral
2 × 2⅞ × ⅞ in.

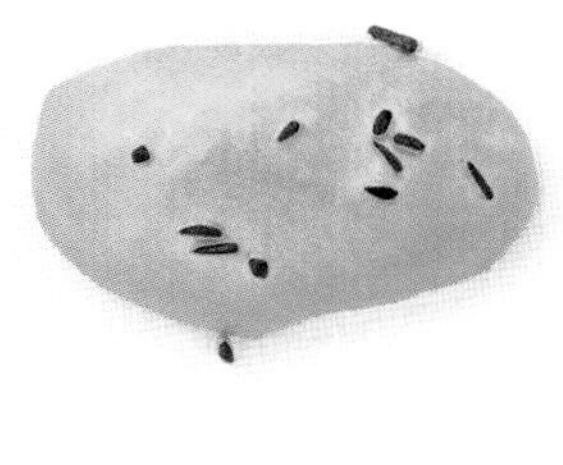

***Pomme de Terre–Pathètique–Tragique* drawing, 2002**
Ink and graphite on paper mounted on board
11½ × 8¼ in.
Photographed with brooch

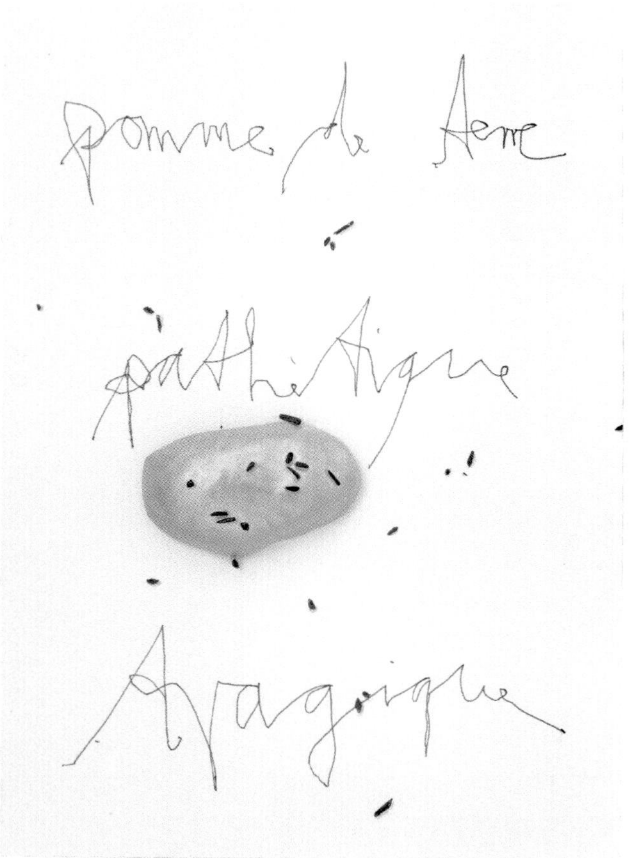

Liv Blåvarp

(b. 1956, Norway)

Necklace, designed 1991, this example made 2001
Birch, alkyd paint, brass, elastic cord
9 ½ × 8 × 3 in.

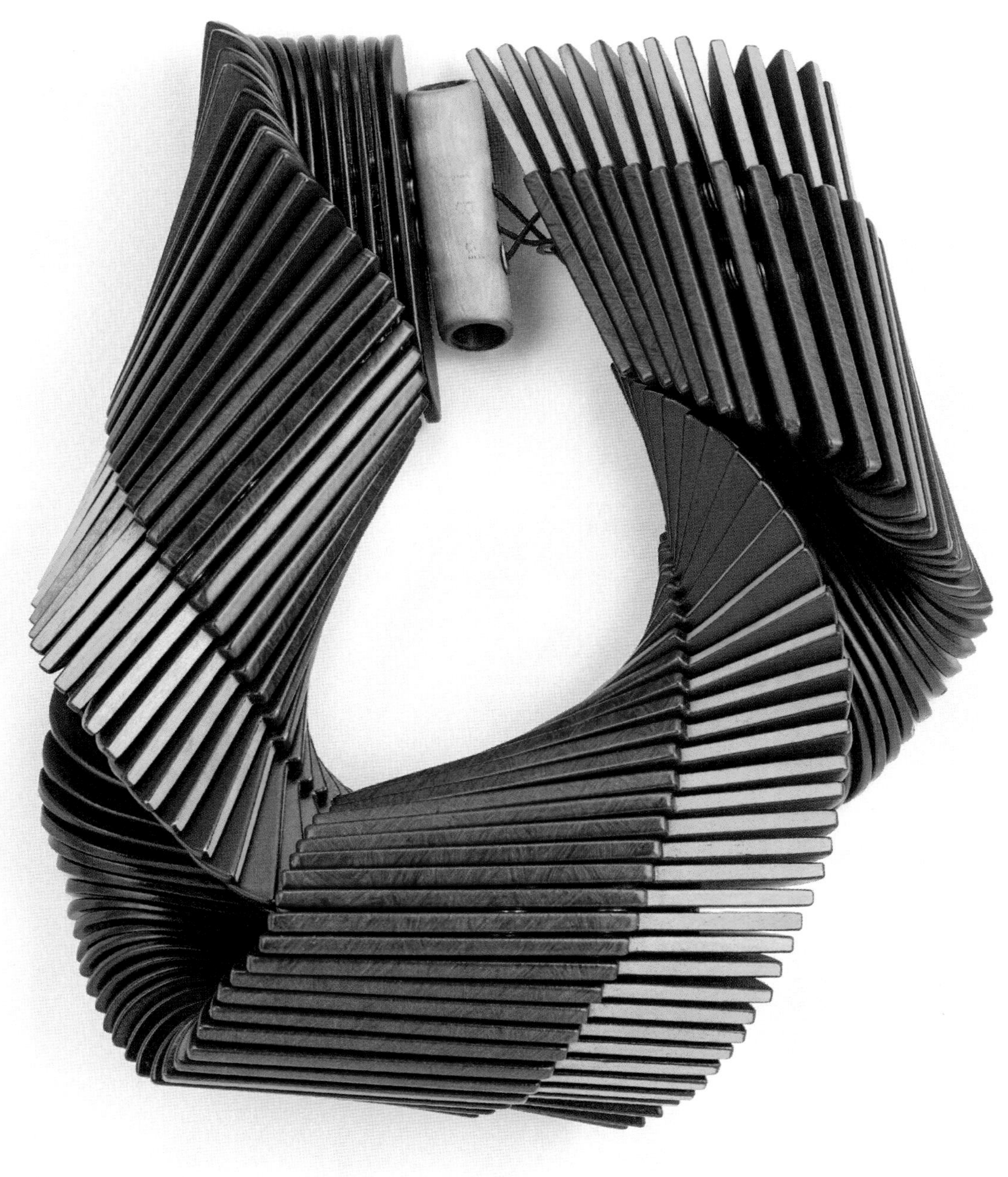

Helen Britton

(b. 1966, Australia, active Germany)

***Last Bird* brooch, 2006**
Silver, onyx, glass, paint
4 × 3¾ × ¾ in.

***Strange* brooch, 2006**
Silver, glass
1½ × 2¼ × ⅝ in.

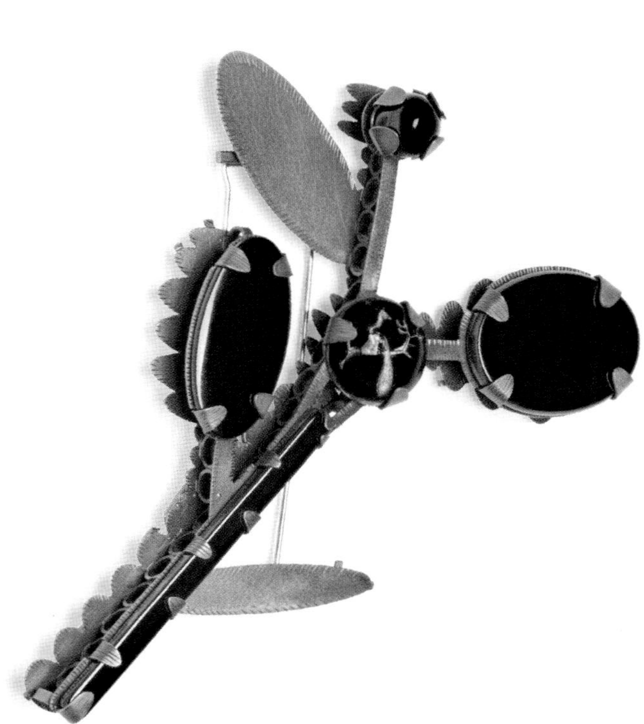

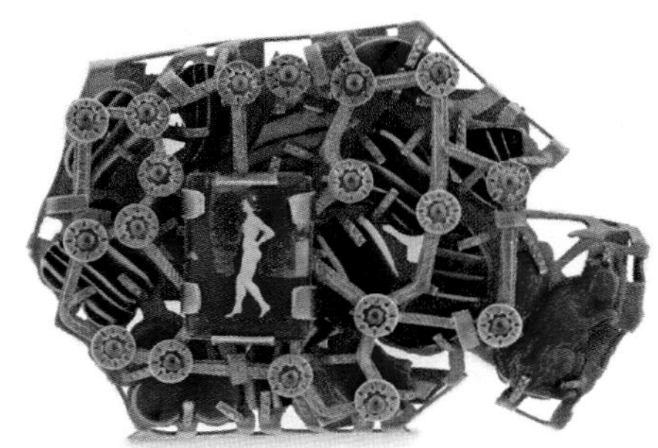

Doug Bucci

(b. 1971, United States, active Pennsylvania)

***Islet* | *Stainless* bracelet, designed 2010, this example made 2012**
Number 6 from an edition of 20, plus 2 artist proofs
Bronze-infiltrated stainless steel
4 ¼ × 4 ¼ × 1 in.

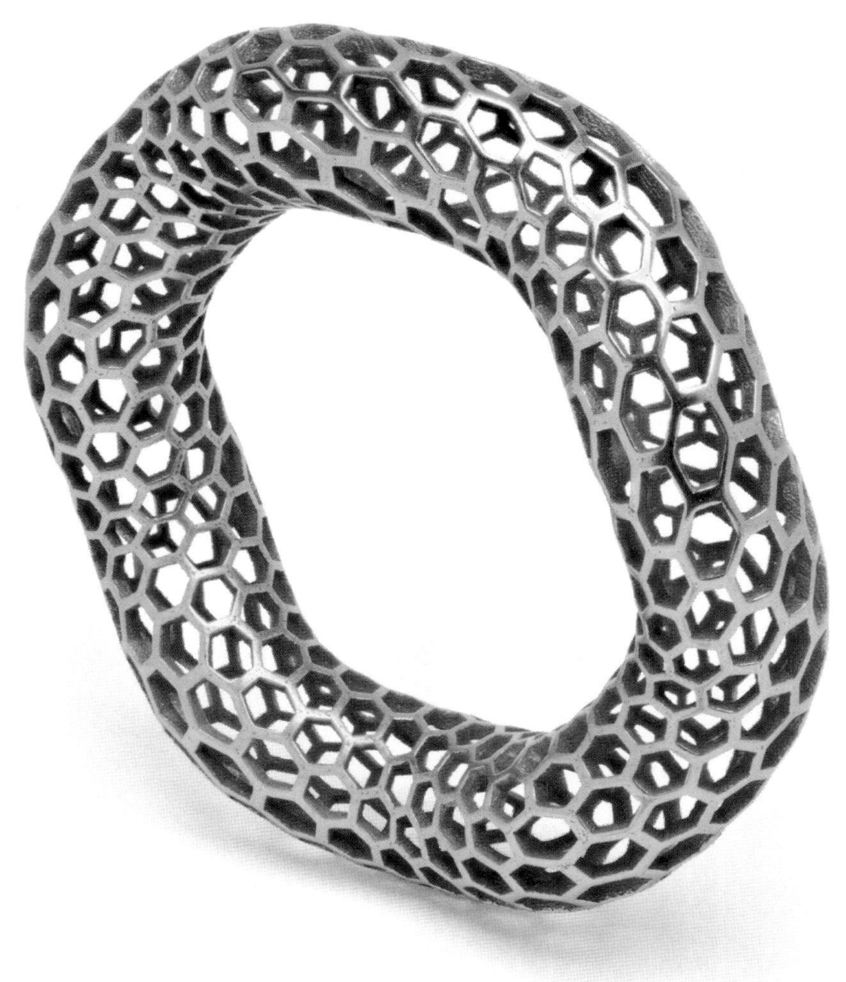

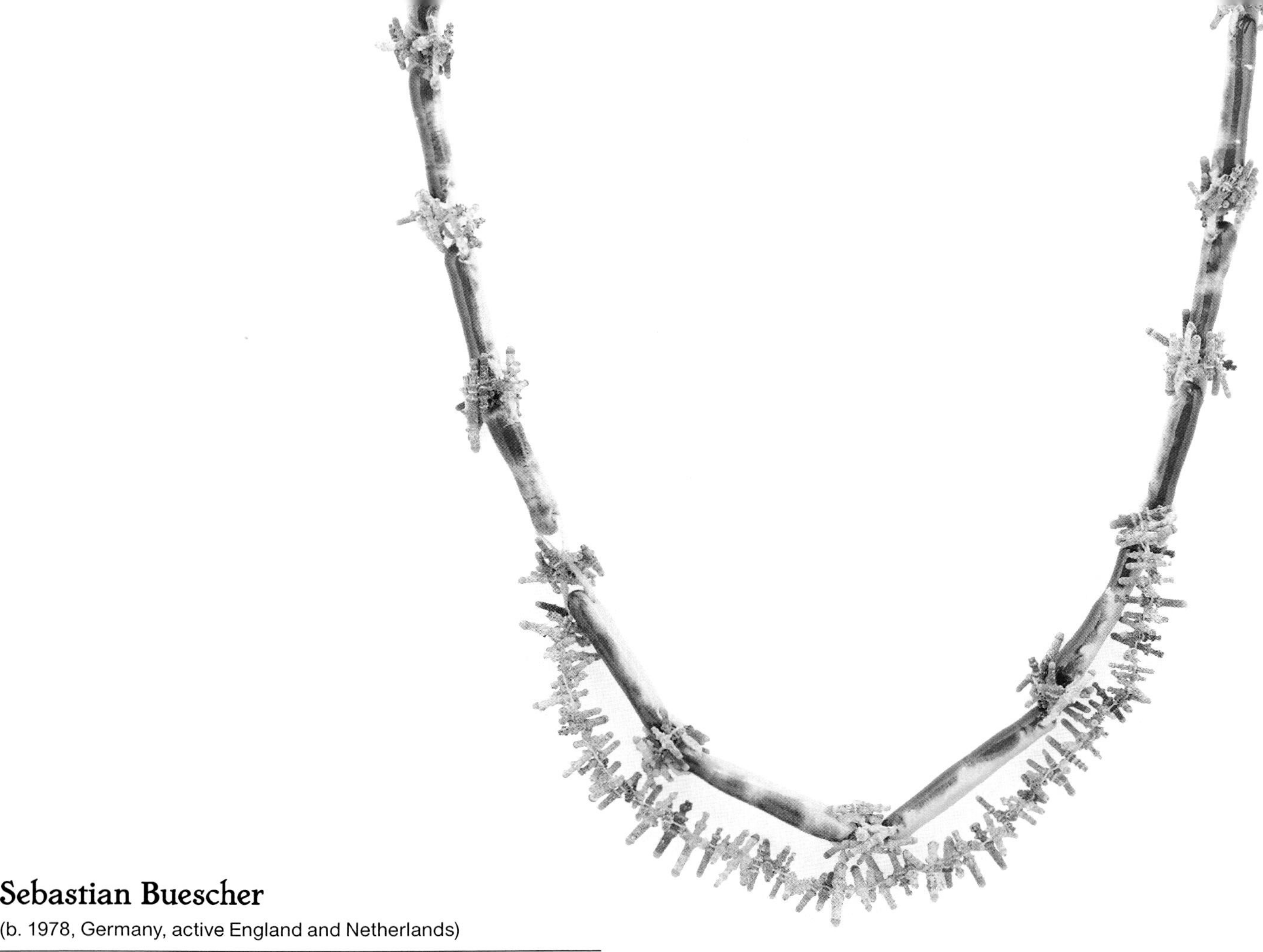

Sebastian Buescher

(b. 1978, Germany, active England and Netherlands)

***Octocoralia* necklace, 2008**
From the series Hadal Realm,
2008–09
Ceramic, sea urchin spines,
wool yarn, synthetic thread
17 × 10 × 1 in.

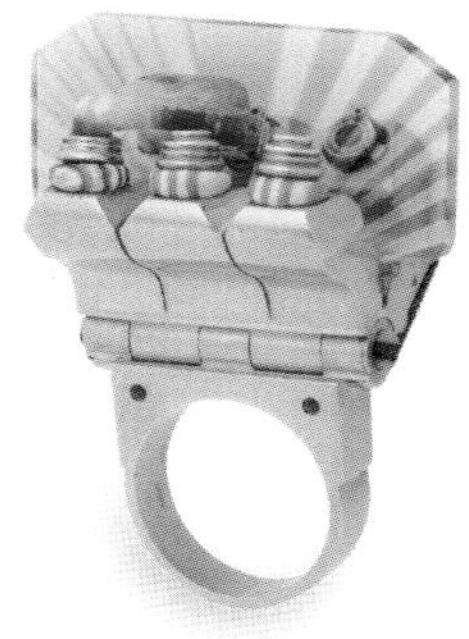

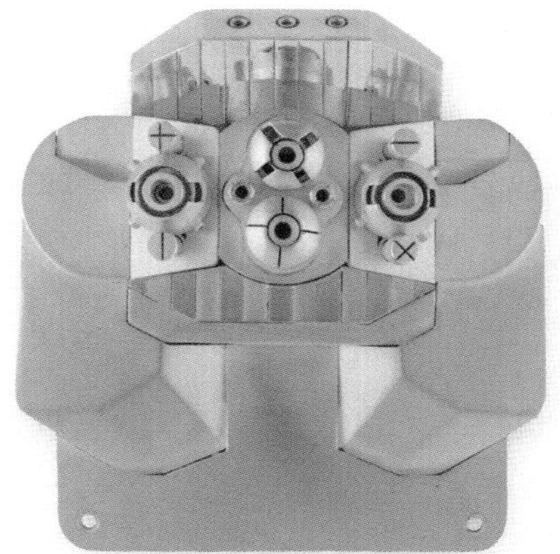

Claus Bury

(b. 1946, Germany)

Ring, 1971
Gold, PMMA
$1\frac{7}{8} \times 1\frac{7}{16} \times \frac{7}{8}$ in.

Brooch, 1973
Varicolored gold
$2\frac{5}{8} \times 2\frac{7}{16} \times \frac{1}{2}$ in.

Metallzeichnung
brooch, 1977
Gold, silver, copper alloy
$2 \times 4\frac{1}{4} \times \frac{1}{4}$ in.

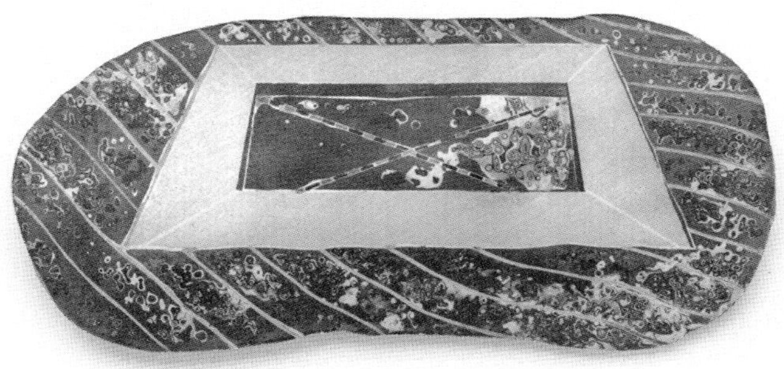

Pierre Cavalan

(b. 1954, France, active Australia)

Brooch, c. 1990–95
Silver-plated brass,
rhinestones, found objects
6¾ × 3½ × ½ in.

***Semaphore Necklace #1*, 1997**
Copper alloy, found objects
8½ × 9¼ × ½ in.

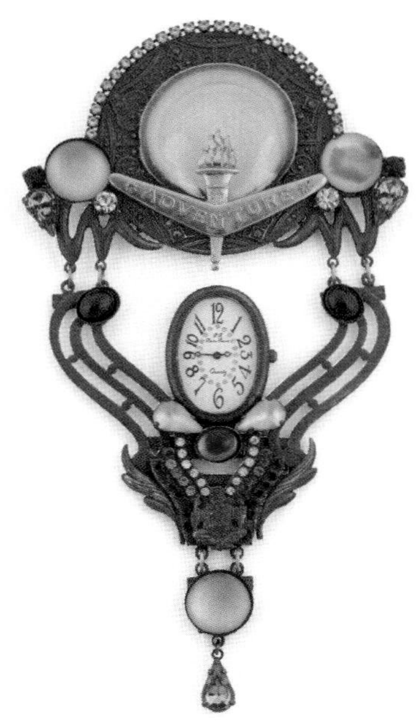

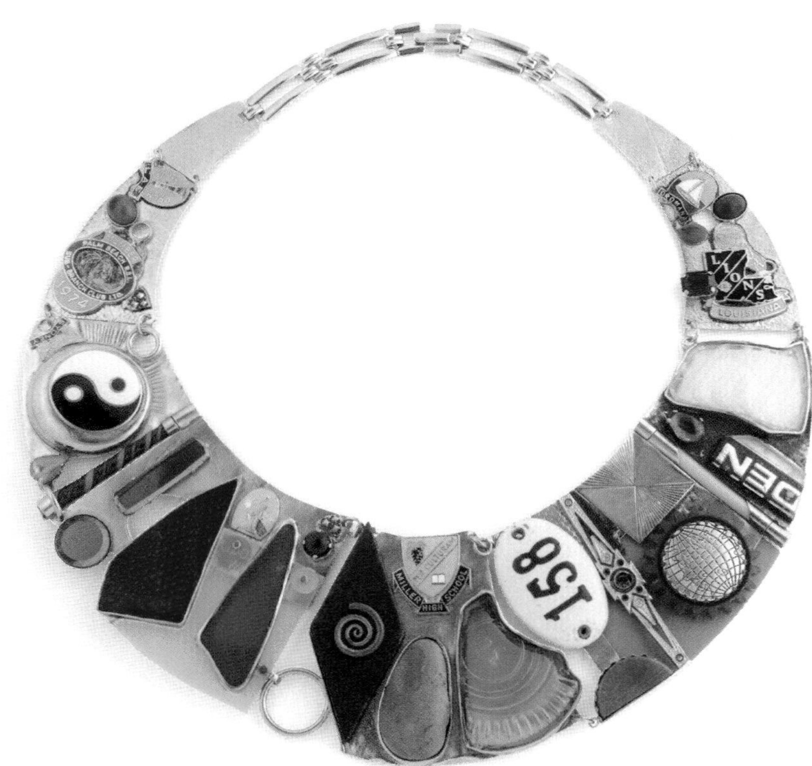

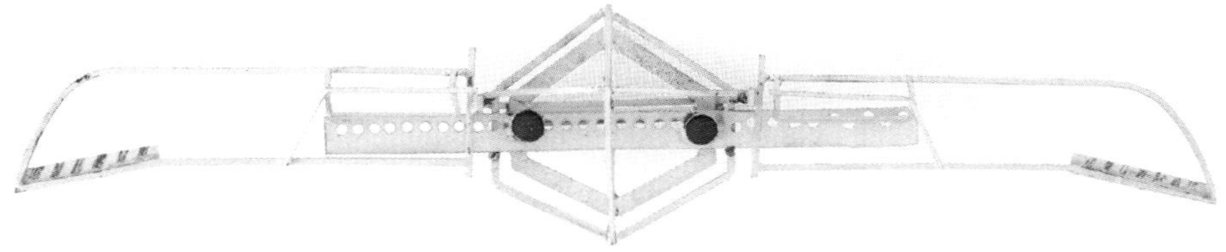

Anton Cepka

(b. 1936, Czechoslovakia [now Slovakia])

Brooch, 1986
Silver, PMMA
1 × 4½ × ½ in.

Peter Chang

(b. 1944, England, active Scotland)

Bracelet, 1989
PMMA and plastic grout
on polystyrene foam
6 × 6 × 2 in.

Bracelet, 1995
PMMA and resin on
polystyrene foam
6 × 6 × 3 in.

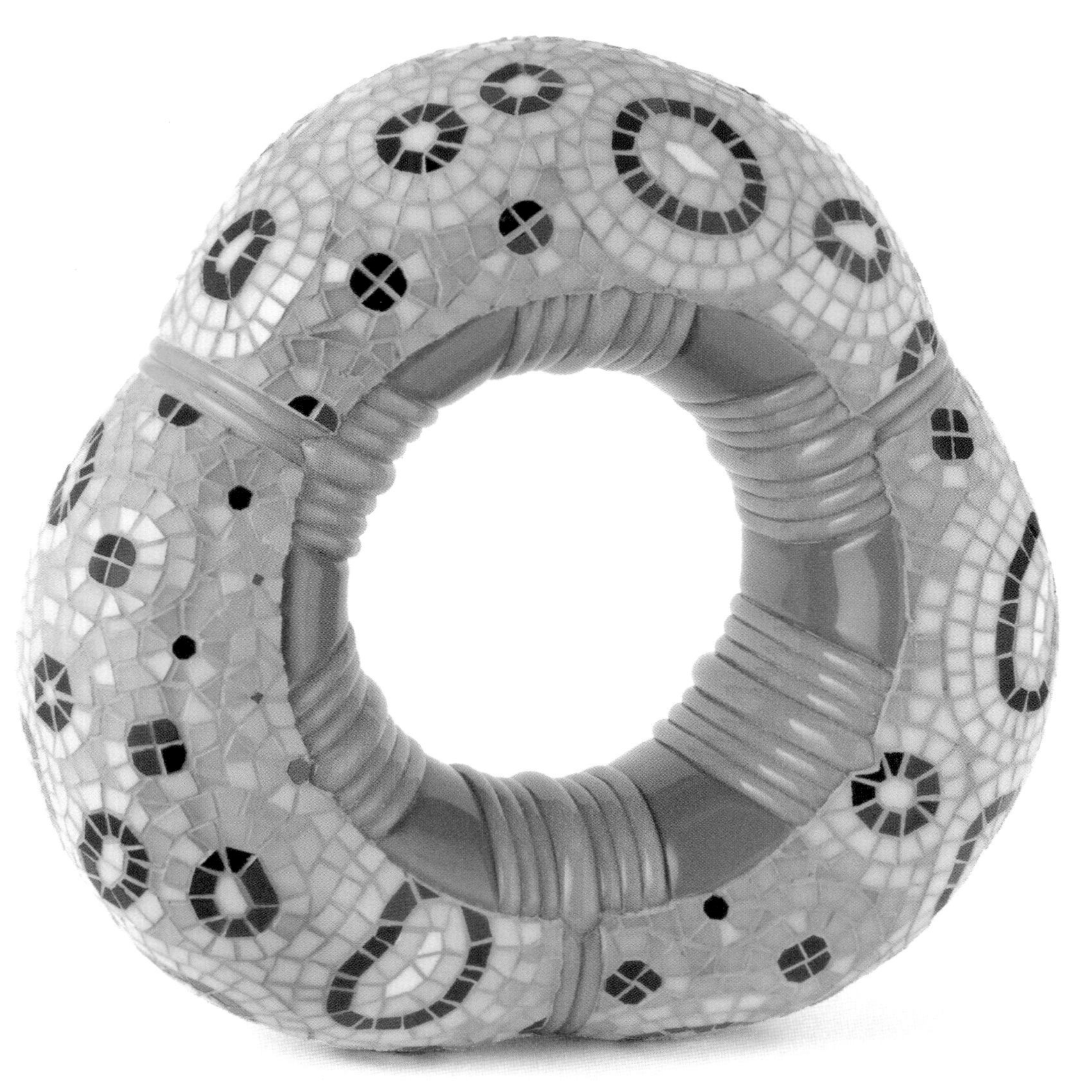

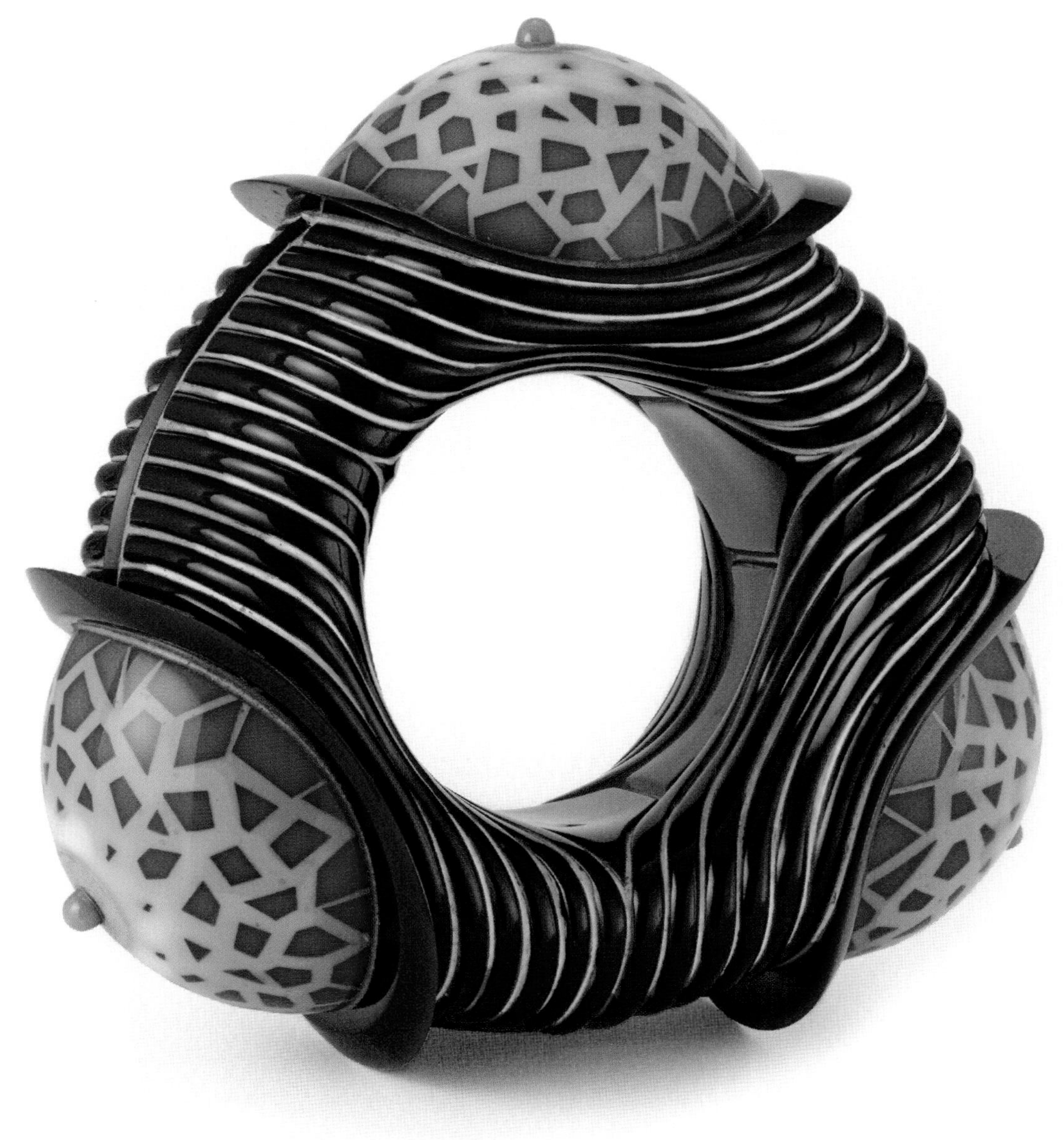

Sharon Church

(b. 1948, United States, active Pennsylvania)

***Long Chain* necklace, 1986**
Silver, onyx, diamonds
16 ¼ × 11⅜ × ⅞ in.

***Foliate Harness* necklace, 1997**
Silver, leather
6 × 10 × ¾ in.

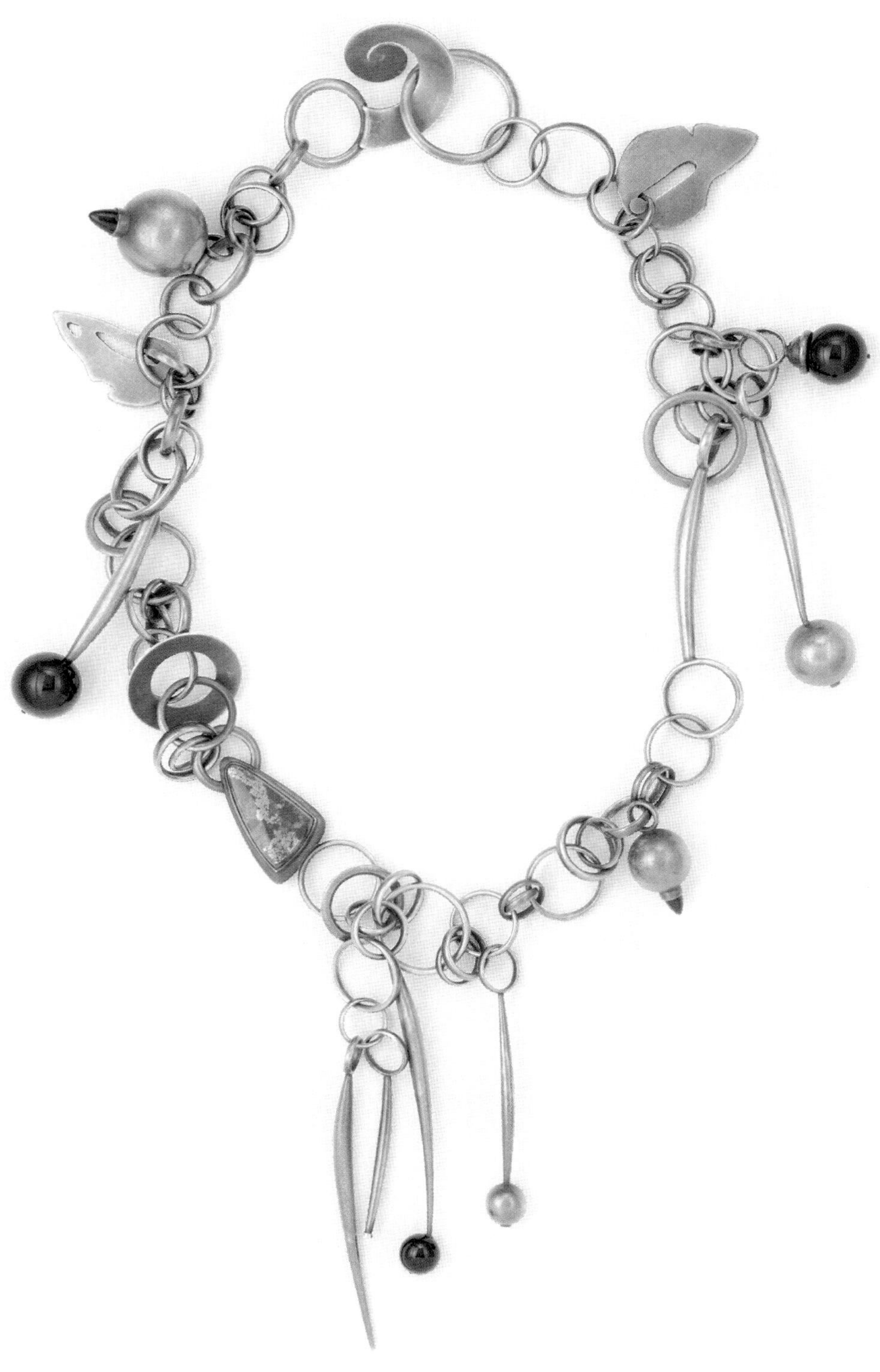

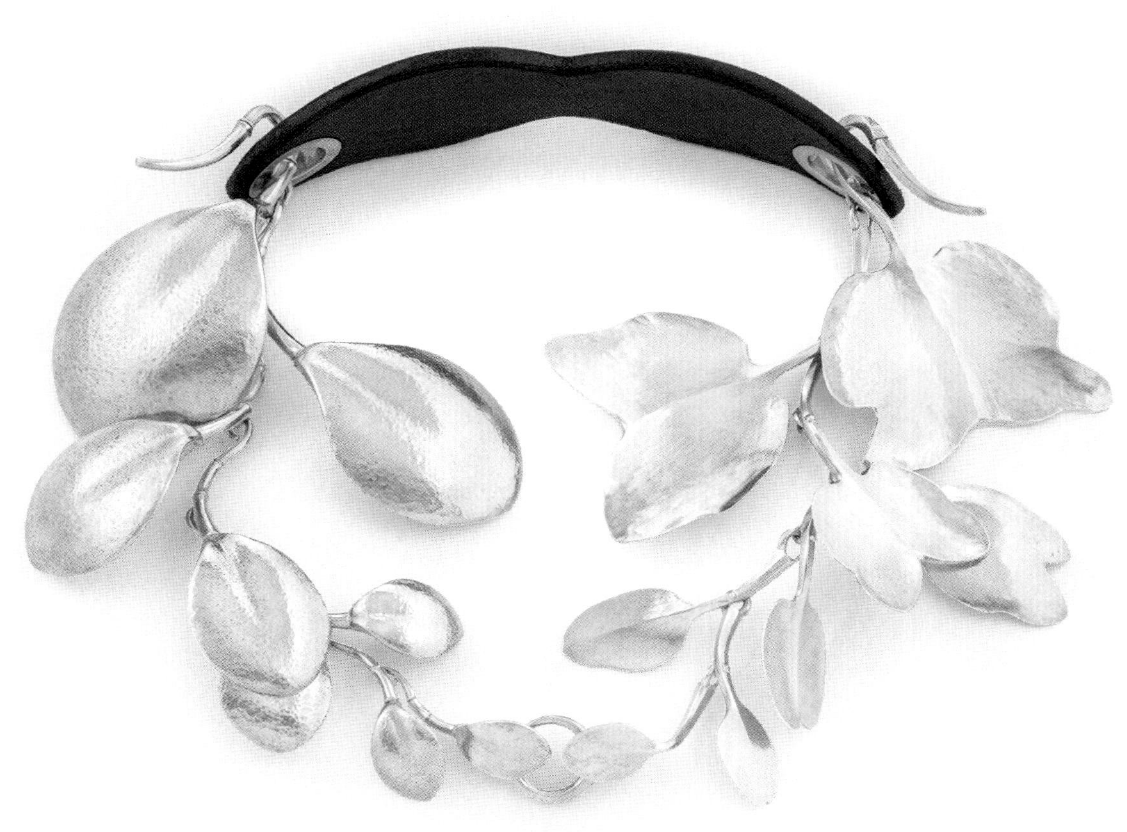

Sharon Church

(continued)

***Scatter Pins*, 1998**
Lemonwood, gold, buffalo horn, diamonds
Hand pin: 2¾ × 1¼ × 1 in.; each diamond pin: ⅜ × ⅜ × ⅜ in.

***Lion's Head* necklace, c. 1999**
Silver, boxwood
9½ × 6½ × 1⅞ in.

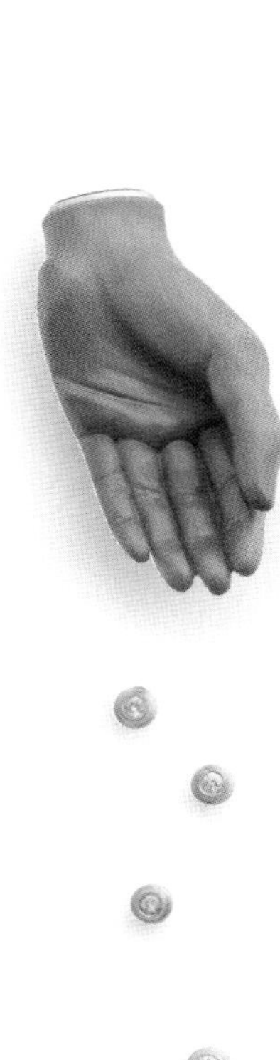

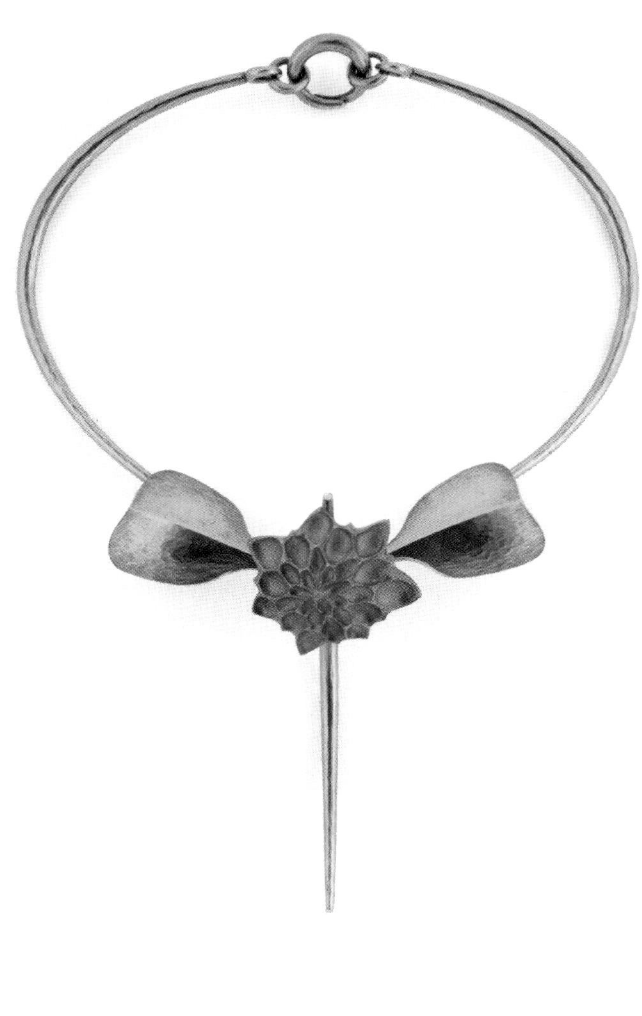

Susan Cohn
(b. 1952, Australia)

***3 tooth-saw* bracelet, 1985**
From the series Saw, 1984–85
Anodized aluminum alloy
6 ¼ × 6¾ × 1¼ in.

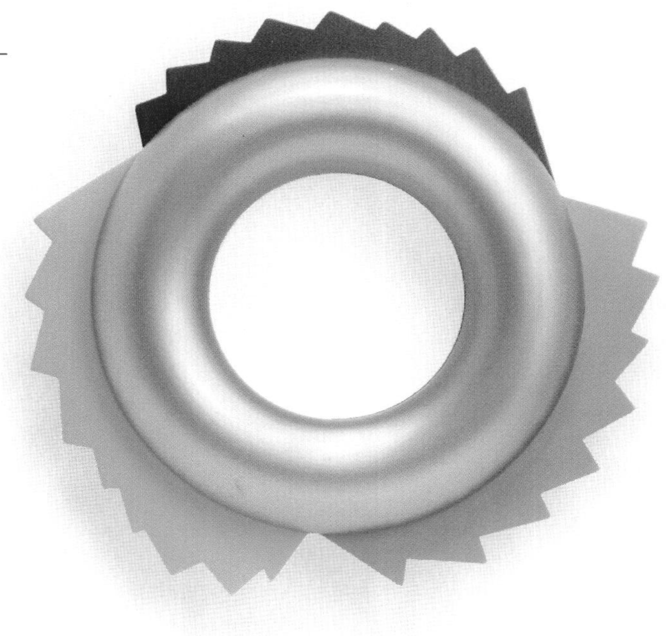

Ros Conway
(b. 1951, England)

Hugh O'Donnell
(b. 1951, England)

***At the Snare III* brooch, 1984**
Enamel on silver, gold
3 × 2 × ⅛ in.

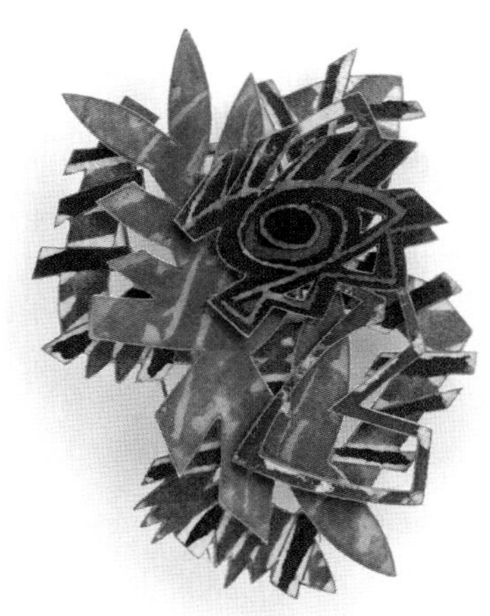

Crown Jewels for a Philosopher King

Blake Gopnik

Imagine a world where the Metropolitan Museum of Art collected the kitsch of Thomas Kinkade ("Painter of Light") and gave him major shows. Or a world where the Museum of Modern Art (MoMA) featured the goofy-realist bronzes of J. Seward Johnson. That is what the world of jewelry risks looking like to a critic trained to consider fine art. I've been in love with the work of our most serious jewelers for many decades now; I've been surprised for just as long at how little cultural leverage it has outside its own circles, compared to the other disciplines a mass-media critic is asked to cover.

When it comes to painting and sculpture and all the new media that have joined them, the notion of a "serious" cutting edge has dominated museums and the public square for something like the last hundred years. Curators have, at least in principle, aimed to buy and show only the most exciting and daring of contemporary art; if you attack one of their choices, the defense will always be that you have not recognized the work's innovations and significance—not that you have somehow set the bar for creativity too high.

And then there's jewelry. The public's notion of serious jewelry tends to be built around karat and cut, glitter and weight. "Bigger is better" is pretty much the average person's guiding aesthetic when it comes to this art form.

The view from the museum may not be much better. In 2013 the Met itself put on a show of splashy gewgaws by the Parisian *bijoutier* Joel A. Rosenthal (a.k.a. JAR), which included such things as lifelike(-ish) butterflies smothered in rubies and a diamond-bridled zebra brooch. The justification for the exhibition was not—could not have been—phrased in terms of the work's conceptual advances or formal radicalism or bold content or critique of fine art. It was all about technical skill, rarefied materials, and the imprimatur JAR's pieces gained from the social elites that buy and wear them (and that funded the show and sit on the Met's board).

This commitment to bling can be found even in museums dedicated to design. In 2011 pieces by the venerable jewelers Van Cleef & Arpels, in thrall to centuries-old traditions, were shown at Cooper Hewitt, the Smithsonian's design museum in New York. The exhibition was sponsored by the company itself. These "treasures" may have been impressively crafted, but they were more or less interchangeable with any number of other *bijoux* sold by similar firms over the last century. Their makers

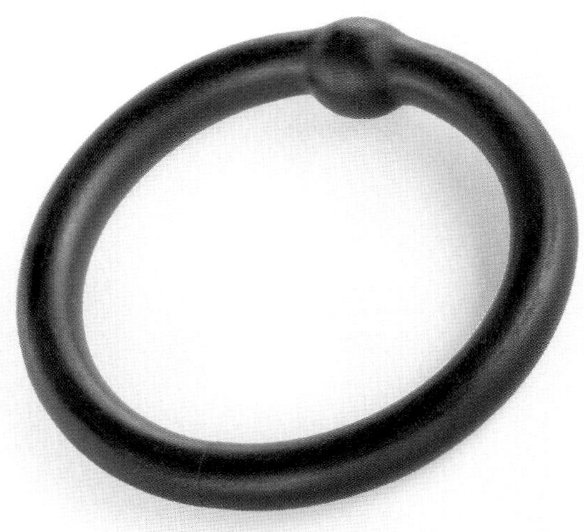

FIG. 1
Otto Künzli, *Gold Macht Blind* bracelet, designed 1980, this example made c. 1986

seemed blissfully unaware of the cutting-edge daring of twentieth-century figures such as Picasso and Calder, whom we've officially crowned as our cultural heroes. The fine-art equivalents of JAR and Van Cleef & Arpels—figures like Kinkade or Johnson—would never get through MoMA's front door.

Now if that sounds like a depressing context for LACMA's *Beyond Bling: Jewelry from the Lois Boardman Collection* exhibition, it shouldn't. The parlous situation that contemporary jewelry finds itself in, out in the larger world, can only make a show like this one that much more important.

You could say that jewelry's Tiffany-and-Cartier mainstream finds itself where the Paris Salon did in the 1860s, when it was dominated by slick, sentimental, expensive works such as the jailbait angels painted by William-Adolphe Bouguereau and the noble lions sculpted by Antoine-Louis Barye. And if JAR and Van Cleef & Arpels are our current *pompiers*, then the makers included in *Beyond Bling* are the Courbets, Manets, and Monets of art that is worn on the body.

In fine art, the lack of any visible opposition to what counts as today's cutting edge can make the stakes feel pretty low. At MoMA the public fully expects to see the likes of Jeff Koons or Cindy Sherman on display; they'd be surprised to find society portraitists instead. Any debate about what should or should not be on view at an art museum takes place within a fairly narrow range of work that, by a pretty broad consensus, counts as "serious" contemporary art. Gallerygoers might debate where any given artist fits within that category—Koons or Sherman might be seen as ranking at its top or its bottom—but they don't expect to deal with work that is engaged in a completely different discussion.

With jewelry, by contrast, the cutting edge remains largely unknown outside a tiny circle of specialists, the way "difficult" modern art did for its first decades. A show like *Beyond Bling* is mounting the kind of thrilling polemic that was still needed at the Salon des Refusés in Paris in 1863 or in MoMA's 1939 Picasso survey, which toured the country like a revival meeting for Modernism. The public's perception of the art of contemporary jewelry needs almost complete rejiggering.

Your local Kay Jewelers will have plenty of JAR-ish brooches, but almost certainly nothing at all like the oversize necklace that Gijs Bakker made in 1982 from a hyperrealistic, plastic-laminated image of a red rose (see p. 19). It will offer its shoppers a heavy bangle made of gold, but would never think to present a bauble of precious metal encased in a black rubber bracelet, so that the glint of its bullion lies hidden from view, as in *Gold Macht Blind* by Otto Künzli from the 1980s (fig. 1). Any branch of Tiffany & Company will stock gold-and-sapphire rings, but none that look as though they were drawn by a three-year-old, cast by a ten-year-old, and then run over by a truck—which is pretty much the look of a Karl Fritsch ring from 2005 (fig. 2). The gap between popular tastes in jewelry and what happens on its cutting edge is vast—and that much more in need of bridging.

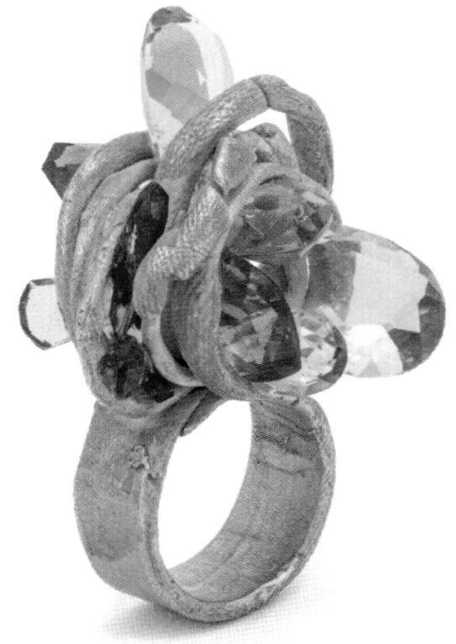

FIG. 2
Karl Fritsch, ring, 2005

An astute reader will have noticed something about the *Beyond Bling* examples I have just given: the most recent one is more than ten years old; the other two are triple that. As every insider knows, the battle for the hearts and minds (and bulging wallets) of the jewelry-wearing public has been going on for many decades now, often in precisely the same terms in which it's conducted now. My own interest in the field began fully thirty years ago, when my linguistics-professor mother began a sideline in avant-garde "wearable art" (the most popular term at the time). Her first pieces were mostly made from commercial embroidery thread wrapped around roofing slate she picked up off the street. She had some success with this work. It was shown by Suzanne Greenaway at Prime Gallery in Toronto, as well as by the great Helen Drutt in Philadelphia, source of many pieces in *Beyond Bling*. But thinking back, I realize that my mother's preference for found slate over worked gold was mostly framed in formal terms: gold just seemed less interesting, and more cliché-bound, than slate; it had an element of ostentation that was hard to overcome. In our current world of gross income gaps, however, the contemporary jeweler's long-standing rejection of precious materials can carry a political weight.

A jeweler's brazen refusal to work in traditional modes can now count as a full-blown repudiation of our new Gilded Age, whose values dominate the world of elite *bijoutiers*. As today's most radical jewelry takes on a more and more conceptual edge—becomes interested more in what it's about than how it looks—it can also engage more directly with our most pressing social issues.

A recent favorite example is a project titled Wilhelm Tell's Shot, in which the Swiss jeweler Johanna Dahm has used an assault rifle to blast holes through the gold coins and little gold

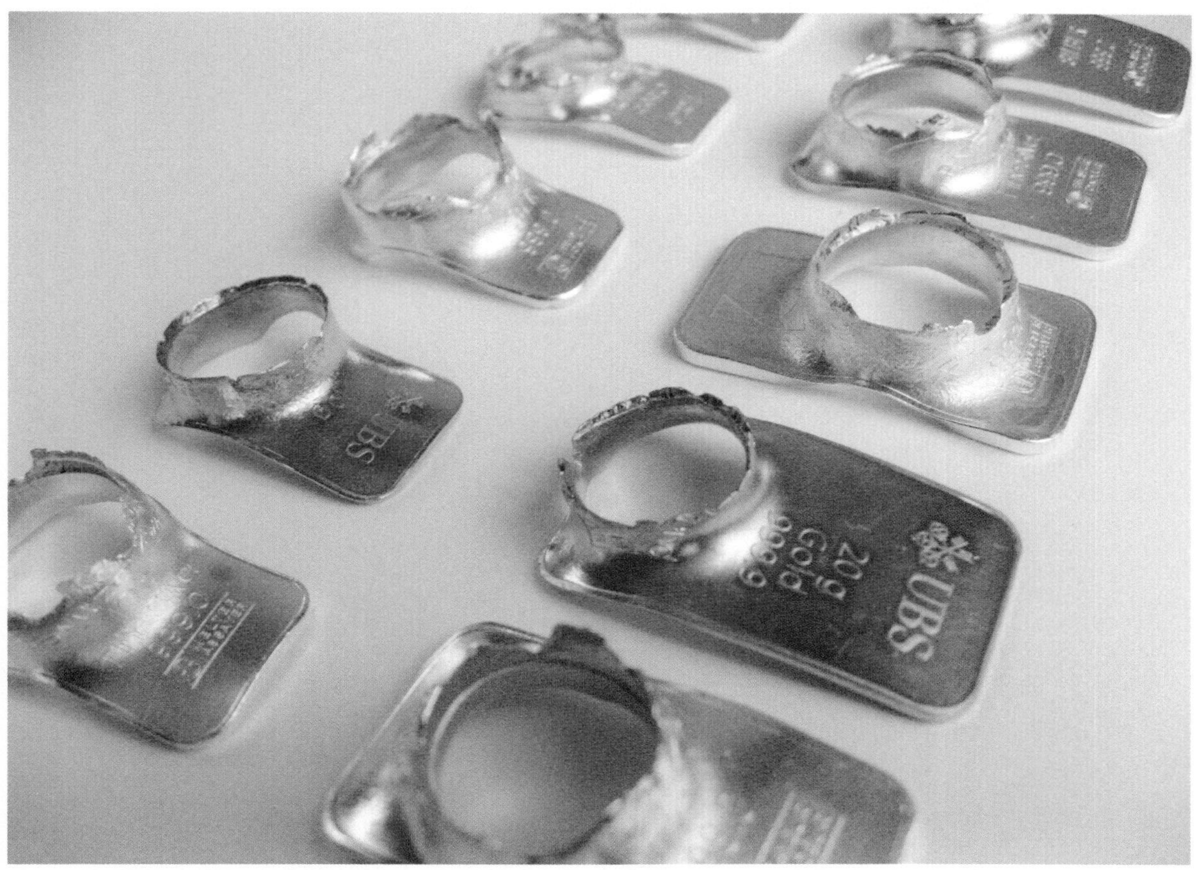

FIG. 3
Johanna Dahm, rings from the series Wilhelm Tell's Shot, 2011, silver and gold, 1¼ × ⅞ × ⅜ in. (3.2 × 2.1 × 1.1 cm) each, courtesy of the artist and Ornamentum Gallery, Hudson, New York

bars that are usually a store of wealth (fig. 3). You can put your finger through your bullet-pierced ingot, ringwise, or wear it around your neck as a pendant, but the shot that made it cannot be ignored. The piece is bound to stand for the violence involved in procuring gold in the first place, and the violence that gold and gross wealth then propagate in the world.

Maybe jewelry like Dahm's has not achieved the popular acceptance of equivalent works by Koons or Sherman because, in a sense, it matters too much. Day to day, it is easy enough to ignore fine art's cutting edge; for most people, it lives in its own, far-off world of museums and galleries and art fairs, doing its own way-out thing. If contemporary art is supposed to be strange and radical, it is also supposed to be remote—that is what makes its strangeness acceptable. Whereas jewelry lives on almost every woman's body, almost every day. If Dahm and Bakker and Künzli really managed to occupy that intensely intimate, familiar space, it would represent one of the greatest artistic revolutions of modern culture—as though Bruce Nauman's art videos were to play in rerun on the nation's TVs.

If that's too much to ask of any contemporary jeweler, no matter how brave and ambitious, it's nevertheless the kind of vision that *Beyond Bling* hopes to conjure. It's a vision of a future, however unlikely, in which our culture's most intimate art form could be one of its most powerful and trenchant ones.

Peter de Wit

(b. 1952, Netherlands, active Sweden)

Necklace, 1983
Silver, anodized aluminum
8¾ × 9¾ × 1 in.

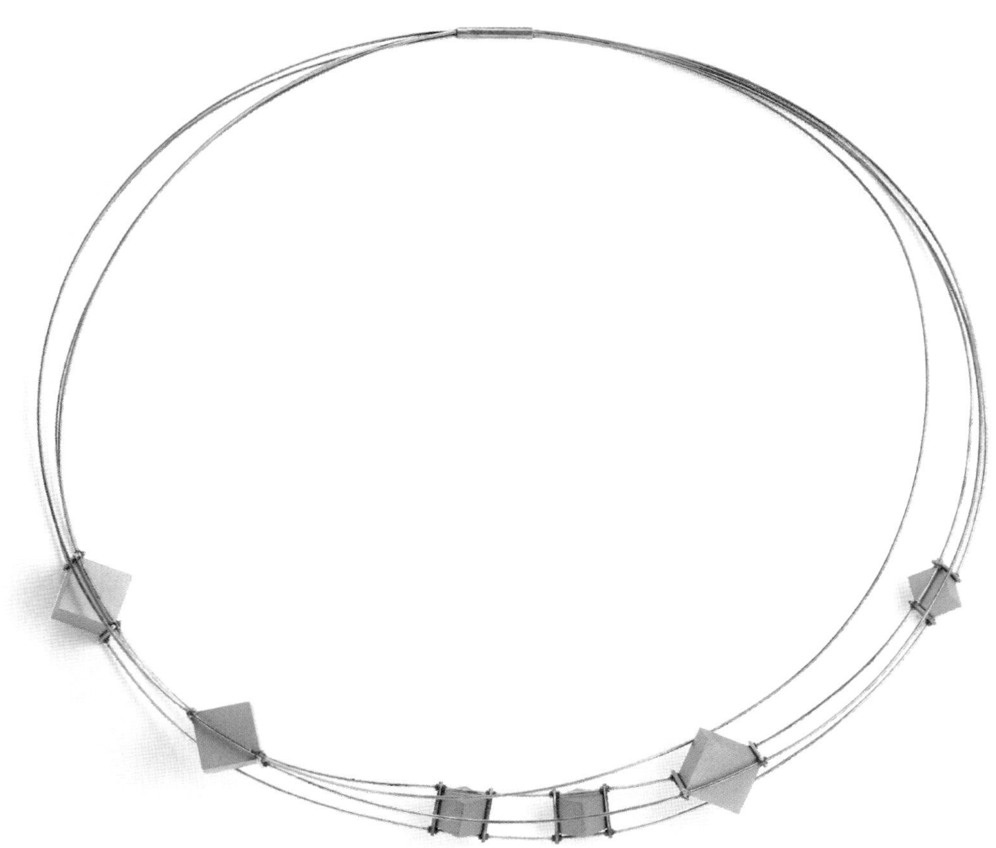

Lam de Wolf

(b. 1949, Netherlands)

Headdress, 1986
From the series Hommage
à la Libre Pensée, 1986
Cotton fabric, kindling sticks,
paint
30 × 23 × 14 in.

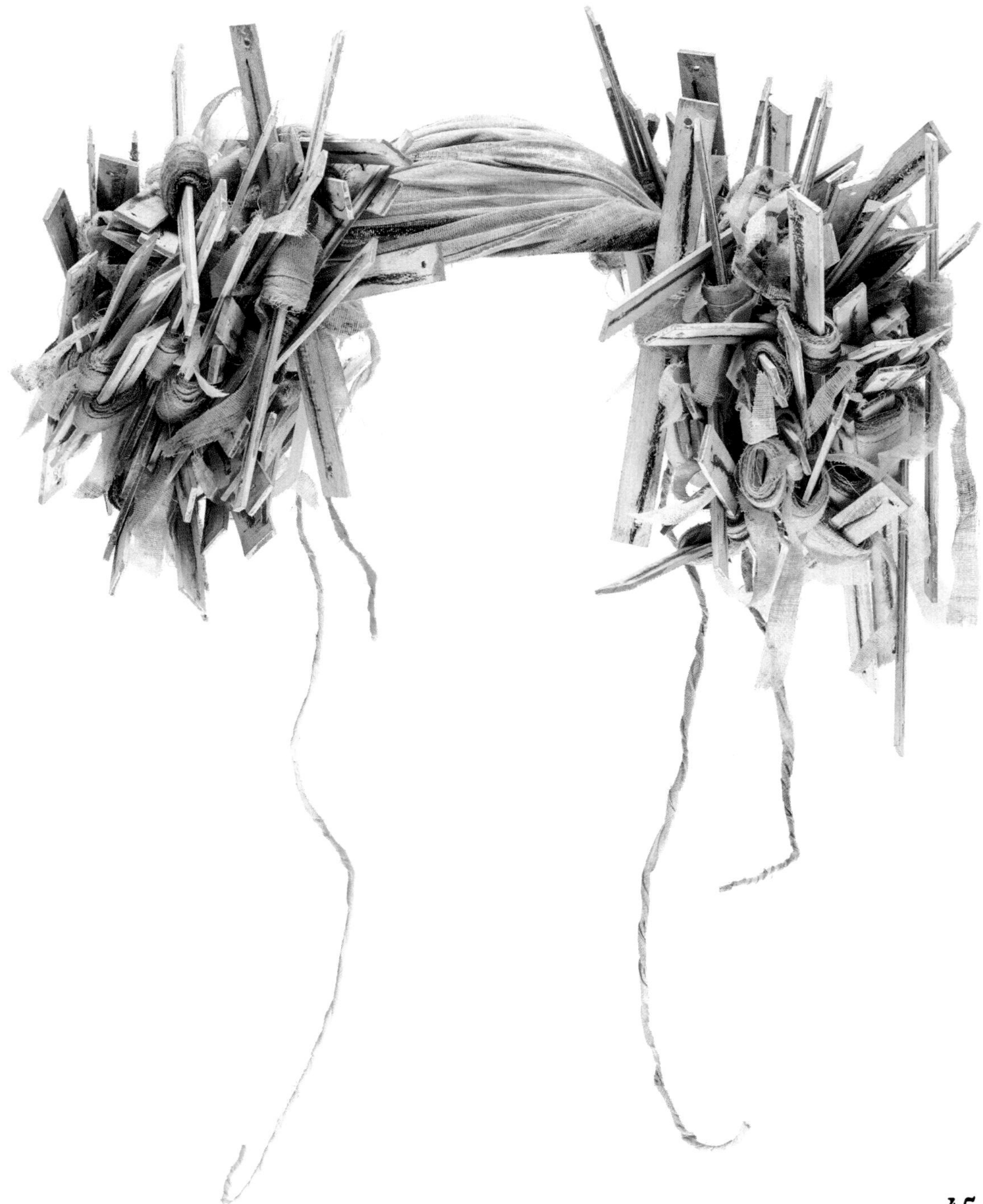

Elisabeth Jesus Guennaibim Defner

(formerly Elizabeth Kodré-Defner, b. 1931, Austria)

Rodent Skull **necklace, 1984**
Gold, steel, silver, opal,
emerald, diamond, rubies
7 13⁄16 × 6 1⁄8 × 1⁄2 in.

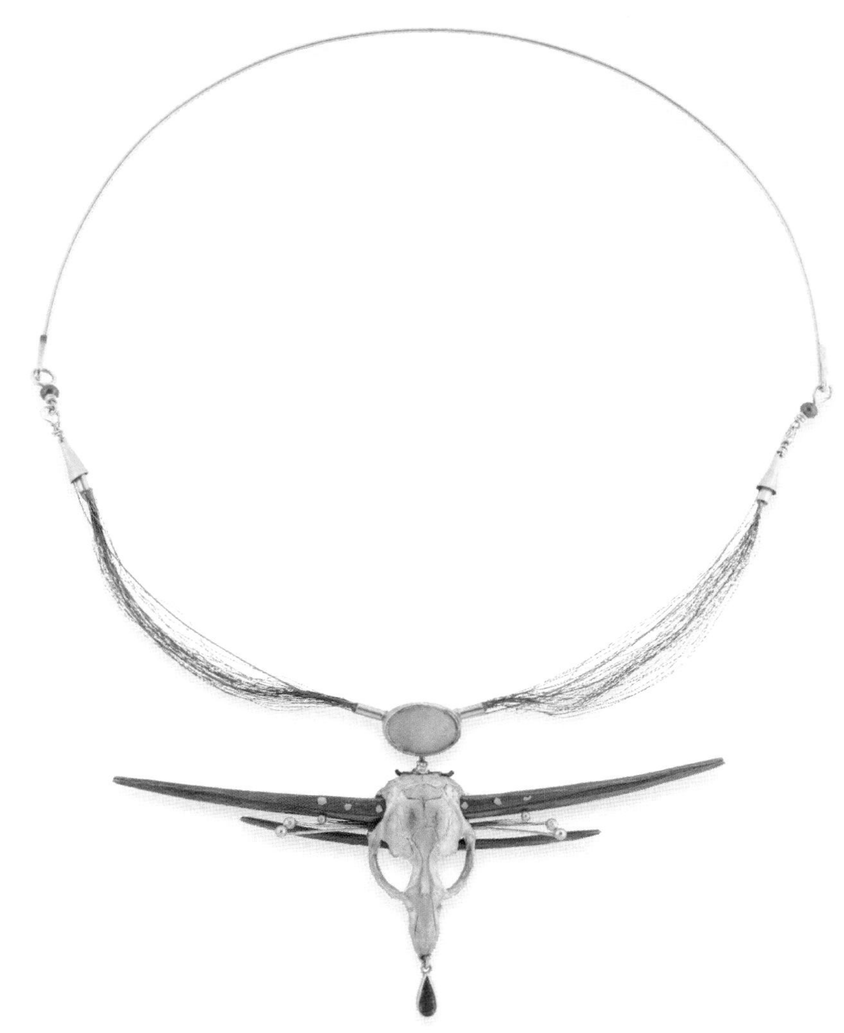

Paul Derrez

(b. 1950, Netherlands)

***Pebble Collar*, 1985**
Cork with spray paint,
cotton cord
18 × 14½ × 2 in.

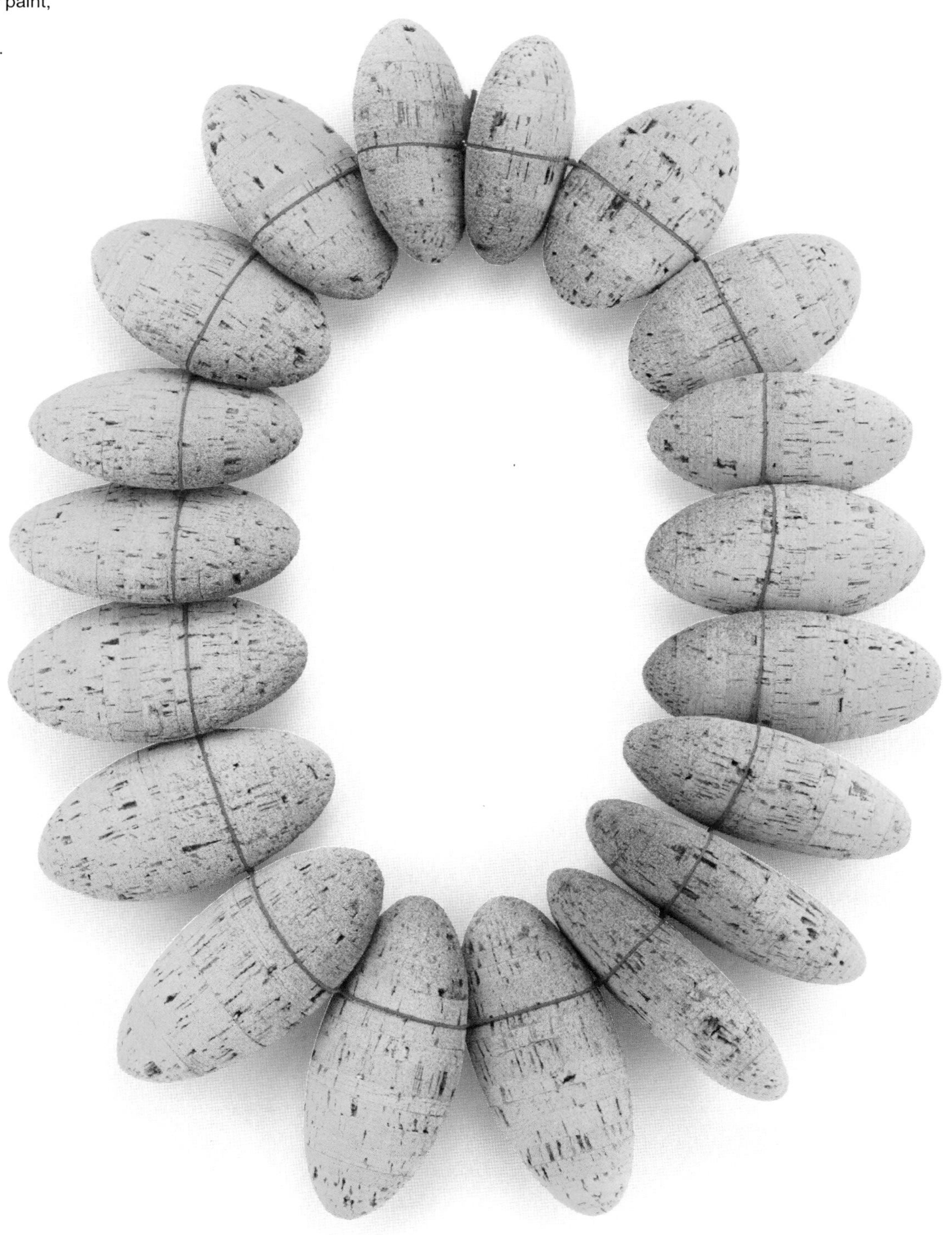

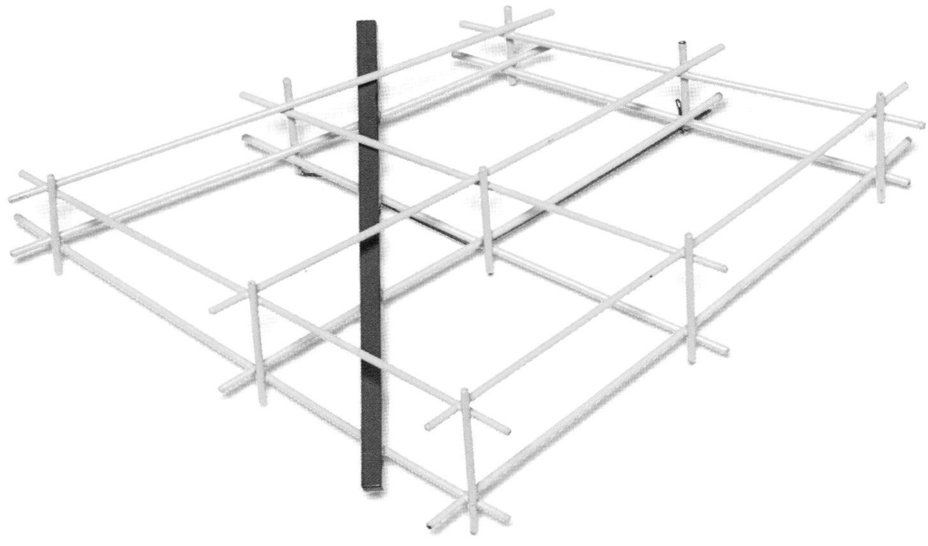

Georg Dobler

(b. 1952, Germany)

***3-D Illusion* brooch, designed 1980, made 1981**
Acrylic-coated copper alloy
3 ¼ × 5 ⅜ × ⅞ in.

***Wassily K.* brooch, 1986**
Silicon-coated stainless steel
6 ½ × 11 × 1 ¼ in.

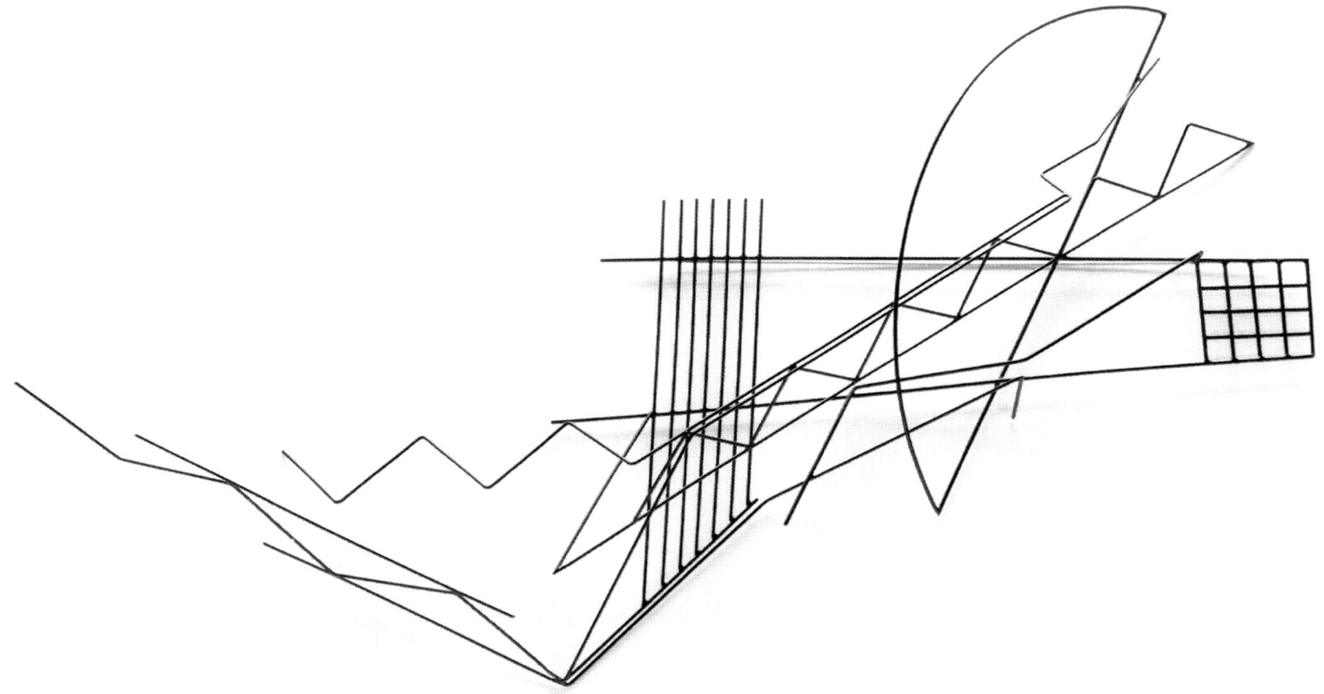

Georg Dobler

(continued)

Brooch, 1998
Gold, silver
1 15/16 × 1 15/16 × 3/16 in.

Brooch, 1998
Gold, blue topaz
1 5/8 × 2 7/8 × 1 3/16 in.

Happiness of Grapes
brooch, 1998
Silver, amethyst
2 × 4 × 3/4 in.

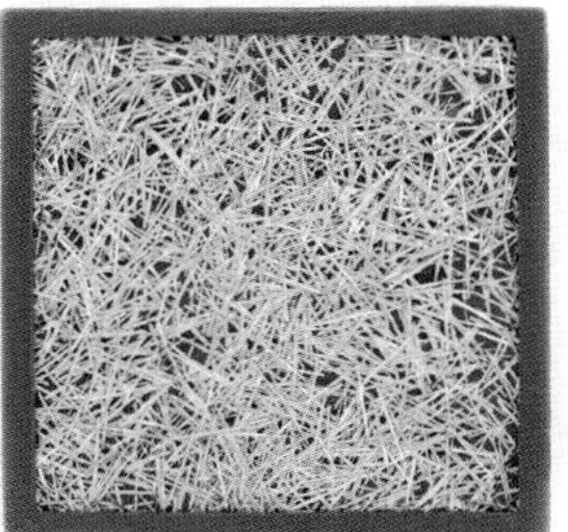

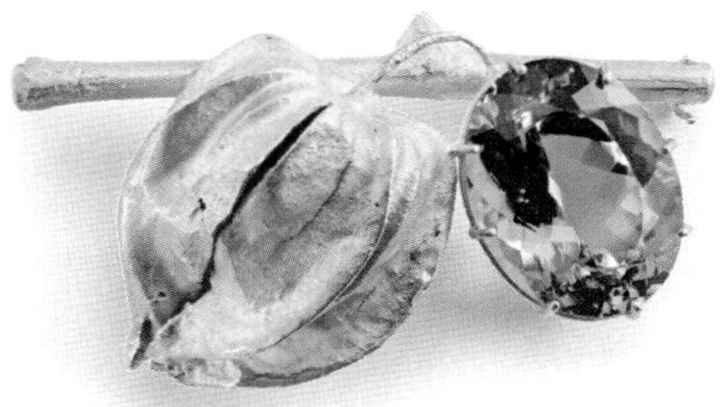

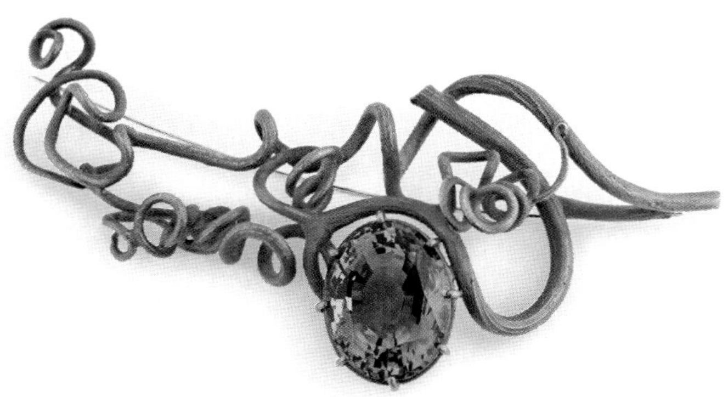

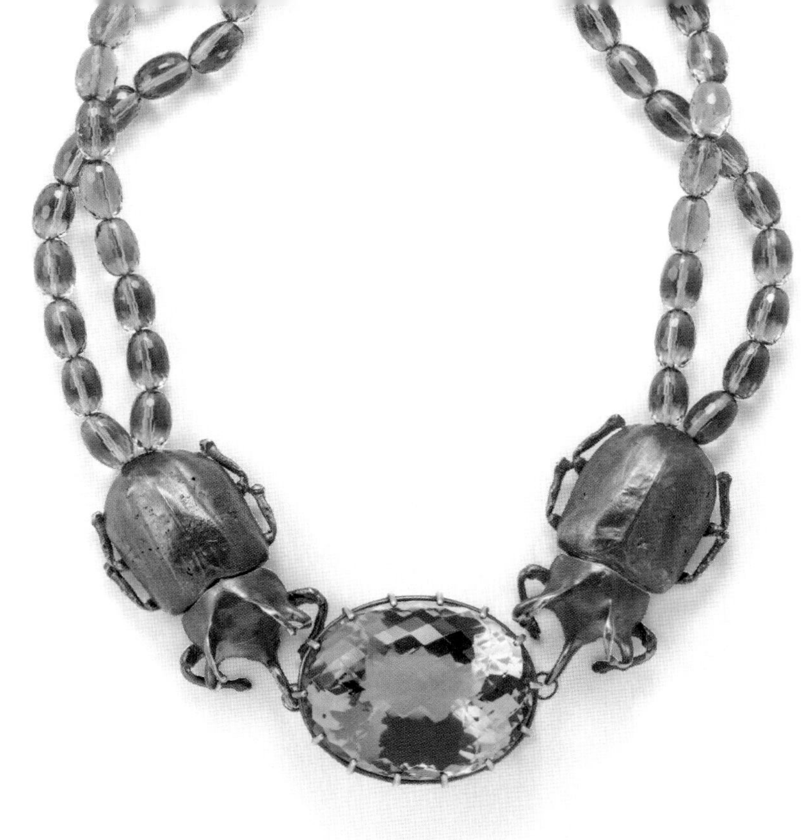

***Trouble with Beauty* necklace, designed 2004, made 2006**
Silver, citrine, smoky quartz, rutilated smoky quartz
8 ½ × 7 ½ × 1 3⁄16 in.

Gemma Draper

(b. 1971, Spain)

Brooch, 2012
From the series Strain's rhetoric, 2012
Copper alloy, silver alloy
5 × 4 ¾ × ¼ in.

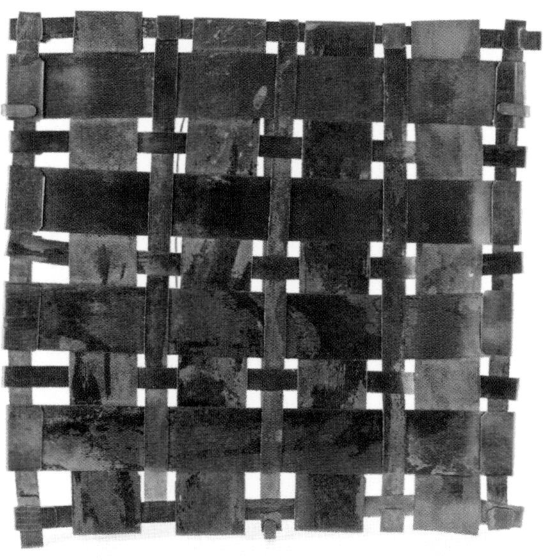

Robert Ebendorf

(b. 1938, United States, active Georgia, New York, and North Carolina)

Necklace, designed 1984, made 1984–85
Chinese newspaper on Styrofoam, gold foil, acrylic lacquer, copper, plastic
12 ½ × 9 ½ × 2 in.

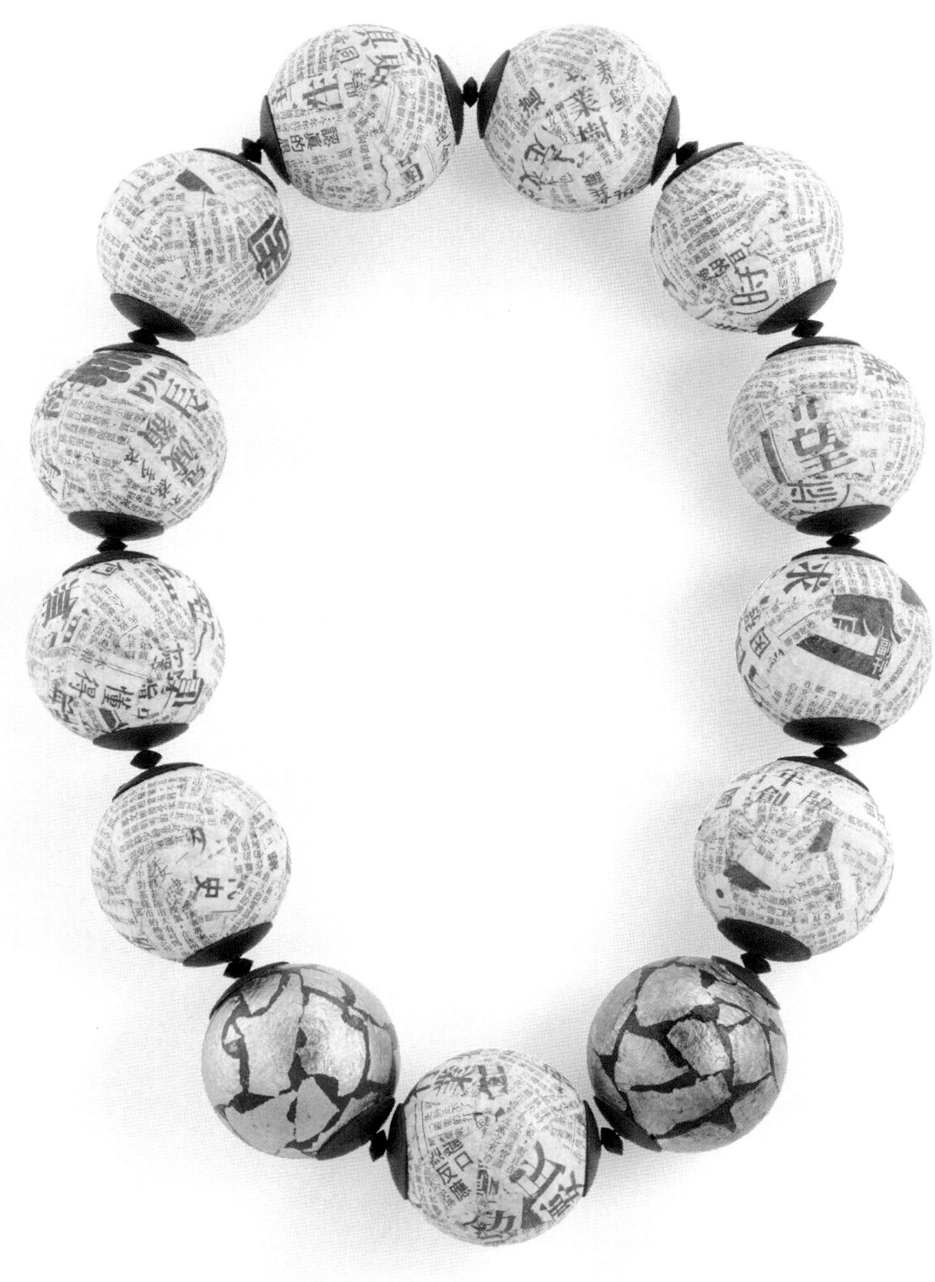

Eva Eisler

(b. 1952, Czechoslovakia [now Czech Republic], active New York)

Brooch, 1987
Slate
1⁹⁄₁₆ × 4¾ × ⅝ in.

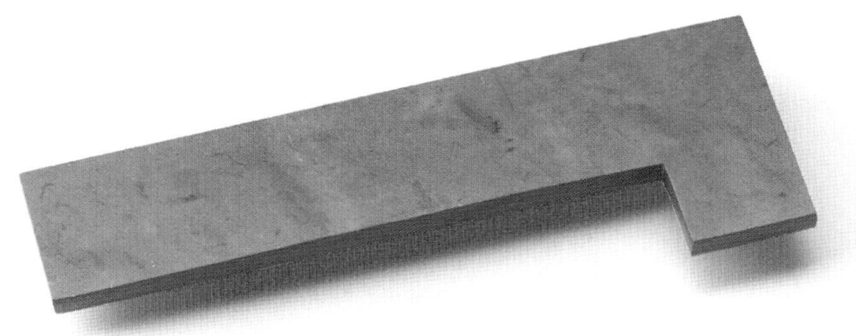

Sandra Enterline

(b. 1960, United States, active California)

***Queen Bee* brooch, 1998**
Gold, queen yellow jacket,
pollen, glass
1½ × 1½ × ⅝ in.

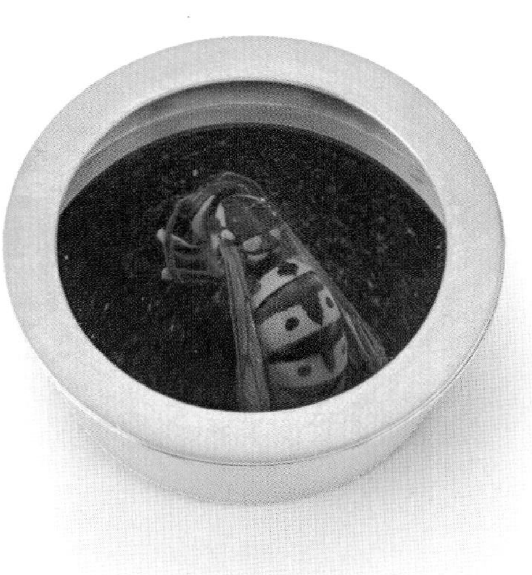

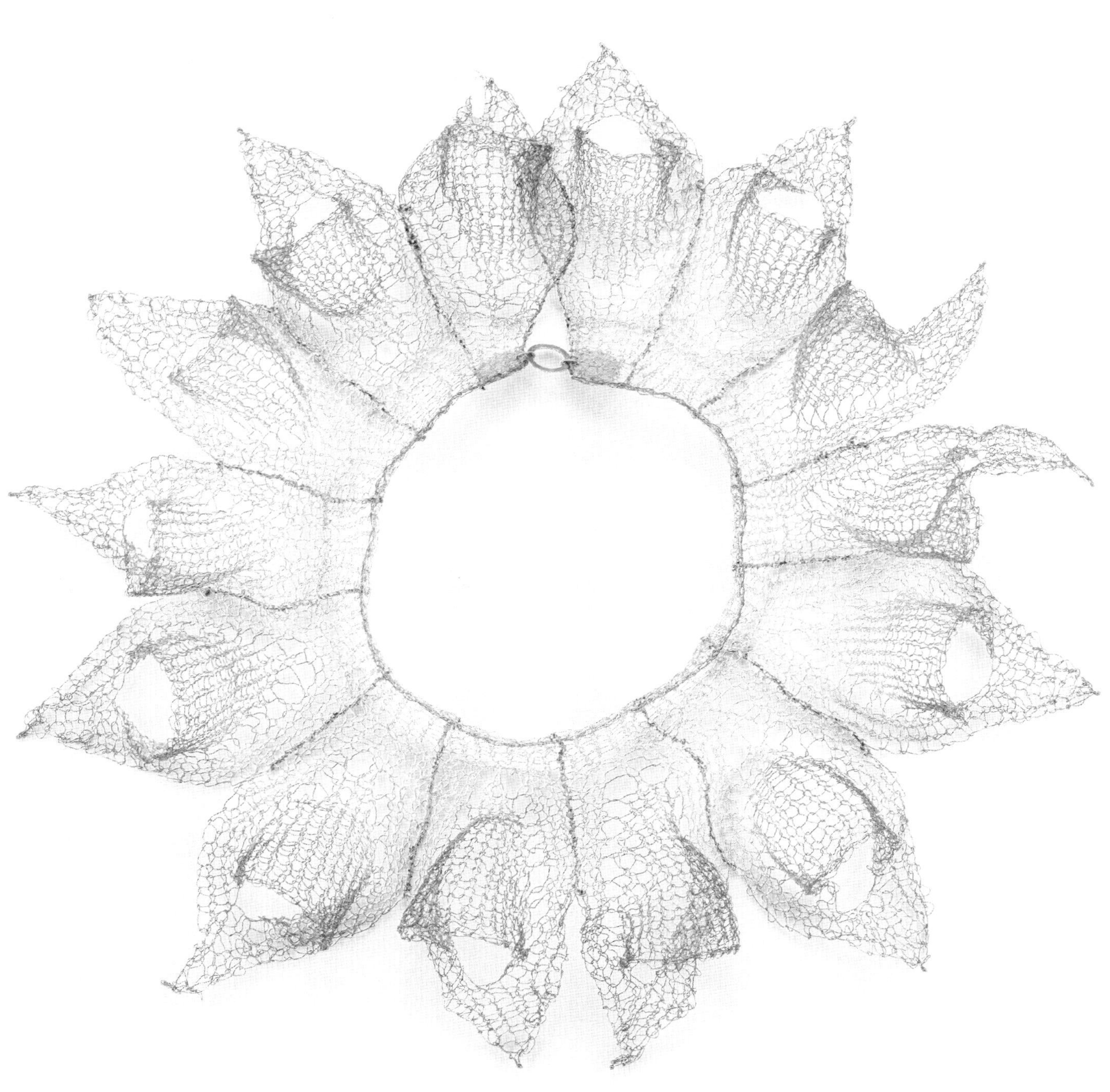

Arline Fisch

(b. 1931, United States, active California)

Bell Frills **necklace, 1985**
Silver, gold
13 × 13 × 2 in.

Long Cuff **bracelet, 1995**
Color-coated copper, silver
5¾ × 5¾ × 11 in.

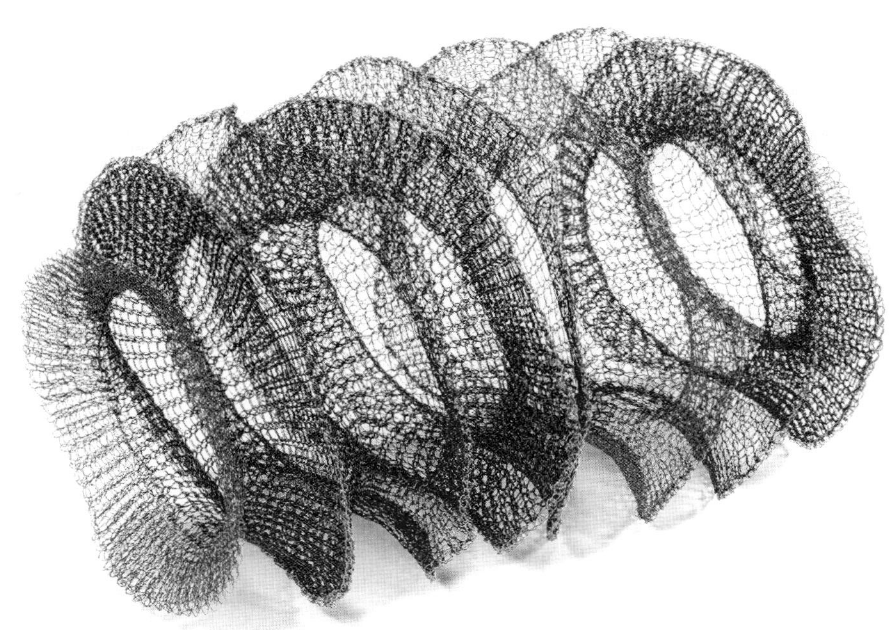

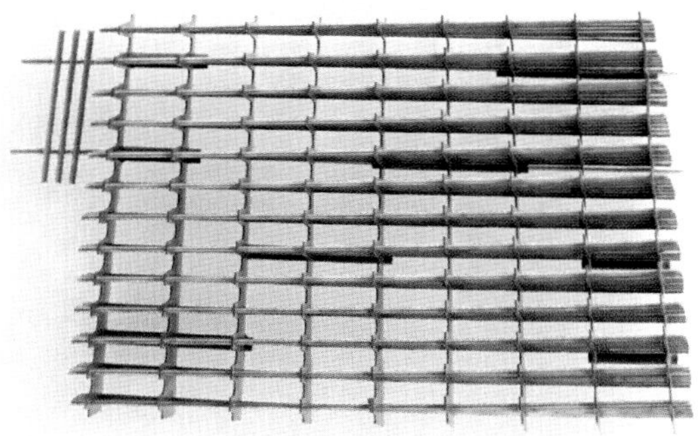

Anna Fraling

(b. 1955, Germany)

Brooch, 1987
Stainless steel, brass
2 × 3 ¼ × ½ in.

Max Fröhlich

(1908–1997, Switzerland)

Ring, 1985
Silver
1 ⅛ × 2 × ⅞ in.

Brooch, 1997
Gold
2 ⅛ × 2 ⅛ × ¼ in.

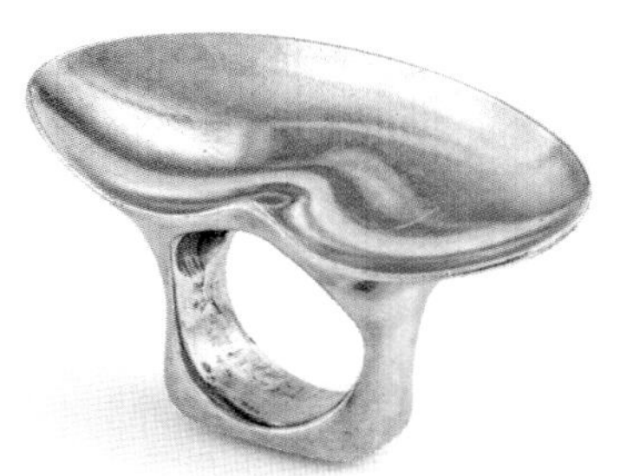

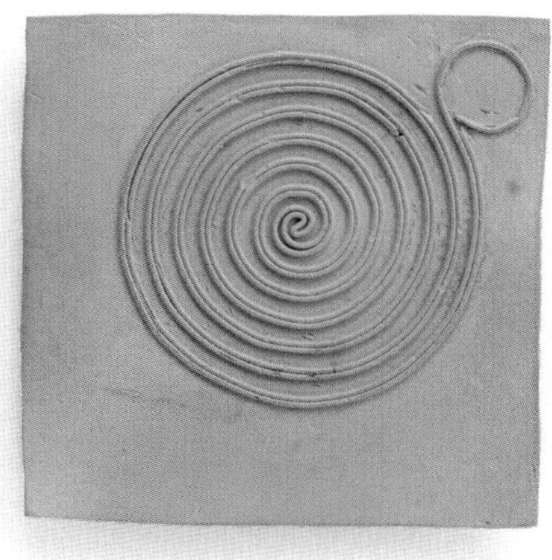

Susie Ganch

(b. 1970, United States, active Virginia)

***Static Orbital Model #3 (Menorah)*, 1999**
From the series About Space, 1997–2003
Silver, stainless steel
15 ½ × 19 ½ × 14 ½ in.

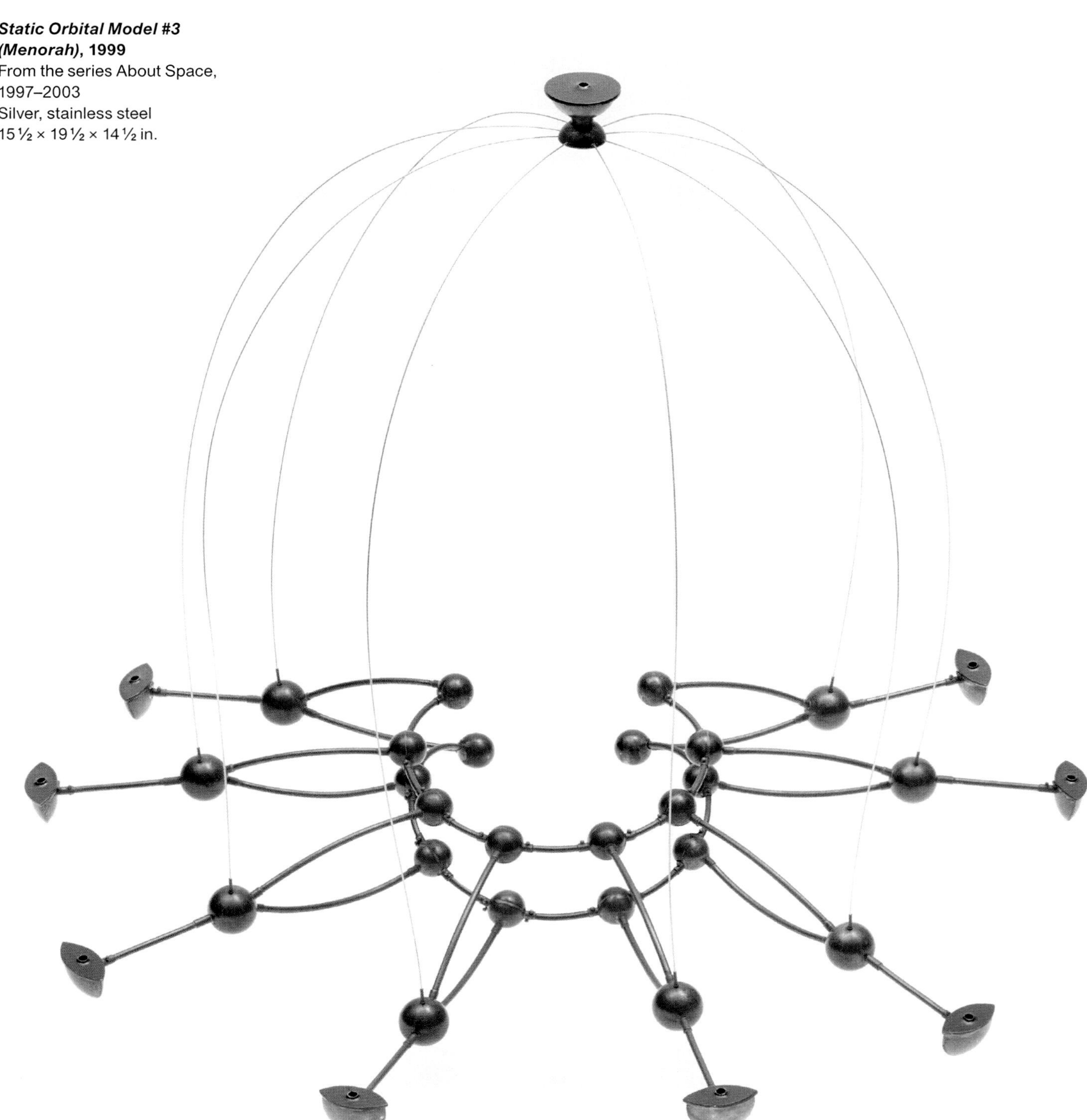

Elizabeth Garrison

(b. 1952, United States, active Florida and New York)

***Under the Fish* brooch, 1982**
Silver, brass, enamel, found object, agate, bone
2 × 3 × ⅜ in.

***Nightshrine* brooch, 1987**
Number 1 of 3 from the series Nightshrine, 1987
Silver, copper, enamel, mother of pearl, gold
2½ × 1½ × ¼ in.

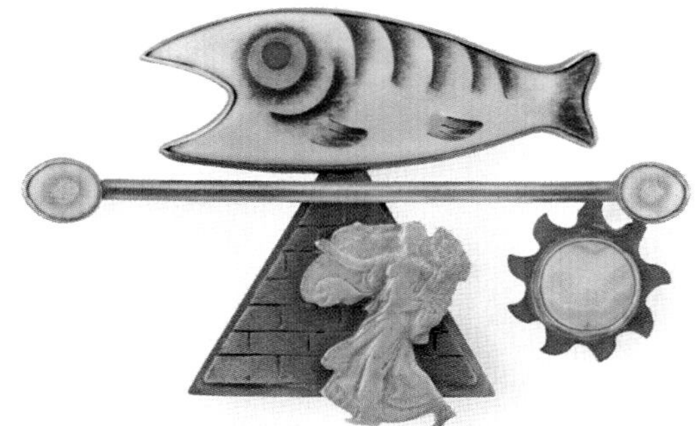

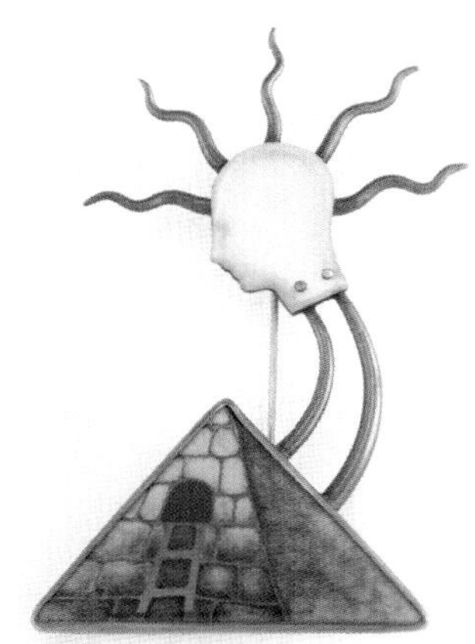

Thomas Gentille

(b. 1936, United States, active New York)

Pin in three parts, c. 1968
Copper, alabaster epoxy resin, ebony epoxy resin, ostrich eggshell, gold
Each: 2¼ × 2½ × ¼ in.

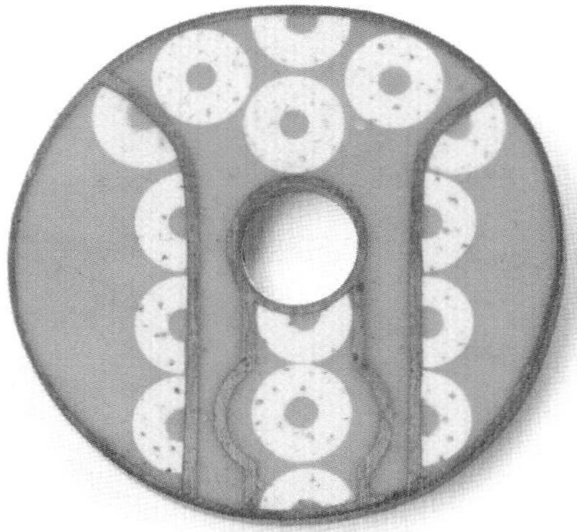

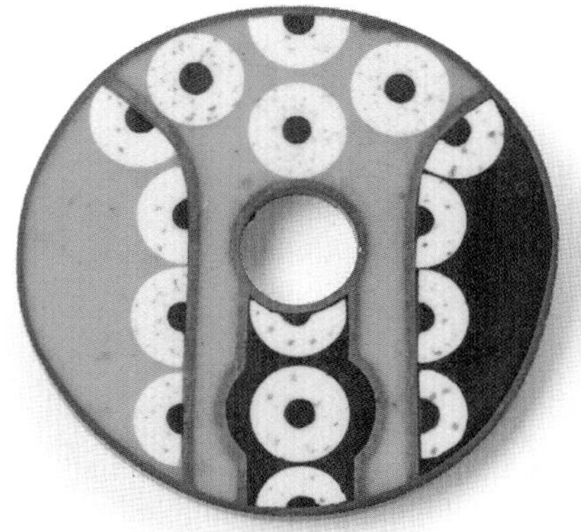

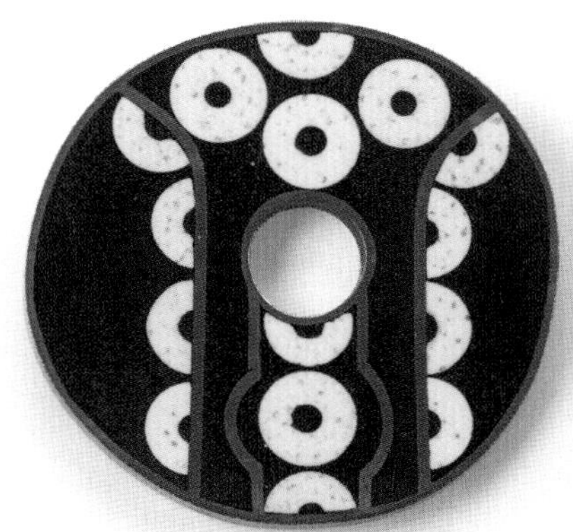

Toni Goessler-Snyder

(1942–1982, b. Germany, active Pennsylvania)

Brooch/pendant, 1975
Silver with gilding, enamel
2⅝ × 3 13⁄16 × 11⁄16 in.

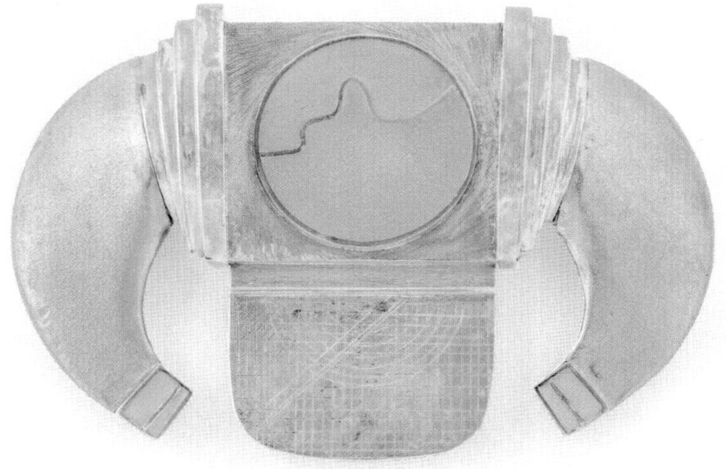

Lisa Gralnick

(b. 1956, United States, active New York and Wisconsin)

Brooch, 2000
Gold
1½ × 2¼ × ½ in.

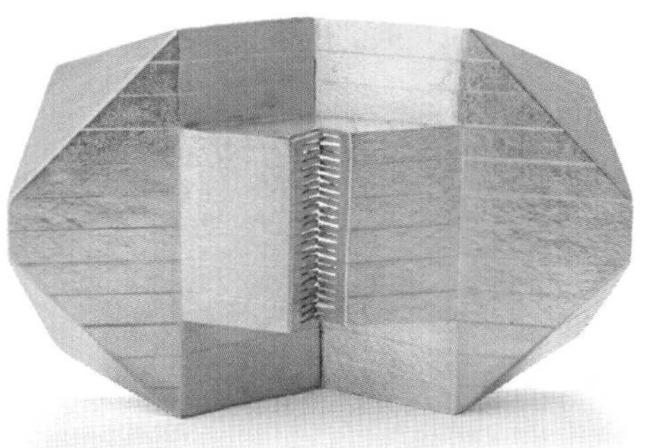

Gésine Hackenberg

(b. 1972, Germany, active Netherlands)

***Delft Blue "Plooischotel" Necklace*, 2012**
1943 Royal Delft earthenware dish, nylon cord, gold
Necklace: 47 ½ in. length;
dish: 14 ¼ × 14 ¼ × 2 ¾ in.

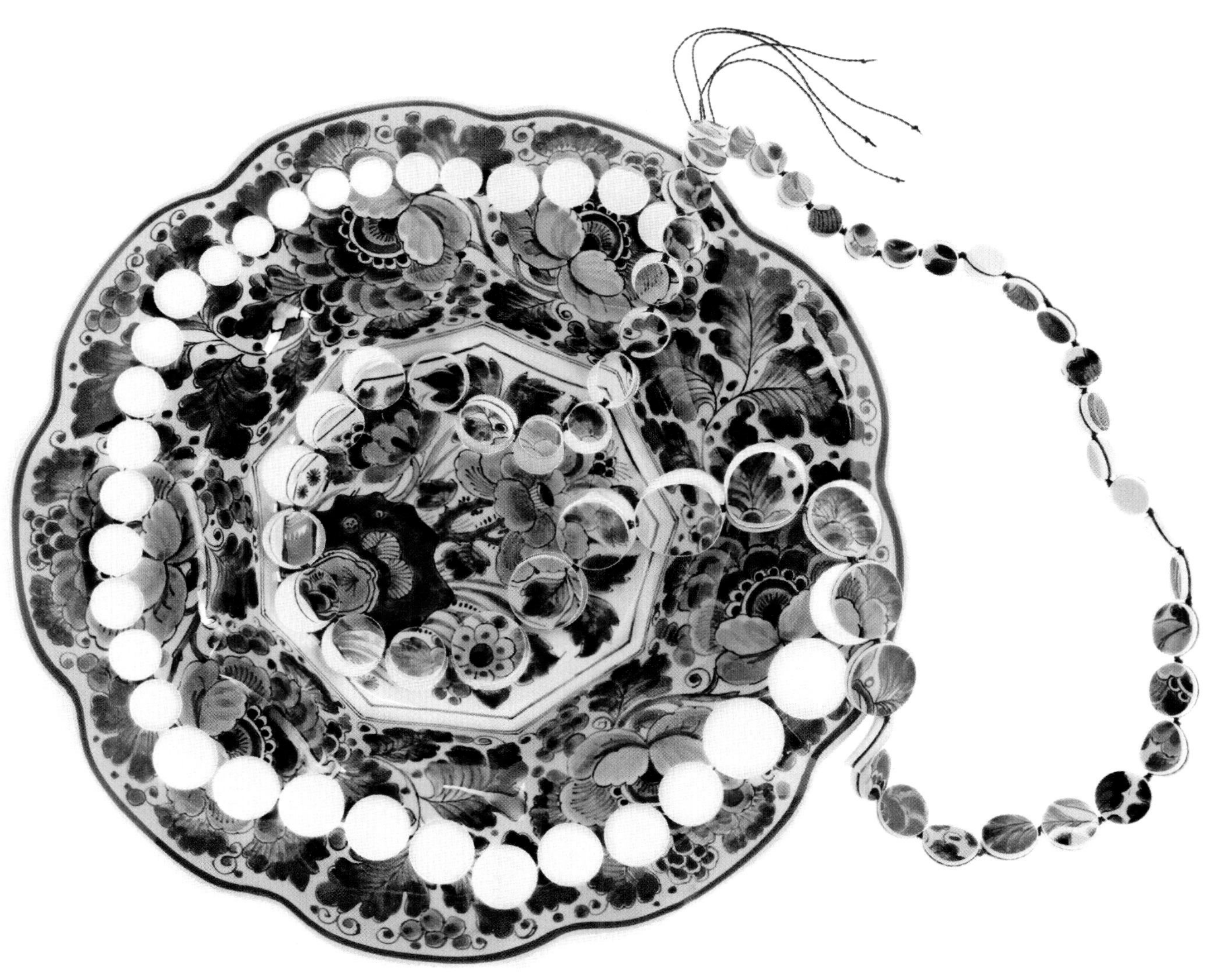

Laurie J. Hall

(b. 1944, United States, active Washington and Oregon)

Bubble-Tea **necklace, 2005**
Silver, coral, paper tea label, PMMA, styrene plastic, glass beads
14 ½ × 7 × ½ in.

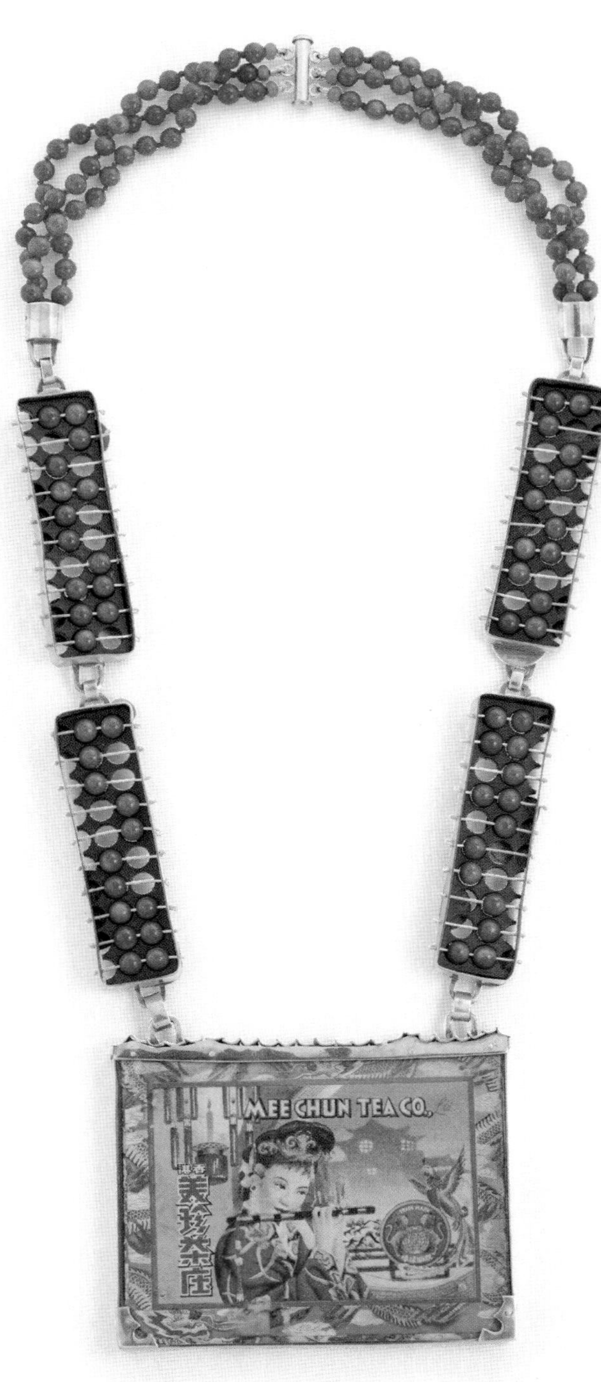

Andrea MAXA Halmschlager

(b. 1961, Austria, active Germany)

Great Spiral **bracelet, 1986**
From the series Paperwork, 1986
Silk paper, brass, copper,
stainless steel
8 × 8 × 5 in.

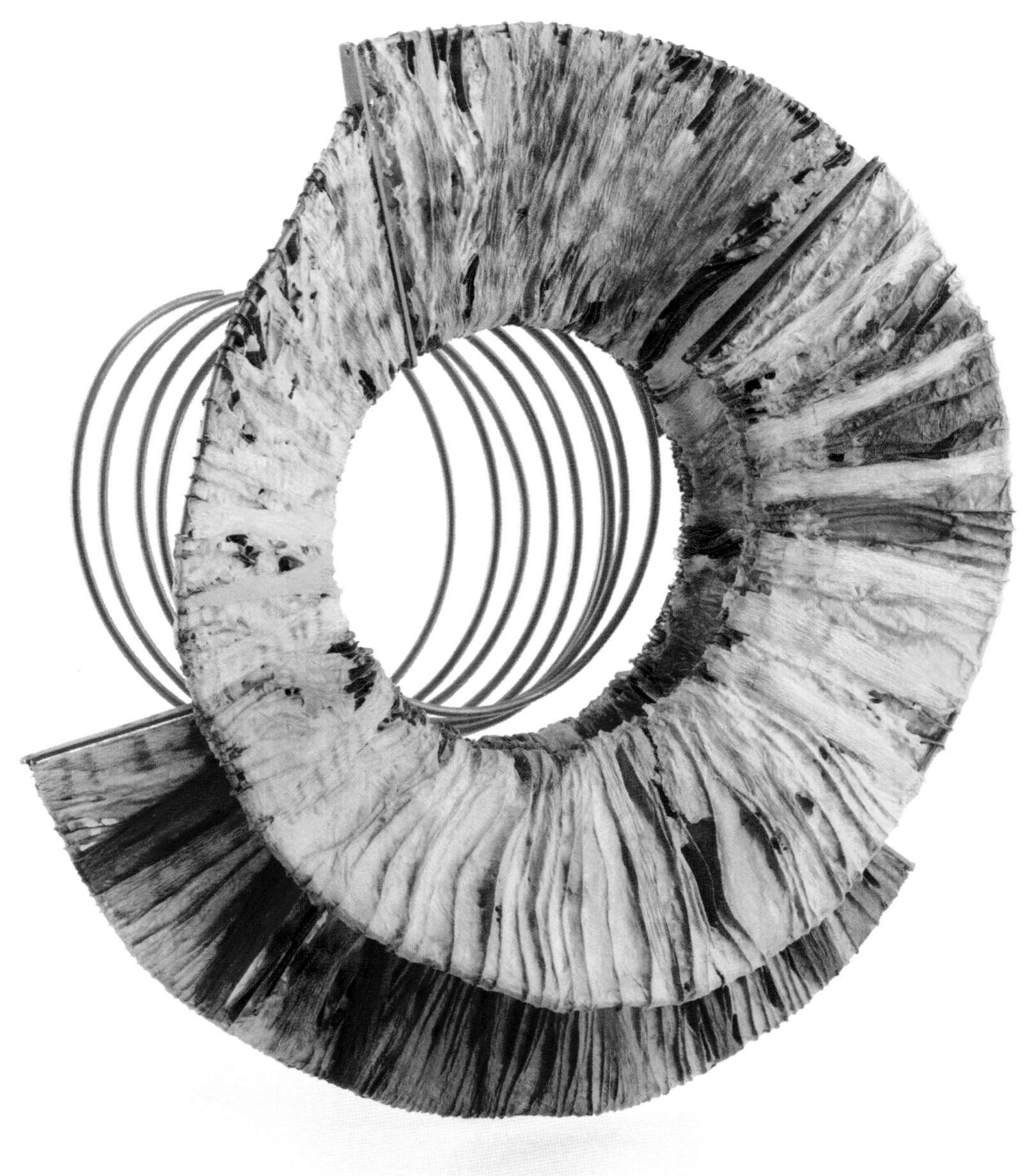

Susan H. Hamlet

(b. 1954, United States, active New York and Massachusetts)

***Shim Bracelet #1*, 1983**
Stainless steel, polyethylene tubing, silver, PMMA, electrical wire insulation
3⅝ × 3⅝ × ½ in.

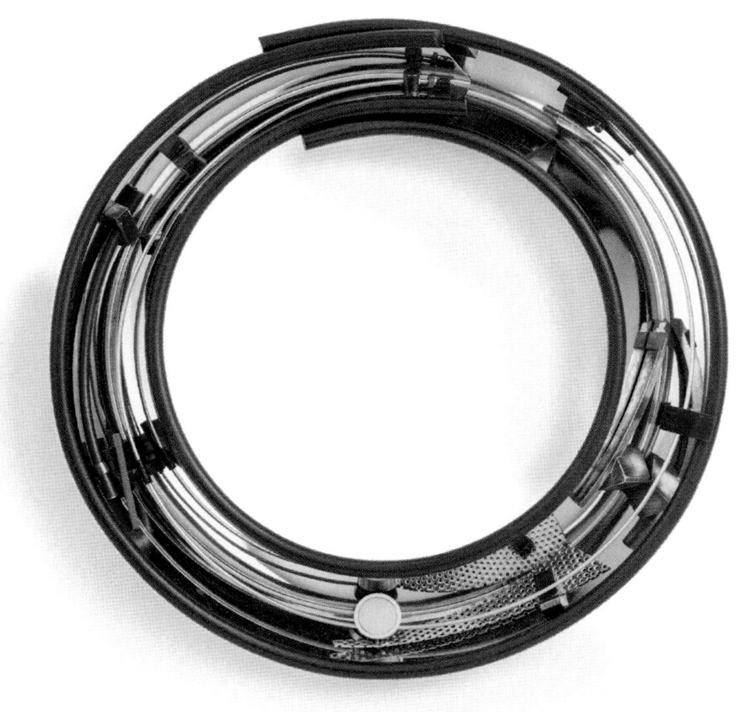

William Harper

(b. 1944, United States, active Ohio and Florida)

***Barbarian Bracelet #1*, 1980**
Silver with gilding, enamel
on copper, gold
4¾ × 4¾ × ¹³⁄₁₆ in.

Brooch, 1983
Silver, gold, enamel on copper,
pearl, moonstone
4¼ × 1½ × ⁵⁄₁₆ in.

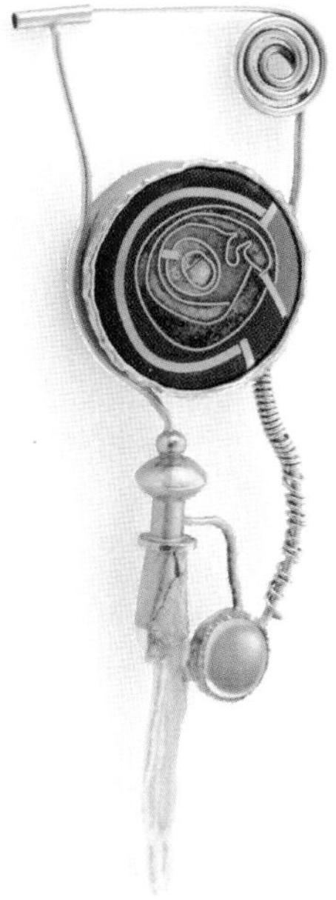

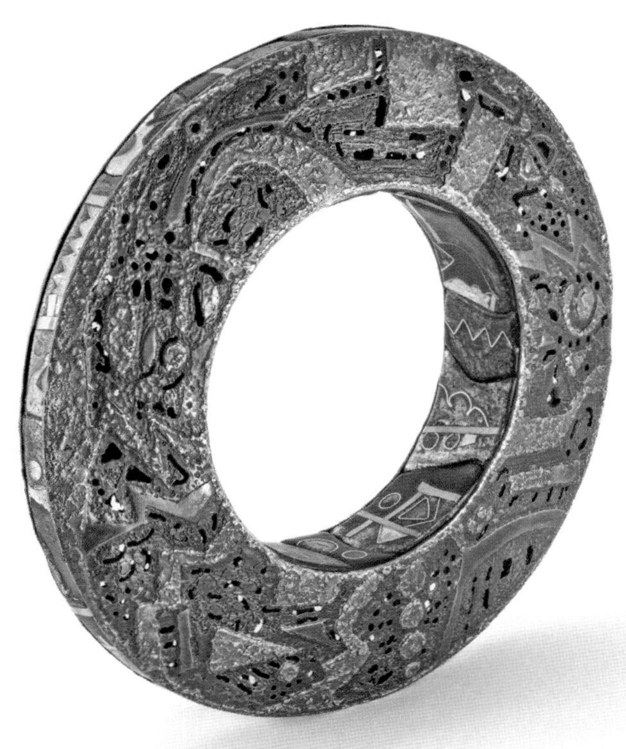

Mirjam Hiller

(b. 1974, Germany)

***Loperenias* brooch, 2012**
Powder-coated stainless steel
8 ¼ × 7 × 2 ½ in.

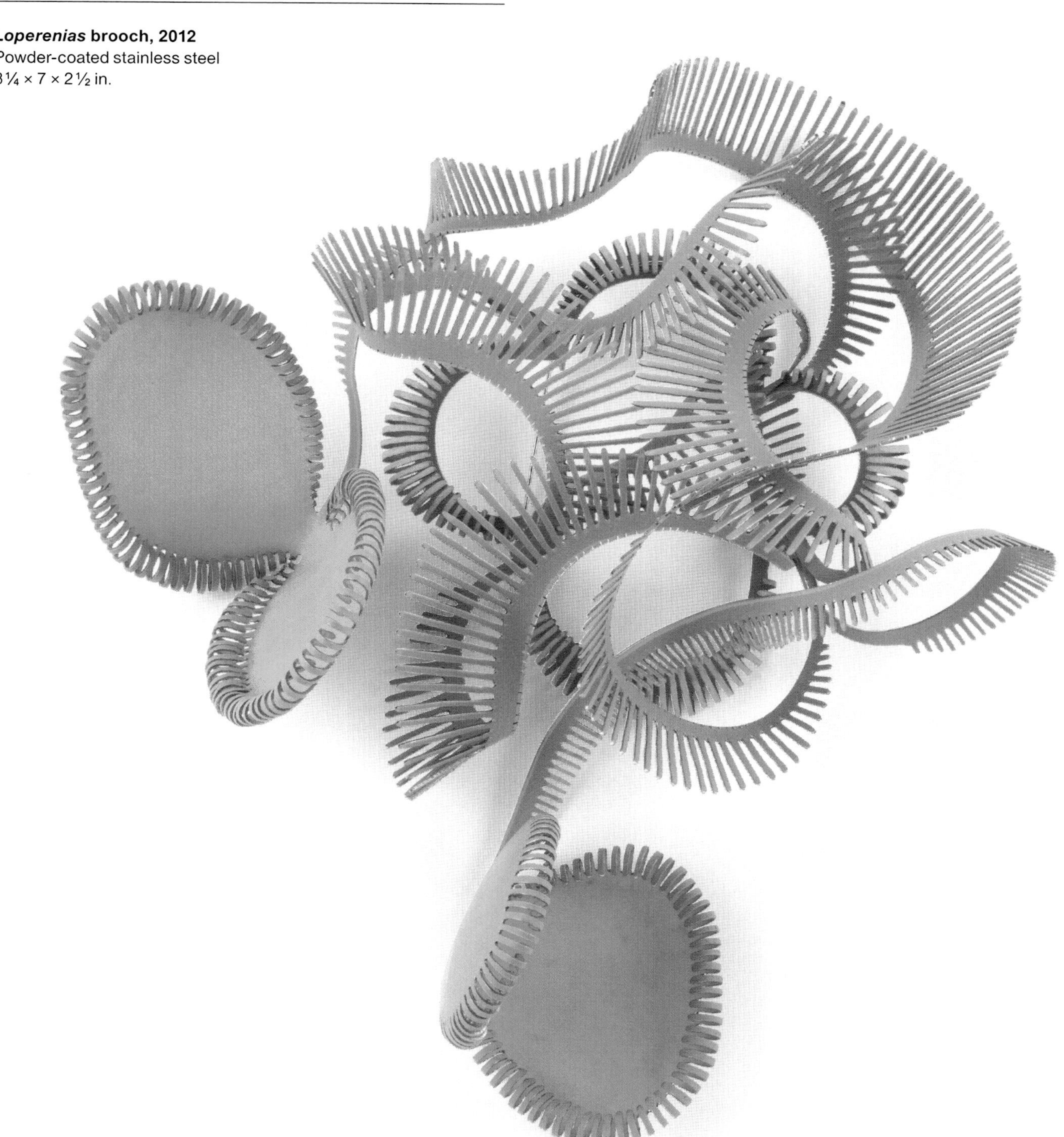

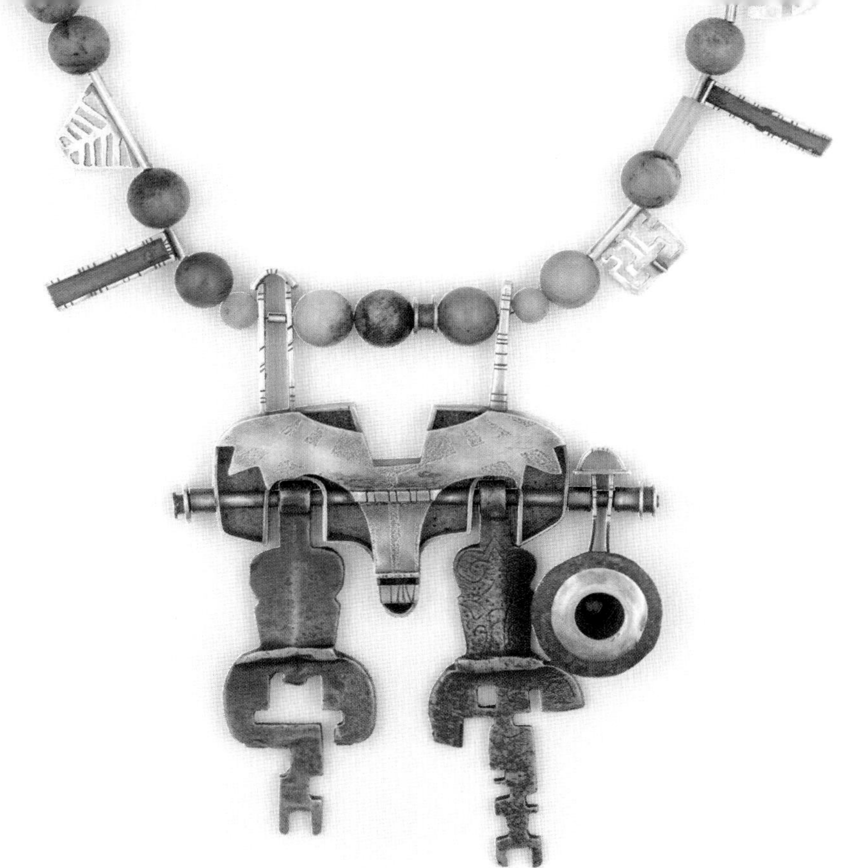

Hiramatsu Yasuki

(1926–2012, Japan)

Ring, n.d.
Gold
1¼ × ¾ × ⅜ in.

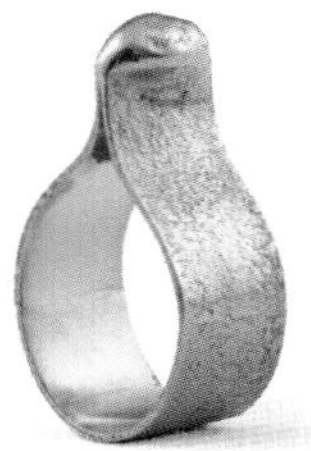

Ron Ho

(b. 1936, United States, active Washington)

***Tibetan Reliquary* necklace, 2012**
Silver, stone beads, Tibetan iron keys, stone earplug
14½ × 7¾ × ⅞ in.

Marian Hosking

(b. 1948, Australia)

***Leaf litter WA* brooch, 2009**
Silver
3 ¼ × 3 ¼ × 1 in.

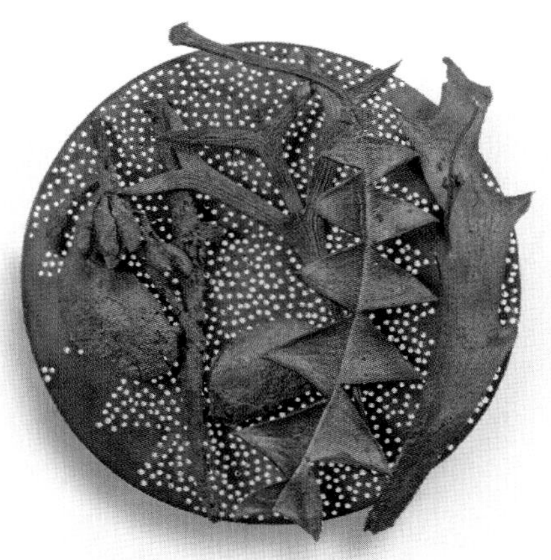

Mary Lee Hu

(b. 1943, United States, active Washington)

***Bracelet #20*, 1983**
Silver, gold
3¾ × 3 × ½ in.

John Iversen

(b. 1953, Germany, active New York)

***Circle Pin*, 1988**
Enamel, gilded copper alloy
4 ½ × 4 ½ × ¼ in.

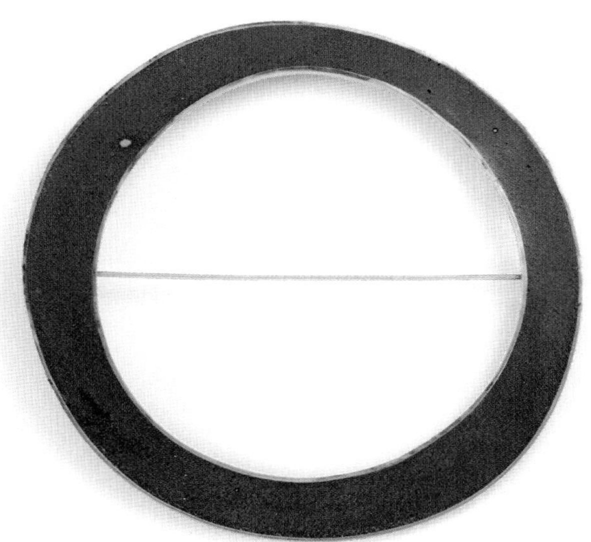

Fantasy, Dreams, Directions, Possibilities, or Even Repudiations: Contemporary Studio Jewelry on the West Coast

Bobbye Tigerman

Several centers of jewelry making and education flourished on the West Coast of the United States in the decades following World War II. While each was influenced by different historical and cultural developments and each spawned individual legacies, these communities of jewelers and metalsmiths were part of, and shaped by, a broader culture of jewelry and craftsmanship. Their shared location in the American West, a place long associated with utopian ideals and embedded with mythologies about possibility and promise, informed their approach. Through an examination of the major jewelry centers—San Francisco and San Diego in California; Seattle and Ellensburg in Washington; and smaller pockets of activity in Long Beach and Santa Cruz, California—this chapter will demonstrate how several distinct traditions of jewelry making evolved independently on the West Coast (largely due to extensive networks of teachers and students) but were also in concert with international developments in the field.[1]

The utopian idea of the West is characterized by deeply held beliefs of independence and self-determination that have long attracted both Americans and foreigners to the region. Freedom from the yoke of tradition, an openness to unconventional methods of working and expression, and a willingness to ignore or break with established social customs and roles all constitute aspects of this Western idealism. Amplifying these long-standing associations reinforced for generations by civic boosters and cultural critics alike, the West became the locus of the counterculture movement in the late 1960s and 70s, a time when many jewelers were just forming their artistic identities.[2]

The "counterculture," a designation popularized by Theodore Roszak in his 1969 book *The Making of a Counter Culture: Reflections on the Technocratic Society and Its Youthful Opposition*, would become a disparaging term for a hedonistic and carefree lifestyle, but its original meaning described a group whose beliefs and values challenged those of the dominant society.[3] In contrast to mainstream artists, those in the counterculture transgressed disciplinary boundaries, emphasized process and experience over finished product, and fostered a distrust of authority and centralization. Instead they embraced irreverence, satire, and a healthy sense of play. All of these characteristics were shared to varying degrees by jewelers on the West Coast, whether in the San Francisco Bay Area, where the countercultural influence was most concentrated, or in other urban and rural areas. And just as the counterculture came to be associated with esoteric forms of spiritual enlightenment, many jewelers likewise explored such practices.

Part of the counterculture movement was deeply concerned with environmentalism and advocated for sustainable practices that improved rather than damaged the earth.[4] Some jewelers working on the West Coast recognized these concerns, especially with regard to the ethical selection of materials. Both leading by example and raising awareness through publication and advocacy, they sought to temper the destructive potential inherent in working with precious materials. California jeweler Susan Kingsley, for example, has worked extensively to raise consciousness about material sourcing. She cofounded Ethical Metalsmiths, a group whose mission is "to lead jewelers and consumers in becoming informed activists for responsible mining, sustainable economic development, and verified, ethical sources of materials used in making jewelry."[5]

The geographical location of jewelers on the West Coast gave them a sustained exposure to the cultures and traditions of Asia. Whether they could trace their family history to the region, or had traveled or come into contact with immigrant communities in the United States, the influence of South and East Asian cultures is often palpable in their art. Working against the backdrop of the devastating political events of the 1960s and 70s (the Vietnam War and assassinations of major political and cultural figures), and informed by a sense of utopianism and the license to defy authority and societal expectations, jewelers on the West Coast contributed significantly to the development and expansion of the international studio jewelry movement.[6]

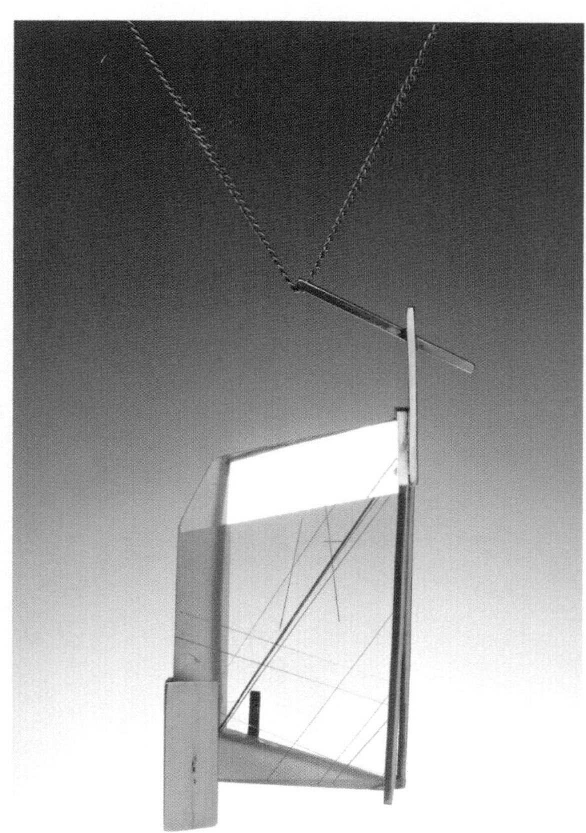

FIG. 1
Margaret De Patta, pendant necklace, 1948, gold and rutilated quartz, pendant: 3¼ × 1⅛ × 13⁄16 in. (8.3 × 2.9 × 2 cm), Margaret De Patta Archives, Bielawski Trust, Point Richmond, California

Margaret De Patta, Progenitor

Any story about avant-garde jewelry on the West Coast must begin with Margaret De Patta, a seminal influence on and mentor to countless jewelers and metalsmiths. Born in 1903 in Tacoma, Washington, and raised in San Diego, De Patta studied painting at the San Diego Academy of Fine Arts, the California School of Fine Arts (now the San Francisco Art Institute), and the Art Students League of New York before settling in San Francisco in 1923.[7] De Patta's interest in jewelry was piqued in 1929 by a frustrated search for a modern wedding ring for herself. Determined to make her own, she apprenticed with San Francisco jeweler Armin Hairenian.

De Patta's jewelry from the 1930s demonstrates a fascination with ancient and foreign cultures, especially the art of Egyptian, Turkish, and pre-Columbian civilizations. The direction of her work would change radically, however, after a 1940 summer course at Mills College in Oakland, California, taught by Bauhaus émigré artist and designer László Moholy-Nagy, followed by study with him at the School of Design in Chicago in 1940–41. Moholy-Nagy famously urged De Patta to "catch your stones with air. Don't enclose them. Make them float in space."[8] Thus encouraged, she became one of the first craftspeople on the West Coast to apply elements of modern design to jewelry, explaining, "I find work problems as set for myself fall into these main directions: space articulation, movement to a purpose, visual explorations with transparencies, reflective surfaces, negative–positive relationships, structures, and new materials. A single piece may incorporate one or many of these ideas."[9] De Patta's fundamental ideas about privileging form and innovative structures and using nonprecious materials have remained important tenets of contemporary jewelry to this day. In a piece such as her 1948 pendant, she demonstrated several of her enduring formal concerns: transparency and the optical effects of gemstones (especially uncommon ones like rutilated quartz[10]); interaction between the piece and the wearer; and a customized, open setting that allows the quartz to be cut in a nonstandard way, thereby permitting the pattern of the clothing worn beneath it to show through (fig. 1).

De Patta actively exhibited her work in national and international exhibitions throughout her lifetime, and was included in such landmark postwar shows as *Modern Handmade Jewelry* at the Museum of Modern Art (New York, 1946) and *Modern Jewelry under Fifty Dollars* at the Walker Art Center (Minneapolis, 1948). She was also one of only a handful of Americans to be included in the show credited with heralding the contemporary studio jewelry movement, the *International Exhibition of Modern Jewellery, 1890–1961* at Goldsmiths' Hall in London in 1961.[11] Her work was shown extensively, and thus became widely known both on the West Coast and farther afield. In California alone she had solo exhibitions at the Fine Arts Gallery of San Diego (now the San Diego Museum of Art) in 1951, the Mills College Art Department in 1955, a dedicated display as part of the exhibition *The Metal Experience* at the Oakland Museum in 1971, and a posthumous retrospective at the same institution in 1976.[12]

In addition to the enormous impact of her work, De Patta also left a lasting legacy as the founding president of the Metal Arts Guild, a professional organization that fostered a collegial community of jewelers and metalsmiths in the San Francisco Bay Area. The group was founded by a handful of jewelers in 1951 with a mission to protect and advise members on legal and business affairs, to create a forum for the exchange of technical and practical information, to promote the field of contemporary metalwork by organizing exhibitions of members' art, and to provide a venue for social interaction.[13] Members of the Metal Arts Guild formed a core of active jewelers that would go on to shape the field for the next several decades. In addition to De Patta, founding members included such influential figures as Irena Brynner, Imogene Gieling, Peter Macchiarini, merry renk, Byron Wilson, and Bob Winston.[14] The group had forty-five members by the end of its first year, and although membership has fluctuated over the years, it now numbers around two hundred. The mission and activities remain true to the founders' vision: it provides programming about the technical and business aspects of professional metalsmithing, fosters exhibition opportunities, and organizes community outreach events and social gatherings throughout the Bay Area.

Jewelry in the Pacific Northwest

Concurrent with Margaret De Patta's most active years, a tradition of jewelry making was forming in the Pacific Northwest. With a strong basis in technique, this jewelry also drew upon an interest in found objects as well as motifs and materials borrowed from a wide range of cultures.

A contemporary of De Patta, jeweler and artist Ruth Penington grew up and spent her career in Seattle, but her extensive travels domestically and abroad were critical to the development of her work. Penington combined the highly refined Scandinavian-influenced metalworking traditions so prevalent in the mid-twentieth century with the use of objects from the Puget Sound region, such as beach pebbles. A student at the University of Washington in Seattle, she later served on the faculty from 1930 to 1970, working as a jeweler, enamelist, textile designer, and printmaker. Her wide range of formative experiences included study at Teacher's College, Columbia University, in New York in 1929; work in industrial designer Gilbert Rohde's New York office in 1944; participation in the Handy and Harman silver workshop at the Rhode Island School of Design in 1947; and training in the Copenhagen silversmith shop of A. Michelsen in 1952, the combination of which gave her a firm grounding in design approach and metalwork techniques.[15] Her students

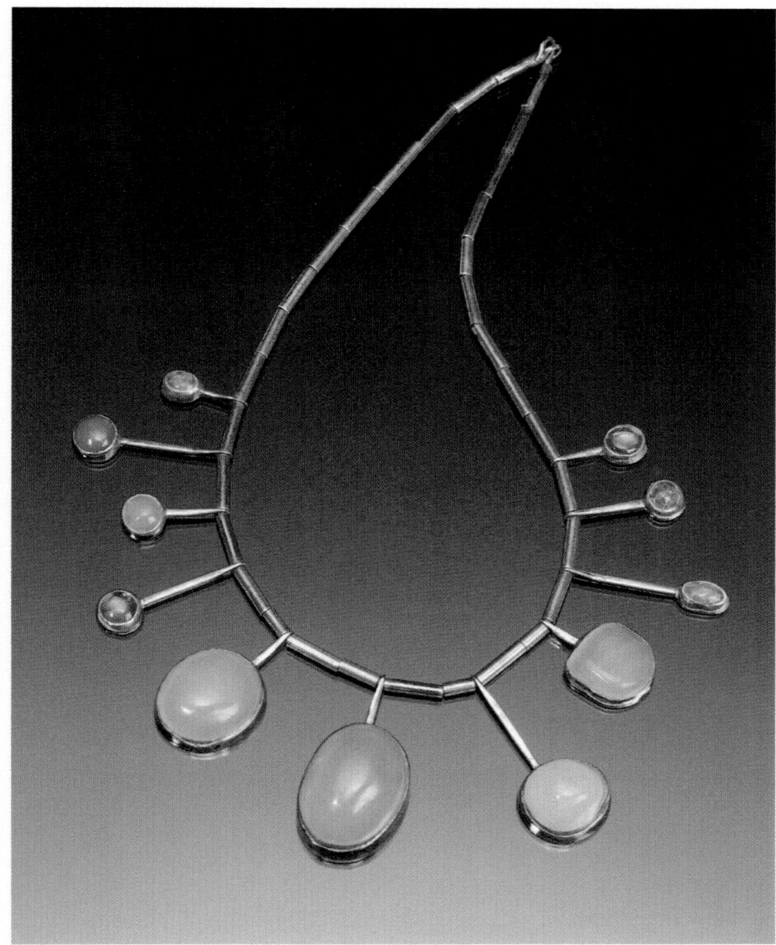

FIG. 2
Ruth Penington, necklace, early 1960s, silver, opals, moonstones, and agates, 14⅛ × 1½ in. (35.9 × 3.8 cm), Tacoma Art Museum, gift of Gene and Liz Brandzel, 1998.6

have recalled that she was a formidable teacher who emphasized the dutiful honing of technique and cultivation of a refined precision.[16] She encouraged them to nurture their curiosity, saying, "It behooves the designer to broaden his understanding of the needs of his time and the technology available to him." In her view, a designer should also carefully study the past, thereby "evaluat[ing] and absorb[ing] the ideas expressed [in historical work] . . . [as] his own expression becomes richer because of this."[17] Penington's early 1960s necklace (fig. 2) reflects many of these artistic ideals. The piece is masterfully wrought in sterling silver with an array of opals, moonstones, and agates framing the face. While the necklace shape is fairly conventional, the bold starburst pattern of semiprecious gemstones gives the work a distinctly modernist sensibility.

In addition to her artistic output and teaching, Penington was an incredibly active member of the national crafts community and was truly devoted to promoting her field. She had strong connections to Aileen Osborn Webb, the influential founder of the American Craftsmen's Council (now the American Craft Council), and served as a craftsman-trustee of the organization from the Northwest region of the United States for many years. In Seattle she was a founder and key member of many art and design professional associations, including the Northwest Designer Craftsmen, which held juried exhibitions at the Henry Art Gallery that gave craftspeople such as Peter Voulkos (then living in Montana) and Don Tompkins early recognition.[18] The legacy of her own work is matched by the contributions of her students, the most prominent being jewelers Russell Day,

Tompkins, Imogene Gieling, and the indefatigable Ramona Solberg.

Day earned a master's degree in fine arts at the University of Washington under Penington and was a professor in the art department at Everett Community College (formerly Everett Junior College) in a northern suburb of Seattle from 1948 to 1976. He was renowned for his phenomenal sense of color and his early experiments in both jewelry and studio glass, notably as a mentor to famed glass artist Dale Chihuly. He is fondly remembered as a teacher of many artists, the most significant jewelry student being Don Tompkins, whom he taught at both Everett High School and Everett Community College, and who would become his faculty colleague at the latter institution.[19]

After studying with Day, Tompkins transferred to the University of Washington in Seattle where he studied under Penington, earning a master's degree with a specialization in metal, jewelry, and sculpture in 1958.[20] He was part of an early generation of jewelers that included J. Fred Woell and Robert Ebendorf, all of whom incorporated aspects of pop culture and politics into their jewelry. In Tompkins's work this is most clearly exemplified by his Commemorative Medals series (1965–76), a group of pendants that feature artistic and political figures that shaped his life for good or ill, such as Jackson Pollock, Janis Joplin, J. Edgar Hoover, and Richard Nixon (fig. 3).[21] Tompkins displayed them as part of his doctoral dissertation requirements at Teachers College, Columbia University, in 1972.[22] He was an early proponent of using the medium of jewelry to express personal convictions and states of mind, thereby liberating it from its traditional role as a symbol of power and wealth.

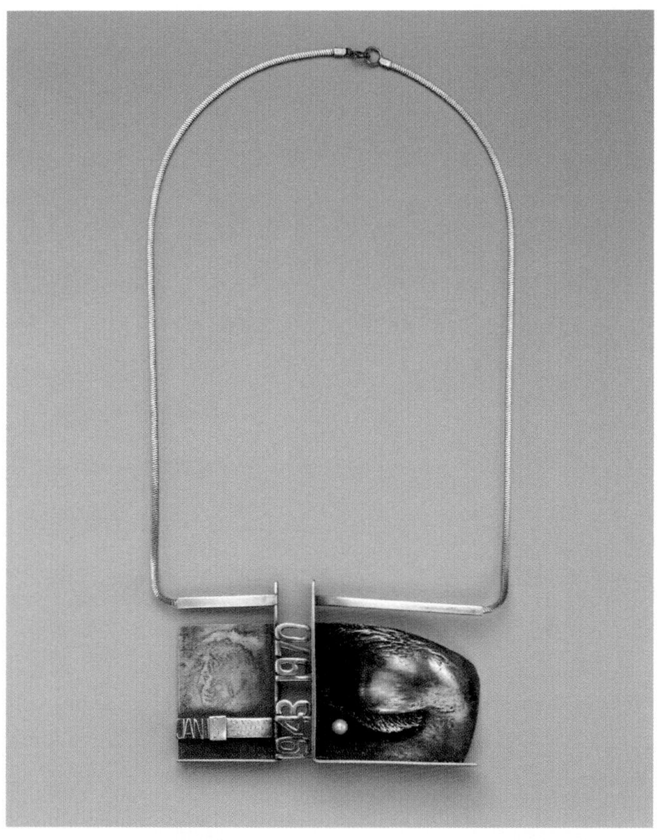

FIG. 3
Don Tompkins, *Janis Joplin Commemorative Medal* from the series Commemorative Medals, 1970, silver, brass, and pearl, 9¾ × 4¼ × ¾ in. (24.8 × 10.8 × 1.9 cm), The Museum of Fine Arts, Houston, Helen Williams Drutt Collection, gift of Helen Williams Drutt English

Tompkins, a native of Washington, moved back and forth between the state and the East Coast several times. In addition to his undergraduate and master's education in Seattle, he taught art, design, and jewelry at Central Washington State College (now Central Washington University [CWU]) in Ellensburg from 1966 to 1972 and returned to the region from 1975 until his death in 1982. In addition to the legacy of his many students, he maintained a strong network of family and friends in the jewelry field, including his sister Merrily Tompkins, Ken Cory, Nancy Worden, and Ramona Solberg.

Solberg was actually the reason that Tompkins returned to his home state in 1966. She had known him through Day and recruited him to teach with her in Ellensburg, where she had held a post since 1957. Solberg credited Tompkins with having an indelible impact on her work. She began to incorporate

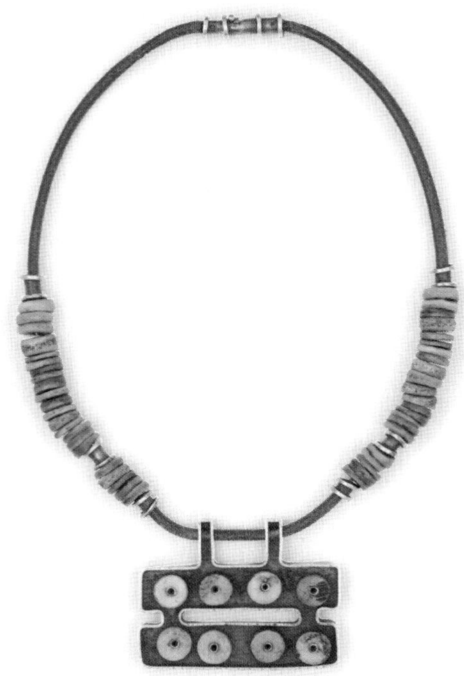

FIG. 4
Ramona Solberg, *Tantric* necklace, c. 1970, silver, bone, and leather; pendant: 2⅝ × 3 × ¼ in. (6.7 × 7.6 × .6 cm), Los Angeles County Museum of Art, gift of Nancy Worden, M.2014.110.3

found and unconventional objects shortly after his arrival, a practice that became her trademark. "Don influenced me with what I was using in my jewelry perhaps more than anyone," she said. "It kind of loosened me up, and I could see that I didn't always have to use beads, or I didn't always have to use stones."[23]

Prior to this transformation, Solberg had volunteered for the Women's Army Corps during World War II and served in Germany in the mid- to late 1940s. She returned to the United States in 1950 and received her bachelor's degree in art education and later her master's in jewelry at the University of Washington in Seattle, where she studied with Penington. Solberg began teaching art at a Seattle high school but used opportunities afforded by the GI Bill to study jewelry and enameling in Norway in 1953–54 before beginning her teaching career in Ellensburg.[24]

While certainly not the first jeweler to incorporate found objects,[25] Solberg is largely credited with popularizing the use of everyday objects and ethnic souvenirs in jewelry. She shared this approach with her many students and in 1972 published *Inventive Jewelry-Making*, a compendium of materials and techniques that could be used in the creation of jewelry. As she explained in the introduction, "This book is devoted to jewelry of the inexpensive and expendable variety. . . . Taking a cue from today's inventive jewelers, who are inspired by the past, the present, and visions of the future, we can see how to draw upon the ingenious, inexpensive materials and discards of our affluent, disposable world to create humorous, spontaneous jewelry."[26] Illustrated with a combination of ethnic jewelry and pieces made by herself and her students (Ron Ho figures prominently), the book was an early manual in jewelry design using unconventional materials and found objects. Solberg gained a national reputation from the book and received many invitations to lead workshops as a result.

In her own work, Solberg used a variety of materials, including found objects, beads, silver, and even the children's craft material Doodley-Doo in one piece made entirely of the brightly colored, pliable plastic (including the clasp). For her 1972 *Tantric* necklace (fig. 4), Solberg strung disc-shaped mottled bone beads separated by hand-forged silver spacers on a brown leather cord. For the pendant, she arranged the same beads in a graphic composition, placing them on an oxidized silver ground. The beads thus serve as both structure and decoration. The contrasting color palette of the oxidized silver and bone recalls the dark-and-light compositions of her celebrated domino pieces, and as she did for nearly all of her work, Solberg fashioned a custom silver clasp. The reference in her title to Tantric art and culture remains opaque but the piece was made in 1972, a time of widespread countercultural interest in Indian spirituality in general and Tantra in particular. The rectangular pendant may suggest Indian amulet boxes.

Solberg was recruited back to the University of Washington in Seattle in 1967 during Penington's sabbatical. Offered a permanent post, she taught there until 1983. In addition to her teaching, prolific output, and book, she participated in important exhibitions, including the seminal 1969 *Objects: USA* show that heralded a new generation of craftspeople as it traveled to more than twenty venues across the country. She also curated the hugely popular *Ubiquitous Bead* exhibitions at the Bellevue Art Museum (now Bellevue Arts Museum) in Washington in 1987 and 1998, respectively. An avid traveler, she led many art- and craft-oriented group trips to Turkey, Afghanistan, India, and Thailand. Solberg's multiple visits to these areas resulted in a sustained knowledge of contemporary artistic production as well as deep personal relationships. Jeweler Kiff Slemmons recounts that while she was traveling once with Solberg in the remote city of Jaisalmer, in the Indian state of Rajasthan, a teenage boy emerged from a small shop and proclaimed, "Hi, Ramona!"[27] The trips also gave her the opportunity to acquire objects for use in future pieces. Solberg's influence was felt most strongly (like Penington and Day before her) through her mentoring and friendships with a close-knit group of Seattle jewelers that included Ho, Slemmons, Worden, and Laurie J. Hall.

Ho, one of Solberg's earliest and most dedicated students and friends, first met her in a summer workshop she led at the University of Washington in Seattle in 1968. He was born in Hawaii in 1936 to a family of Chinese descent and moved to Seattle to enroll at Pacific Lutheran College (now Pacific Lutheran University) in Tacoma, Washington, where he earned a bachelor's degree in art education in 1958.[28] Solberg had a revelatory impact on Ho, as she did on so many others, exposing him to the possibility of incorporating common objects into jewelry. Ho recounted, "I had never envisioned making jewelry from anything other than precious stones and materials. The idea of using simple found objects to make art was, at that time, a new experience for me.... Ramona introduced me to the beauty and power of ethnic jewelry, which she had picked up on her world travels. This had a profound effect on my vision and the way I began to look at all jewelry."[29]

Solberg and Ho remained lifelong friends and travel partners, with Ho eventually leading the international trips after Solberg retired. While he continued to use a rich variety of ethnic objects collected during his travels, in 1990 Ho began to mine his ancestral Chinese culture for subject matter, casting and forging in silver and copper miniature dim sum steamers, teapots, pagodas, and auspicious Chinese symbols. Ho's 2012 *Tibetan Reliquary* necklace (fig. 5) demonstrates his interest in both Asian culture and found artifacts: the steel keys in the pendant were found in Tibet and the stone earplug is from Mexico. The chain is made of green stone beads acquired in China, which are interspersed with silver ornaments that he describes as "doodles in silver." Several of the beads are boxed in silver (a technique borrowed from examples in his Southeast Asian jewelry collection), relieving the repetition of the round bead.[30]

Solberg's student Laurie J. Hall also went on to have a distinguished jewelry career. She studied with Solberg while earning her master's degree in teaching at the University of Washington in 1974. It was Solberg who introduced Hall to the idea of using unconventional objects in her jewelry but unlike her mentor (and like Ho and other fellow Pacific Northwest jewelers), she imbues her work with autobiographical meaning. The *Wheelbarrow* brooch of 2004 (fig. 6) was inspired by her and her family's love of gardening and commitment to the land. Her grandfather was a vegetable farmer who cultivated one hundred acres in Shedd, Oregon. Her family had always used wheelbarrows in the garden, and Hall is an avid gardener herself. An inveterate tinkerer, she is also fascinated by mechanical structures and often makes miniature working machines. In this piece, the wheelbarrow has a functioning, spinning wheel.[31] The unusual placement of the pin allows it to be worn on the top of the shoulder like an epaulet, a ceremonial marker of military rank.

Solberg also touched many artists who were not her formal students, the most prominent being Slemmons and Worden. Slemmons was active in Seattle from 1969 to 2002 (when she moved to Chicago) and her work ranges widely in its inspiration and approach. She has used strategies such as found objects and appropriation but does not embrace a particular material or technique. All of her work is conceptually driven, and as a student of literature, language and poetry underlie most of her work; she even considers poetry a model for the visual effect she hopes to achieve.[32] Her work runs the gamut from the Hands of the Heroes series (1987–91), which

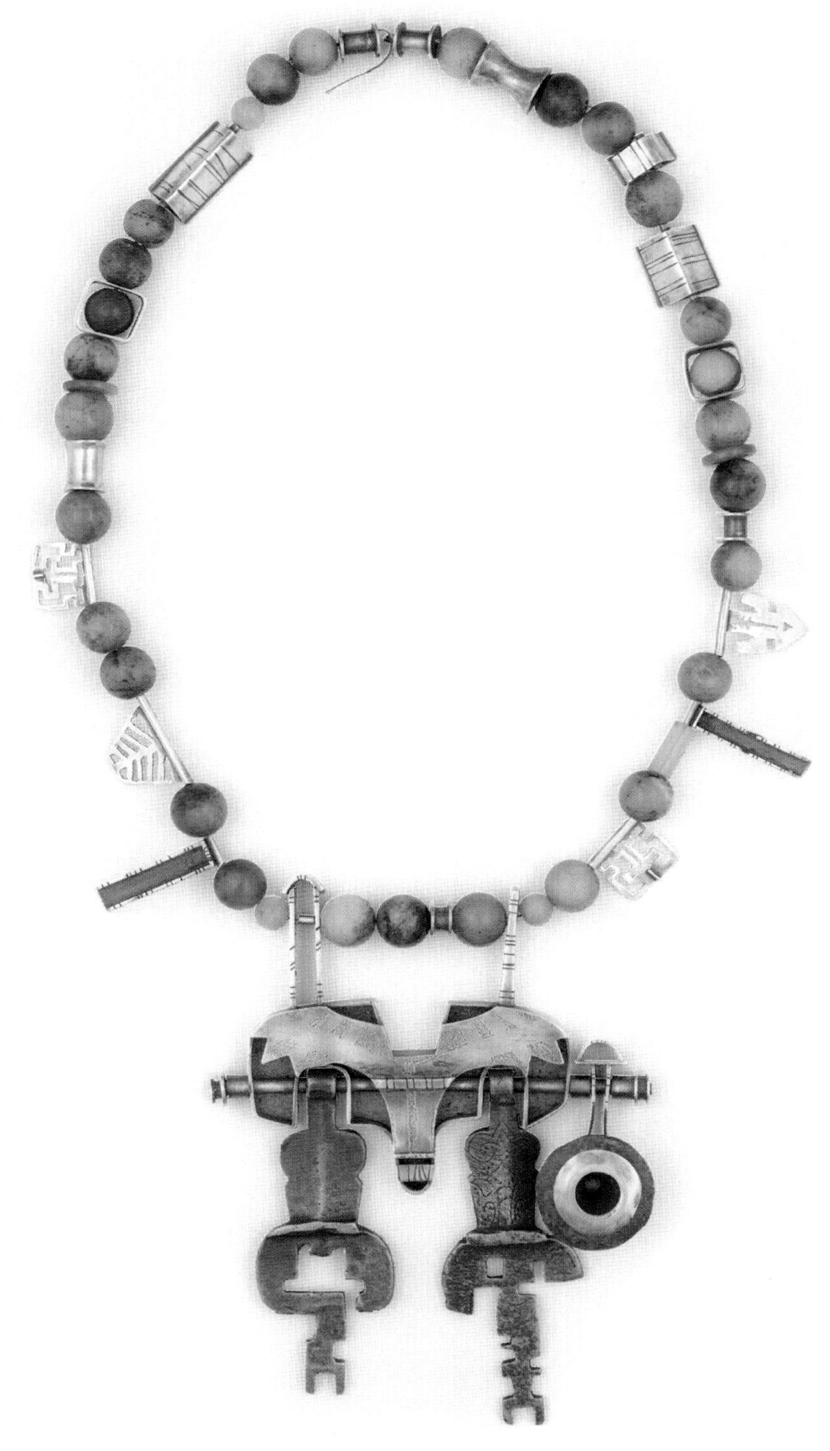

FIG. 5
Ron Ho, *Tibetan Reliquary* necklace, 2012

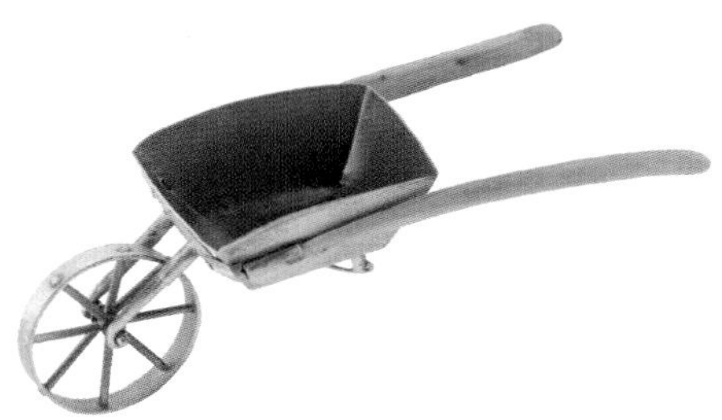

FIG. 6
Laurie J. Hall, *Wheelbarrow* brooch, 2004

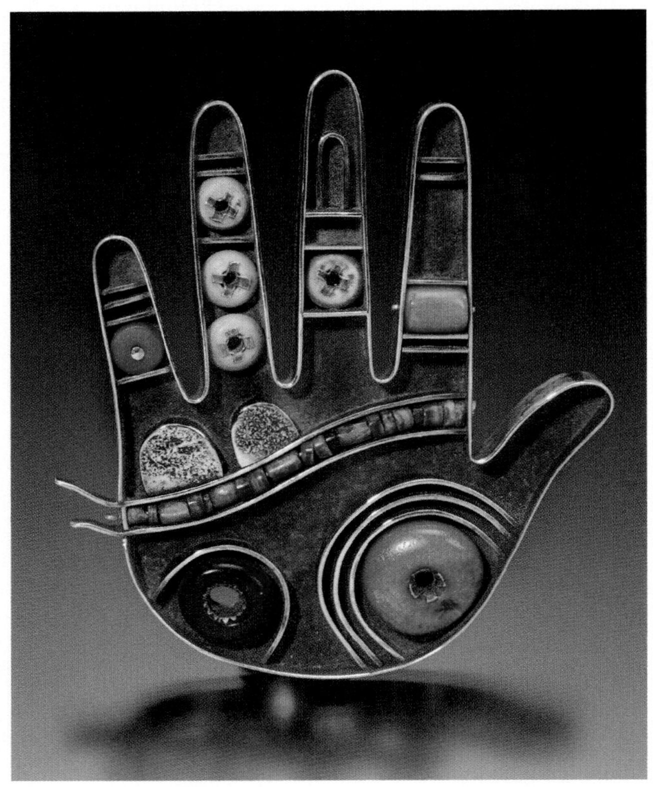

FIG. 7
Kiff Slemmons, *Ramona Solberg* brooch, from the series Hands of the Heroes, 1991, silver, amber, bone, coral, glass, and pre-Columbian stone beads, 3 1/4 × 2 7/8 × 7/16 in. (8.6 × 7.3 × 1.1 cm), Tacoma Art Museum, gift of Ramona Solberg, 1998.33

consists of more than fifty hand-shaped brooches relating to her personal heroes, each with unique attributes, to her Re:Pair and Imperfection series (2004–06), in which she asked eighteen prominent jewelers to send her "a broken, incomplete, or inconclusive fragment" that she then modified and adapted into new work.[33] For the Hands of the Heroes brooch dedicated to her great friend and inspiration Solberg (fig. 7), Slemmons used a string of small pre-Columbian beads that she had kept since finding them on her first trip to Oaxaca, Mexico, in the late 1960s.[34] Solberg's passion for and extensive knowledge of beads are well documented; she was a consummate collector and organized several exhibitions on the subject. Slemmons used the Oaxacan beads to form the metaphorical life line of Ramona's palm, emphasizing the shared central role that beads played in their work and the long history of beads in jewelry, ritual practices, and as currency.

Slemmons also knew Penington's work well through their mutual membership in the Northwest Designer Craftsmen, and her appreciation deepened after an exhibition of Penington's work at the Bellevue Art Museum in 1990. Slemmons held Penington's intellectual rigor and technical mastery in high esteem, but it was Solberg with whom she had a close personal bond and shared many common interests in jewelry making. While their approaches differed markedly—Solberg emphasized visual form and was famously reserved about explaining her work while Slemmons's process generally begins with an idea and later considers the materials to execute the vision— they shared a mutual passion for non-Western jewelry and foreign cultures.

Funk and Funky: The Bay Area and Washington

The generation of artists that matured under De Patta and Penington developed approaches and values that diverged from their mentors. By the 1960s the San Francisco Bay Area had entered a period of great artistic ferment. Informed by Beat poetry, bohemian music, and radical politics, the art scene was flourishing. The Bay Area artists who came of age in the 1950s and 60s employed a broad range of strategies, including gestural assemblage and critiques of pop culture and consumerism, and generally rejected a hierarchy of materials. As the counterculture movement unfolded in the 1960s and early 70s, there was a deepening disregard for established art world institutions and critical approbation; visual manifestations of this alternative outlook emerged in art and craft.

The Bay Area–based Funk movement, which would inspire a number of jewelers, comprised a group of artists who shared an emerging sensibility, and sometimes aesthetic, that was partly a reaction to the perceived slickness of 1960s Minimalism, Pop Art, and "Finish Fetish" art prevalent in Southern California. The movement—documented in the landmark *Funk* exhibition at the University Art Museum of the University of California, Berkeley, in 1967—was also an expression of disdain for mainstream art criticism. Curator Peter Selz described it as "hot rather than cool; it is committed rather than disengaged; it is bizarre rather than formal; it is sensuous; and frequently it is quite ugly and ungainly."[35] The show consisted largely of multimedia sculptures that often incorporated industrial materials such as aluminum, fiberglass, and vinyl, with a handful of works made exclusively of clay. Robert Arneson, Bruce Conner, James Melchert, Ken Price, and Voulkos were among the prominent artists whose work was included in the exhibition.

The bulbous shapes, ungainly proportions, and raw sexual references of Funk would influence many jewelers who also challenged the art establishment and sought to assert an alternative, independent voice. The unorthodox approach to materials in Funk appealed to jewelers. As the artist Harold Paris wrote, "The meaning of the art was not in any way related to the intrinsic worth of the materials. Funky artists were essentially assemblage people."[36] The exhibition and the zeitgeist it captured especially resonated with Ken Cory, a Washington State native who encountered the creative upheavals of the Funk artists as a student at the California College of Arts and Crafts (CCAC, now California College of the Arts) beginning in 1963.

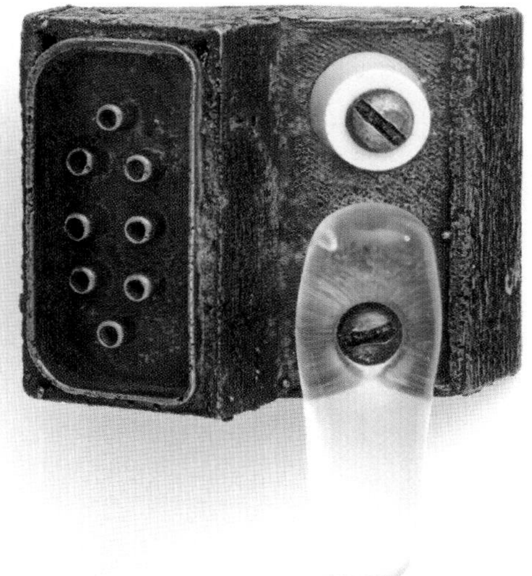

FIG. 8
Ken Cory, Brooch, 1968, bronze, Plexiglas, found object, 1¾ × 1½ × 1 in. (4.5 × 3.8 × 2.5 cm), Los Angeles County Museum of Art, gift of Beverly Cory, M.2015.23.5

While in the Bay Area a few years later, Cory made a group of small brooches that embodied his enduring interests: machines (especially cars); Euclidean geometries contrasted with organic, almost primordial shapes; and provocative, often sexually suggestive, imagery. Attesting to the continuing links between the Pacific Northwest and the Bay Area, he cited De Patta's belief in the evocative power of jewelry and her embrace of unconventional materials and techniques as a critical influence.[37] In his 1968 brooch (fig. 8), Cory used a process he had developed for copper-casting balsa wood to create a textured surface in the bronze.[38] The coarse metal and small protrusions that suggest the male end of a plug on the left side of the brooch complement the phallus-shaped piece of clear Plexiglas and the white cylinder above (held in place with a prominent screw). These elements, along with the engine-like appearance of the shape conveyed a charged masculinity more in line with the Funk movement than with modernist jewelry.

In 1972 Cory began teaching jewelry and metalsmithing at Central Washington State College (now CWU) in Ellensburg, replacing Don Tompkins. This move brought him back to his home region and allowed him to draw directly on a familiar landscape and way of life. Cory had a definitively Western point of view, finding inspiration and imagery in the expansive terrain, the richness of native Pacific Northwest cultures, and the solitude allowed by a reclusive life in rural Washington far from major cities and jewelry centers. Fellow jeweler and close friend Mary Lee Hu recalled: "In all this work there is a sense of place. Very few metalsmiths do work that is about and from the place they live. He knew the West was marginalized [by the art world]. But it was *his place*."[39]

Despite Ellensburg's remoteness, Cory found ways to engage with the larger jewelry and artistic worlds. He was a regular participant as both instructor and attendee at the annual Summervail Workshop for Art and Critical Studies held between 1971 and 1984 near Vail, Colorado. Established by jeweler Jim Cotter and artist Randy Milhoan, the workshop brought together artists and craftspeople from around the country, with many representing Western states. Each summer hundreds of students would arrive for weeklong sessions in glass, ceramics, enameling, metalsmithing and jewelry making, blacksmithing, fiber design, sculpture, drawing, printmaking, photography, film, and dance. Faculty members taught one-week sessions consisting of both presentations and demonstrations. Intended to be less formal and structured than other similar workshops, the atmosphere of Summervail was rustic and relaxed. Attendees lived in tents and shared communal cooking and cleaning responsibilities. The most anticipated social event of the year was the Black and White Rainbow Ball, an elaborate costume party. Other activities included themed Sunday dinners cooked and decorated by workshop participants (memorable ones included a Chinese banquet by jeweler Mary Lee Hu and an Italian feast by enamelist Jamie Bennett) and the annual creation of a float for the Fourth of July parade in Vail.[40]

Summervail also hosted an annual metalworking symposium organized by Cotter and jeweler and educator Lane Coulter. A microcosm of the larger conference, it offered a further opportunity for metalsmiths and jewelers to meet and learn from each other. Cotter and Coulter invited ten metalsmiths each year to give talks, slide presentations, and demonstrations over the course of three or four very intense days. The speakers were all accomplished artists, some just beginning their careers and others (like J. Fred Woell, L. Brent Kington, and Alvin Pine) more established practitioners. The organizers included enamelists and blacksmiths in order to represent a range of metalworkers. Participants came from all over the United States (a handful were even from other countries), though the majority came from Western states.[41] The only similar gathering was the annual Society of North American Goldsmiths (SNAG) conference, which was decidedly more formal and structured and, in the Summervail organizers' opinions, did not leave enough time for spontaneous interactions. A highlight of the symposium for many attendees was the Saw, File, and Solder Sprints, in which teams of three metalsmiths competed to create a ring in the shortest period of time.[42] The legacy of Summervail was the extraordinary exposure participants received to the range of metalworking in America and the connections forged, which often resulted in invitations to teach workshops around the country.[43]

The hundreds of participants who flocked to Summervail each year were seeking an unconventional kind of art education and were hungry for the informal atmosphere and communal lifestyle of the workshop. Cory was one of the first metal-symposium instructors and returned every summer, driving his MG convertible through the back roads of central Washington. For him, as well as many other Western artists who felt isolated in their academic departments or independent studios, Summervail was a rare chance to bond with and learn from peers who shared their passions and pursuits.

Though powerful, Cory's work was often small-scale, consisting mainly of brooches and belt buckles. *How to Fix Your Snake* from 1976 (fig. 9) demonstrates his tendency to depict cryptic and suggestive scenes in enamel. Set in a river landscape that could be the Pacific Northwest, the image combines the phallic symbol of the snake with the lower torso and thighs of a person. Such subject matter reflects a countercultural interest in unusual or transgressive subjects rarely found in more conventional jewelry. Furthermore, the belt buckle is a form associated with the West and cowboy culture and is usually intended for men. Cory was part of a lineage of male Washington jewelers (that includes Ron Ho and Keith Lewis) who addressed the subject of jewelry for men. Rather than using models or standard jewelry sizing,

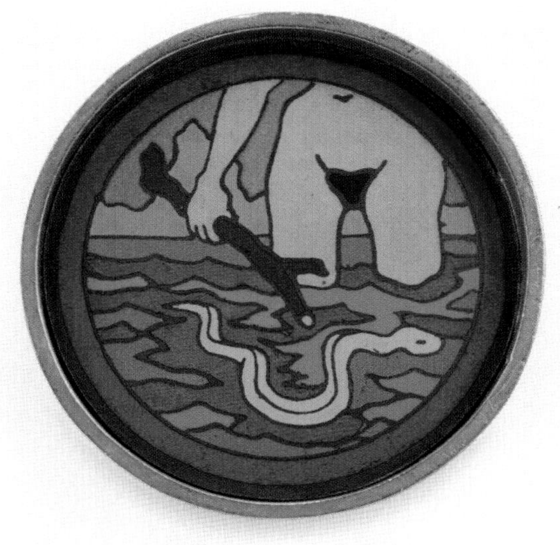

FIG. 9
Ken Cory, *How to Fix Your Snake* belt buckle, 1976

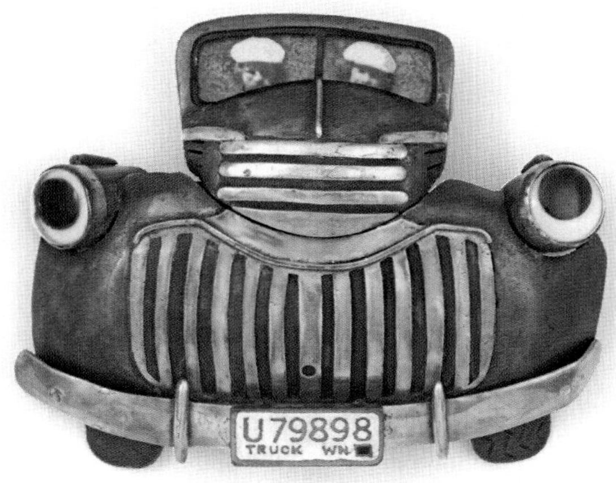

FIG. 10
Merrily Tompkins, *Here Comes Trouble* brooch, 1973

these artists often used their own bodies to determine form and scale.[44]

Cory's strong relationships with other Washington artists extended the legacy of his work. He had a long and fruitful collaboration with artist Leslie W. LePere, whom he met in 1966 and partnered with as the Pencil Brothers to make enameled belt buckles, wall pieces, ashtrays, and switch plates. All depicted their shared interests in cars, the expanse of the American West, and the female form.[45] Cory's colleagues Merrily Tompkins and Nancy Worden also played influential roles in the jewelry field.

Merrily Tompkins, who studied jewelry under her older brother Don Tompkins at Central Washington State College in Ellensburg, was involved with Cory both platonically and romantically in the 1970s. She absorbed from him the tenets of Funk, imbuing her pieces with a raw, provocative sensibility and deriving subject matter from her own experiences. "My main concerns are getting the idea across and making a lovingly crafted, beautiful little heartfelt thing loaded with passion and humor and empathy," she said.[46] In 1973's *Here Comes Trouble* (fig. 10), she depicted the 1946 Chevy pickup truck of friend and Seattle gallerist James Manolides, inserting photographs of Manolides and LePere in the windshield and plastic googly eyes in the headlights. The work's title refers to Manolides's and LePere's mischievous adventures driving around Washington State and is leavened by the kinetic eyes, which both give the piece movement and anthropomorphize the truck. Humorous and sentimental, the piece embodies the spirit of her work.

Manolides was the proprietor of an eponymous gallery in Seattle's Pioneer Square from 1968 to 1986, where he showed a combination of painting, sculpture, and craft. The gallery was an important conduit of the Funk movement to the Seattle area, granting solo exhibitions to Roy De Forest, Clayton Bailey, Robert Arneson, William T. Wiley, Erik Gronborg, and others.[47] Both Worden and Merrily Tompkins credit the gallery with exposing them to this vein of artistic creativity.[48] Manolides, a jeweler himself, also avidly supported craft and exhibited the work of Washington jewelers Cory and both Tompkins siblings.

Cory also exerted a strong influence on Nancy Worden, who incorporates both political and personal statements (and sometimes a combination of both) in her work.[49] As Worden's undergraduate professor at CWU in Ellensburg, Cory encouraged her to imbue her jewelry with elements of personal experience. She believes the honest expressions of masculinity in his work gave her the liberty to address the daily challenges Worden faced as a woman, wife, and mother, as exemplified in her 1992 brooch *Resolution to Lose* (fig. 11). Incorporating real popcorn and casts of baby teeth, it references her struggle to lose weight following the birth of her daughter.[50] After graduating from college, Worden had enrolled at the University of Georgia, Athens, to earn a master's degree with metalsmith Gary Noffke; she intensively studied many technical aspects of making there, including raising and forging. Noffke taught an intuitive, iterative way of working that contrasted with Cory's deliberate development of each piece. Combining the technical skills learned in graduate school with her carefully planned mode of working, she returned to the Pacific Northwest and settled in Seattle.

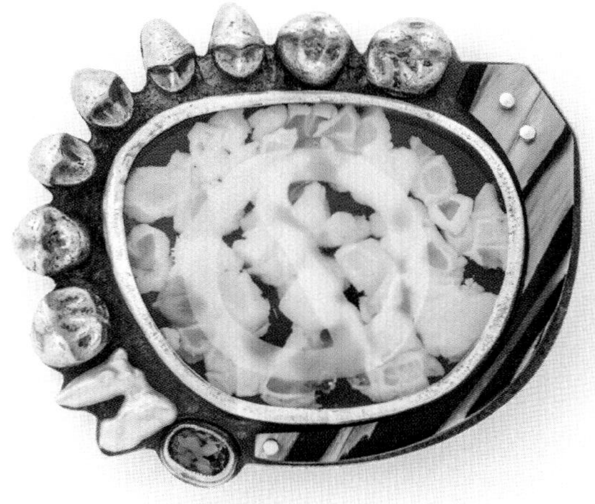

FIG. 11
Nancy Worden, *Resolution to Lose* brooch, 1992, silver, popcorn, glass, pearl, citrine, 2¼ × 2⅝ × ½ in. (5.7 × 6.6 × 1.3 cm), Los Angeles County Museum of Art, gift of the artist, M.2015.305

Worden's *Armed and Dangerous* of 1998 (fig. 12), based on the structure of a Native American squash-blossom necklace, consists of a chain of beads made of coins and fabricated bullets centered on an oversize cross pendant inscribed on the reverse with "They preach the gospel of love; they practice the gospel of hate." The piece refers to the harrowing experience of an extended family member's daughter who was kidnapped by a religious cult. The bullets allude to the violence the cult threatened against both its members and broader society, and the use of American currency—both the coins made into beads with inset dollar bills and the shredded bills stuffed into the cross—symbolize the extortionary tactics to which cults often resort. A condemnation of violence and exploitation, the piece could also be read as a broader statement on how whites treated Native Americans during the settling of this country.

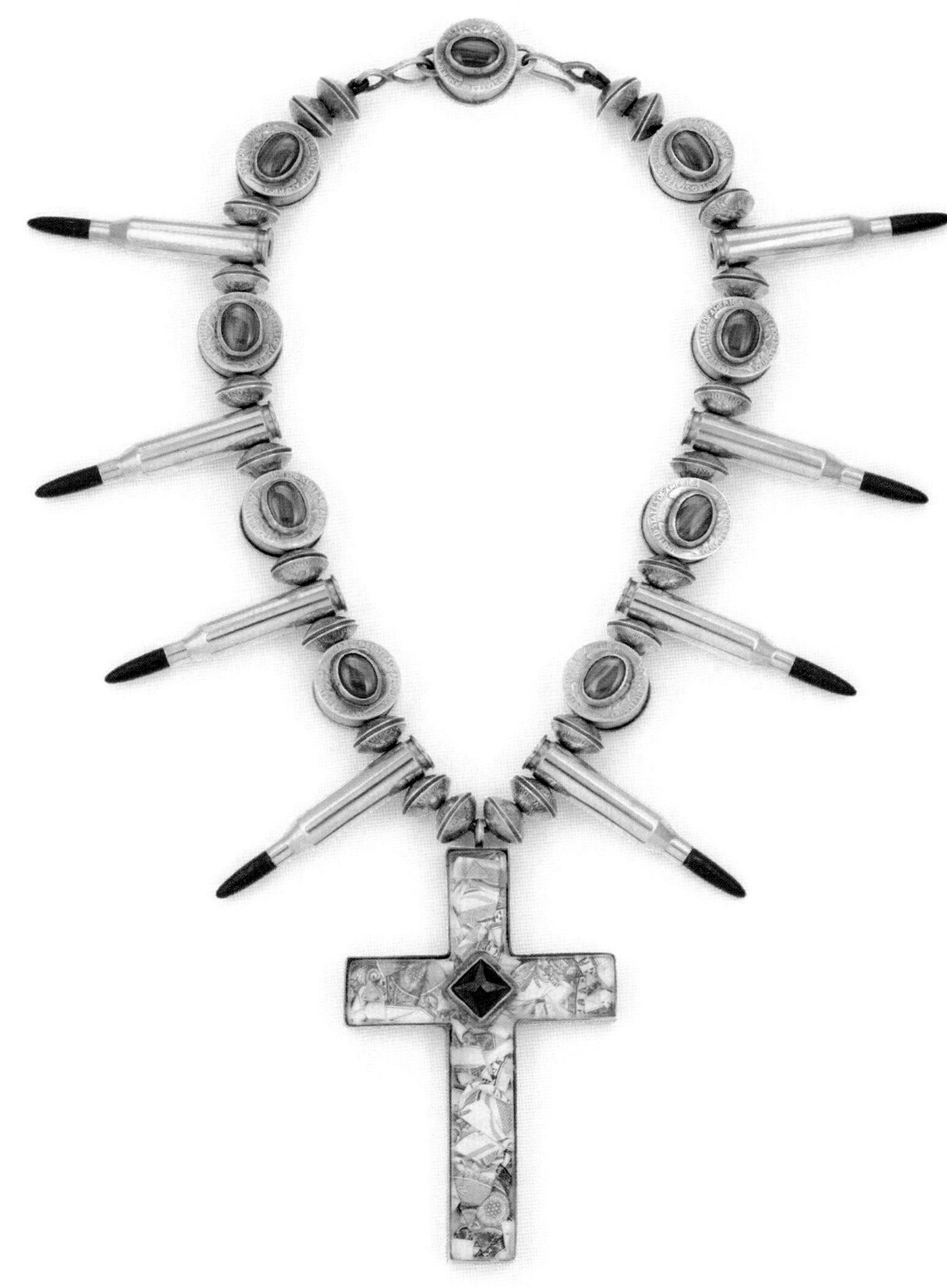

FIG. 12
Nancy Worden, *Armed and Dangerous* necklace, 1998

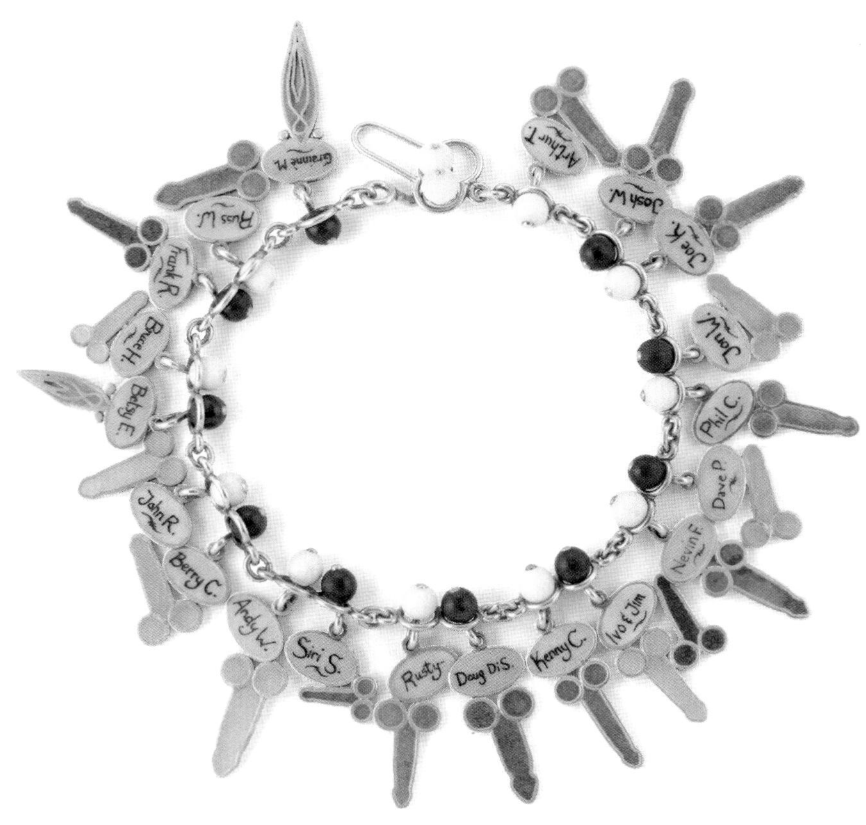

FIG. 13
Keith Lewis, *"Charm" (Sexual Self-Portrait)*, 2002

The coins have additional personal resonance for Worden, as they came from a cache collected by Cory and given to her by his parents after his sudden death in 1994.

Cory's legacy at CWU extends to jeweler and professor Keith Lewis, who acknowledges Cory as an inspiration (although the two never met). Lewis received a master's degree in jewelry and metalsmithing from Kent State University in Ohio and began teaching at CWU following Cory's death in 1994. He was attracted to jewelry making because of its intimate relationship to the body.[51] His early pieces, which he considers works of activism, express outrage that the field had failed to address then-urgent social issues such as the AIDS crisis. Lewis depicts sexual imagery in a much more overt way than Cory's more subtle suggestions did, earning himself both renown and criticism. *"Charm" (Sexual Self-Portrait)* (fig. 13) from 2002, a bracelet of enamel genitalia charms, documents each of his liaisons and is accented with beads made of horn and bone (chosen for the sexual puns). Lewis is also an eloquent spokesman for his field and the craft movement in general, making impassioned pleas for choosing materials sourced in ethical ways (and especially for avoiding elephant ivory) and articulating the value and importance of handmade work.[52]

In 1995 the critic Matthew Kangas named the particular Northwest adaptation of the Bay Area Funk movement "Ellensburg Funky" after the rural college town where Cory, Don and Merrily Tompkins, Worden, and Lewis lived while they taught or attended CWU.[53] This variation maintained the opposition to mainstream art values, the rejection of a hierarchy of materials, the raunchy humor, and the sometimes off-putting forms and textures of Funk but combined them with aspects of autobiography and sentimentality not present in the earlier Bay Area movement.

New Directions: Body Ornament in California

Beginning in the late 1960s, jewelers began to move beyond the conventions of traditional jewelry to create new categories and forms. They increasingly worked at a larger scale, making ornaments for the body, not just for the neck, wrist, fingers, and ears. Although one of the most prominent practitioners of larger body jewelry in the United States was Kansas-based Marjorie Schick—and similar experimentation was occurring in Europe by figures such as Gijs Bakker, Emmy van Leersum, Lam de Wolf, and Caroline Broadhead—there was a concentration of activity in the American West, especially California.

The rise of body ornament in the 1960s was not limited to large-scale works; it included all forms of unconventional adornment and was part of a larger reexamination of social norms relating to acceptable clothing and modes of representation. In 1968 the Museum of Contemporary Crafts (now the Museum of Arts and Design) in New York organized the exhibition *Body Covering.* Its curator Paul Smith "suggest[ed] a variety of approaches to clothing which is suited both to the environment and to individual needs."[54] Comprising mainly avant-garde clothing and high-tech garments, the exhibition featured a small selection of body jewelry, including an electrically heated garment by Vickey Cooper that incorporated a necklace with a rechargeable silver-cadmium battery pack made by San Diego jeweler Arline Fisch. In 1973 Donald Willcox published *Body Jewelry: International Perspectives*, a wide-ranging survey of various new practices by an international roster of jewelers that included such West Coast figures as Cory, Fisch, Hu, David LaPlantz, Marcia Lewis, and Lynda Watson.[55] While much of the jewelry featured is monumental and bold, smaller-scale works were also included. The presence of an artist like Cory, whose output consisted mainly of belt buckles and small brooches, demonstrated the broad range that Willcox encompassed in this snapshot-of-a-moment book.

Certainly a large part of this movement was influenced by the increasing popularity of large-scale, non-Western body ornaments from such diverse cultures as the Maasai of Kenya, the pre-Columbian Aztec and Maya, and Native Americans, all of which were the subject of books and exhibitions in the 1970s. Furthermore, a very fine line divided experimental jewelry and clothing, acknowledged in 1976 when that year's *California Design* exhibition at the Pacific Design Center in Los Angeles included a new section (distinct from the previous jewelry and metalwork displays) called Body Covering. Curator Eudorah Moore explained that it was devoted not to "style, not fashion but fantasy, dreams, directions, possibilities, or even repudiations, possibly even the way it might be."[56] The Body Covering section featured pieces by fashion designers like Rudi Gernreich, as well as those whose work crossed disciplinary boundaries between clothing and adornment like Fisch and Nicki Marx. This impulse to create customized clothing, body adornments, and accessories resonated along the West Coast, particularly in the regions around San Francisco, as documented in such period books as *Native Funk and Flash: An Emerging Folk Art* by Alexandra Jacopetti and Jerry Wainwright and *Creating Body Coverings* by Jean Ray Laury and Joyce Aiken (both 1974).[57] The clothing shown in these publications, mostly unique pieces created for the maker or his/her close friends and relatives, reflected a desire to adapt mass-produced clothing or even avoid the industrial system altogether by making original garments.[58]

K. Lee Manuel was an important figure in this "artwear" or "art-to-wear" field. She was renowned for hand-painted clothing and especially for her painted white goose feathers, which she began to decorate in the early 1980s. She attached single feathers to stickpins, created large face-framing collars, and even assembled the feathers into cape-like garments. Manuel's vibrantly colored designs ranged from the figurative to the purely abstract, though all tended to have a dreamlike quality.[59] Egg and heart motifs, possibly signifying vitality or fertility, were common in her work, as seen in a collar from around 1977 (fig. 14). A native Californian, Manuel studied at the San Francisco Art Institute and set up her studio in the Santa Cruz Mountains, a fertile site for the crossover of clothing and jewelry, as also evidenced in the work of her friend Nicki Marx.

Marx grew up in Los Angeles and was living in Santa Fe, New Mexico, in 1972 when she spotted a bag of feathers intended as fishing flies in a store and felt an instant connection to the material. Shortly thereafter she moved to Santa Cruz and began making feather necklaces and later entire plumed garments and wall hangings.[60] For her, feathers have profound spiritual power—she describes them as sacred—and the birds

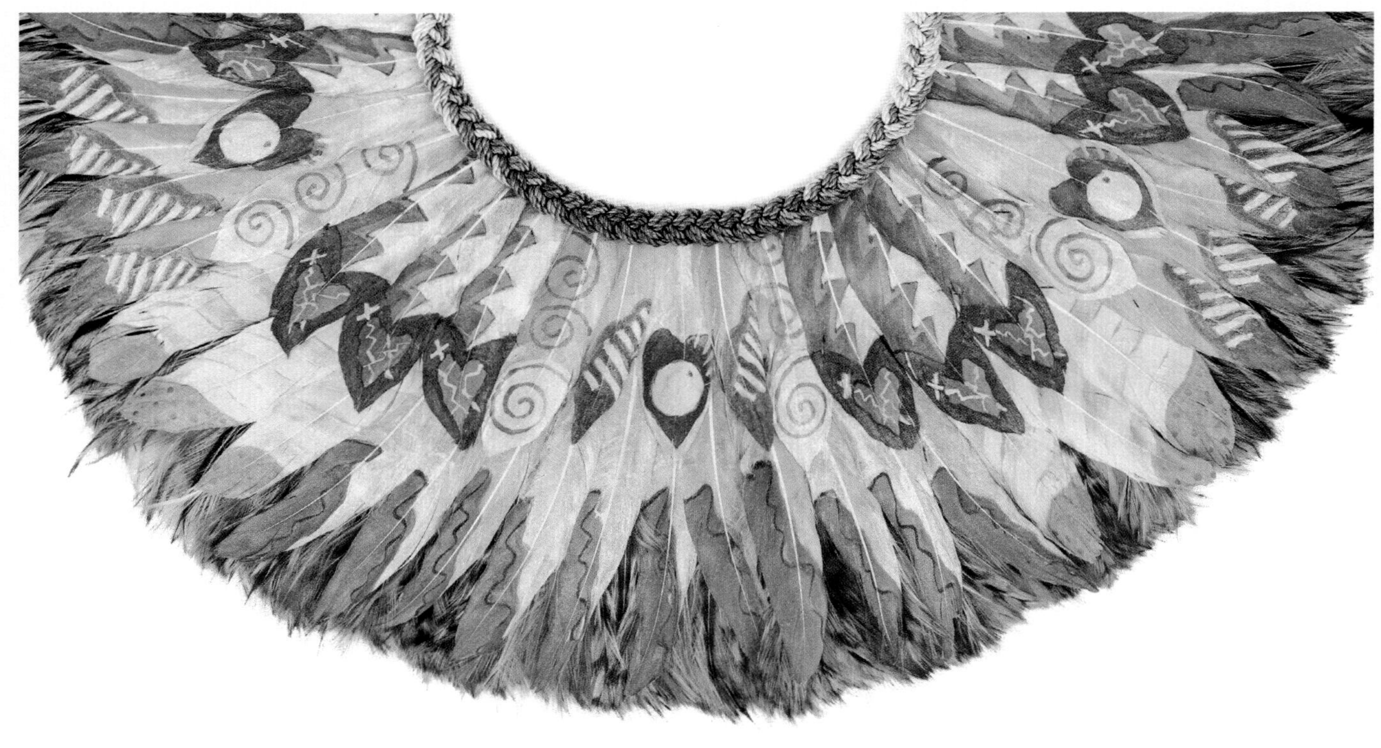

FIG. 14
K. Lee Manuel, necklace (detail), c. 1977

from which they come symbolize freedom. She prefers to use feathers that have been shed naturally or are by-products of birds raised for food, explaining that her work is ecologically sound, with the feathers recycled into art rather than being thrown away."[61] Unlike Manuel, Marx uses the natural colors and patterns of the feathers to create larger designs. In *Royal Raiment* from 1973 (fig. 15) small green peacock feathers are methodically arranged around the breastplate-like garment accentuated with blue feathers. The shape is based on a mandala, a symbol found in many Eastern religions, and a frequent motif in Marx's work. Marx has emphasized the mystical origins of her work, and describes achieving something like a flow state when making: "The ideas are flowing through me but they don't come from me."[62]

Another significant jeweler working in this region was Lynda Watson, who had studied at California State University, Long Beach, with Alvin Pine and went on to establish the metals program at Cabrillo College outside Santa Cruz in 1970. Her early work consists of intricately cast silver ornaments assembled into large, chest-covering necklaces. She would later focus on smaller-scale pieces inspired by her environment, from her own garden or from as far away as Japan and Mexico, where she has traveled.[63]

Bay Area jeweler William Clark also created body-scale work alongside more traditional forms with political and satirical themes, such as his 1969 *Police State Badge*. Star-shaped like a sheriff's badge, it reverses the standard *state police* phrase to suggest the brutality sometimes exercised by law officers.[64]

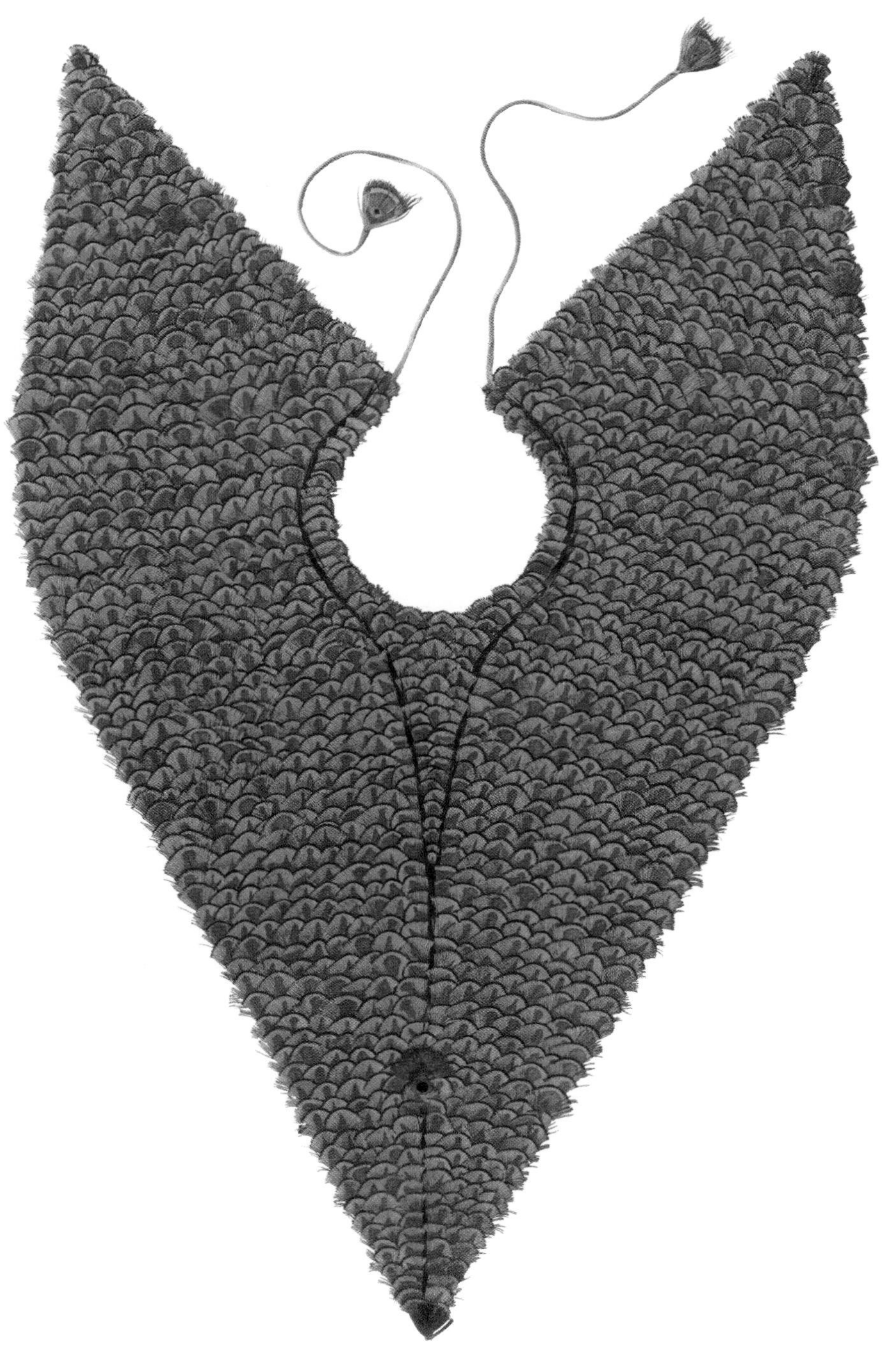

FIG. 15
Nicki Marx, *Royal Raiment* necklace, 1973

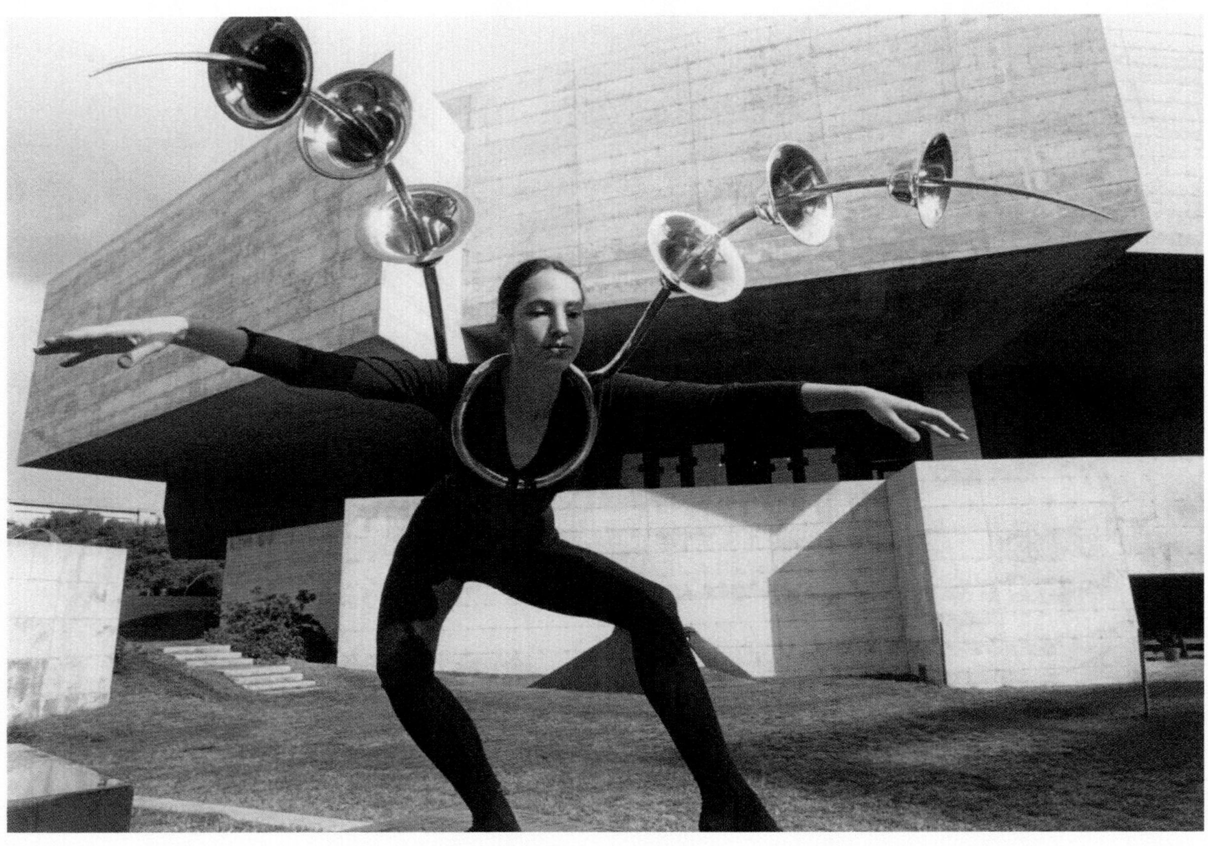

FIG. 16
Performance at the University of California, Berkeley, incorporating William Clark's *Untitled*, a brass body ornament with bells and antlers, 1970s

Although not formally trained, Clark was drawn to jewelry and acquired metalworking skills while living in Saudi Arabia as a teenager and then in the Bay Area and in Vancouver as a young adult. In the mid-1970s, Clark made several large-scale brass body sculptures that sit on the shoulders in the shape of spirals, bells, and antlers (fig. 16). Shown in museums and galleries, they were also used in dance performances at UC Berkeley and the California Palace of the Legion of Honor (now part of the Fine Arts Museums of San Francisco).[65] Such cross-disciplinary undertakings demonstrate the close ties among artists working in different creative fields during this era.

Beginning in the late 1960s and continuing into the 70s, Seattle jeweler Mary Lee Hu made elaborate neckpieces of worked wire, many featuring animal shapes or stylized wings and feathers. Hu had earned a bachelor's degree in metal-smithing at the Cranbrook Academy of Art in Bloomfield Hills, Michigan, in 1965 and a master's in fine arts in 1967 from Southern Illinois University at Carbondale, where she had studied with the renowned blacksmith L. Brent Kington. While her early work was characterized by large-scale, figural imagery, like many jewelers, Hu abandoned this mode of working by the 1980s and has come to be best known for the highly intricate metal twining techniques she developed from textile methods such as weaving and macramé (see p. 67). She stands apart from the majority of Pacific Northwest jewelers, choosing to manipulate precious, high-karat gold rather than incorporate found objects and drawing many of her design motifs from Celtic and Etruscan sources.[66]

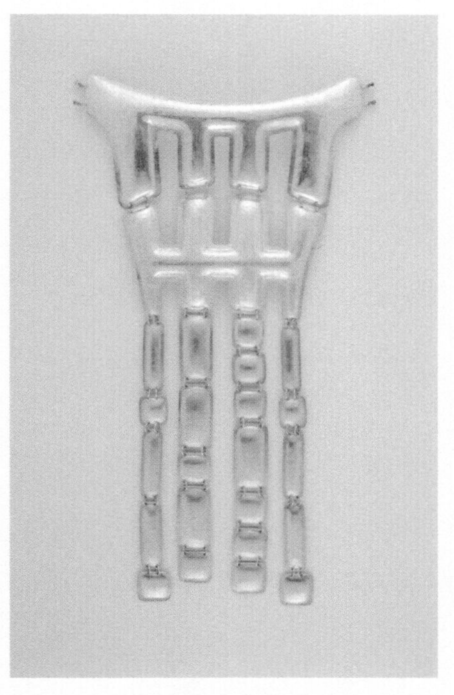

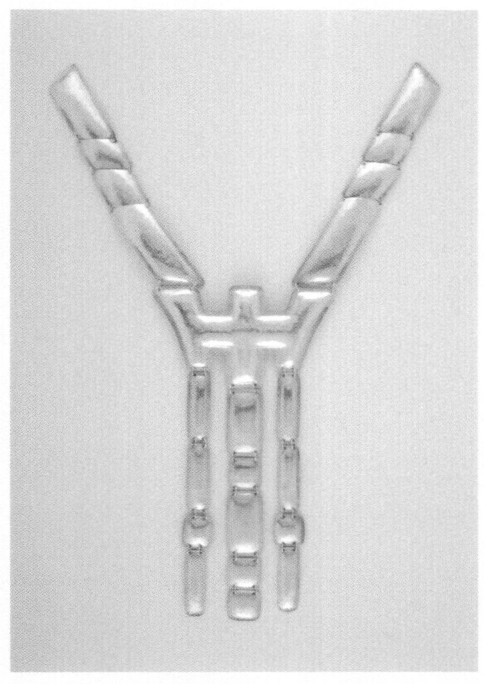

FIG. 17a–b
Arline Fisch, *Front & Back* body ornament, 1971, silver, 17 × 8¾ × 1¼ in. (43.2 × 22.2 × 3.1 cm), Los Angeles County Museum of Art, gift of Allison and Larry Berg through the 2014 Decorative Arts and Design Acquisitions Committee (DA²), M.2014.45a–b

Fisch, the internationally distinguished San Diego jeweler, was an early and frequent proponent of large-scale jewelry, deriving inspiration from her study of pre-Columbian jewelry after a 1963 trip down the western coast of Central and South America from Mexico to Peru.[67] As she explained, "The scale of individual ornaments, the use of beads and feathers, of faces and wings, all relate to the cultures whose work I have studied in great detail: pre-Columbian Peru and Mexico, Egypt, Africa, Eskimo, and American Indian."[68] Exposure to this material led her to create a series of collars, breastplates, and full body ornaments like the 1971 *Front & Back* body ornament (fig. 17a–b), whose geometric designs and decoration were inspired by ancient Peruvian jewelry.[69]

San Diego: A Beachhead for Jewelry

While the jewelry and larger artistic communities in the San Francisco Bay Area and the Pacific Northwest had many links, the contemporary jewelry field in Southern California developed along a different course. Beginning in the 1960s, San Diego became an extremely important node of jewelry making and education on the West Coast, with strong ties to other national and international contemporary jewelry centers. Before then, local craftspeople found support in the Allied Craftsmen of San Diego, which began meeting in 1946 as a subset of the Allied Artists' Council, a larger forum for artists in San Diego.[70] In the early years, jewelers did not make up a significant part of the group, though by 1979 it counted eleven members (out of forty) as jewelers.[71] Much like the Metal Arts Guild of San Francisco, group activities included convivial monthly meetings featuring demonstrations or discussions and two annual exhibitions—a members' show at the Fine Arts Gallery of San Diego (now the San Diego Museum of Art) and a Christmas selling exhibition. The group comprised craftspeople working in a range of media and over the years included a handful of important jewelers such as Fisch, Ruth Radakovich, James Parker, Helen Shirk, Jane Groover, Steven Brixner, and Fennell Wallen.[72] There were also several makers for whom jewelry was just one of many media in which they worked, such as Harry Bertoia, Barney Reid, Jack Rogers Hopkins, James Hubbell, and Svetozar Radakovich. Although the annual exhibitions subsided in the 1980s, and the organization no longer retains the prominence it once had, it continues to meet and foster a community of craftspeople, most recently organizing an exhibition at the Mingei International Museum in 2013–14 that represented thirty-seven of its members.[73]

San Diego's international profile in the jewelry world rose considerably after the arrival of Fisch as a professor of art at San Diego State University in 1961. She had studied art at Skidmore College in New York and earned a master's in the field from the University of Illinois in 1954. A Fulbright grant (1956–57) enabled her to study metalsmithing in the Copenhagen workshop of Bernard Hertz and at the Kunsthaandvaerkskolen (School of Arts and Crafts). Fisch's artistic legacy includes both the creation of large-scale silver body ornaments derived from ancient and ethnic sources (as discussed in the previous section), as well as the application of fiber techniques such as weaving and knitting to metal, which she detailed in her classic 1975 book *Textile Techniques in Metal: For Jewelers, Sculptors, and Textile Artists*.[74] An example of the latter technique is her 1985 *Bell Frills* necklace (p. 54), for which she knit silver and gold wire on standard knitting needles, basing the design on lace collars found in Northern Renaissance paintings.

Fisch was the first of several San Diego jewelry and metalsmithing professors who actively participated in the growing array of exhibitions and conferences about contemporary studio jewelry. She won grants and fellowships to see and study a wide range of jewelry traditions and museum collections around the world and had an extensive network of international connections in the field. As a result of her professional relationships, she was able to bring a succession of internationally prominent jewelers such as Giampaolo Babetto, Gijs Bakker, Albert Paley, and Wendy Ramshaw to San Diego, introducing her students and the artistic community to the dynamic developments in the field in the 1970s, 80s, and 90s.[75]

This was a different kind of worldliness and cosmopolitanism than that of the Pacific Northwest. Jewelers in the Northwest were mainly interested in historical and folk traditions of foreign cultures and often gained information, inspiration, and materials through direct experience. Fisch instead connected the burgeoning international community of avant-garde jewelers to her students and colleagues in San Diego. Through extensive international travel for participation in conferences and exhibitions, and by serving in leadership roles on the American Craft Council, the World Crafts Council, and as a founding member of the Society of North American Goldsmiths, Fisch was not only a connective force, but also helped to shape the nascent field itself. She was especially supportive of her students, often bringing their work to international conferences and advocating for its inclusion in publications and exhibitions.[76] Christina Y. Smith attributes her presence in Susan Grant Lewin's 1994 book *One of a Kind: American Art Jewelry Today* to Fisch's efforts, while Mona Trunkfield credits Fisch for the encouragement to send her *Waist Ornament and Purse*, part of her master's thesis on wearable containers completed under Fisch's direction in 1973, to New York for its consideration and ultimate inclusion in the Museum of Contemporary Crafts's *Baroque '74* exhibition and catalogue.[77]

In 1975 Helen Shirk joined Fisch in the art department at San Diego State University. Like Fisch, she had majored in art at Skidmore College and won a Fulbright scholarship to study metalsmithing in Copenhagen. She later received her graduate training at Indiana University in Bloomington with legendary jeweler Alma Eikerman. Shirk's silver jewelry and metalwork in the 1970s reflected the "constructivist" or additive approach for which Eikerman was well-known, with the distinct metal elements built upon each other to form a sculptural composition (fig. 18). In the early 1980s Shirk moved away from fine metals and initiated a long-term interest in color, first using anodized titanium in her jewelry (see p. 221), and by the mid-1980s, focusing on patinated copper and brass vessels, whose shapes and surfaces were informed by an influential six-month trip to western Australia in 1992, as well as the desert and coastal landscape of her San Diego surroundings.[78]

Fisch and Shirk mentored many students at San Diego State who would go on to earn their master's degrees at California State University, Long Beach, and become teachers in the field. Notable figures include Randy J. Long, who has

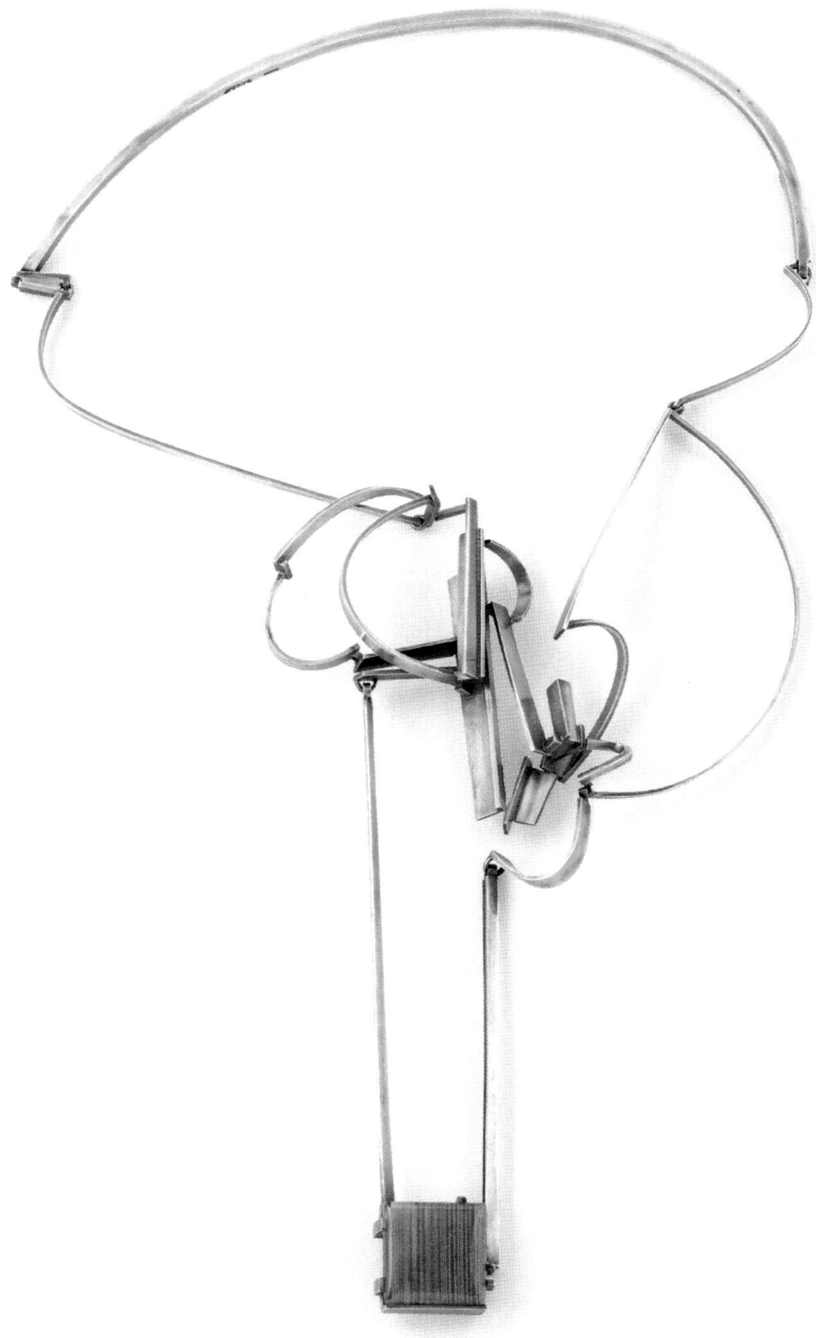

FIG. 18
Helen Shirk, *Pendant with Phantom Quartz*, 1974

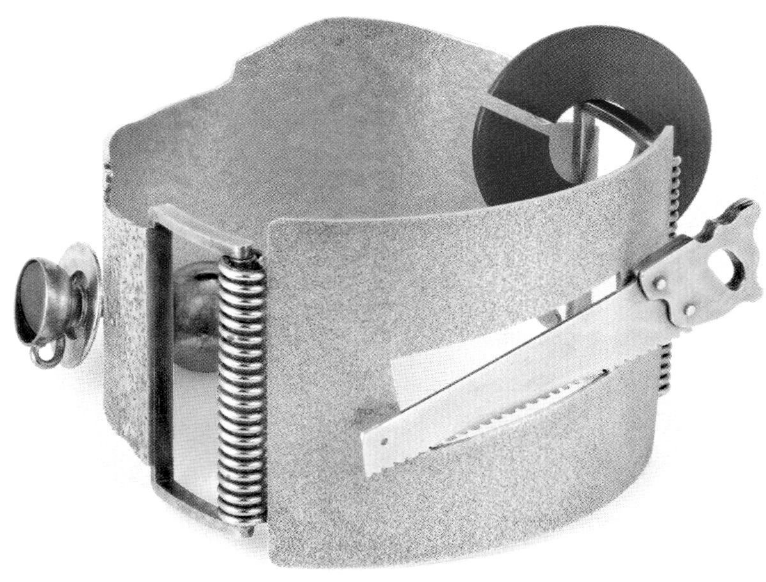

FIG. 19
Christina Y. Smith, *Work, Work, Work* bracelet, c. 1986

taught metalwork and jewelry at Indiana University Bloomington, since 1983 and draws on ancient sources, religious imagery, and natural motifs in her work;[79] Marcia Lewis, who taught at Long Beach City College from 1978 to 2003 and wrote a key guide to contemporary metal chasing;[80] and Christina Y. Smith, who has taught at California State University, Fullerton, since 2001 and whose work is often biographical in nature, as in her late 1980s *Work, Work, Work* bracelet (fig. 19) documenting a period of extreme zeal early in a friend's career, whose three different jobs are represented by three "charms."[81]

As the first Southern California institution where jewelers could receive their master's degrees and thus be eligible for tenured university positions, California State University at Long Beach developed a regionally important jewelry and metalsmithing program under professors Alvin Pine and Dieter Muller-Stach. After receiving an MFA in metalsmithing and jewelry in 1958 from the Cranbrook Academy of Art, two years of army service, and a Fulbright fellowship in Germany, Pine was hired at Long Beach in 1962.[82] The next decade comprised his most active period of work, in which he made delicate, dangling pendant necklaces of forged metal that often incorporated kinetic elements, along with silver holloware and flatware.[83] Born in Munich, Muller-Stach studied at the Akademie der Bildenden Künste under Franz Rickert, followed by several years teaching at the University of Ghana in Kumasi.[84] While in Ghana, he developed an interest and expertise in Ashante casting, which would become his signature technique. After moving to Long Beach in 1968, he focused on casting and forging large metal objects.

The Enduring Influence of West Coast Jewelry

Jewelry and metalworking on the West Coast continue to evolve along distinct regional lines, reflecting a simultaneous engagement with both the immediate environment and the international community of jewelers. Several university metalsmithing programs remain vital centers that attract top professors and students, including those at San Diego State University, California College of the Arts, Central Washington University at Ellensburg, and the University of Oregon at Eugene. The San Francisco Bay Area is also where former gallerist Susan Cummins in 1997 founded Art Jewelry Forum, an organization established "to advocate for the field of contemporary art jewelry... through education, discourse, appreciation, and support for the field."[85] Through its publications, events, and extensive website of interviews, reviews, and general information about contemporary studio jewelry, it has fostered a community for the discussion and advancement of the field, and with a board that draws from both the Bay Area and the wider world, it further weaves the West Coast into the international jewelry community.

The myths that have defined the West for centuries still resonate, though growing awareness of environmental crisis has begun to erode the perception of endless opportunity and growth. Jewelers have accommodated these realities, adapting their working materials and techniques to environmental and ethical restrictions. The advent of the internet has meant that information travels faster and is more accessible. It is possible to be cognizant of current developments even when one's physical location is remote, so the decision to engage with one's immediate environment becomes even more political, not just a function of proximity. Ultimately, the values espoused by De Patta, Penington, Solberg, and their contemporaries—namely the use of nonprecious materials and an emphasis on form and meaning rather than monetary value—remain the fundamental tenets of contemporary studio jewelry in the twenty-first century.

Notes

1. I appreciate the many individuals who helped me construct this story. I would like to thank Susan Cummins for providing guidance from her extensive experience as gallerist, collector, and philanthropist. I am deeply grateful to each of the jewelers who shared their thoughts and memories, and especially to Arline Fisch, who also offered incisive comments on an early draft of this essay. In addition to those cited in the notes, conversations with Jim Cotter, Lane Coulter, Imogene Gieling, Jane Groover, Mike Holmes, Rock Hushka, Diane Kuhn, Randy Milhoan, emiko oye, and Sondra Sherman substantially enriched this text as well.

2. For an in-depth examination of how the counterculture manifested in the West, especially in the realms of art and craft, see Elissa Auther and Adam Lerner, eds., *West of Center: Art and the Counterculture Experiment in America, 1965–1977* (Denver: Museum of Contemporary Art, 2012).

3. Theodore Roszak, *The Making of a Counter Culture: Reflections on the Technocratic Society and Its Youthful Opposition* (Garden City, NY: Doubleday, 1969).

4. For a history of the intersections between the environmental and countercultural movements, see Andrew G. Kirk, *Counterculture Green: The Whole Earth Catalog and American Environmentalism* (Lawrence: University Press of Kansas, 2007).

5. See http://www.ethicalmetalsmiths.org/about-us. Prior to founding Ethical Metalsmiths, Kingsley wrote about the ethical and environmental implications of using gold without knowing its source and the disastrous environmental effects of gold-mining operations. See Susan Kingsley, "The Price of Gold," *Metalsmith* (Summer 2004): 34–45.

6. While a wide range of artists and craftspeople on the West Coast have engaged with the design and production of jewelry as part of a broader artistic practice (some of the most prominent being Claire Falkenstein and Jay DeFeo), this essay focuses on those whose *primary* field is jewelry and metalwork.

7. Biographical information about Margaret De Patta can be found in Ursula Ilse-Neuman and Julie M. Muñiz, *Space Light Structure: The Jewelry of Margaret De Patta*, exh. cat. (New York: Museum of Arts and Design, and Oakland: Oakland Museum of California, 2012).

8. See Yoshiko Uchida, "Jewelry by Margaret De Patta," *Craft Horizons*, March/April 1965, 23.

9. Margaret De Patta, "De Patta," *Design Quarterly* 33 (1955): 6.

10. Rutilated quartz is a type of quartz with rutile (titanium dioxide) inclusions. Also known as Venus's hairstone, it was a preferred material for De Patta and other Bay Area jewelers such as merry renk and Florence Resnikoff. De Patta worked with lapidary Francis Sperisen to find and cut her unconventional stones. His book *The Art of the Lapidary* (Milwaukee, WI: Bruce Publishing Company, 1950) was a standard reference.

11. There was no catalogue for the 1946 exhibition *Modern Handmade Jewelry* at the Museum of Modern Art, but many of the pieces were illustrated in Charles James Martin, *How to Make Modern Jewelry* (New York: Museum of Modern Art, distributed by Simon and Schuster, 1949); "Modern Jewelry under Fifty Dollars," *Everyday Art Quarterly* 7 (1948); *International Exhibition of Modern Jewellery, 1890–1961*, exh. cat. (London: Worshipful Company of Goldsmiths, 1961).

12. Thomas B. Robertson, "Talk on Jewelry Slated at Gallery," *San Diego Union*, November 4, 1951; Hazel V. Bray and Claudia Williams, *The Metal Experience* (Oakland, CA: Oakland Museum Art Division, 1971); *The Jewelry of Margaret De Patta: A Retrospective Exhibition*, exh. cat. (Oakland: Oakland Museum of California, 1976). The Museum of Arts and Design and the Oakland Museum of California also jointly organized the 2012 retrospective *Space Light Structure: The Jewelry of Margaret De Patta*.

13. merry renk and Carrie Adell, "The San Francisco Metal Arts Guild Yesterday and Today," *Metalsmith* 4, no. 3 (Summer 1984): 40–45. Jennifer Shaifer documented the founding of the Metal Arts Guild in "Metal Rising: The Forming of the Metal Arts Guild, San Francisco (1929–1964)" (master's thesis, Corcoran College of Art and Design, 2011). In it, she traces how the primary motivation for founding the group was to protect metalworkers' financial and business interests in much the same way that the Artists Equity Association was designed to protect painters, sculptors, photographers, and graphic artists.

14. A selected list of Metal Arts Guild members between 1951 and 1964, including founding members, is found in appendix B of Shaifer, "Metal Rising."

15. LaMar Harrington, "The Making of a Modernist Metalworker: Ruth Penington," *Archives of American Art Journal* 23, no. 2 (1983): 18–21; Ruth Penington, oral history interview, February 10–11, 1983, Archives of American Art, Smithsonian Institution, Washington, DC.

16. Such impressions of Penington were shared by Ron Ho in a telephone conversation with the author, January 23, 2015, and by Imogene Gieling, interview with the author, February 5, 2015, among others. See also Ramona Solberg, oral history interview, March 23, 2001, Archives of American Art, Smithsonian Institution, Washington, DC.

17. Ruth Penington, "Design and Human Need," in *Research in the Crafts* (New York: American Craftsmen's Council, 1961), 117–18.

18. A history of the Northwest Craftsmen's Exhibitions, along with a consideration of the benefits and drawbacks of juried shows, is found in *Tenth Annual Northwest Craftsmen's Exhibition*, exh. cat. (Seattle: Henry Art Gallery, 1962). See also Lloyd E. Herman, *Looking Forward, Glancing Back: Northwest Designer Craftsmen at Fifty* (Bellingham, WA: Whatcom Museum of History and Art, and Seattle: University of Washington Press, 2004).

19. Diane Wright, "College Honors Former Art Chair with Exhibit," *Seattle Times*, January 2, 2008.

20. Ben Mitchell, "Heart and Hand: The Life and Work of Don Tompkins," *Metalsmith* (Summer 2003): 29–37.

21. Tompkins's medals for Jackson Pollock and Janis Joplin are in the collection of the Museum of Fine Arts, Houston, gift of Helen Williams Drutt English (2006.655, 2006.657).

22. Tompkins's dissertation, "Crafts, the High Arts, and Education," wrestled with the question of the postwar role of personal expression in the craft media, arguing that though contemporary craftspeople may be more concerned with personal expression and less with proper technique and functionality, they remain within the cultural category of "craftsperson." He ultimately advocated for the role of a new type of craftsperson as embodied by ceramic sculptor Peter Voulkos, and his own work is an expression of this new approach in the form of jewelry. See Donald Paul Tompkins, "Crafts, the High Arts, and Education" (EdD thesis, Teachers College, Columbia University, 1972).

23. Solberg, oral history interview, Archives of American Art.

24. Vicki Halper, *Findings: The Jewelry of Ramona* Solberg (Seattle and London: Bank of America Gallery in association with the University of Washington Press, 2001), 5–6.

25. Margaret De Patta, Sam Kramer, J. Fred Woell, Don Tompkins, Robert Ebendorf, and many others used this technique in the 1960s and earlier.

26. Ramona Solberg, *Inventive Jewelry-Making* (New York: Van Nostrand Reinhold Company, 1972), 7.

27. Kiff Slemmons, email to author, April 10, 2015.

28. Ron Ho, Ben Mitchell, and Stefano Catalani, *Dim Sum at the On-On Tea Room: The Jewelry of Ron Ho* (Bellevue, WA: Bellevue Arts Museum, 2006).

29. Ibid., 16.

30. Ho, telephone conversation with author.

31. Laurie J. Hall, telephone conversation with author, December 12, 2014.

32. Slemmons has said: "If I think about Emily Dickinson's poetry, I would feel very good if I made a piece that was like an Emily Dickinson poem ... she does things through a kind of paring down, and a way of hearing words differently, familiar words, but she torques them like bending notes in blues, she calls it truth at a slant." Kiff Slemmons, oral history interview, November 1–2, 2007, Archives of American Art, Smithsonian Institution, Washington, DC.

33. Kiff Slemmons, *Re:Pair and Imperfection*, exh. cat. (Chicago: Chicago Cultural Center, 2006), 18.

34. Kiff Slemmons, email to author, January 28, 2015.

35. Peter Selz, "Notes on Funk," in *Funk*, exh. cat. (Berkeley, CA: Regents of the University of California, 1967), 3.

36. Harold Paris, "Sweet Land of Funk," *Art in America*, March–April 1967, 96.

37. Ben Mitchell, *The Jewelry of Ken Cory: Play Disguised* (Seattle: Tacoma Art Museum and University of Washington Press, 1997), 46–48.

38. Lost-wax casting for jewelry was widely popularized by Bay Area jeweler Bob Winston through both his courses at CCAC (in which Cory may have been enrolled) and his book *Cast Away*. See Bob Winston and Gina Winston, *Cast Away: A Treatise on the Technical Processes and the Aesthetic Development of "Lost Wax" Casting* (Scottsdale, AZ: Shelfhouse Publications, 1970).

39. Mitchell, *The Jewelry of Ken Cory*, 78.

40. Jim Cotter, telephone conversation with author, January 12, 2015; Randy Milhoan, telephone conversation with author, October 15, 2015; Summervail Archive, private collection of Jim Cotter and Randy Milhoan.

41. Lane Coulter, telephone conversation with author, January 27, 2015.

42. Coulter recalls the record being forty-five seconds and the most memorable team name being the "Soldering Gomorrahs."

43. After the demise of Summervail, many participants continued the annual gathering at the Yuma Art Symposium in Arizona, which continues to be held at the time of publication.

44. For example, Keith Lewis reported that he scaled the bracelet *"Charm" (Sexual Self-Portrait)* to his own wrist. Keith Lewis, telephone conversation with author, December 29, 2014.

45. Mitchell, *The Jewelry of Ken Cory*, 58–62, 69–82.

46. Ben Mitchell, "Merrily Tompkins: Over Yonder," *Metalsmith* 26, no. 5 (Winter 2006): 50.

47. James Manolides, telephone conversation with author, January 13, 2015; Manolides Gallery Archive, private collection of James Manolides.

48. Nancy Worden, telephone conversation with author, October 2014; Merrily Tompkins, telephone conversation with author, January 12, 2015.

49. Nancy Worden was the subject of a retrospective exhibition at the Tacoma Art Museum in 2009. See Michelle LeBaron, Nancy Worden, Susan Noyes Platt, and Rock Hushka, eds., *Loud Bones: The Jewelry of Nancy Worden*, exh. cat. (Tacoma, WA: Tacoma Art Museum, 2009.)

50. Worden, telephone conversation with author.

51. Lewis, telephone conversation with author.

52. For examples, see Keith Lewis, "Ethics of Materials," *Metalsmith* 9, no. 3 (Summer 1989): 6; Lewis, "Renegade Ornament," *Metalsmith* 11, no. 3 (Summer 1991): 10, 12; Lewis, "Some Objects Worth Listening To," *Artweek*, November 1995, 14.

53. Matthew Kangas, "Ellensburg Funky," *Metalsmith* 15, no. 4 (Fall 1995): 14–21.

54. Paul J. Smith, introduction, in *Body Covering*, exh. cat. (New York: American Craftsmen's Council, 1968), 3.

55. Donald J. Willcox, *Body Jewelry: International Perspectives* (Chicago: H. Regnery, 1973). Fisch was an important adviser on this book.

56. *California Design '76: A Bicentennial Celebration*, exh. cat. (Pasadena, CA: California Design Publications, 1976), 110ff. *California Design* was an annual series (triennial after 1962) of exhibitions that featured current work by designers and craftspeople in the region and later the entire state. See Jo Lauria and Suzanne Baizerman, *California Design: The Legacy of West Coast Craft and Style* (San Francisco: Chronicle Books, 2005).

57. Alexandra Jacopetti and Jerry Wainwright, *Native Funk and Flash: An Emerging Folk Art* (San Francisco: Scrimshaw Press, 1974); Jean Ray Laury and Joyce Aiken, *Creating Body Coverings* (New York: Van Nostrand Reinhold, 1974).

58. In 2005 curator Melissa Leventon organized *Artwear*, an exhibition with international scope but a decided focus on the Bay Area, that brought together these various strands of creative production. See Melissa Leventon, *Artwear: Fashion and Anti-fashion* (London: Thames & Hudson, 2005).

59. Jean Williams Cacicedo, "In Memoriam: K. Lee Manuel," *Ornament* 27, no. 3 (2004): 13; Barbara Hamaker, "K. Lee Manuel's Splendid Ceremonial Raiments," *Ornament* 12, no. 4 (1989): cover, 40–45, 81, 83.

60. Gay Weaver, "Artists' Work Centers around the Body," *Palo Alto Times*, September 8, 1976, 15.

61. Bea Miller, "Fine Feathers," *Los Angeles Times Home Magazine*, June 24, 1973, K50.

62. Weaver, "Artists' Work Centers around the Body," 15.

63. See Pasadena Art Museum, *California Design 10*, exh. cat. (Pasadena, CA: Pasadena Art Museum, 1970), 140; and Lee Nordness, *Objects: USA*, exh. cat. (New York: Viking Press, 1970), 222; Lynda Watson, telephone conversation with author, April 9, 2015; see also www.lyndawatsonart.com.

64. *Police State Badge* is in the collection of the Museum of Arts and Design in New York, gift of Diane Kuhn (2012.20).

65. An undated poster showing a dancer wearing Clark's body piece publicized the performance *Memories for a Bivouac Passage*, which was choreographed by David Wood for a University Dance Theatre production at UC Berkeley. And on September 7 and 8, 1974, two performances incorporating his pieces were held in the Little Theater at the California Palace of the Legion of Honor in conjunction with the exhibition *Metal Sculpture by William Clark*.

66. Mary Lee Hu and Stefano Catalani, *Knitted, Knotted, Twisted & Twined: The Jewelry of Mary Lee Hu* (Bellevue, WA: Bellevue Arts Museum, 2012).

67. Arline Fisch, David Revere McFadden, Ida Katherine Rigby, Robert Bell, Denny Stone, and Anna Beatriz Chadour-Sampson, *Elegant Fantasy: The Jewelry of Arline Fisch* (San Diego: San Diego Historical Society; and Stuttgart: Arnoldsche, 2001), 14; Arline Fisch, oral history interview, July 29–30, 2001, Archives of American Art, Smithsonian Institution, Washington, DC.

68. Willcox, *Body Jewelry*, 57.

69. My thanks to Rosie Chambers Mills for pointing out this connection to Peruvian jewelry.

70. Craftspeople continued to meet after the Allied Artists' Council folded and formally established the Allied Craftsmen of San Diego in 1947. "History of the Allied Craftsmen," n.d., folder 1, Allied Craftsmen of San Diego Records, MS 162, San Diego History Center Document Collection (hereafter ACSDR).

71. Isabelle Wasserman, "Allied Craftsmen—Thirtieth Annual Spring Exhibition," folder 23, ACSDR. It was the thirtieth anniversary of the first annual exhibition at the Fine Arts Gallery of San Diego in 1949, not the thirtieth anniversary of the organization.

72. Allied Craftsmen membership lists are preserved in folder 3, ACSDR. For further information on San Diego jewelers in the midcentury period, see Toni Greenbaum, "Tea and Jewelry: Modernist Metalsmithing in San Diego, 1940–1970," *Metalsmith* 22, no. 3 (Summer 2002): 26–33.

73. *Allied Craftsmen Today* (San Diego: Allied Craftsmen of San Diego, 2013).

74. Fisch et al., *Elegant Fantasy*, 118; Arline Fisch, *Textile Techniques in Metal: For Jewelers, Sculptors, and Textile Artists* (New York: Van Nostrand Reinhold, 1975).

75. Arline Fisch, telephone conversation with author, November 26, 2014.

76. Jane Groover and Christina Y. Smith, interview with author, December 23, 2014.

77. Mona Trunkfield, telephone conversation with author, February 23, 2015; American Crafts Council, *Baroque '74*, exh. cat. (New York: Museum of Contemporary Crafts of the American Crafts Council, 1974); Mona Trunkfield, "Five Wearable Containers in Precious Metals" (master's project, California State University, San Diego, 1973).

78. Marjorie Simon, "Helen Shirk: At Home in Nature," *Metalsmith* 31, no. 1 (2011), 36–43; Helen Shirk, telephone conversation with author, September 12, 2015.

79. Randy J. Long, telephone conversation with author, April 7, 2015.

80. Dave Hampton, *San Diego's Craft Revolution: From Postwar Modern to California Design* (San Diego: Mingei International Museum, 2011), 127–30, and Erica Goebel, "Marcia Lewis's Flights of Fancy," *Ornament* 11, no. 1 (Autumn 1987): 48–51; Marcia Lewis, *Chasing: Ancient Metalworking Technique with Modern Applications* (Long Beach, CA: LarMar Productions, 1994); Marcia Lewis, telephone conversation with author, April 3, 2015;

81. Kate Wagle, "Chris Smith: The Luxury of Stolen Images," *Metalsmith* 19, no. 2 (Spring 1999), 12–21.

82. "Alvin Pine," obituary, *San Francisco Chronicle*, February 7, 2010.

83. Sarah Bodine, "Benchmark: Al Pine's Conceptual Exploration," *Metalsmith* 9, no. 4 (Fall 1989): 34–37; Beverly Johnson, "He Turns Metal into Magical Forms," *Los Angeles Times*, April 23, 1967, 36.

84. "Dieter Muller-Stach," obituary, *Los Angeles Times*, October 31, 2011; "Edith Eva Muller-Stach," obituary, *Daily Pilot*, July 10, 2007.

85. See http://www.artjewelryforum.org/about-ajf.

Hermann Jünger

(1928–2005, Germany)

Brooch, c. 1970
Gold, opals, enamel
1⅞ × 1½ × ⅜ in.

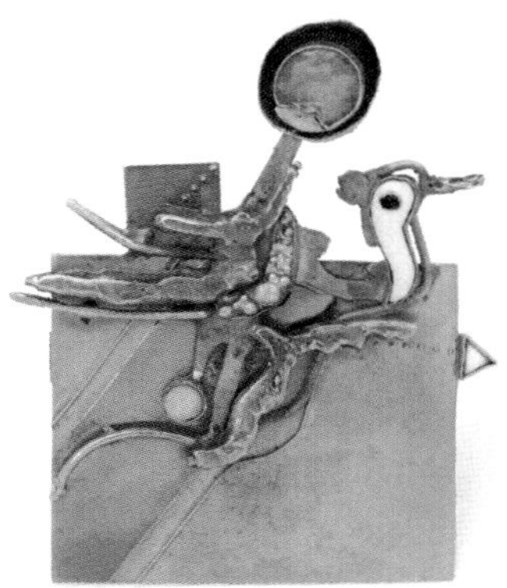

Necklace, 1993
Silver, gold, hematite, granite, wood box for storage
Wire: 19½ in. length;
box: 5¾ × 5¾ × ⅞ in.

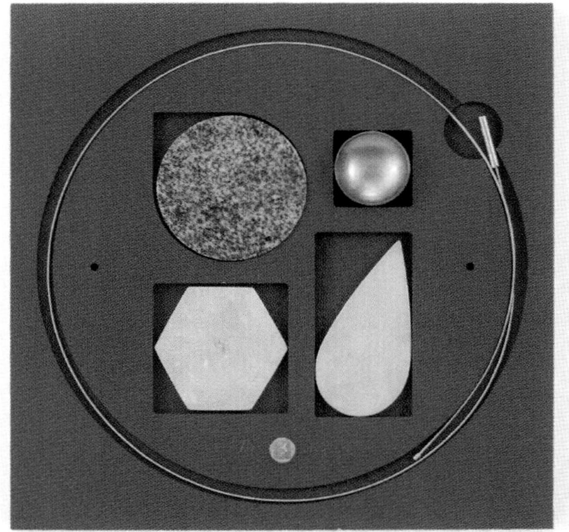

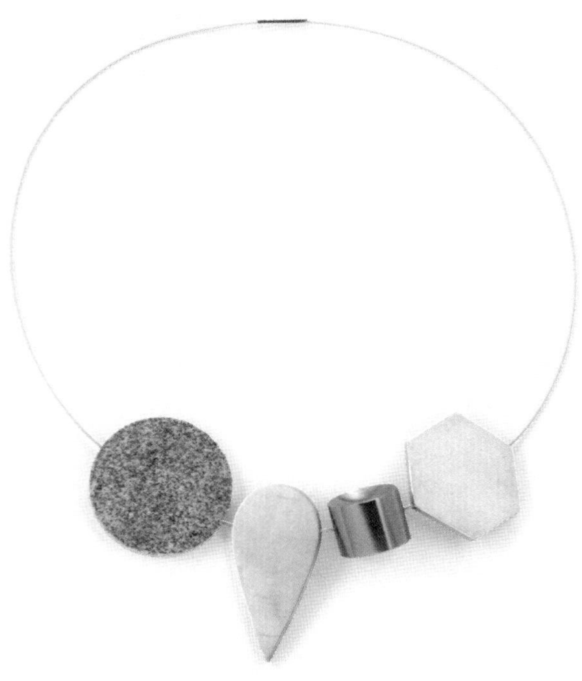

Brooch, 1997
Gold, semiprecious stones, possibly resin
2 1/4 × 2 1/16 × 1/2 in.

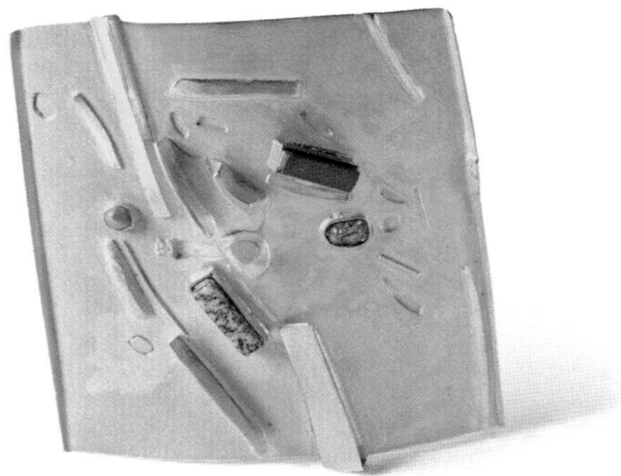

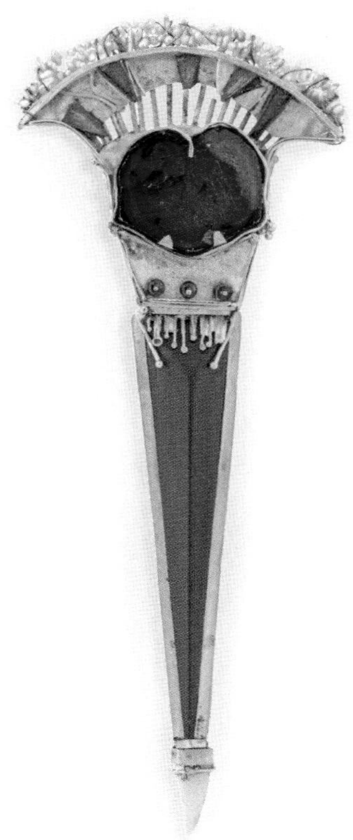

Judith Kaufman

(b. 1955, United States, active Connecticut)

Point of Woods **brooch, 2002**
Gold, tourmaline, onyx, silver, pearls, spinels, shell
5 11/16 × 2 1/8 × 1/2 in.

Betsy King

(b. 1953, United States, active Virginia and New Jersey)

***Chicago City Bolo*, 1988**
Silver, copper, brass, plastics, postcard, synthetic spinel
Cord: 36 ½ in. length; slide: 6 ¼ × 2 13/16 × 7/8 in.

***Earth Angel* brooch, 1994**
Silver, copper, brass, paper, polycarbonate sheet, foil, ivory
3 11/16 × 4 1/16 × 3/8 in.

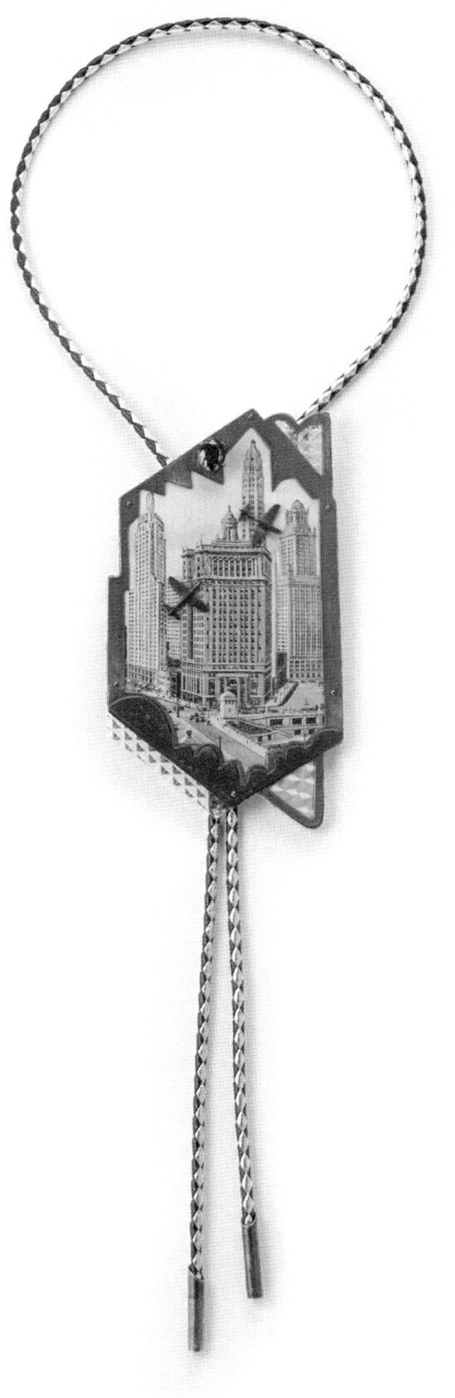

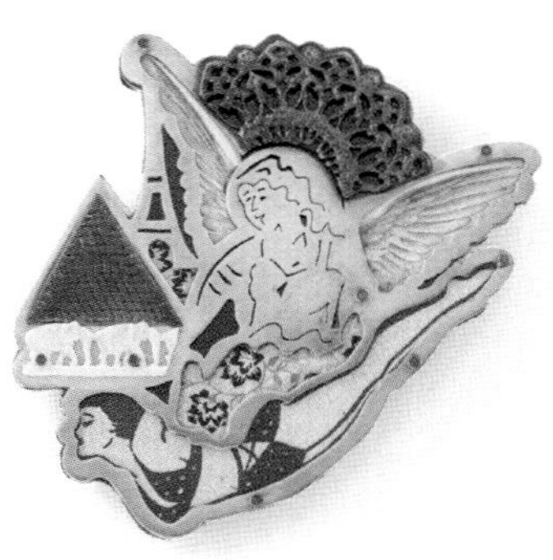

Alice H. Klein

(b. 1956, United States, active Pennsylvania, Wisconsin, and Delaware)

Necklace, 1982
PMMA, Cratex wheels, copper alloy (nickel silver), silver
9 1/8 × 6 3/4 × 3/4 in.

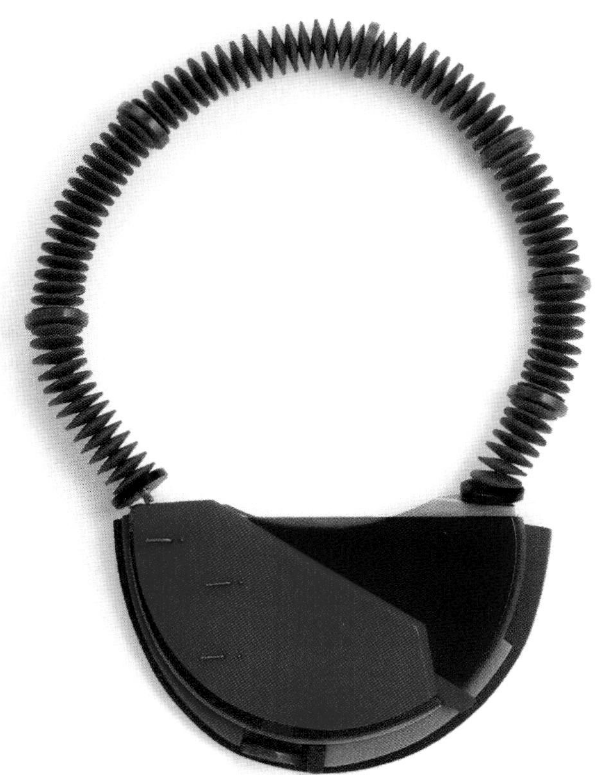

Esther Knobel

(b. 1949, Poland, active Israel)

Brooch, mid-1980s
From the series Warrior, 1982–87
Steel can, alkyd paint, elastic cord, stainless steel
4 1/2 × 6 1/2 × 1/4 in.

***A Kit for Mending Thoughts* pin set, 2005**
Gold, silver, paper-lined tin box for storage
Square piece: 2 5/16 × 2 3/8 × 1/16 in.; box (closed): 3 × 7 1/8 × 3/4 in.

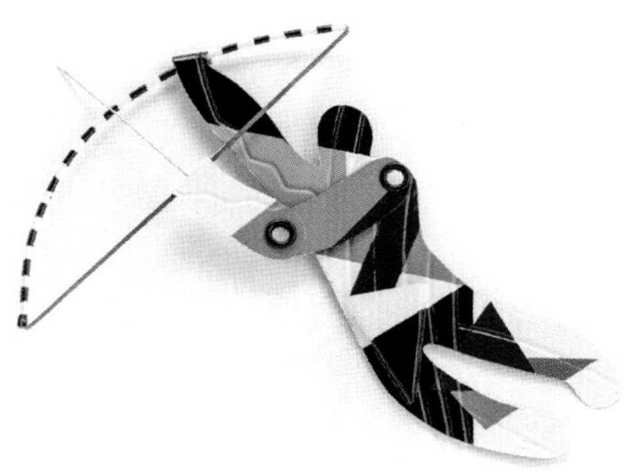

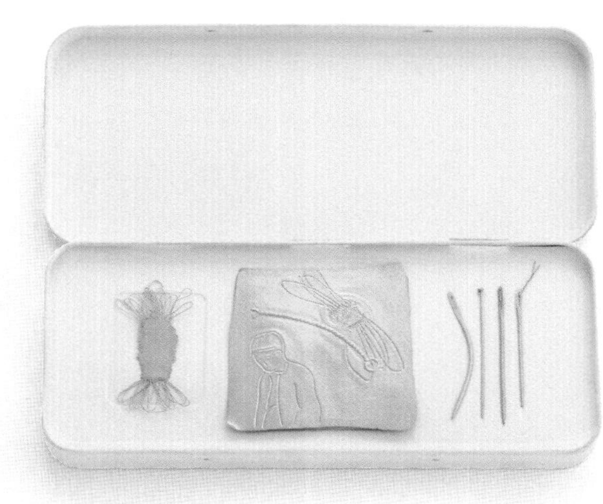

Friedrich Knupper

(1947–1987, Germany)

Necklace, 1984
Silver, iron, cellulose nitrate
on brass and silver
12 × 8 1/16 × 1/2 in.

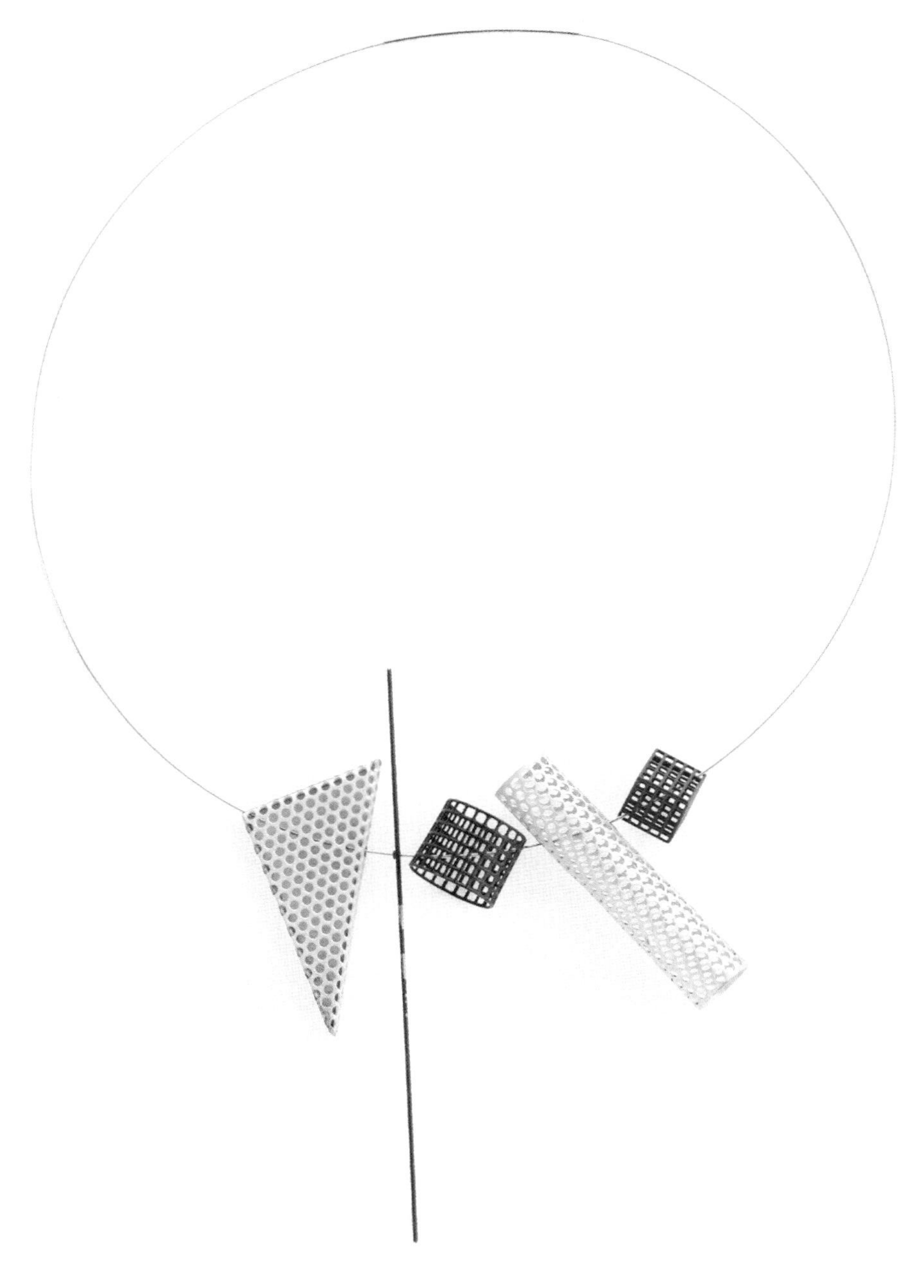

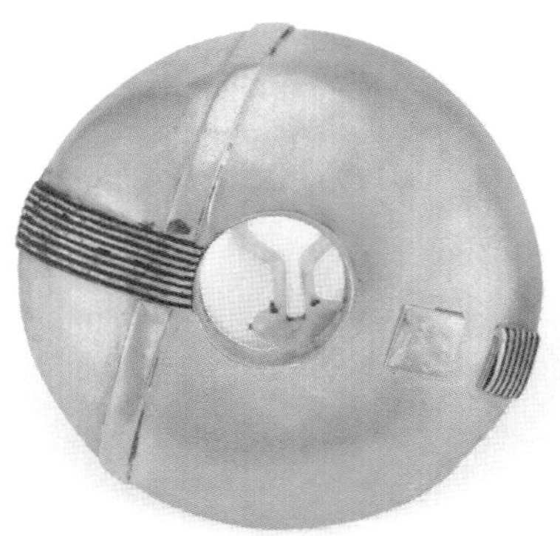
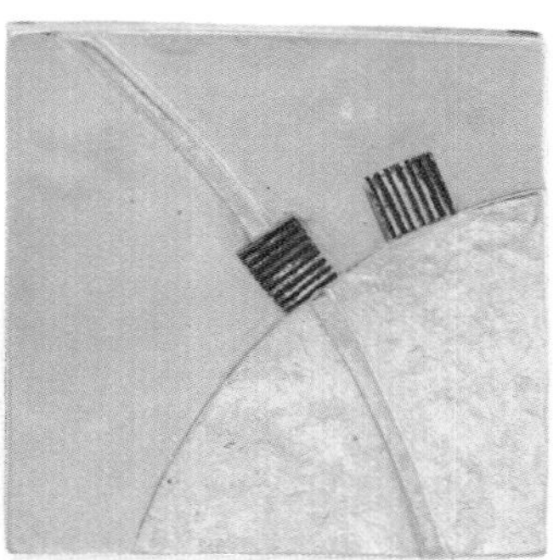

Rena Koopman

(b. 1945, United States, active Massachusetts)

Earrings, 1990
Varicolored gold
Round earring: 1⅝⁄16 × 1⁵⁄16 × ½ in.;
square earring: 1³⁄16 × 1³⁄16 × ⅜ in.

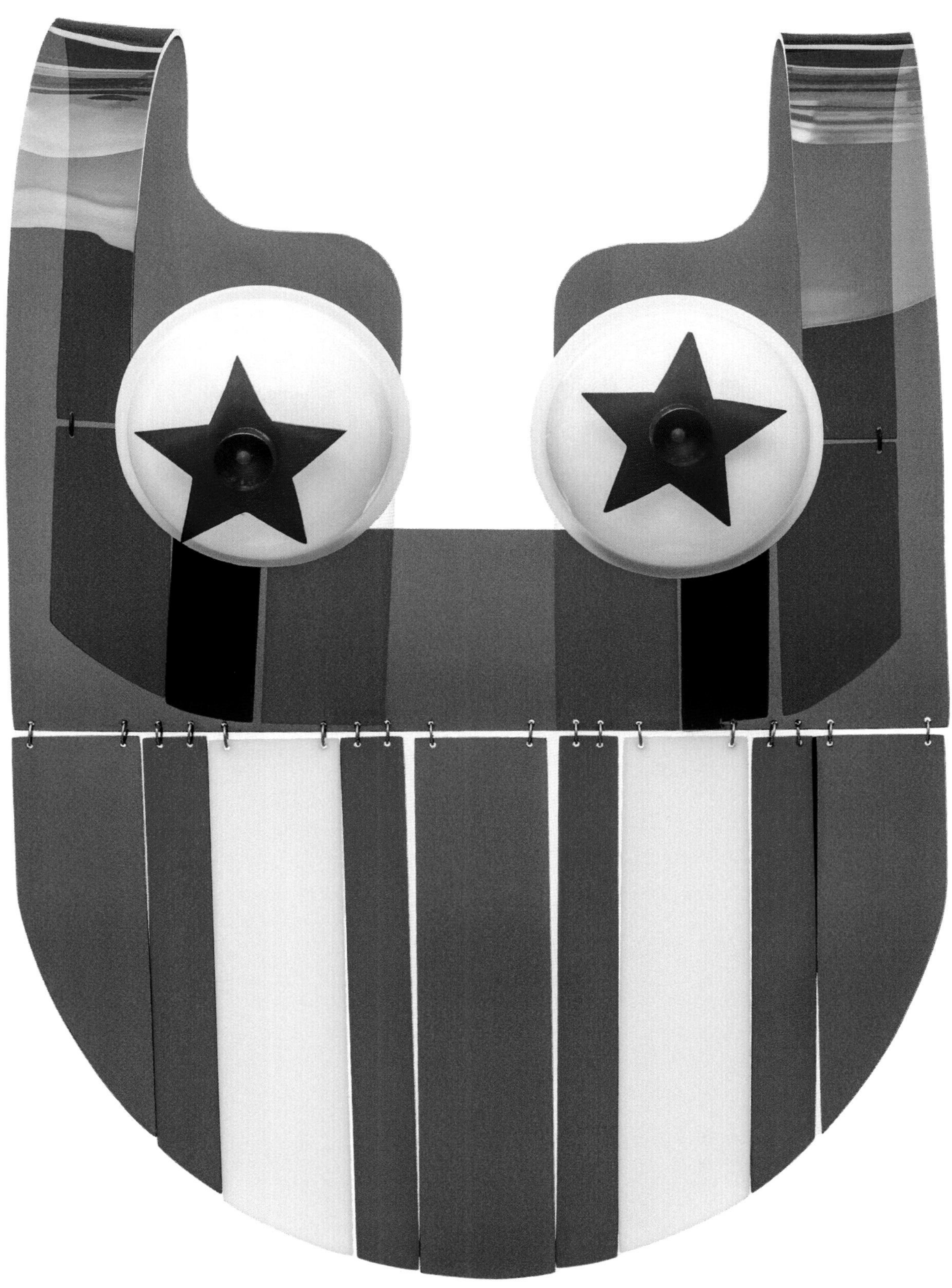

Carolyn Kriegman

(1933–1999, United States, active New Jersey)

Necklace, 1969
PMMA, metal rings
19¾ × 13¾ × 10½ in.

Necklace, 1969
Silver, smoky citrine
13 × 5⅛ × ⅝ in.

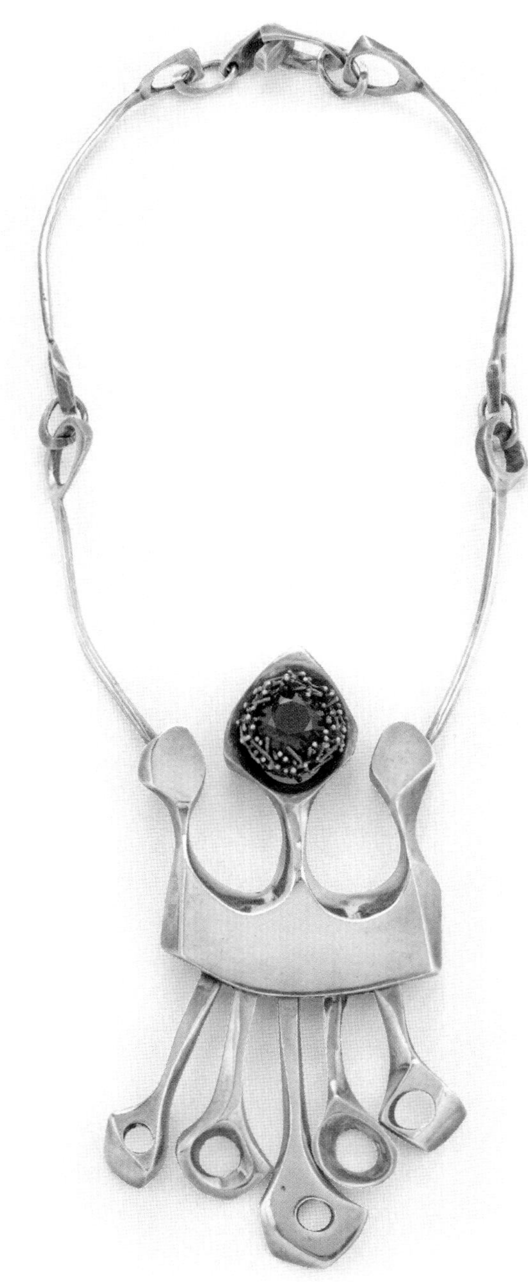

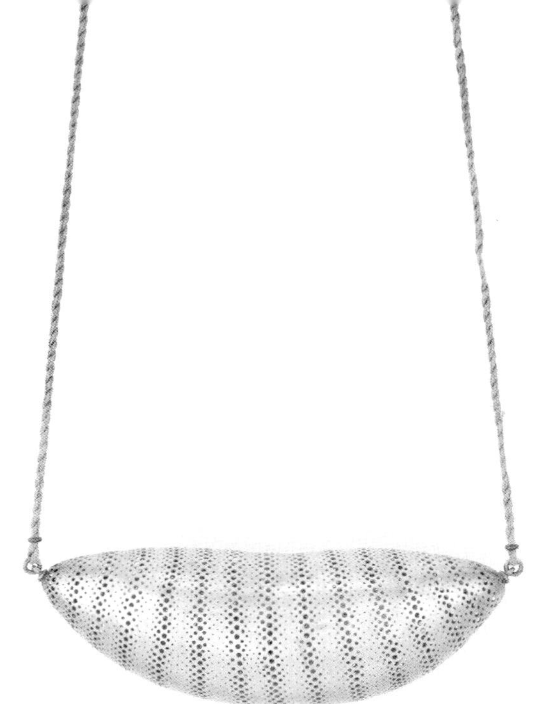

Daniel Kruger

(b. 1951, South Africa, active Germany)

Necklace, 1984
Silver, silk cord
Cord: 24½ in. length;
pendant: 1½ × 4½ × 1½ in.

Necklace, 1987
Gold, mirror and glass
fragments
8½ × 8½ × ½ in.

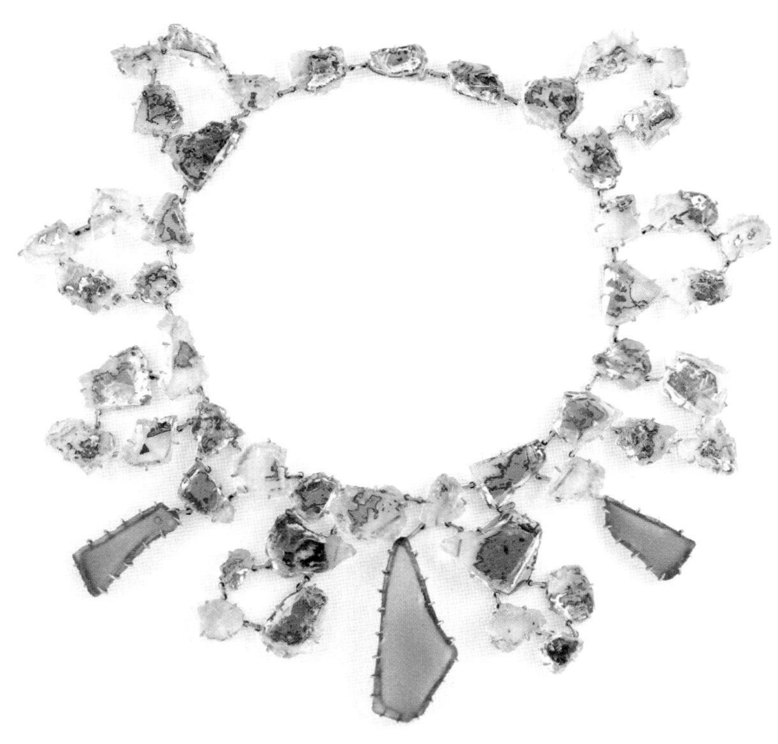

Otto Künzli

(b. 1948, Switzerland, active Germany)

***Centifolia* brooch, 1983**
From the series Wallpaper Brooches, 1982–85
Wallpaper on polymeth-acrylimide foam
5 1/8 × 3 1/2 × 2 1/2 in.

***Heart* brooch, 1985**
Number 4 from an edition of 10
Acrylic lacquer on polymeth-acrylimide foam
3 3/4 × 3 1/2 × 1 3/4 in.

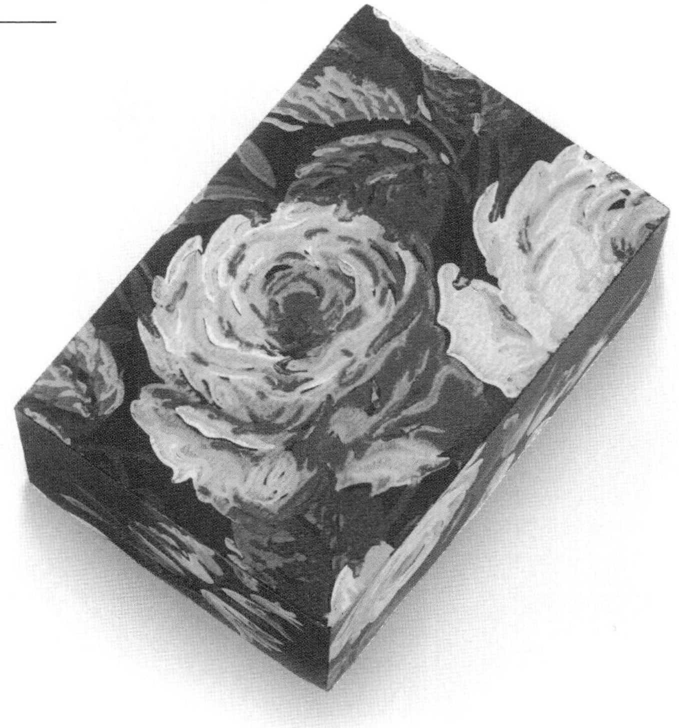

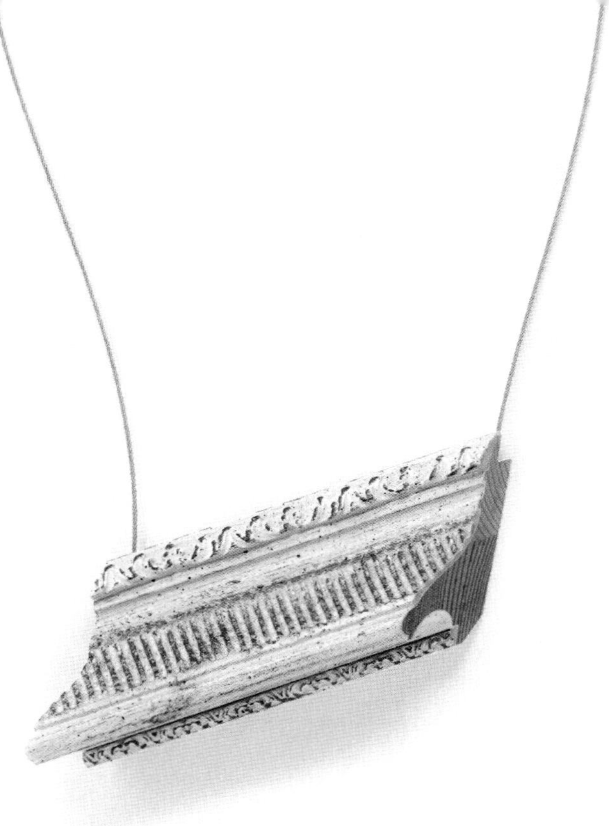

Otto Künzli

(continued)

Fragment necklace, 1986
From the series Fragments, 1986–88
Wooden frame, stainless-steel wire
15¾ × 6 × 1¼ in.

Rebekah Laskin

(b. 1955, United States, active New York)

Brooch, 1984
Enamel on copper, silver
1¾ × 1¾ × ¼ in.

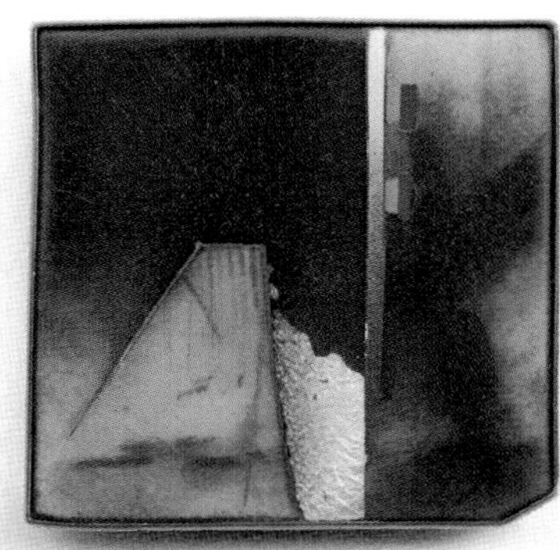

Stanley Lechtzin

(b. 1936, United States, active Pennsylvania)

***Ring #18 C-5*, designed 1968, made 1981**
Gold, watermelon tourmaline
1 5/16 × 15/16 × 9/16 in.

***Brooch #70 C*, 1970**
Gilded silver, hessonite grossular garnet
2 × 6 1/2 × 3/4 in.

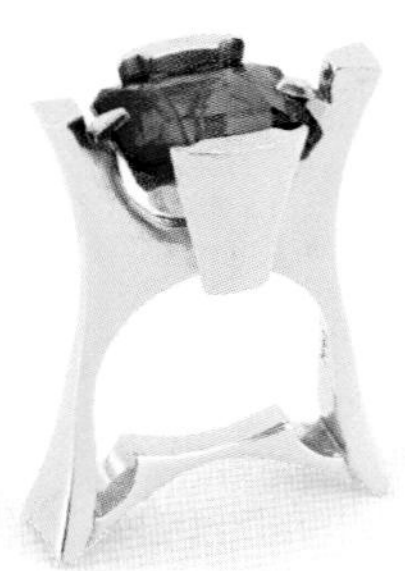

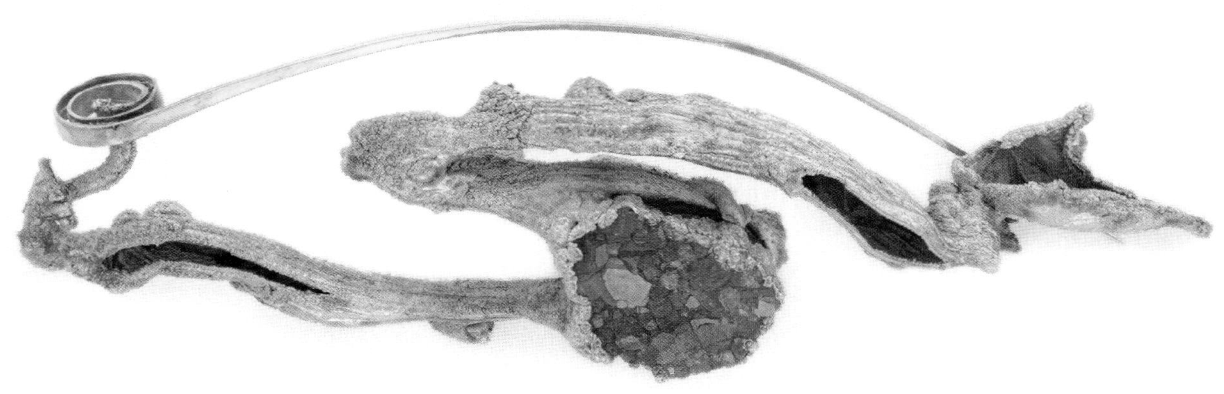

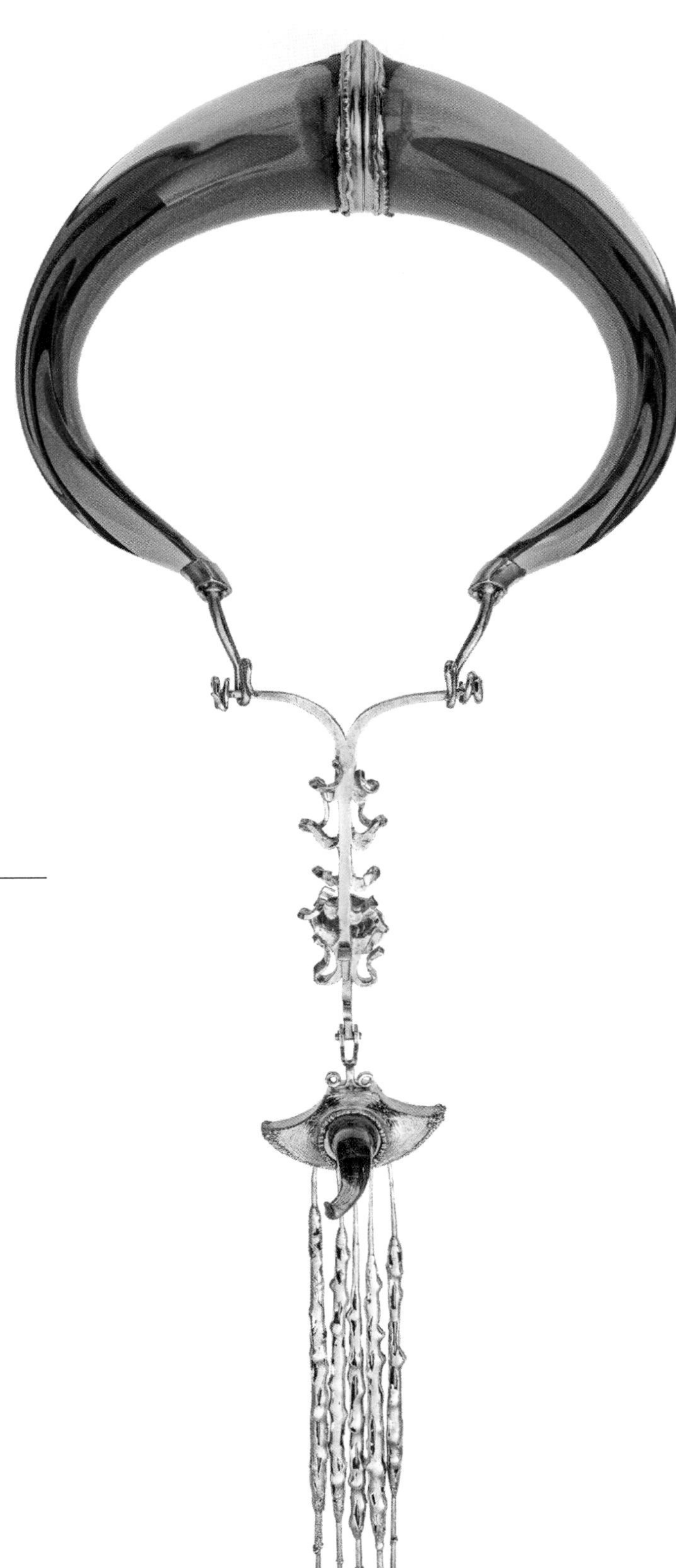

Stanley Lechtzin

(continued)

***Torque #40 D*, 1973**
Gilded silver, polyester resin,
freshwater pearls
19 × 7 ¼ × 2 in.

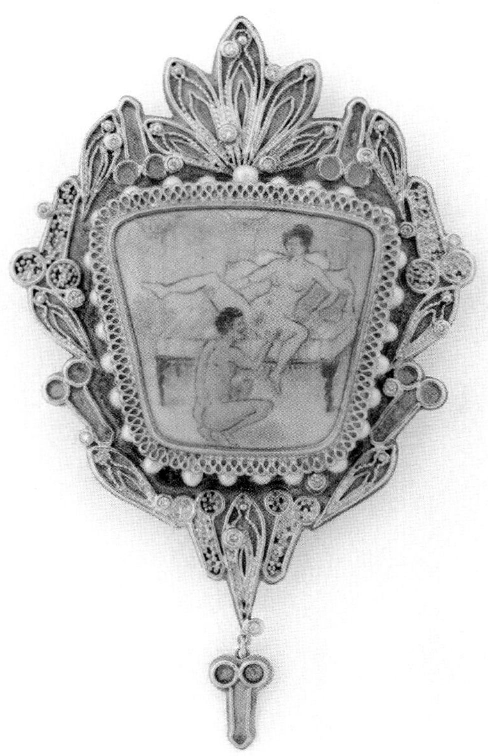

Keith Lewis

(b. 1959, United States, active Washington)

***Maritimus cunnum lingit assibus IIII* brooch, 2002**
Gilded silver, enamel,
pearls, diamonds
4 × 2⅜ × ⅝ in.

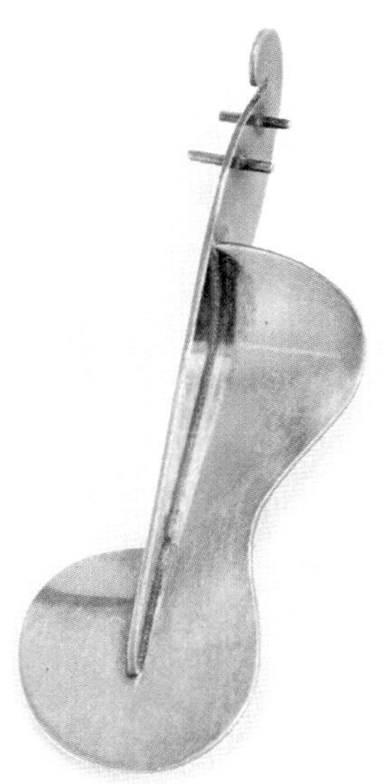

Paul Lobel

(1899–1983, Romania, active New York)

***Stradivarius* brooch, c. 1945**
Silver
3 × 1 × ½ in.

Linda MacNeil

(b. 1954, United States, active Massachusetts)

***Elements Necklace (26–84)*, 1984**
Number 26 from the series Elements, 1979–present
Glass, Vitrolite glass, gold
9¾ × 7½ × ⅝ in.

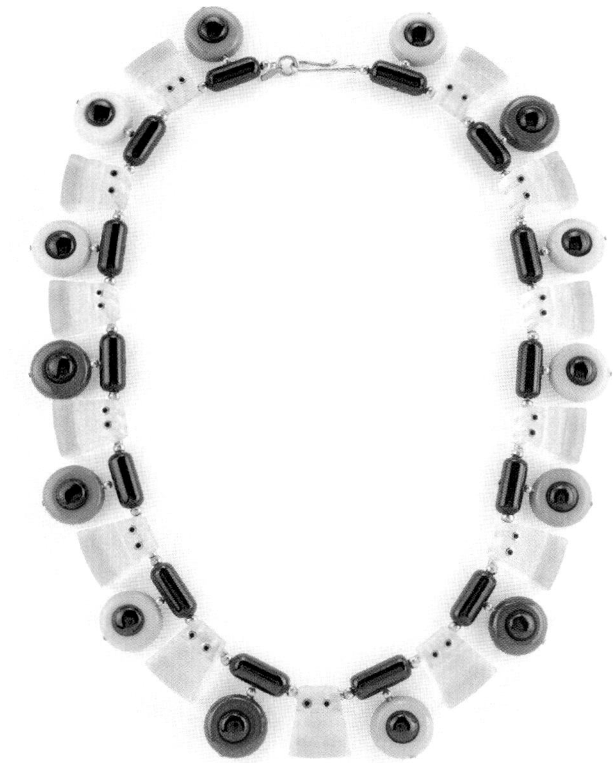

Fritz Maierhofer

(b. 1941, Austria)

Brooch, 1977
Silver, gold
2 ¼ × 2 ¼ × ½ in.

Ring, 2009
Silver
3 × 2 ¼ × 1 ¾ in.

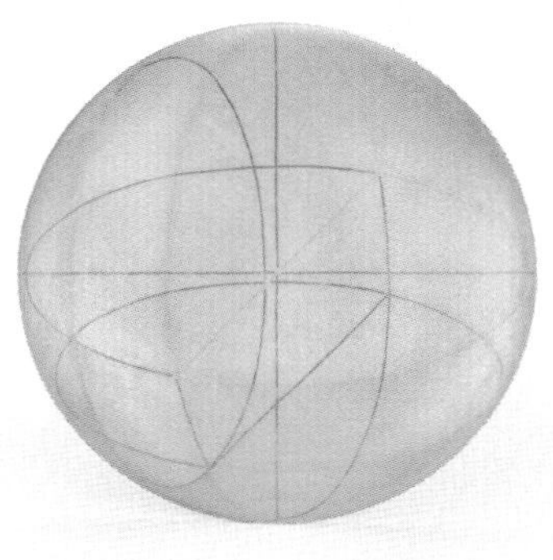

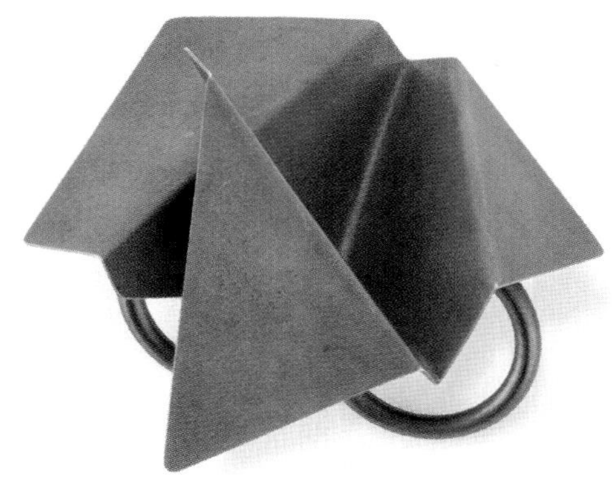

Carlier Makigawa

(b. 1952, Australia)

Shrine for Kanzaburo
brooch, 1987
Stainless steel, silver,
papier-mâché with gilding
3 ¼ × 2 ¾ × ¾ in.

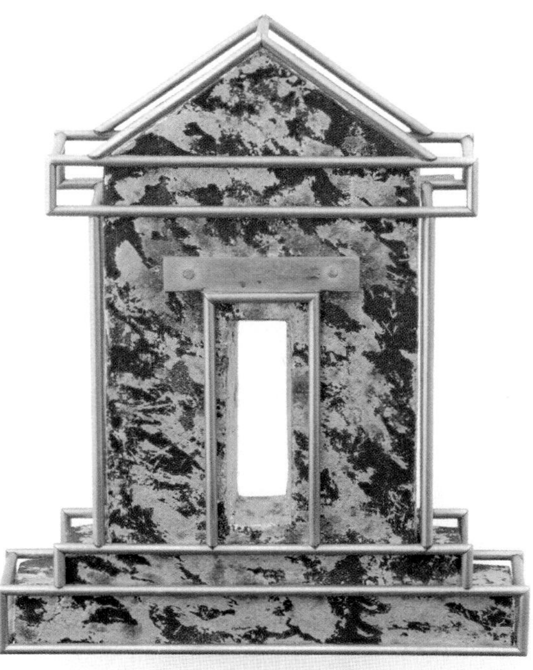

K. Lee Manuel

(1936–2003, United States, active California)

Necklace, c. 1977
Feathers, acrylic and fabric paint, leather, nylon
15 × 17 ½ × ½ in.

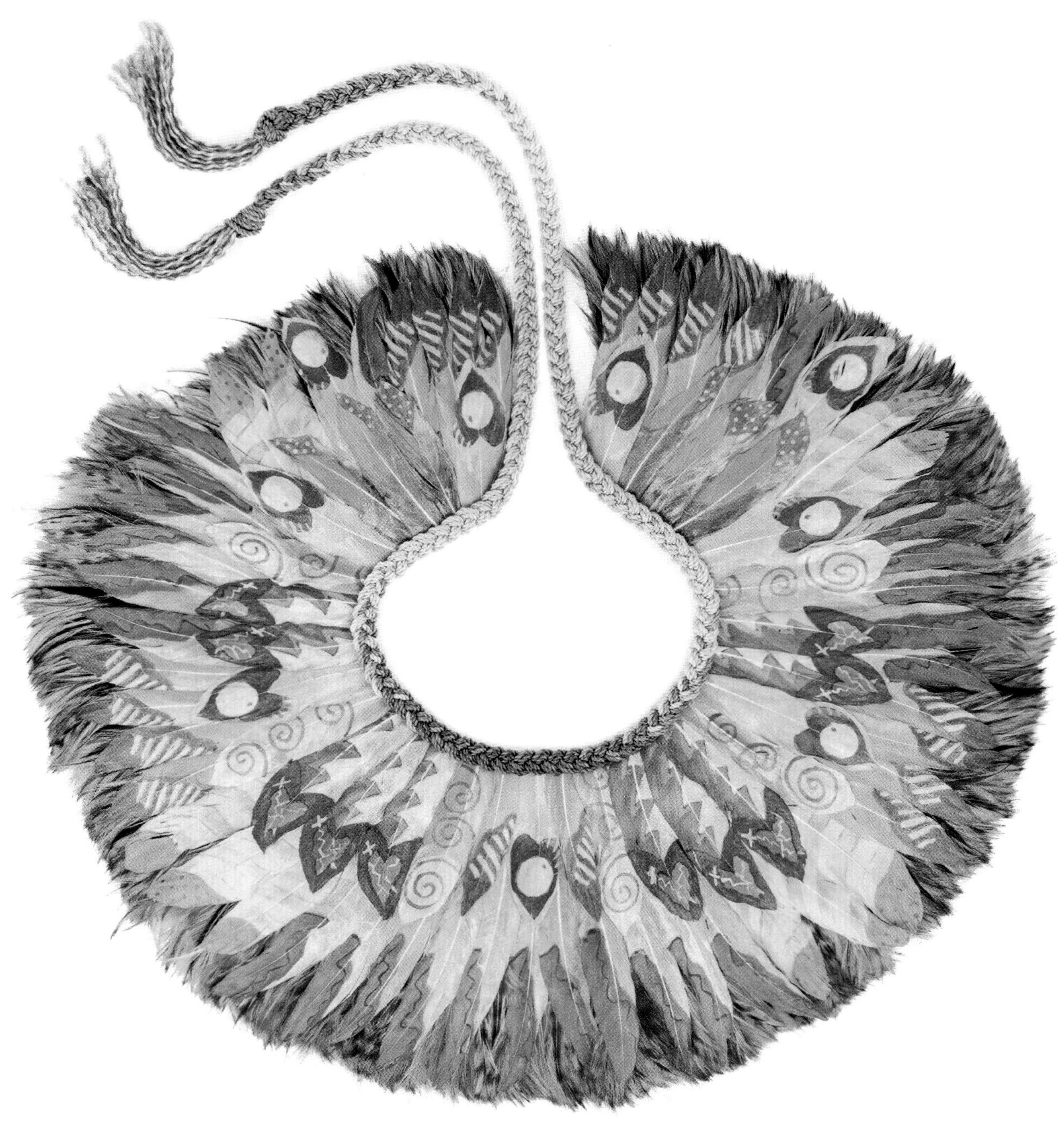

Stefano Marchetti

(b. 1970, Italy)

Brooch, 2004
Gold, silver
2⅝ × 2½ × 1 in.

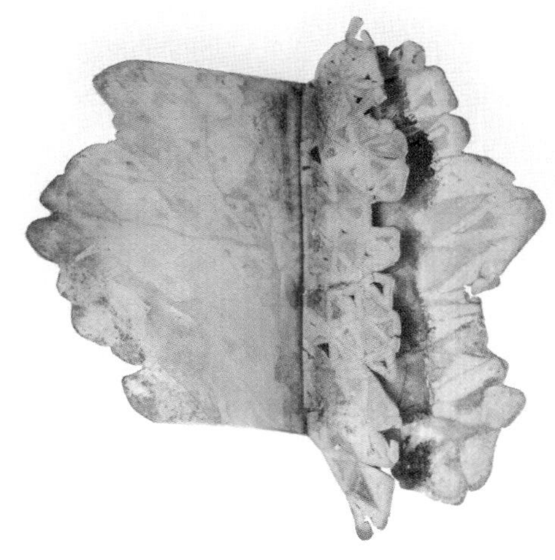

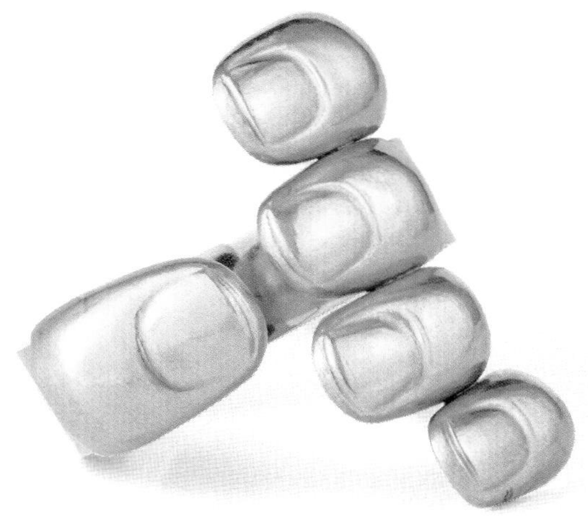

Bruno Martinazzi

(b. 1923, Italy)

***Goldfinger* bracelet, designed 1969, made 1970**
Number 9 of 12 left-hand *Goldfinger* bracelets
Varicolored gold
2 ⅞ × 2 ⅜ × 2 ⅛ in.

***Venus* brooch, 1980**
Gold
2 × 2 × ¾ in.

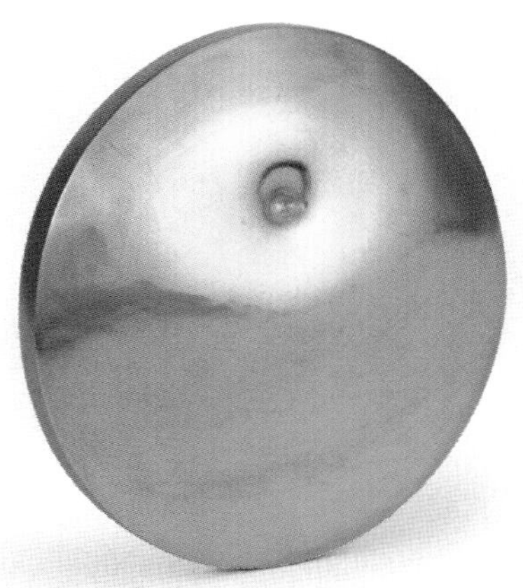

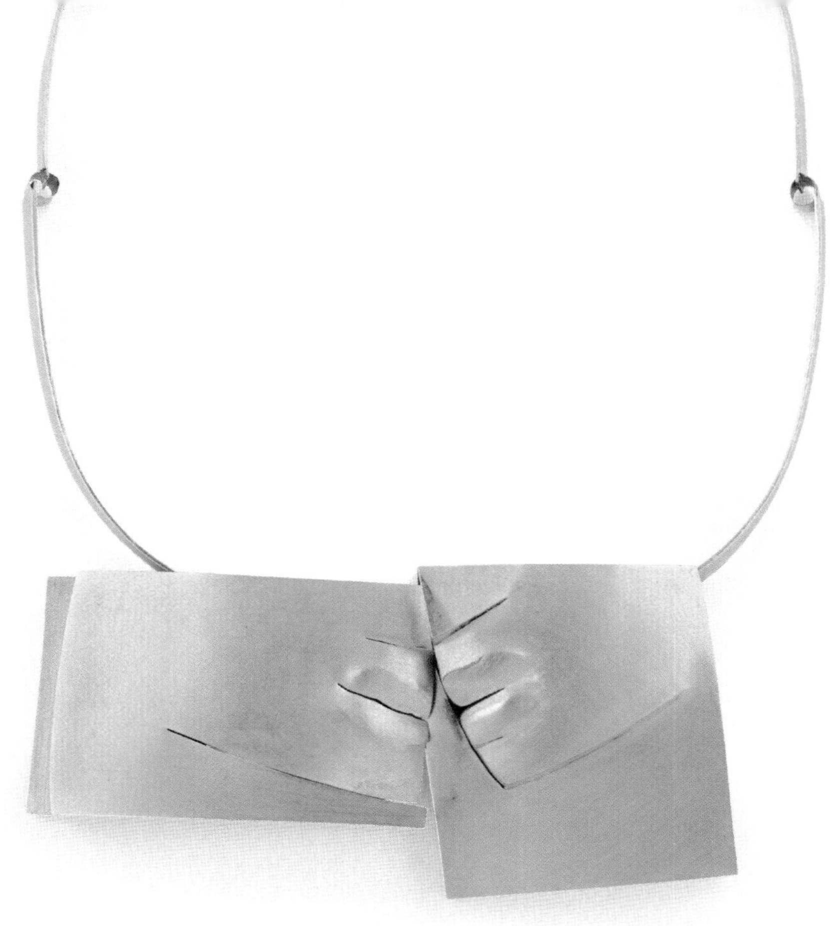

***Mito/Logos* brooch, 1989**
Varicolored gold
1 7/16 × 2 5/16 × 1/2 in.

***E se, rivolto, inver' di lei si piega, quel piegare è amor* necklace, 1999**
Gold
8 × 5 1/4 × 3/4 in.

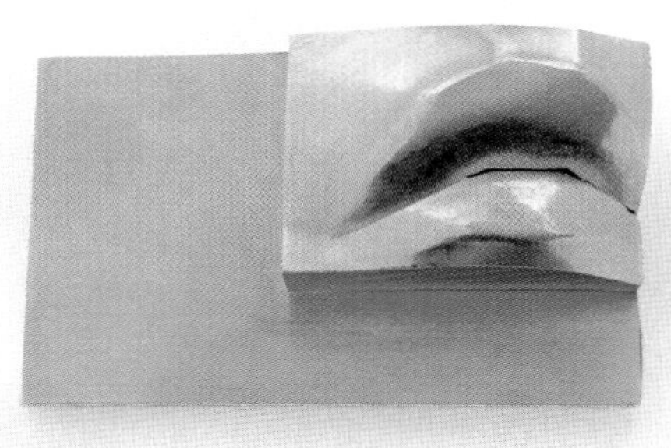

Falko Marx

(1941–2013, Germany)

Brooch, 1989
Athenian pottery fragment, gold, diamond
1½ × 2¾ × ⅝ in.

Brooch, 1989
Gold, plastic-coated steel, emeralds, diamonds, ruby
1¾ × 2¾ × ¼ in.

Ring, 1989
Gold, porcelain, metal filings, liquid, glass
1¾ × 1¼ × 1 in.

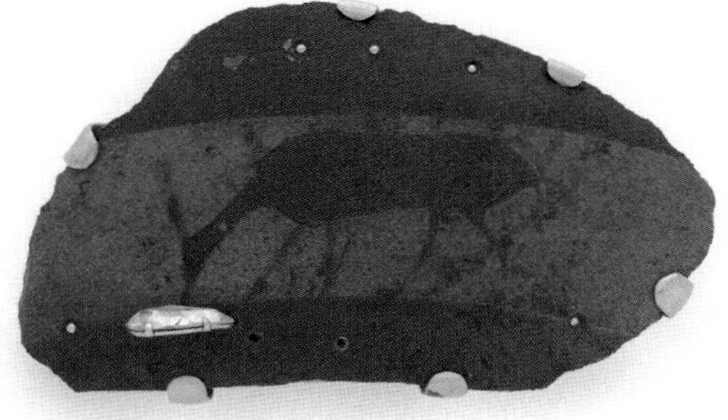

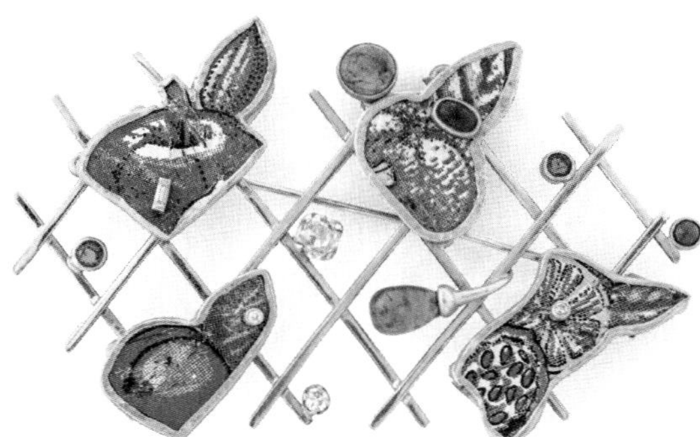

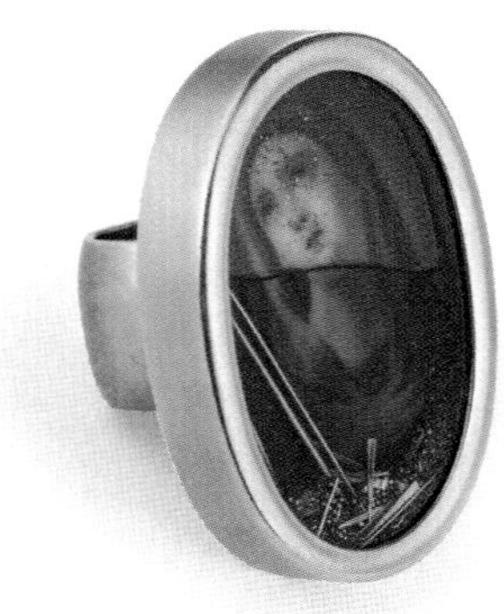

Nicki Marx

(b. 1943, United States, active California and New Mexico)

***Royal Raiment* necklace, 1973**
Peacock feathers, suede
27 ½ × 17 × ⅛ in.

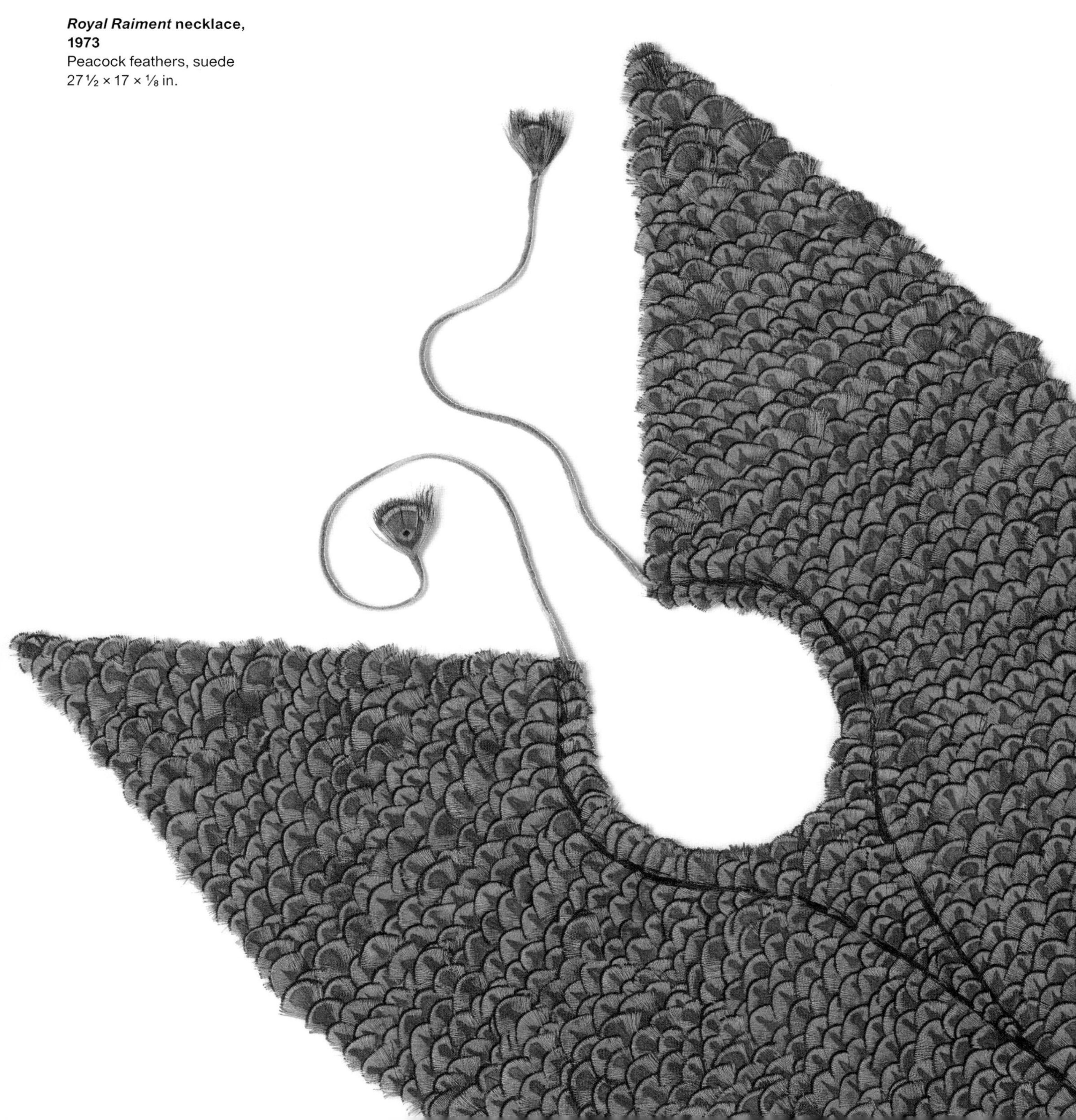

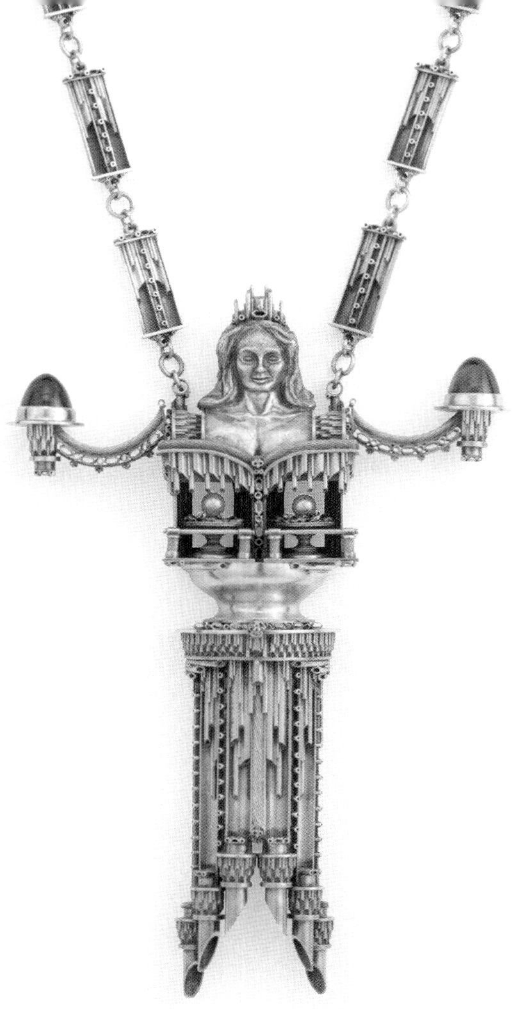

Richard Mawdsley

(b. 1945, United States, active Kansas and Illinois)

Wonder Woman in Her Bicentennial Finery
necklace, 1975
Silver, pearls, smoky quartz
13¾ × 5½ × ¾ in.

Albatross Boston Tea Medal
necklace, 1999–2000
Silver with gilding
13¾ × 5½ × ⅞ in.

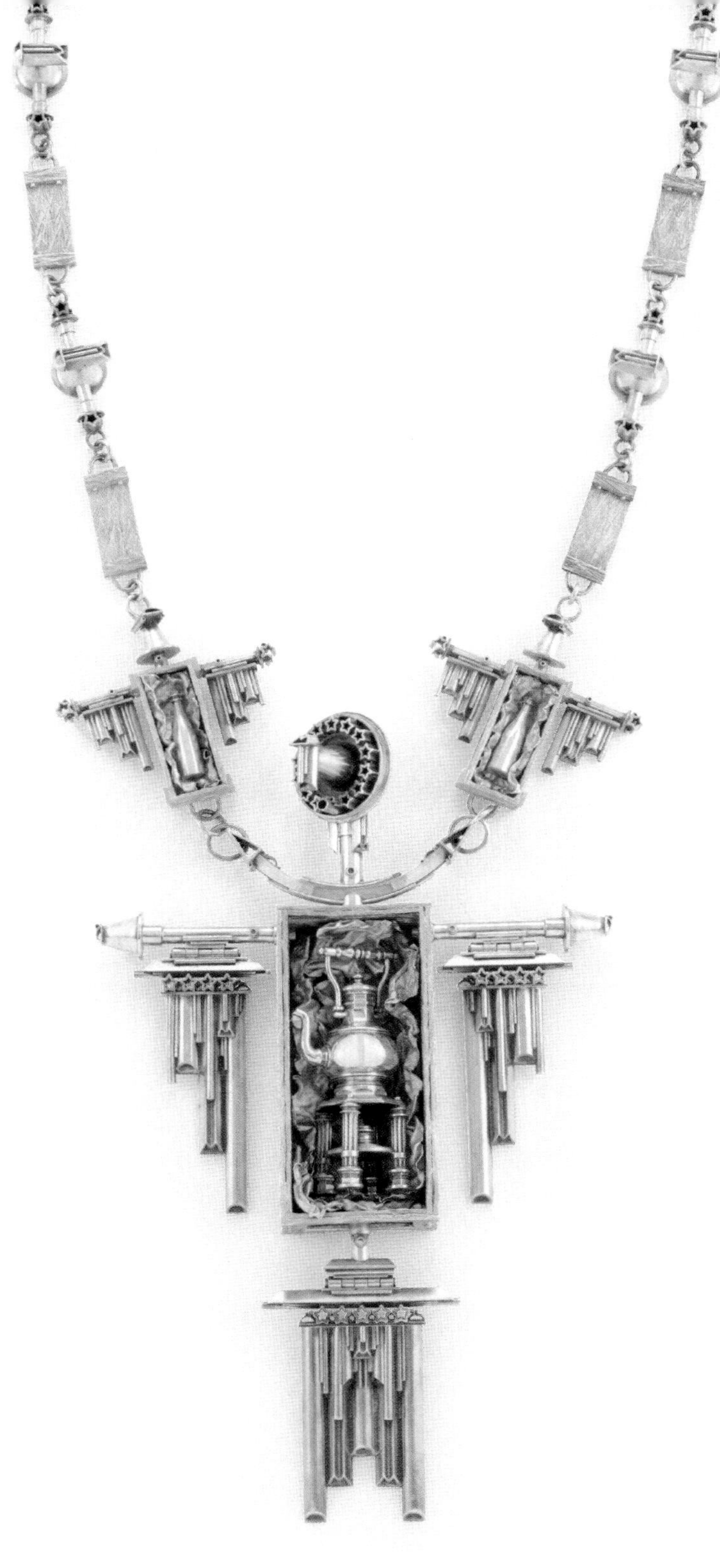

Peter McKay

(b. 1951, New Zealand)

***Dark Plain* set of ten brooches, 2006**
Silver with gilding
Largest brooch:
$1\frac{11}{16} \times 1\frac{3}{8} \times \frac{1}{4}$ in.

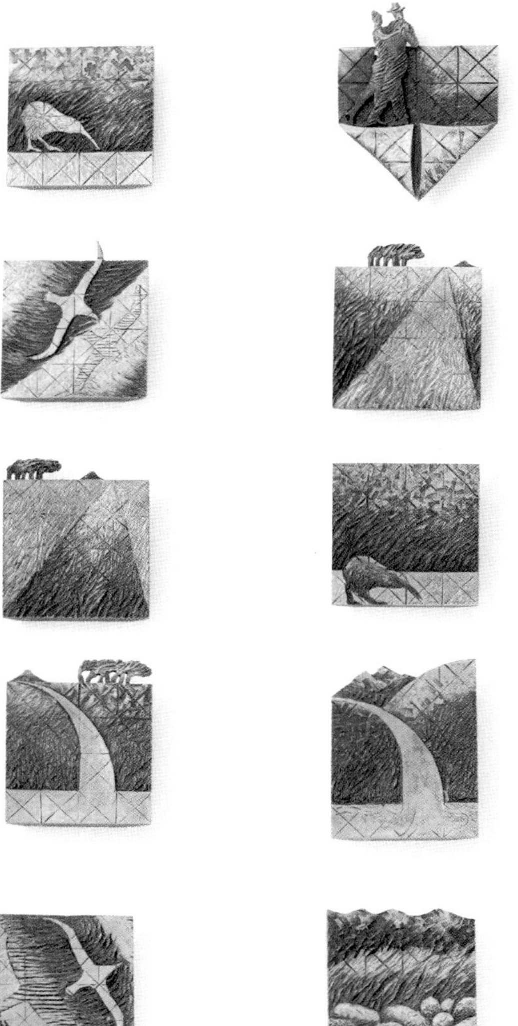

Bruce Metcalf

(b. 1949, United States, active Pennsylvania and Ohio)

***Swimming Blind in a Sea of Moons* brooch, 1986**
Silver with paint, brass, PMMA, colored pencil on Mylar®
$3\frac{1}{2} \times 4\frac{5}{8} \times \frac{5}{8}$ in.

***Handwork Necklace*, 1999**
Beech, holly, mahogany, cork, brass, silver, gold
$14\frac{1}{2} \times 9\frac{1}{2} \times 2$ in.

***Think Too Much* brooch, 1986**
Silver, brass
$2\frac{7}{8} \times 3\frac{1}{8} \times \frac{1}{2}$ in.

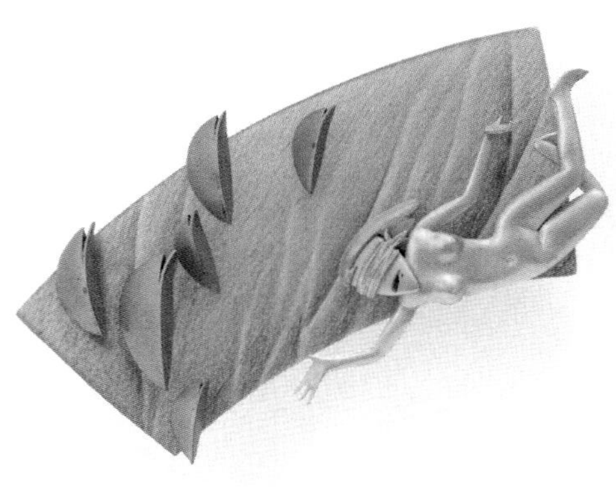

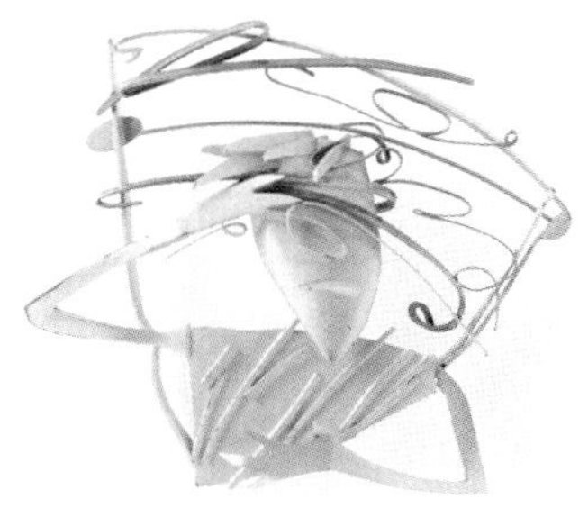

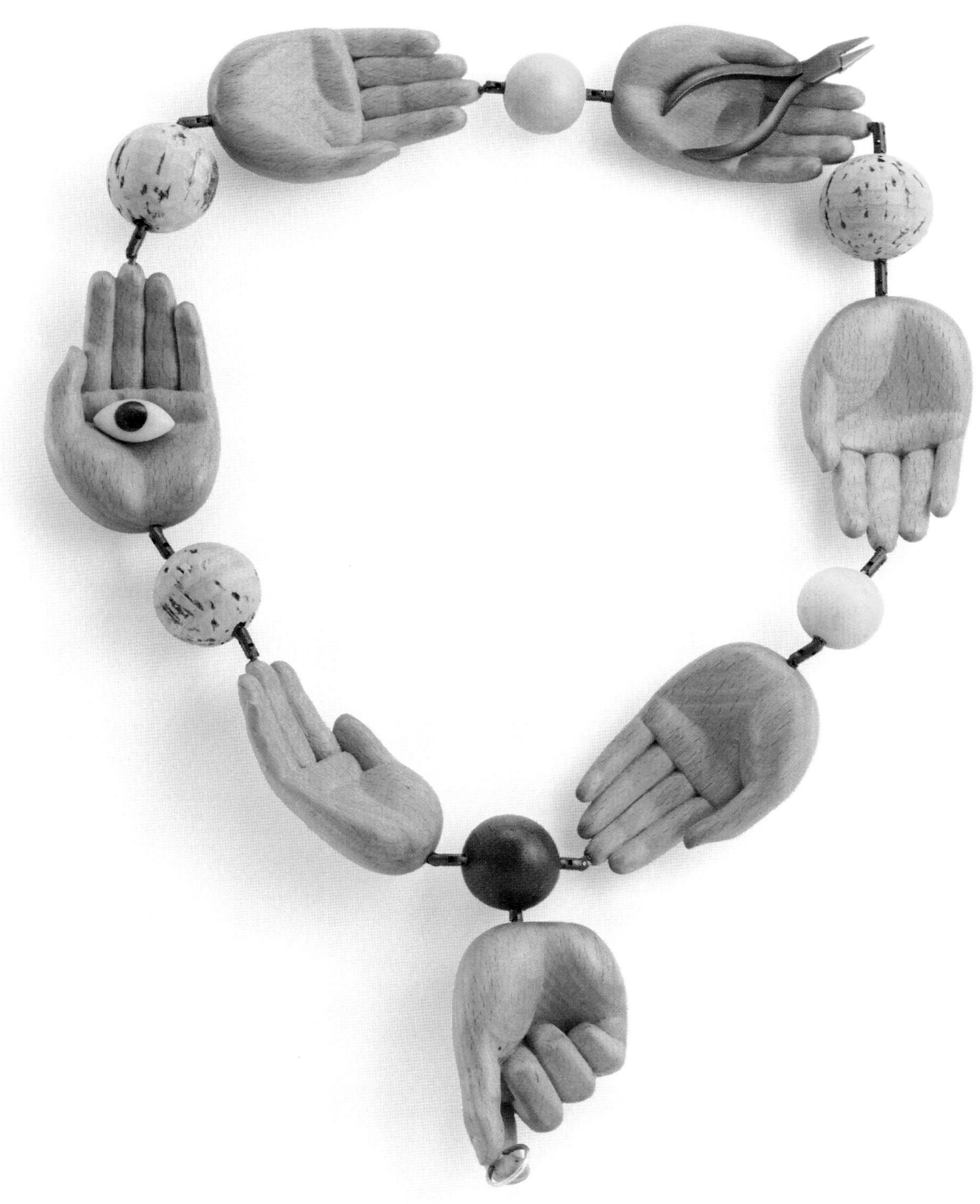

Louis Mueller

(b. 1943, United States, active California, Rhode Island, and New York)

***Crossword 3* brooch, 1986**
Number 3 of 7 from the series Crossword, 1986
Gilded silver, onyx, lapis lazuli, amethyst, agate
2 3/16 × 2 3/16 × 5/16 in.

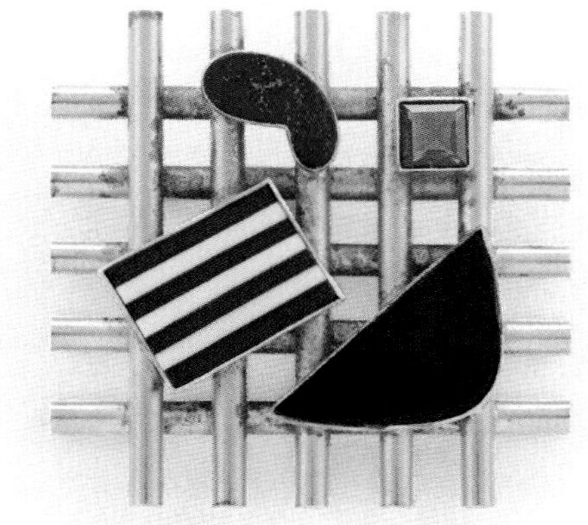

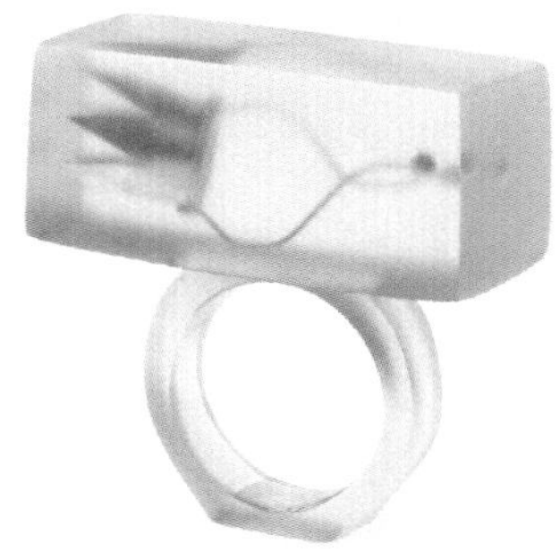

Ted Noten

(b. 1956, Netherlands)

***Crown-Ring*, 1997**
Number 2 from an edition of 2
PMMA, gold
1 5/8 × 1 9/16 × 11/16 in.

***Fashionista Golden Girl* necklace, 2010**
From the series Fashionista Golden Girl, 2010
Glass-infiltrated nylon, gold
15 × 15 × 1 in.

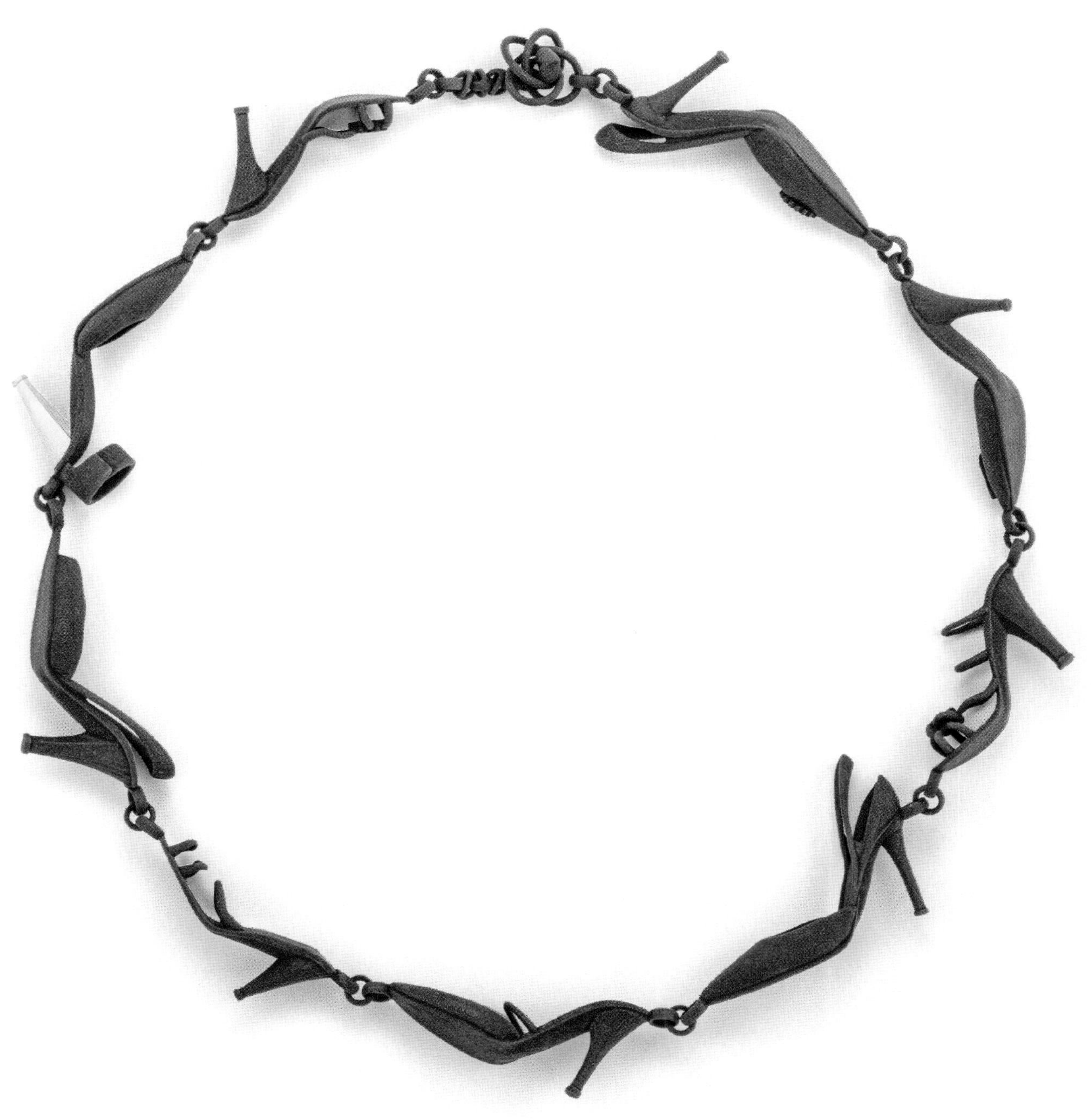

Rarities before Riches: The Boardman Collection as a Cabinet of Curiosities

Rosie Chambers Mills

In Praise of the Extraordinary

A salamander, a chameleon, a pelican... a flying squirrel, another squirrel like a fish, all kinds of bright colored birds from India, a number of things changed into stone, amongst others a piece of human flesh on a bone, gourds, olives, a piece of wood, an ape's head, a cheese, etc.... all kinds of shells, the hand of a mermaid, the hand of a mummy, a very natural wax hand under glass, all kinds of precious stones, coins, a picture wrought in feathers... the robe of the King of Virginia, a few goblets of agate... the Passion of Christ carved very daintily on a plum stone... [and] a hatband of snake bones.

Georg Christoph Stirn, on the collection of John Tradescant

Eclectic collections have stimulated curious minds for centuries. Known as "The Ark," the extraordinary and wide-ranging objects assembled by John Tradescant (c. 1570s–1638) and his son John (1608–1662) in London south of the River Thames seem to have constituted the first "museum"[1] open to the English public, "entertaining and receiving all persons, whose curiosity shall invite them to the delight of seeing his rare and ingenious collections of art and nature."[2] It attracted local and foreign visitors alike. In 1659 schoolmaster Charles Hoole (1610–1667) noted the educational advantage that children living in London could gain "once a year, by walking to Mr. John Tradescant's,"[3] and University of Altdorf student Georg Christoph Stirn (1616–1669) (who traveled through Switzerland, France, England, and Holland while studying for a doctorate in civil and canon law) was impressed by the diversity of its contents.[4] Stirn's diary entry detailing what he saw in July 1638 is full of unexpected juxtapositions: "a piece of wood, an ape's head, a cheese." Although the items listed in the 1656 catalogue *Musaeum Tradescantium, or A Collection of Rarities* can be divided into two principal categories (natural and artificial),[5] it is clear from Stirn's account that he experienced it as a delightfully intermixed, rather than strictly ordered, collection. For him, the impact of each individual object was heightened by the diverse array of the totality.[6]

The Tradescants' appetite for the incongruous and the unusual exemplified a wider collecting phenomenon that emerged across Europe in the sixteenth and seventeenth centuries. Holy Roman Emperor, King of Bohemia, and

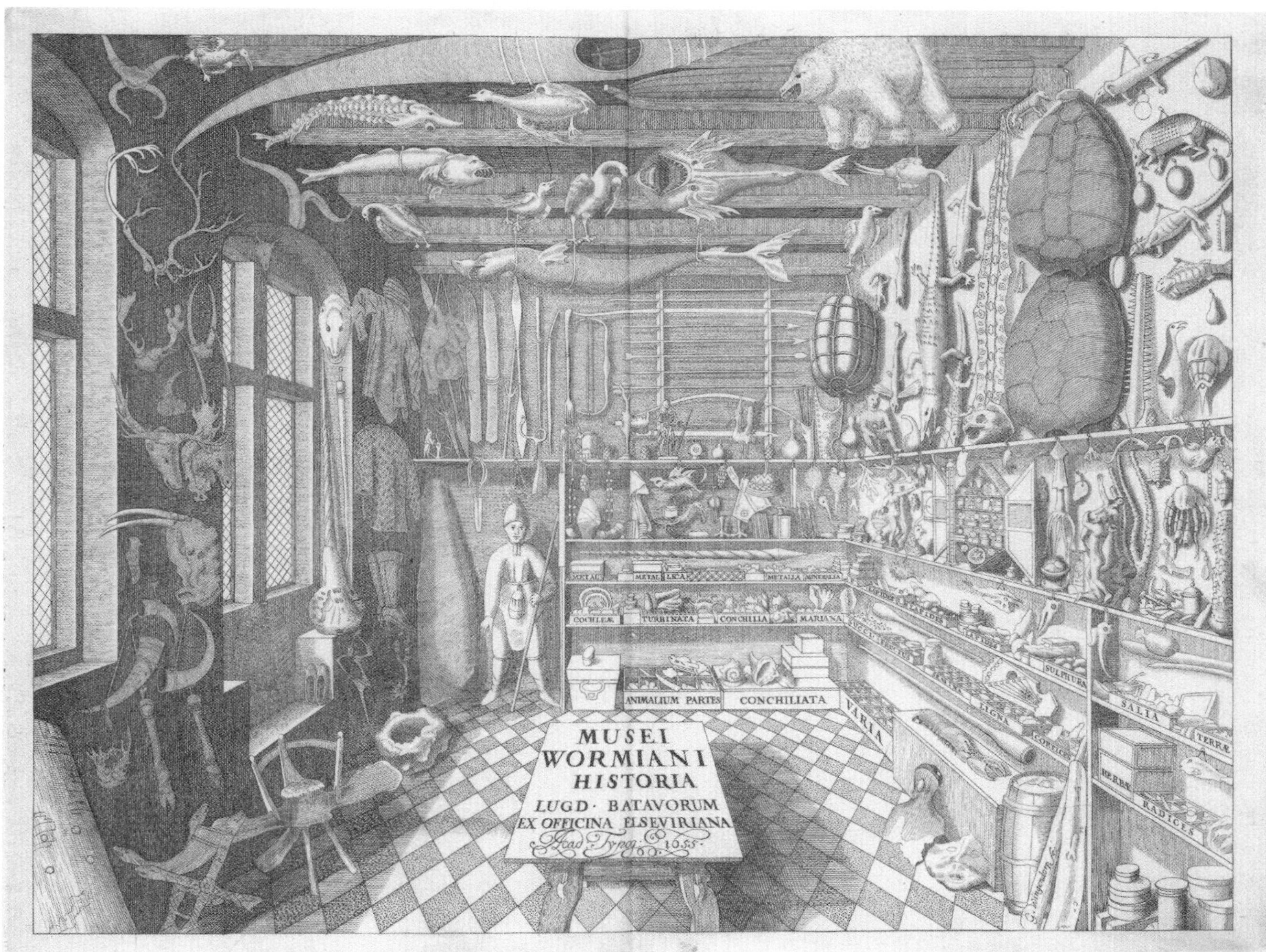

FIG. 1
Frontispiece of Ole Worm's *Museum Wormianum*...
(Amsterdam: Lowijs and Daniel Elzevier, 1655)

Archduke of Austria Rudolph II (1552–1612) amassed instruments of magic and alchemy, curiosities of nature, and extraordinary works of art in his palace in Prague. In Rome the historian and antiquarian Francesco Angeloni (before 1575–1652) owned a "sea-man's skin"[7] as well as ethnographic and natural history collections. At Schloss Ambras near Innsbruck, Austria, Archduke Ferdinand of Tirol (1529–1595) had eighteen cabinets individually decorated according to their contents, which ranged from metalwork, minerals, corals, porcelain, glass, wood carvings, and historical portraits to ivories from Benin and paintings from China. In Denmark the collection of physician Ole Worm (1588–1654) comprised animals (including "sea unicorns" and parts of mermaids), plants, fossils, Egyptian antiquities, ethnographic tools and weapons, and a mechanical human puppet powered by a wheel (fig.1). Renaissance and Baroque princes, bankers, merchants, doctors, and scholars strove to represent anything and everything that could spark fascination and amazement.[8]

In Italy these unusual collections tended to be displayed separately from contemporary paintings and sculptures, but north of the Alps such collections remained integrated with fine art. The German words *kunstkammer* (art chamber), *wunderkammer* (chamber of wonders), and *raritatenkammer* (chamber of rarities) functioned as alternative and equivalent terms. While the English *cabinets* of *wonder*, *rarities*, and *curiosities* were also interchangeable.[9] This broadening of traditional collections of art, ancient antiquities, and historical portraiture to encompass exotic specimens, foreign artifacts, and strange works of man and nature was spurred by burgeoning international exploration. It was through the elder Tradescant's career as gardener to a series of influential patrons (the Earls of Salisbury, the first Earl of Buckingham, and eventually the King of England himself), that he gained the extensive access to and generosity of donors needed to build the contents of his Ark. His collection grew through networks of like-minded patrons interested in foreign exploration as well as through his and his son's pursuit of botanical specimens in continental Europe, North Africa, and the New World.[10] Several benefactors acknowledged in the Tradescants' museum catalogue can be tentatively identified as being involved with the major international trade enterprises of the day, such as the East India and Virginia companies active in Asia and North America. The desire for large assemblages of "rarities" only grew as their known world expanded.[11]

Early collections of rarities are often invoked as antecedents to modern encyclopedic museums. Institutions that represent a broad range of cultures and historical periods—such as the British Museum in London, the Metropolitan Museum of Art in New York, and the Los Angeles County Museum of Art (LACMA), just to name a few—reflect the spirit of intellectual inquiry and desire for a greater understanding of the wider world that these early collections embodied. The model of the cabinet of curiosities has continued to provide a useful lens through which museums and art galleries can offer insights about extraordinary but dissimilar things. The recent exhibition *Curiosity: Art and the Pleasures of Knowing*, curated by Brian Dillon, created points of comparison between contemporary works of art, historical artifacts, and natural specimens for visitors to ponder as it toured venues across England and the Netherlands.[12] Experiencing a wunderkammer (because it is an important part of the history of the types of object it included) is in fact still a consideration in the design of permanent museum galleries that display Renaissance and Baroque decorative arts. In 2015 Baron Ferdinand de Rothschild's (1839–1898) nineteenth-century bequest of kunstkammer objects to the British Museum, which includes such objects as miniature busts of Margaret of Austria and Philibert of Savoy from the kunstkammer of Rudolf II, was redisplayed in a new gallery designed by architectural firm Stanton Williams to evoke the type of presentation in which the objects were originally admired.[13]

Like these early collections and encyclopedic museums, contemporary art jewelry incorporates a dizzying array of disparate materials in varied and strange forms, gathered from places near and far. Its diversity and intention distinguishes it from other categories of adornment: costume, fashion, folk, fine, mourning, traditional, and tribal jewelry. Contemporary art jewelry overlaps with all of these categories and is informed by them, of course, but is broader in scope and ambition because of its independence from them.[14] In the decades following World War II, avant-garde jewelers experimented with alternative materials and techniques, drawing upon industrial as well as traditional resources.[15] Perceptions of what jewelry could be made from, and how it could be crafted, expanded rapidly in the second half of the twentieth century, and this change was manifested in different centers around the world with a wide range of results.

In 1967 Dutch design duo Gijs Bakker and Emmy van Leersum staged a performance of their futuristic aluminum body pieces with lights and electronic music at the opening of *Edelsmeden 3* (Goldsmiths 3) at the Stedelijk Museum Amsterdam.[16] In New Jersey in the late 1960s, Carolyn Kriegman heated and manipulated acrylic sheets using her kitchen stove to create her fabulous necklaces (see p. 100), one of which featured among only a handful of pioneering plastic pieces in *Objects: USA*, the touring exhibition that brought the American studio craft movement to national attention.[17] Yugoslavian-born jeweler Peter Skubic in 1974 organized an international symposium in Austria on new artistic applications for steel, *Schmuck aus Stahl* (Jewelry in Steel).[18] And in 1975 San Diego–based jeweler Arline Fisch set out for Australia on a teaching tour following the publication of what would become her seminal book, *Textile Techniques in Metal: For Jewelers, Sculptors, and Textile Artists*.[19] Although the emancipation and democratization of contemporary art jewelry occurred long before the emergence of the global connectivity made possible by the internet, it was still a remarkably international phenomenon. Fascinated, intrepid collectors, gallerists, and curators pursued pieces across the globe. And like Cambridge-trained physician William Butler (1535–1617/18), a likely benefactor of the Tradescant Museum, Lois and Bob Boardman "preferred [these] rarities before [any] riches."[20]

The powerful and enduring aesthetic appeal of historic cabinets of rarities has been very apparent in 2015 museum exhibitions of luxury items, especially those including jewelry. Alexander McQueen's *Armadillo* boots (Spring/Summer 2010), the butterfly headdress Philip Treacy made for him (Spring/Summer 2008), and the skeletal body piece known as the

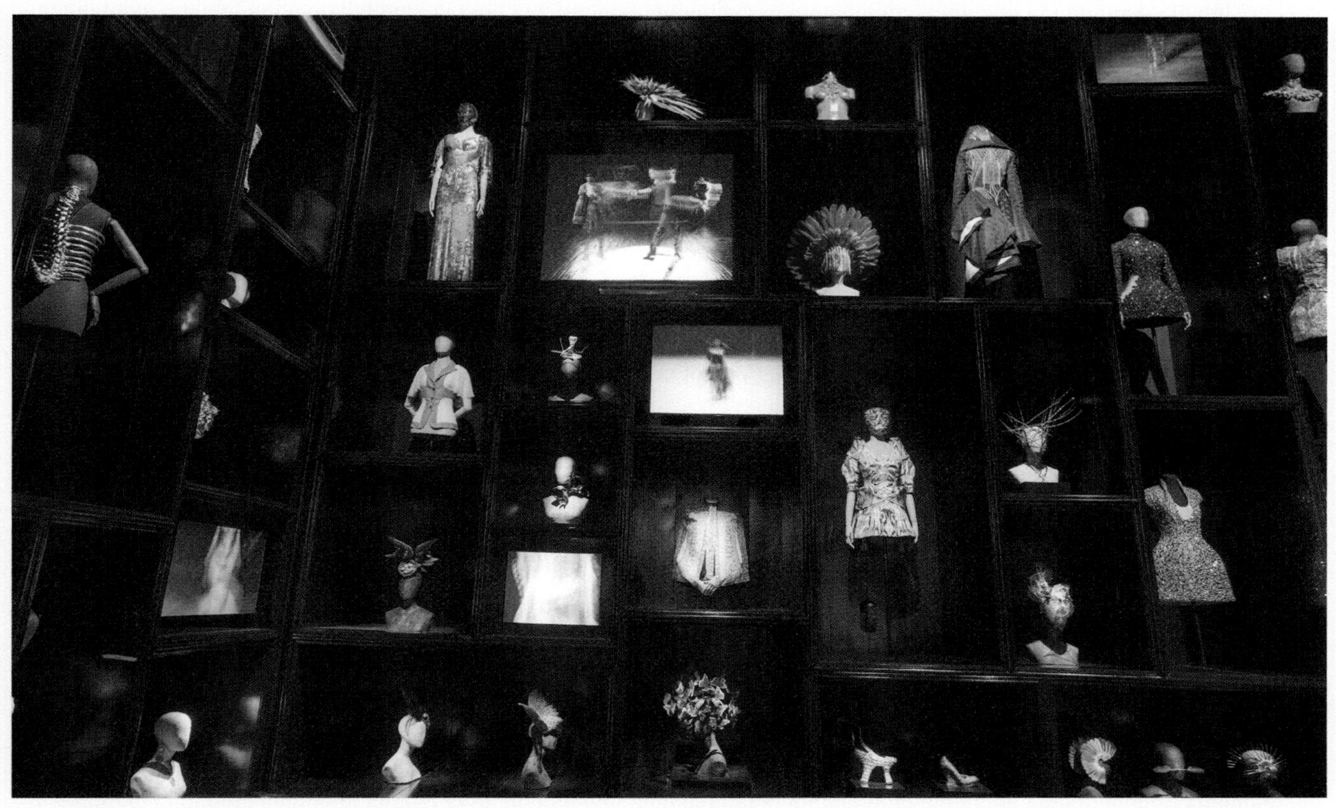

FIG. 2
Cabinet of Curiosities room in the exhibition *Alexander McQueen: Savage Beauty*, 2015, Victoria and Albert Museum, London

Spine corset (Spring/Summer 1998) that McQueen commissioned from jeweler Shaun Leane populated the Cabinet of Curiosities room of compartmentalized shelving in the blockbuster homage to his outlandish genius, *Alexander McQueen: Savage Beauty*, at the Victoria and Albert Museum (fig. 2).[21] It gave visitors the pleasure of experiencing the strangeness of his artistic vision and the omnivorous reach of his inspiration. At the Museum Arnhem in the Netherlands, the first room in *Beauty of the Beast: Jewelry and Taxidermy* was titled Curious Creatures; it presented each piece as a unique object of fascination, heightening the effect by placing the objects beneath individual bell jars. Curator Eveline Holsappel chose the wunderkammer aesthetic to elicit wonder at the beauty of the animals on display and to provoke thought about the relationship between them and humans (many pieces were made by vegetarians using skins gathered from roadkill, industrial waste, and pest management).[22] At the Auckland Art Gallery, *Wunderrūma* (the German *wunderkammer* updated with *rūma*, the Maori word for "room") mixed works of fine art and Maori *taonga* (treasures) with contemporary jewelry from New Zealand in order to highlight direct or metaphorical relationships across these different categories of objects. Its aim was to demonstrate the richness and variety of the nation's jewelry-making practices.[23]

The history and aesthetics of the wunderkammer model make it particularly apt for exploring contemporary art jewelry. The field could most benefit from its dynamic and idiosyncratic perspective, however. While all three exhibitions discussed above utilized the heterogeneous nature of the wunderkammer to excite the curiosity of their audiences, Auckland's *Wunderrūma* also harnessed the historic format's uncanny ability to reveal hidden affinities across disparate materials. Curators Warwick Freeman and Karl Fritsch, both formidable jewelry artists in their own right, used the analogy of a fishing trip to describe their process of selecting works for the exhibition. As they reeled them in, so to speak, the pieces began to form clusters that resonated with each other. Unexpectedly, a previously unrecognized body of work made from or about cigarettes and smoking emerged.[24] Freeman and Fritsch's extended fishing metaphor parallels the kind of close attention to detail that Stirn's list also invites. It is this potential for seeing objects in different ways, and for perceiving new connections between them, that makes the cabinet of curiosities such an ideal framework for exploring the Boardman collection. We could start with a list: an ornamental carp with scales made out of thumbtacks, a gold bauble encased in rubber, sea-urchin spines, a collar knitted in gold and silver wire, a Venus's hairstone borne aloft on the back of a phoenix, and a potato, among many other things.[25] Or we could start, as collectors so often do, with the objects themselves.

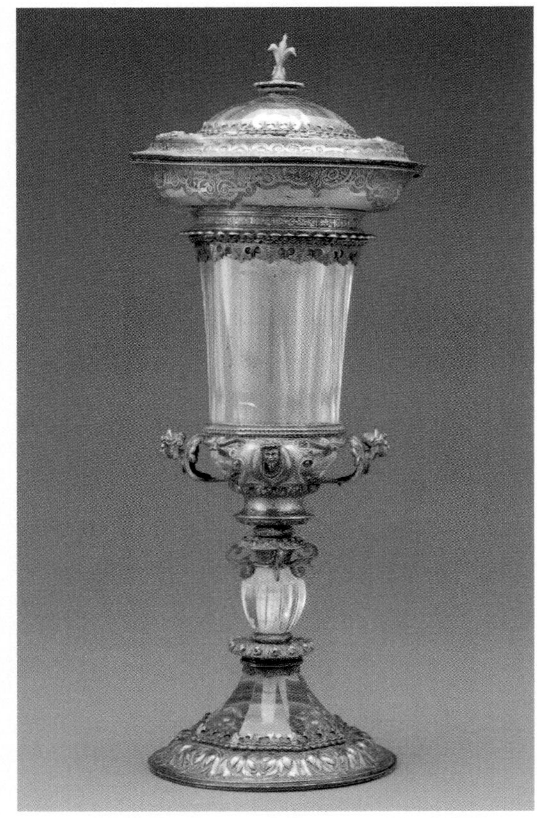

FIG. 3
Diebolt Krug, cup and cover, c. 1560, rock crystal and gilded silver, 11³⁄₁₆ × 4⁷⁄₁₆ × 4⁷⁄₁₆ in. (28.4 × 11.3 × 11.3 cm), Los Angeles County Museum of Art, gift of Varya and Hans Cohn, AC1992.152.104a–b

Art and Nature

A resistance to classification was often a key feature of objects in Renaissance and Baroque collections.[26] Despite the fact that many catalogues of wunderkammern attempted to divide collections into *naturalia* and *artificialia*, or perhaps precisely because of this tendency, objects that fell between these categories proved supremely desirable.[27] Merchant and collector Philipp Hainhofer (1578–1647) commented that, in particular, vases carved from rock crystal were "a great pleasure for princes, since they have nature and art side by side."[28] Rock crystal (the purest form of quartz) was worked by hand and embellished with precious metal in objects that embody the very height of the goldsmith's and lapidary's art, to the delight of those who could procure such treasures (fig. 3). The notion in European culture that art and nature were opposed dates back to Greek philosopher Aristotle (384–322 BCE), who observed in his treatise *Physics* that "of the things that exist, some exist by nature, some from other causes."[29] Objects that could blur the line between art and nature were therefore remarkable. Perhaps this explains why French antiquarian Boniface de Borilly (1564–1648), who otherwise collected Roman medals, also had "a small picture made of the root of an olive tree upon which is naturally represented a human figure."[30] Evidence of the commingling of art and nature—or a challenge to the viewer to identify which was which—made some objects virtually irresistible. San Diego jeweler Sondra Sherman's 2010 *Flowers and Still Life* piece can be interpreted as an elaborate meditation on this allure. It reproduces the bouquet motif embossed on the cover of a book of the same title and is set in a circular cavity cut through the book's pages (fig. 4). Despite this disruption of the text, a statement about the appeal of the interconnectedness of nature and art can still be gleaned at the bottom of the first page of the introduction: "About all painting there is something mysterious which is a condition of its artificial and self-sufficient existence, and the expression of the familiar in terms of the mysterious is

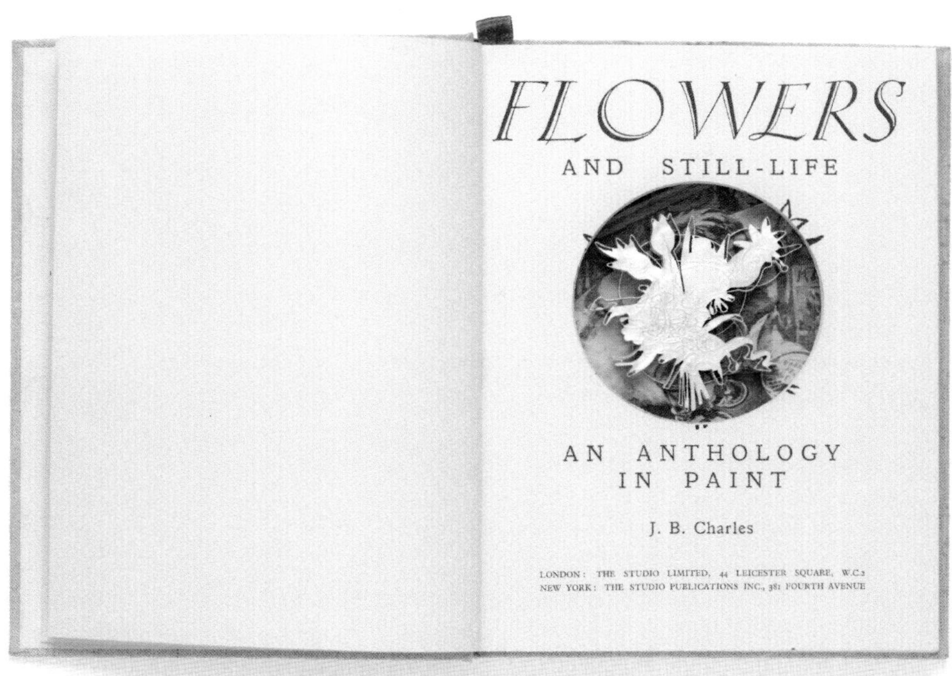

FIG. 4
Sondra Sherman, *Flowers and Still Life* brooch and box, 2010

an important part of its attraction."[31] In short, the attraction of flower painting is the representation of things familiar from the natural world in the mysterious, artificial medium of painting. Sherman's presentation of the brooch neatly demonstrates the ongoing legacy of the wonderfully anomalous objects of the wunderkammer.

As the intention of cabinets of rarities was not to gather representative examples but extraordinary ones, wunderkammern actually have more in common with internet search engines (where unusual and surprising data can rise to the top) than with traditional printed encyclopedias in which information is presented in a classified, ordered, and layered fashion. More resource than reference, these early collections supported an almost infinite number of associations. In 1994 Bruce Robertson and Mark Meadow, professors at the University of California at Santa Barbara, mounted the exhibition *Microcosms: Objects of Knowledge (A University Collects)* with the goal of fostering a better understanding of the multifarious objects used as teaching resources across the nine campuses of the UC system. Exploring the associative potential of cabinets of curiosities, they presented the common pairing of a pangolin (a zoological specimen) and a pinecone (a botanical specimen) to show how the similarity of their spiky-plated forms (despite their classification in different categories) could lead to a deeper understanding of the protective strategies of both. The pineapple from a set of plastic fruit and vegetables used in French-language instruction further highlighted the etymological link between *pine*cone and *pine*apple. The exhibition demonstrated how the formal comparison of seemingly unrelated objects that occurs in heterogeneous collections (like cabinets of curiosities) paradoxically can reveal hidden similarities that lead to fresh insights.[32]

As the Boardman collection joins LACMA's encyclopedic holdings (which include everything from an Egyptian mummy coffin to a couch designed using a computer algorithm that imitates bone growth),[33] we should consider it in terms of this early model of collecting that continues to inform museums' understandings of the experiences and functions of their objects. The different ways that the jewelers featured in the collection have incorporated, manipulated, imitated, and evoked nature will provide an alternative way of looking at the impact of their art. By examining the interconnections between art and nature in works that straddle both categories, we can see patterns relevant both to the past and the present, and become aware of a longer history of human inquiry to which these works are a part. Through a series of juxtapositions with historic types of objects from cabinets of curiosities, unexpected correspondences and insights will emerge. What might at first seem like a comparison of unjustifiably different things—"apples and oranges," as the English idiom goes—can inspire creative interpretations.

Apples and Oranges

In postmedieval Europe, natural specimens were ingeniously incorporated into larger, more complex objects to form some of the most mesmerizing objets d'art. LACMA's seahorse cup (fig. 5), probably made by Leipzig goldsmith Elias Geyer (1560–1634) around 1590–1600, utilizes an exotic conchological example: the spiral of the *Turbo marmoratus* shell serves as the coiled tail. Elector Christian II of Saxony (1583–1611) purchased a similar work in 1602 for his kunstkammer, the Grünes Gewölbe (green vault) in Dresden, where it can still be seen today.[34] Both illustrate the height of achievement in the Baroque practice of using recognizable specimens as analogs for the things they resemble. In the same manner, J. Fred Woell's 1990 brooch *Arctic Setdown* incorporates a natural specimen; the quartz crystal in his composition represents ice (fig. 6). It is hard to see Sandra Enterline's *Queen Bee* brooch of 1998 as anything other than a natural history specimen (fig. 7). Yet viewed alongside Woell's glacial landscape and Geyer's frisky seahorse, the insect is like a precious jewel in its glazed golden setting. "Such conventionally beautiful

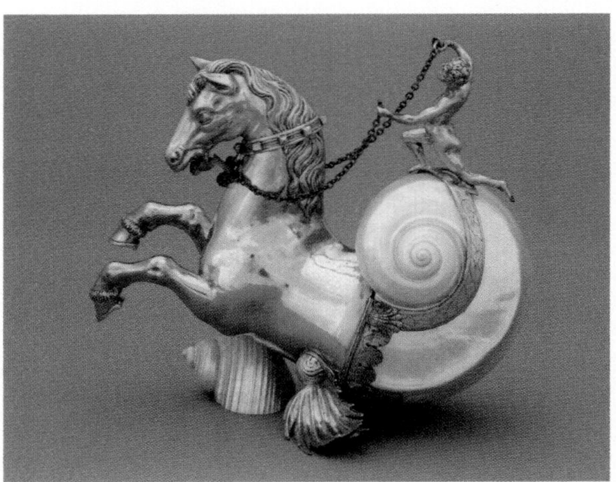

FIG. 5
Attributed to Elias Geyer, seahorse cup, c. 1590–1600, shells and gilded silver, 7 × 7⅞ in. (17.8 × 20 cm), Los Angeles County Museum of Art, gift of Varya and Hans Cohn, AC1992.152.108a–b

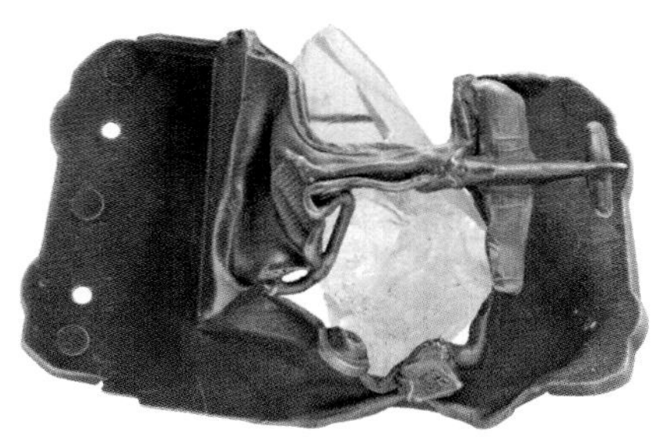

FIG. 6
J. Fred Woell, *Arctic Setdown* brooch, 1990

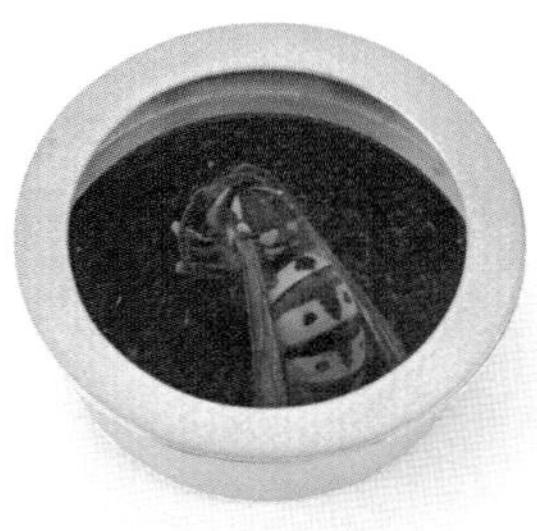

FIG. 7
Sandra Enterline, *Queen Bee* brooch, 1998

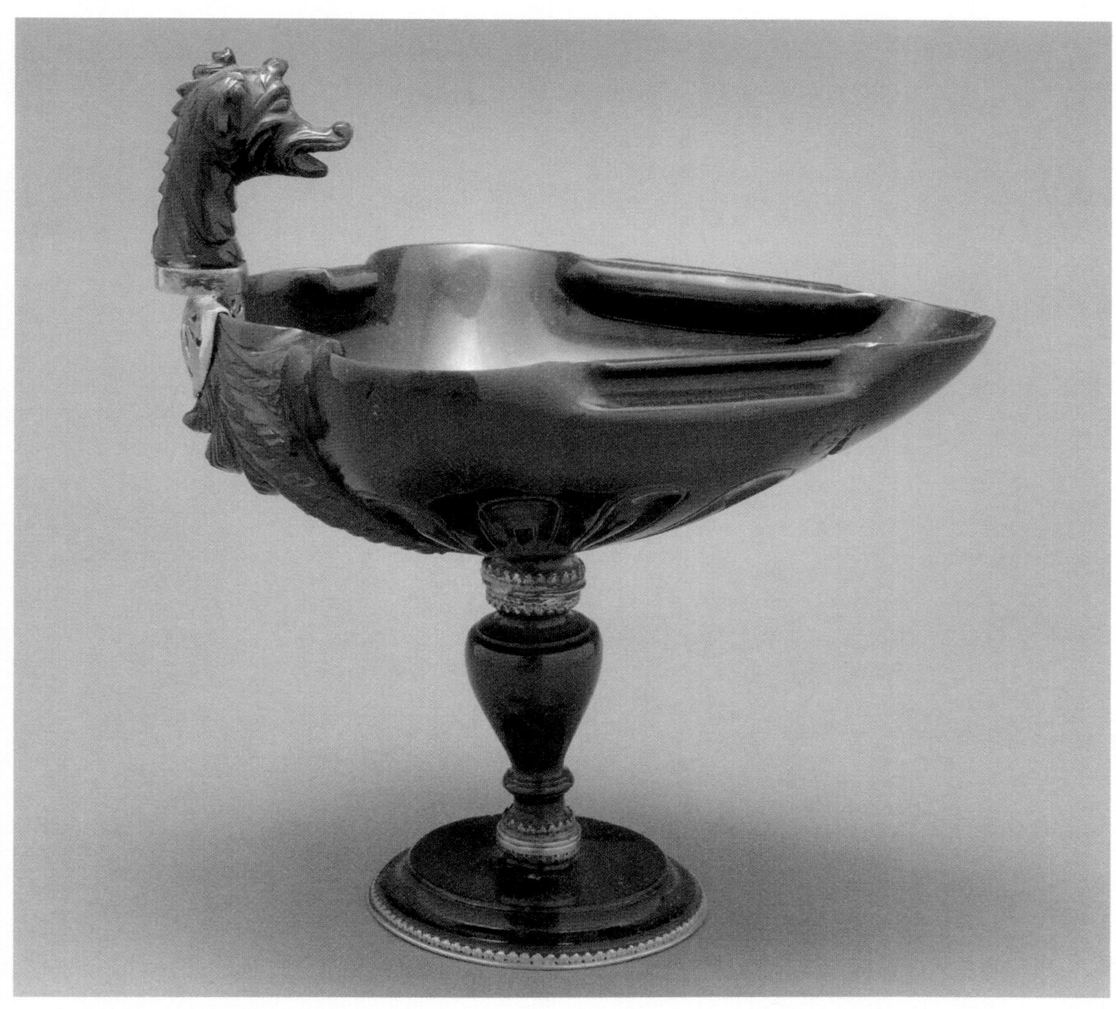

FIG. 8
Cup with dragon's head finial, early 17th century, bloodstone and gilded silver, gilded silver, 6⅞ in. (17.5 cm), length: 6¾ (17.2 cm), Los Angeles County Museum of Art, gift of Varya and Hans Cohn, AC1992.152.111

natural objects assume a quality of 'otherness' when they are lifted from their context in the natural world," wrote Patricia Harris and David Lyon of the Bay Area jeweler's work.[35] Enterline herself says it is about recognizing the beauty in ordinary things and ensuring they are "encased, cherished, protected."[36] So in addition to the analogy of the bee as the jewel, we can also understand Enterline's gold setting as an expression of esteem for the object it contains. Looking again at Woell's brooch, we can conclude from his use of costly silver rather than base metal that like Enterline's precious specimen, the quartz crystal should be treasured for its natural beauty. The rare and coveted turban shell's aesthetic value is likewise conveyed by the precious metal used to shape the highly wrought seahorse cup into which it has been incorporated. Through a series of unlikely comparisons, we derive a wealth of meaning.

Intriguing zoomorphic vessels also celebrated natural resources both local and exotic. Southern Germany, an area rich in natural deposits of semiprecious stones, was a great center for the production of hardstone carvings.[37] Exquisitely cut drinking cups destined for the collection cabinets of princes writhe with decorative monsters. In an early seventeenth-century example from LACMA's collection, the carver has achieved a high polish to maximize the vividness of the stone's natural green color flecked with red (fig. 8). Similarly, ebony and ivory (both exotic and familiar outside Africa and Asia) create a sumptuous contrast when used side by side. However, Czech jeweler Pavel Opočenský took the chromatic possibilities

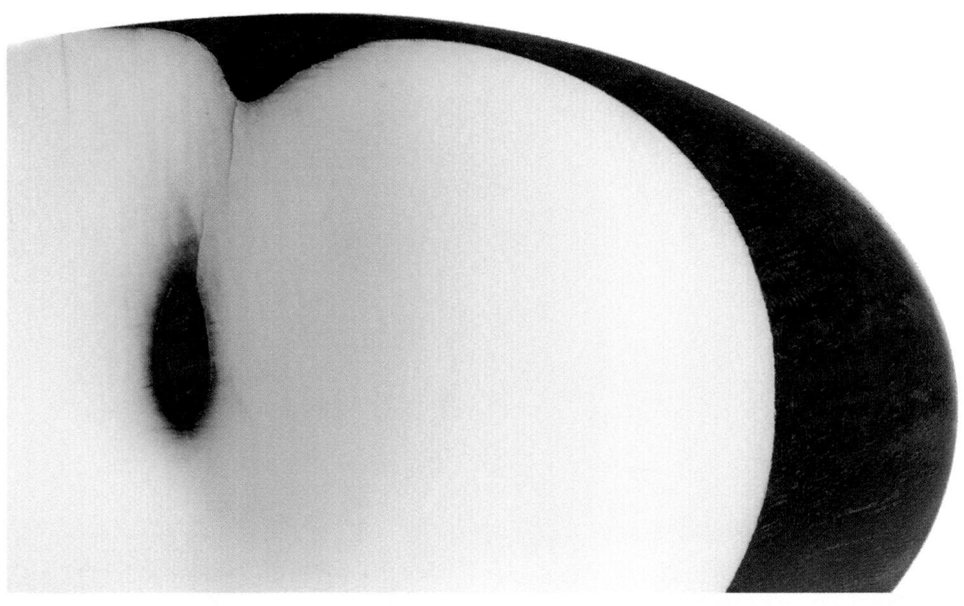

FIG. 9
Pavel Opočenský, brooch (detail), 1986

of these luxury materials to a higher level in a series of brooches he produced in 1986.[38] Close examination of the brooch in the Boardman collection reveals how, by varying the thickness of the ivory veneer, he achieved modulations in hue from white to grayish blue where the ivory is thin enough for the ebony to show through underneath (fig. 9). Equally rich in color, the Boardman *Lure* brooch by Warwick Freeman (fig. 10) dazzles with an iridescent rainbow of polished pāua shell (New Zealand abalone, *Haliotis iris*). Its attenuated form corresponds to the rim of the shell but also intentionally recalls the beguiling pearly fishhooks produced from similar materials across the Pacific. Freeman's explorations of indigenous materials and forms in the 1980s became powerful symbols as New Zealand articulated a national identity more closely aligned with the South Pacific than with Europe.[39] His title may also allude to the *allure* of the piece and how its colorful surface can captivate the viewer.[40] When compared with Freeman's, the brooch by Opočenský can also be seen as playing with the functional associations of its materials. Today found most frequently on the keyboard of a piano, the familiar opposition of ebony and ivory is bridged by the subtle beauty of the tonal possibilities in between. Turning again to functional associations, we might reflect that the bloodstone of the Baroque cup with which we began this discussion was highly valued in the Renaissance for its supposed ability to change color when exposed to poison.[41] The dragon's head that rears up from the rim of the cup could therefore be understood as not only decoration but a guardian figure protecting its owner

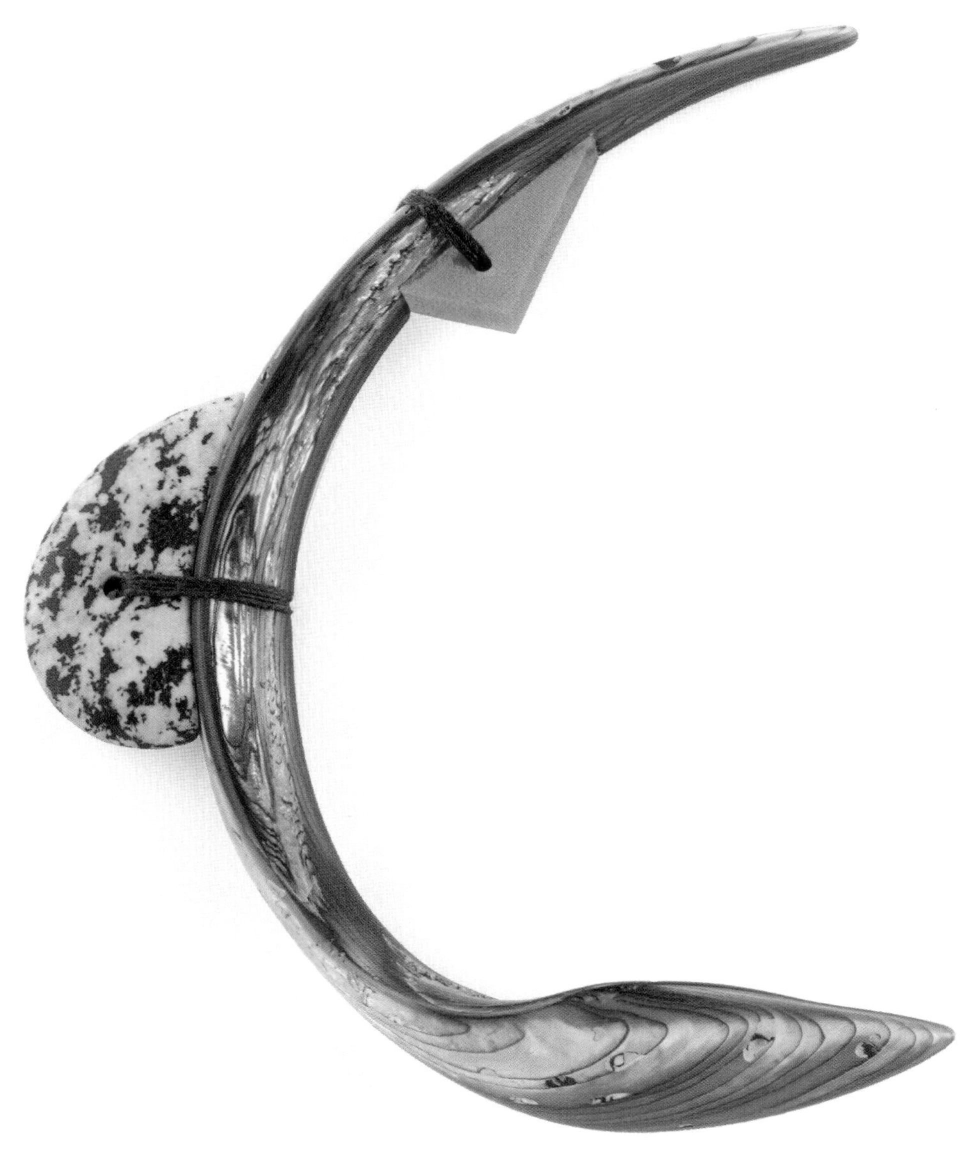

FIG. 10
Warwick Freeman, *Lure* brooch, 1984

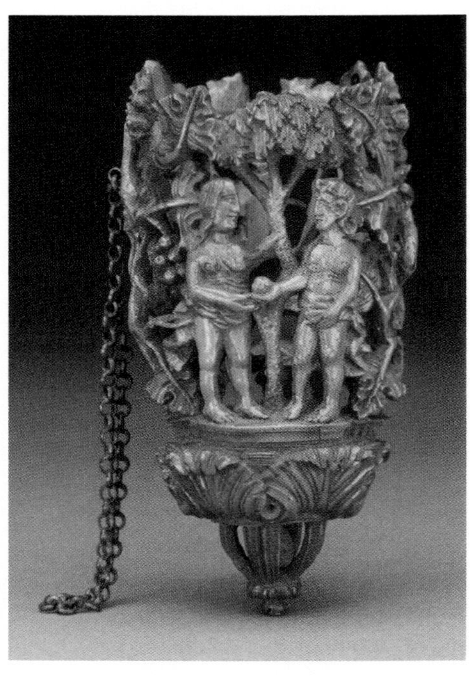

FIG. 11
Bouquet holder, c. 1600, boxwood with metal chain, height: 2 7/8 in. (7.3 cm), Los Angeles County Museum of Art, anonymous gift, 52.20.5

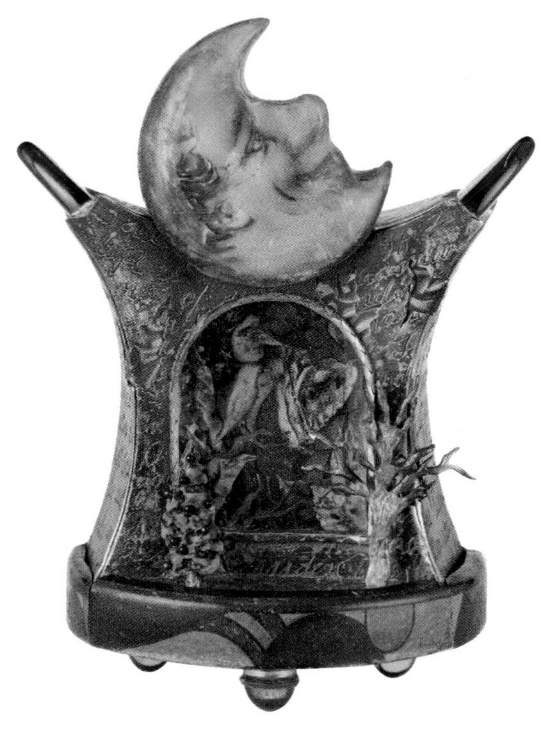

FIG. 12
Robin Kranitzky and Kim Overstreet, *Night Garden* brooch, 1990

from harm and signaling the magical function of the raw material. Comparing approaches and natural resources of the past and present thus is mutually illuminating.

Representing the natural world at different scales can also have a powerful psychological impact on the viewer. Virtuosic carvings in miniature, like the scenes from Christ's Passion on a plum stone described in the epigraph above by Stirn, were staples of the wunderkammer. LACMA's Flemish bouquet holder made around 1600 depicts Adam and Eve in the Garden of Eden carved from very hard and fine-grained boxwood (fig. 11). With a captive wooden ball in the cage-like carving at its tip (although on inspection it can be seen to have been pushed through from a hole inside rather than carved in situ), it imitates grander examples from cabinets of curiosities. Similarly, Robin Kranitzky and Kim Overstreet create the illusion of virtuosity by seamlessly combining carved elements with found objects to achieve the miniature scene in their *Night Garden* brooch of 1990 (fig. 12). By contrast, Gijs Bakker altered scale in the opposite direction, magnifying an image of a red rose in full bloom and using PVC to laminate it (fig. 13). His oversize *Dew Drop* necklace (1982), worn like a lace ruff, is so named for the droplets of condensation that become a key detail in the fantastically enlarged, high-resolution photograph. Yet rather than diminishing the visual impact of the flower by dramatically expanding its size, Bakker instead has intensified the bloom by allowing us to scrutinize the texture of the petals and the glassiness of the dew. On reexamination, Overstreet and Kranitzky have similarly distilled the power of their scene

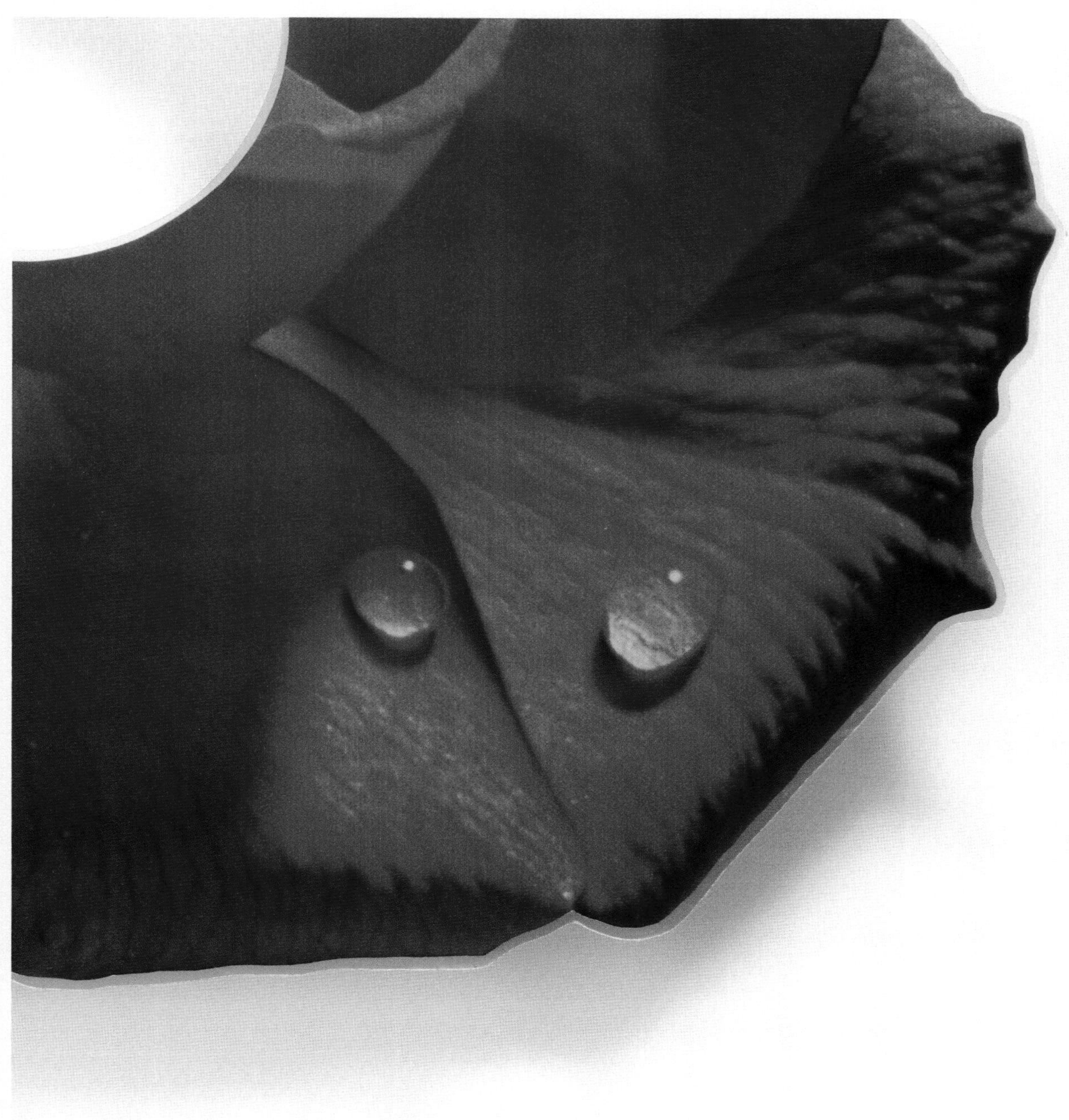

FIG. 13
Gijs Bakker, *Dew Drop* necklace (detail), 1982

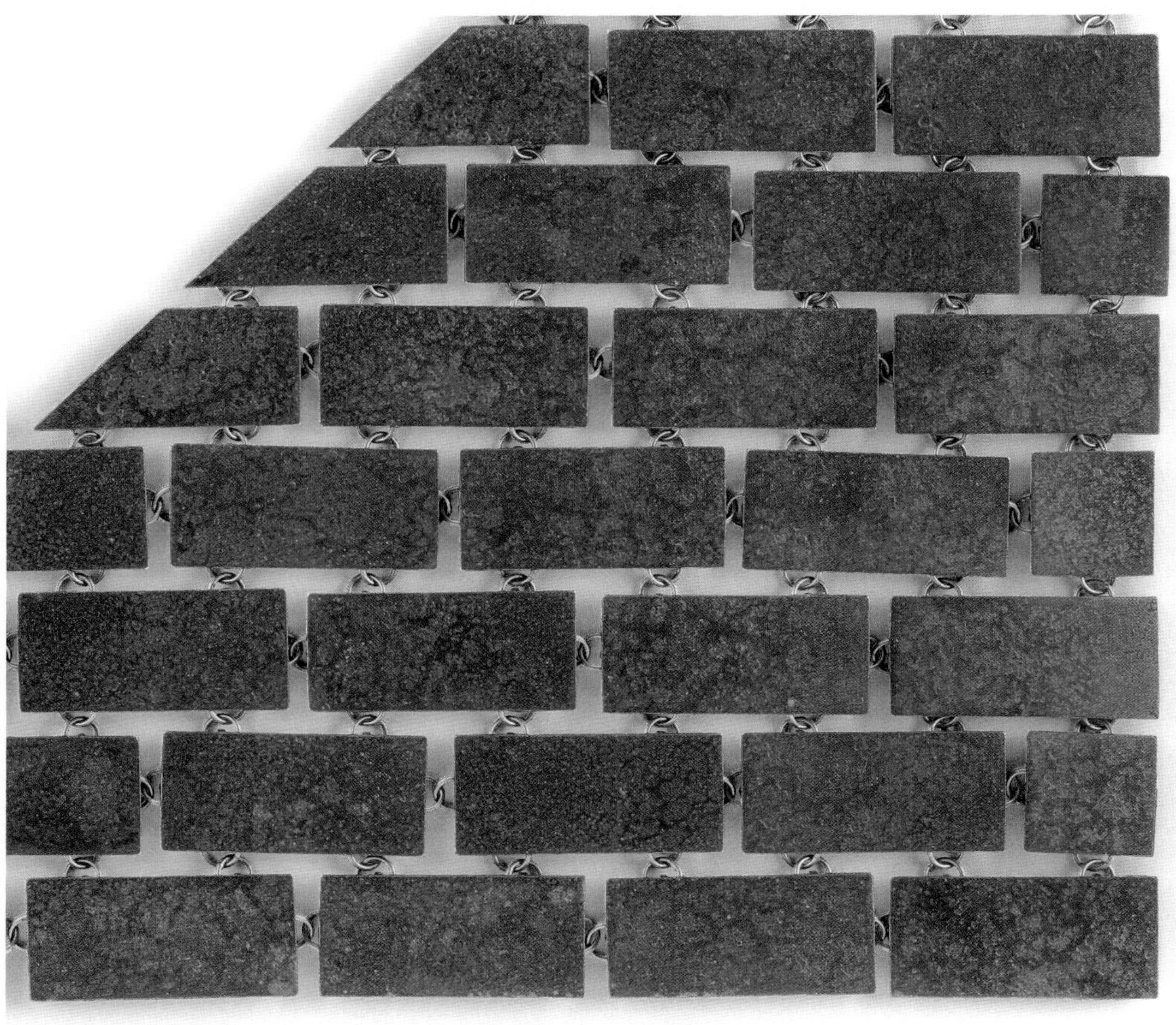

FIG. 14
Ralph Bakker, necklace (detail), designed 2001, made 2007

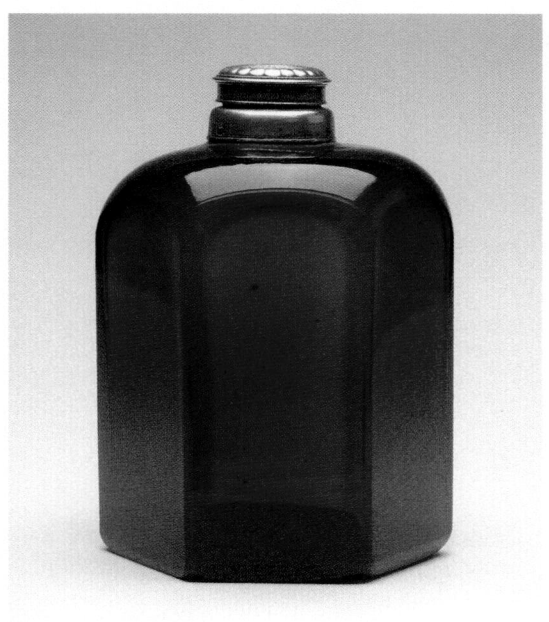

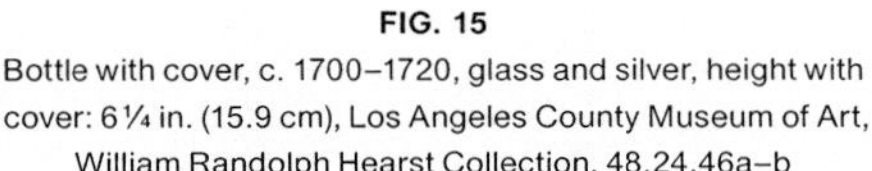

FIG. 15
Bottle with cover, c. 1700–1720, glass and silver, height with cover: 6 ¼ in. (15.9 cm), Los Angeles County Museum of Art, William Randolph Hearst Collection, 48.24.46a–b

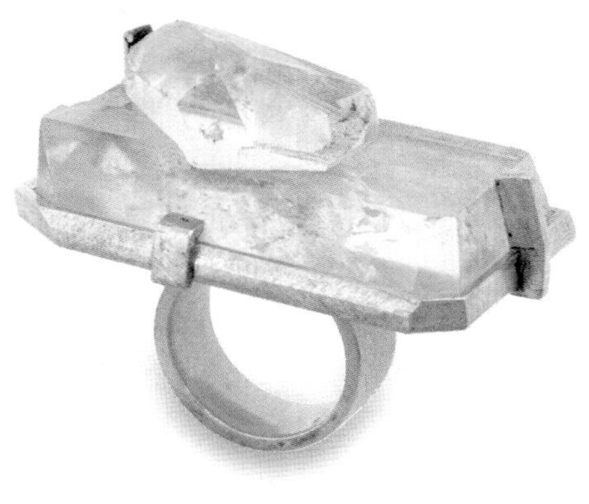

FIG. 16
Barbara Seidenath, hand ornament, 2003

by demanding our full attention to perceive all its details. LACMA's Baroque bouquet holder can also be understood as amplifying the potency of its imagery; close scrutiny is required just to identify the extraordinary moralizing scene selected for the posy: Adam accepting the forbidden apple from Eve. Although diverse examples, each is scaled for maximum effect and all demand to be viewed intently.

Altering the appearance of otherwise naturally occurring materials is another way in which artists and craftspeople have created marvelous objects that tread the line between art and nature. In the late seventeenth-century, Johann Kunckel (1630–1703) revived the production of ruby glass in Europe (fig. 15), rediscovering the process of turning clear glass red by mixing in gold filings for the production of magnificent vessels prized by rulers across Europe.[42] Like Kunckel, Barbara Seidenath manipulates natural materials, introducing color and reflectivity to the stone in her 2003 hand ornament by adding an enamel underlay between the rock and the setting (fig. 16).[43] Ralph Bakker also manipulated natural materials, although he transformed precious metal into something that resembles a much cruder, slate-like substance (fig. 14). In his necklace made in 2007, he fused niello (an alloy of copper, silver, and lead) over the surface of each individual silver plaque. Traditionally used as an inlay,[44] Bakker here used niello as a coating, concealing the more conventional silver substrate beneath and achieving an edgier look. While not a simulation of something more expensive, the intervention nonetheless adds value. Like Bakker's nielloed silver, Seidenath's intervention increases the desirability of the natural material as it complicates it. Ruby glass also vastly raised the prestige of the materials from which it was composed. Prized as if it were a newly discovered gemstone, it even became associated with the red philosopher's stone sought by alchemists.[45] Finding similarities of approach in these differing examples helps us appreciate anew why they have been so admired.

Another colored glass, *calcedonio* or "chalcedony" glass, also was created to resemble a natural material. First developed in the late fifteenth century, it was intended to mimic agate and other banded semiprecious stones. Ancient carved hardstone vessels like the chalice of the emperor Romanos in the Treasury of San Marco were likely the inspiration, and Venetian glassmakers used the technique to produce luxury objects destined for display rather than practical use (fig. 17).[46] Here the value of the material depends upon the viewer recognizing what it imitates. The resemblance of Ted Noten's clear acrylic pieces to the most valuable type of amber (with insects and small animals trapped within) is likewise unmistakable (fig. 18). His *Crown-Ring* (1997) encases a piece of disposable festive wear—a tiny gold party hat with dangling straps that tie under the chin—in frosted resin like a fly. Doug Bucci's inspiration from the natural world for his *Islet | Stainless* bracelet (2010, fabricated 2012) is also immediately recognizable (fig. 19). The reference to the hexagonal cell walls of a honeycomb is quite pleasing but it is not arbitrary. The bracelet is part of a larger body of work that documents his sometimes dangerously elevated blood sugar and includes pieces generated using computer-aided design (CAD) from real data gathered by a continuous glucose-monitoring system that took regular readings of the diabetic artist's blood-sugar level. Bucci chose the honeycomb structure for *Islet | Stainless* because it recalls the full name of the disease he lives with every day, diabetes mellitus (literally "siphon-honey" in Latin);[47] the work is a poignant externalization of his internal health and the challenges it presents. The mimicking of nature in Noten's ring is intentional as well. By preserving a piece of party ephemera as if it were an insect in amber, he emphasizes how fleeting such moments of high spirits can be. Returning to LACMA's chalcedony glass beaker, we notice that it is rather later in date than the earliest production of the material and bears striking inclusions of copper crystals. This glass is in fact a further development of *calcedonio* called aventurine, from the Italian *a ventura* meaning "by chance," a reference to its invention through experimentation. In an extraordinary

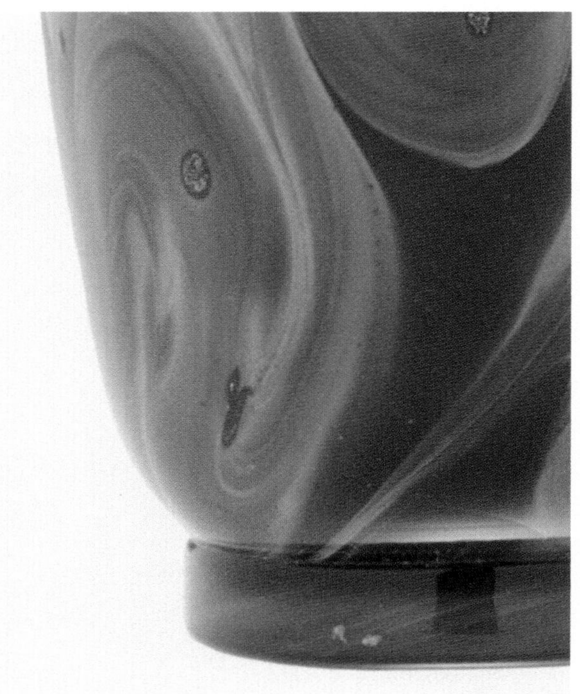

FIG. 17
Beaker (detail), c. 1775–1800, glass, height: 3 5/16 in. (8.4 cm), Los Angeles County Museum of Art, gift of Varya and Hans Cohn, M.82.124.7

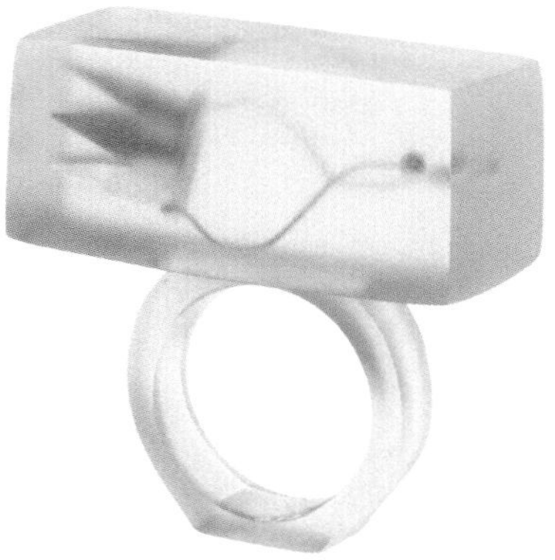

FIG. 18
Ted Noten, *Crown-Ring*, 1997

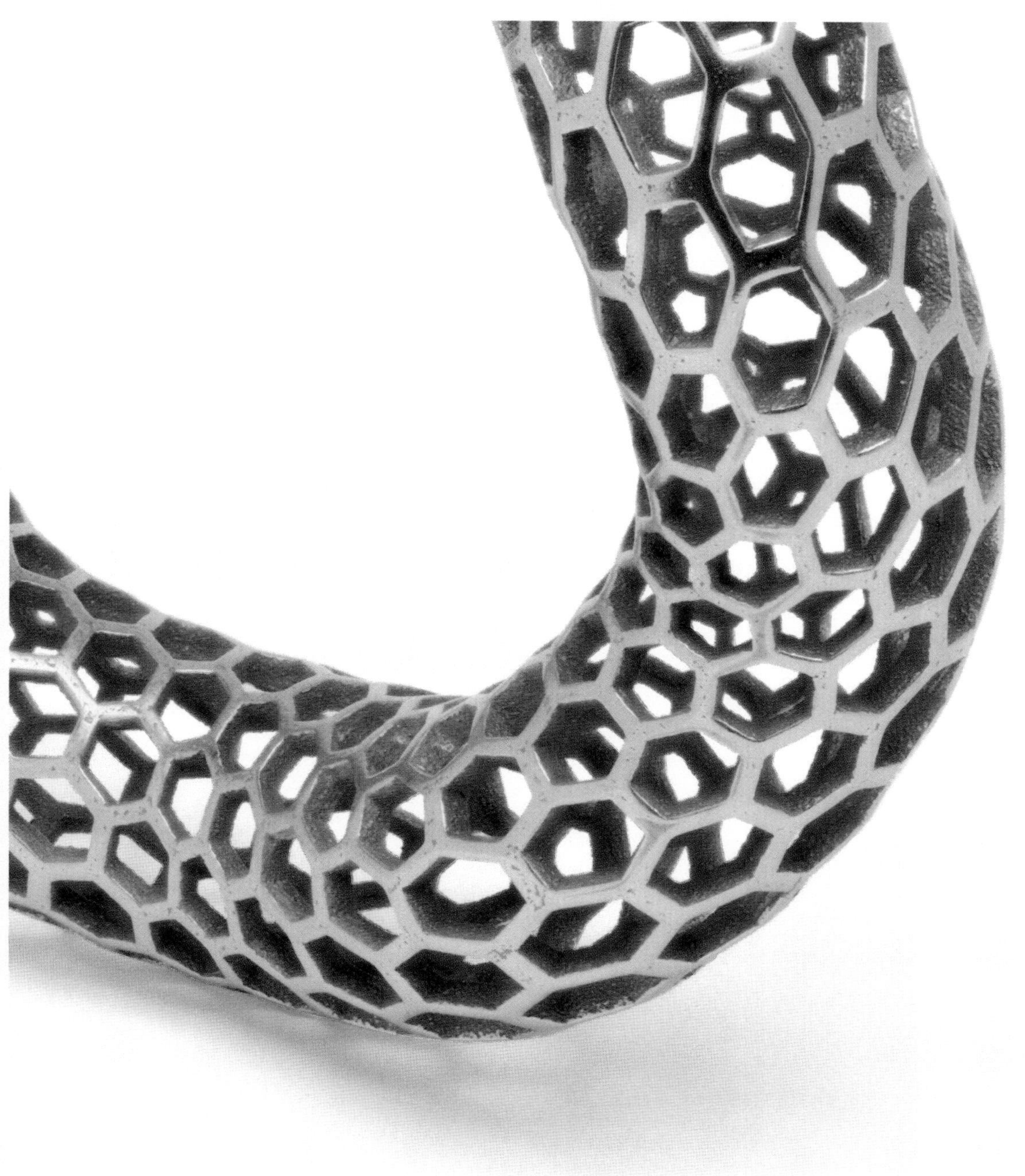

FIG. 19
Doug Bucci, *Islet* | *Stainless* bracelet (detail),
designed 2010, this example made 2012

reversal of expectation (and of the thinking that equated ruby glass with gemstone), a naturally occurring stone that resembles the glass was subsequently named "aventurine" after its similar appearance to the artificial product. From these comparisons we learn that resemblances to forms in nature can be much more than straightforward imitations.

Whether in the precious metals of the Nuremberg goldsmiths or the uncannily watery tin-glazed earthenware developed by Bernard Palissy (1509–1590), decorative details cast from life held a particular appeal for early collectors as well (fig. 20). Constructing an elaborate grotto for French Queen Marie de Médicis (1573–1642), Palissy claimed his majolica molded from real reptiles, fish, crustaceans, and amphibians would surpass their living models in longevity and retain the vibrant colors even fossils would lose through petrification.[48] The specific charm of this so-called *stil rustique*[49] was precisely its convincing improvement on ephemerality in nature. Contemporary jeweler Gerd Rothmann harnessed the historic fascination for life casts to create modern pieces that celebrate the living (see pp. 162–63). His ornaments capture not only the unique and evocative physical characteristics of individuals, but the lifelike texture of their very skin.[50] Marian Hosking cast from life to preserve ephemeral details of nature gathered while traveling in the state of Western Australia in her 2009 *Leaf litter WA* brooch (fig. 21). In addition to celebrating biodiversity, preserving the appearance of these examples of indigenous flora (banksia leaves and grevillea pods) allows her to identify with Australia's early colonial female artists who forged careers in botanical illustration.[51] In this light, we can turn to appreciate the powerful affirmation of identity that comes with wearing a piece that only the person it was cast from can wear, such as Lois Boardman's golden nose (see p. 9). And we can understand how Palissy, who immortalized local flora and fauna in Gallic clays and inspired subsequent generations of makers, was elevated almost to the status of French national hero in the nineteenth century.[52] All cast from life, these objects unexpectedly resonate with each other and with us in their affirmations of collective and individual identity.

Some of the most spectacular objects gathered and treasured by early collectors mimicked nature through mechanical movement. The motions of elaborately automated models of animals, people, and mythological beings, as well as the hands of a clock like LACMA's example made by seventeenth-century master craftsman Georg Metzner (fig. 22), were things at which to marvel.[53] With the flick of a switch, Vernon Reed's

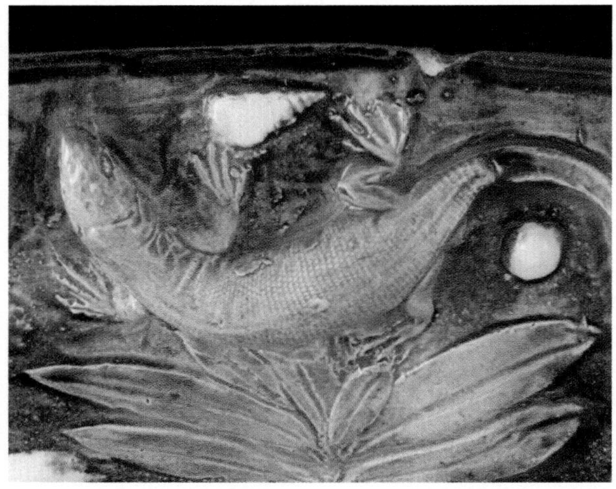

FIG. 20
After Bernard Palissy, large oval dish (detail), 17th–19th century, lead-glazed earthenware, diameter: 20 ¼ in. (51.4 cm), Los Angeles County Museum of Art, gift of the Hearst Foundation, 49.26.2

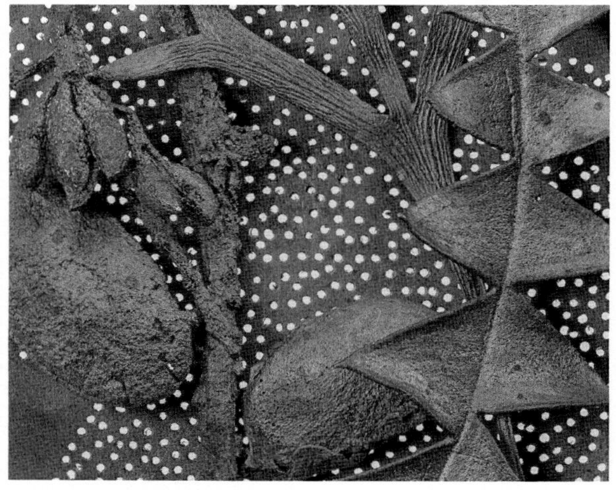

FIG. 21
Marian Hosking, *Leaf litter WA* brooch (detail), 2009

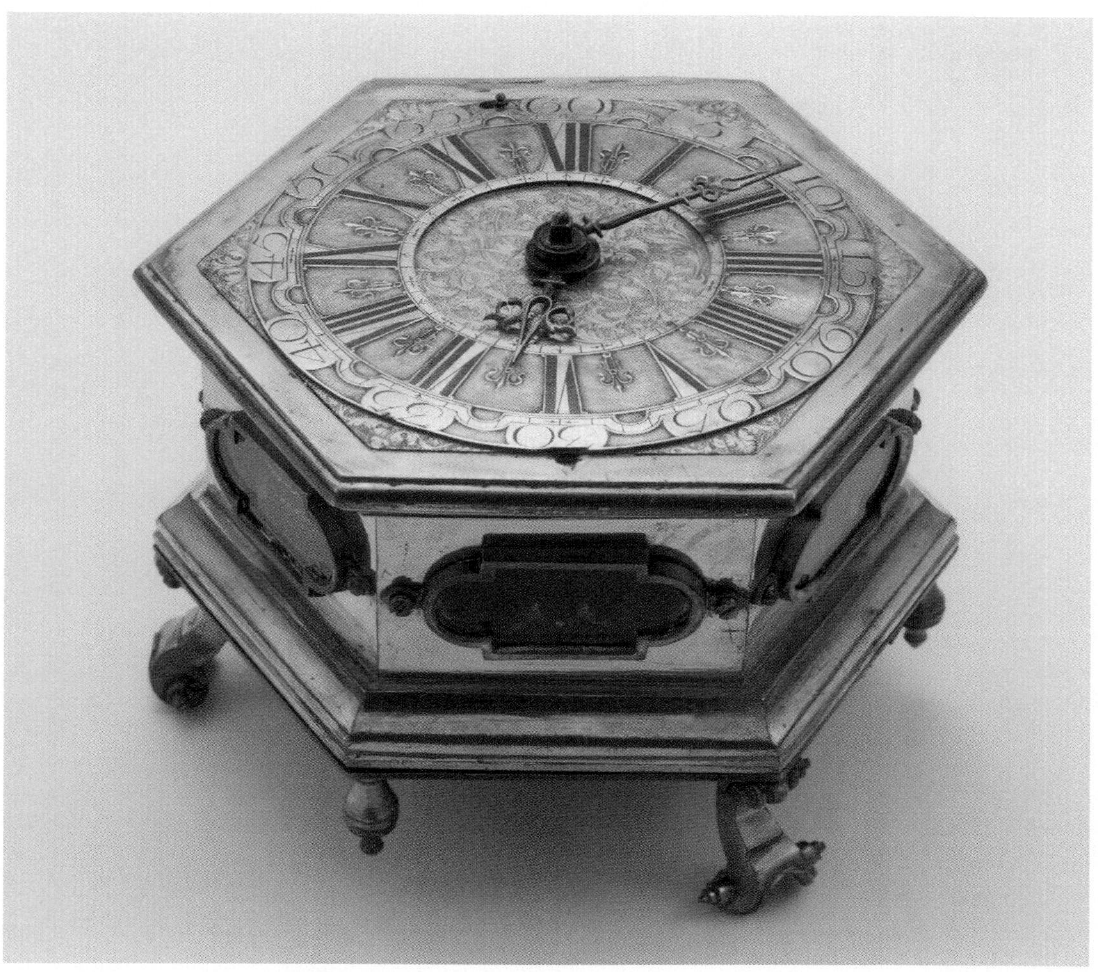

FIG. 22
Georg Metzner, table clock, c. 1650, silver and gilded bronze, diameter: 5 in. (12.7 cm), Los Angeles County Museum of Art, William Randolph Hearst Collection, 49.3.4a

electronic jewelry—controlled by software on a microcomputer inside—is similarly automated as it displays the motion of changing images (fig. 23). And with the aid of manual power to rotate the wheel on the stand of Kranitzky and Overstreet's *Salmon Dream* (1999), an endless arc of fish charmingly leaps upstream (fig. 24). Yet rather than embodying a lack of technological sophistication, the work is a nostalgic homage to bygone kinetic toys. The old-fashioned engineering is central to its appeal. Likewise, Reed's 1987 *Visage Mnemonique* necklace aestheticizes cybernetics' capacity for disorder by displaying parts of a face at random, while Metzner's seventeenth-century table clock is specifically designed to allow curious viewers to see its inner workings: glazed openings around its middle provide gratifying glimpses of the then-modern mechanism inside. Technology, not just the motion it produces, is a source of delight in all these objects.

Yet objects in the form of composite creatures (like "the hand of a mermaid" listed by Stirn after his visit to the Tradescants' museum) remain the most compelling items found in cabinets of curiosities. The seahorse cup, with which we began our exploration, represents a hybrid creature composed of two animals (fig. 5). Also known as a hippocamp—the mythological steed of Greek and Roman marine deities—it is composed of the upper body of a horse and the lower body of a fish. In addition to the related hippocamp cup already mentioned, Elector Christian II of Saxony also purchased cups in the form of a sea unicorn, a Triton with Nereids, and a basilisk for his Dresden kunstkammer in 1602. Juhani Heikkilä's 1997 *Homo*

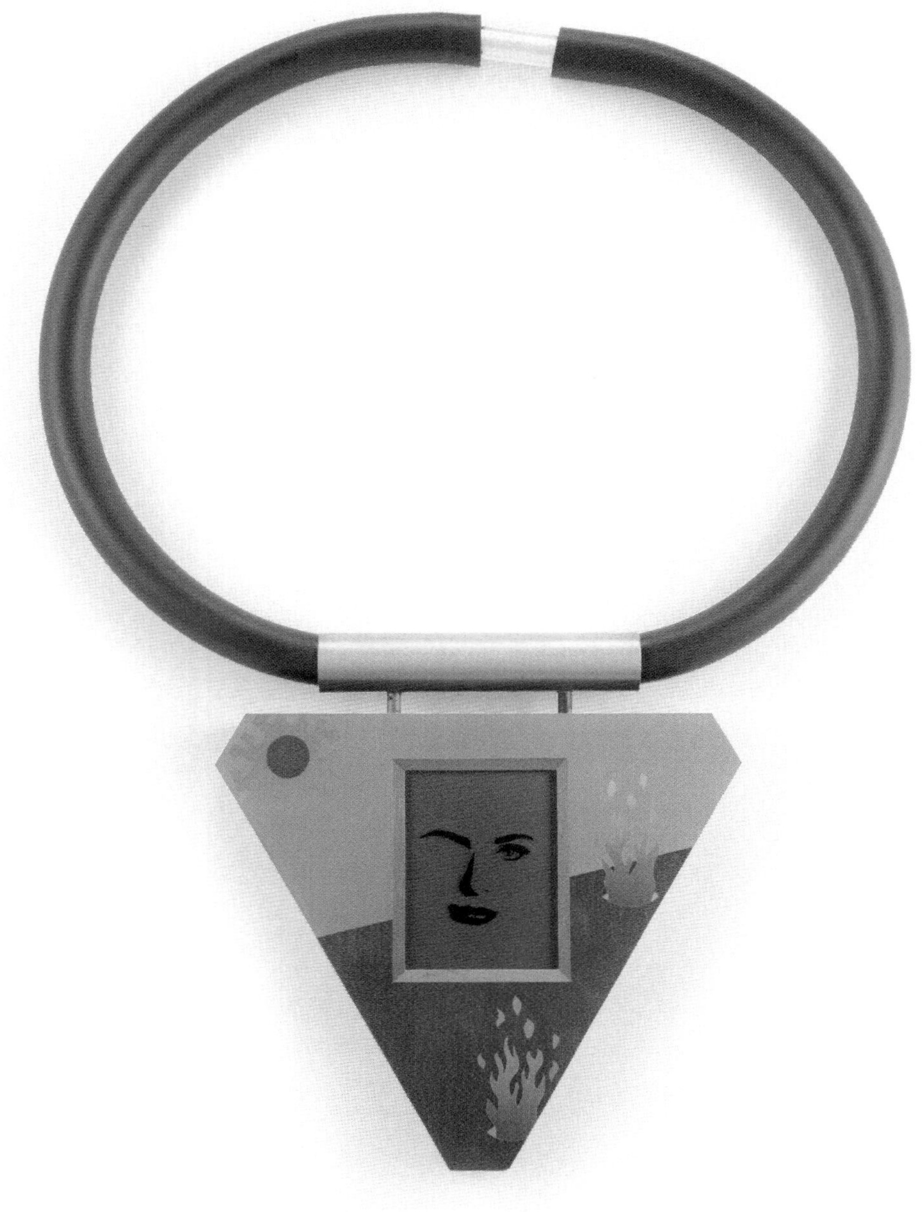

FIG. 23
Vernon Reed, *Visage Mnemonique* necklace, 1987

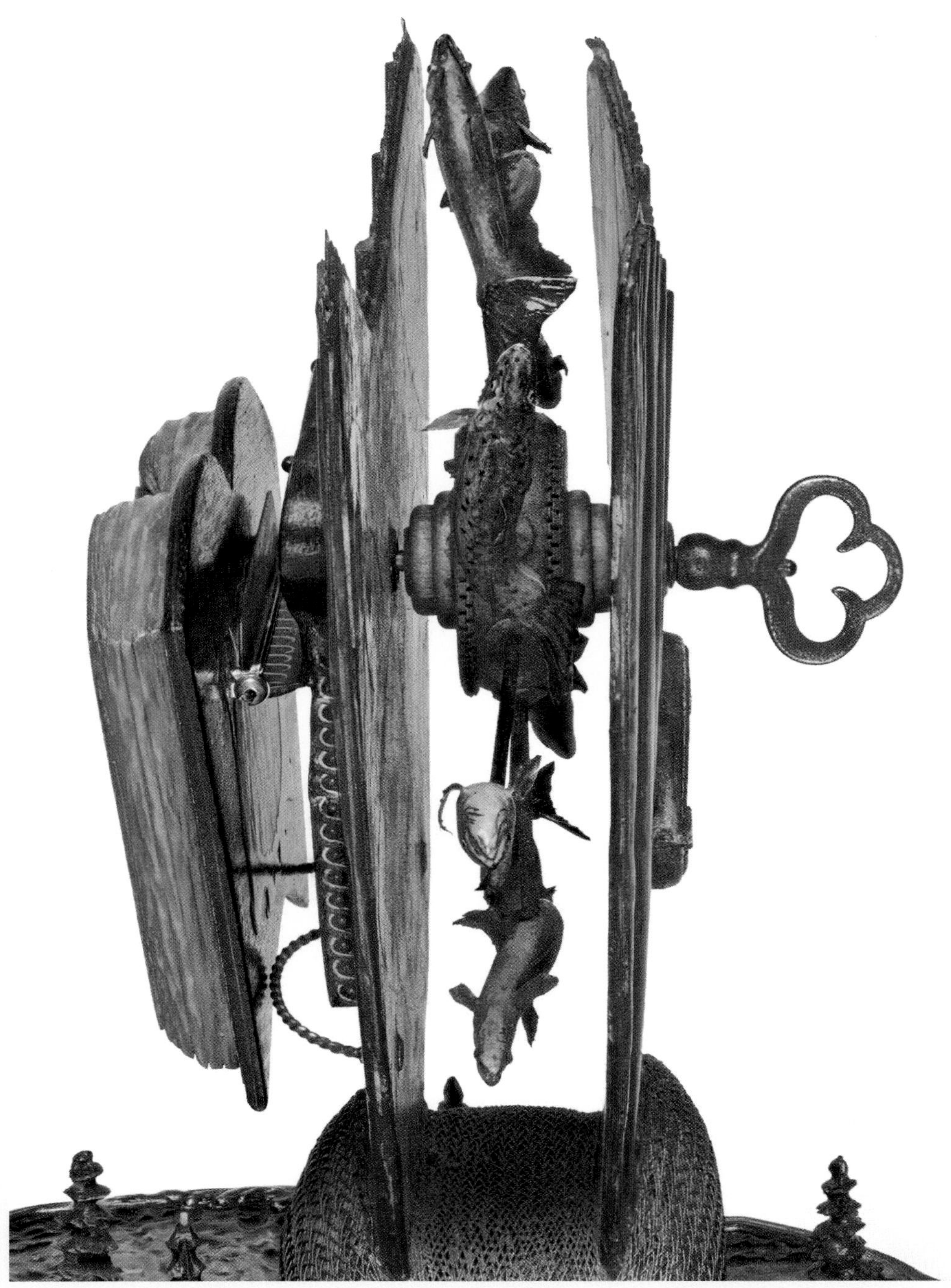

FIG. 24
Robin Kranitzky and Kim Overstreet, *Salmon Dream* brooch and stand (detail), 1999

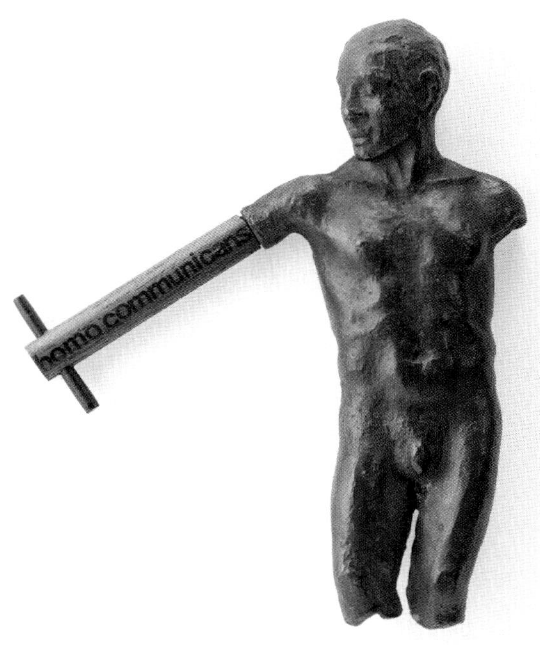

FIG. 25
Juhani Heikkilä, *Homo Communicans* brooch, 1997

Communicans brooch similarly combines disparate parts, a male torso with a piece of wood replacing one arm (fig. 25). *Pregnant Tree Boy*, made by Sebastian Buescher in 2006, is composed of a number of distinct parts joined together: a twig, a pearl, a porcelain head, and wet specimens of black-widow spiders in a bubble-shaped vial (fig. 26). The strangeness of Buescher's title stresses that these are unrelated components, assembled like the "exquisite corpse" of the parlor game promoted by Surrealists, in which a drawing is circulated for each successive participant to add the next section of the body without consideration for what it is attached to.[54] If the purpose of such games was to trigger free associations, what ideas might Buescher's hybrid provoke? The components are so utterly contradictory, yet the title insists they are conjoined, confounding the limits of human reproduction, biology, and development. By comparison, Heikkilä's selections are very deliberate. The prosthesis on which the eponymous inscription appears has a rod inserted—for "twisting the arm" rather than "shaking hands." It was made for an exhibition inspired by US Secretary of State Madeleine Albright's autobiography, in which she detailed her use of jewelry in international diplomacy.[55] The brooch thus offers a commentary about human vulnerability to coercion. It can also be understood as a reflection upon human limitations, just as the hippocamp cup can. In the opening passage of his *Ars Poetica*, Horace (65–8 BCE) counseled against excessive poetic license, which he compared to the absurdity of hybrid composite creatures. By the Middle Ages, his advice was understood as drawing a distinction between

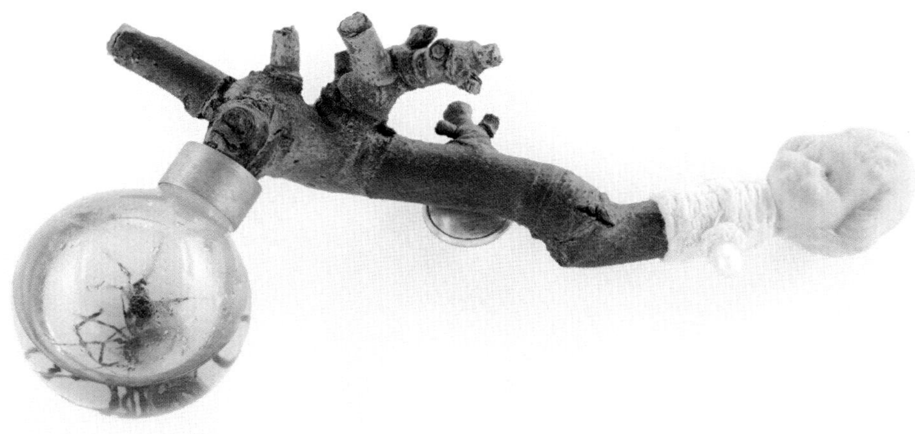

FIG. 26
Sebastian Buescher, *Pregnant Tree Boy* brooch, 2006

the abilities of the divine to create nature and the limits of human creativity to recombine only what already exists.[56] LACMA's hippocamp cup therefore demonstrates the limits (or the height) of human artistry. We thus come full circle, with our appreciation of works from the Boardman collection enriched by associations across it and the wider holdings of the museum.

A Cabinet for Everyone

The kunstkammer, or cabinet of curiosities, draws us in through imaginative reasoning. There is something undeniably appealing about great assemblages of disparate things that seem to speak to each other, and to us. The visual relationships we perceive between otherwise unassociated objects can be understood as a kind of game or a form of play.[57] They inspire the enjoyable generation of new knowledge. Contemporary art jewelry therefore appeals to the human imagination in a way that has deep historical parallels. It embraces an unusually diverse array of forms and media akin to the best rarities found in Renaissance and Baroque collections. It inspires the same wonder as wunderkammern and excites the same curiosity as any cabinet of curiosities. Brought together as a collection, these pieces will continue to reveal insights as they are examined and presented alongside each other and the other works of the museum.

LACMA's encyclopedic reach can provide both broad and specific contexts for the Boardman collection. The pottery

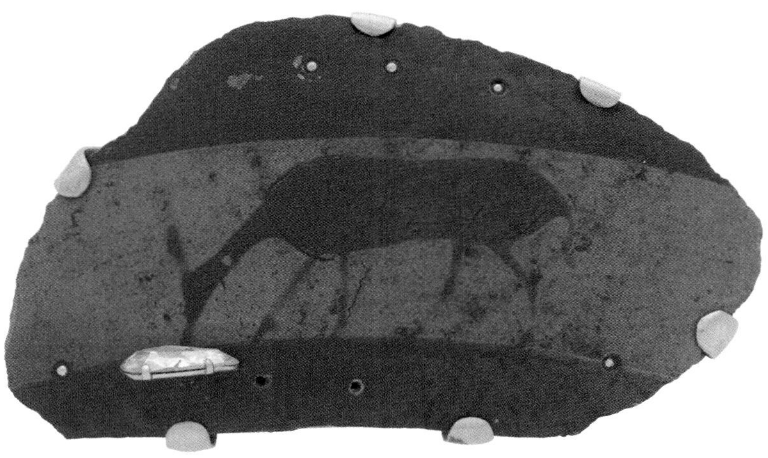

FIG. 27
Falko Marx, brooch, 1989

fragment cleverly transformed (by the unusual positioning of a teardrop diamond) into a scene of a hind drinking from a spring in the brooch by Falko Marx (fig. 27), for example, can be compared with the type of Athenian black-figure band cup from which it probably derives (fig. 28).[58] Ancient examples of the fibula brooch form used by Albert Paley are among LACMA's holdings of Greek, Roman, and Etruscan art.[59] Word drawings that accompany some of Manfred Bischoff's pieces resonate with Pop art wordplay,[60] and work by "Ellensburg Funky" jewelers[61] can be compared with the museum's examples of California Funk art.[62] A ring from 1974 by merry renk joins a hairband of hers from the 1950s and a crown from the 1980s already at the museum, and Arline Fisch's necklace and bracelet are complemented by two of her earlier modernist works in silver.[63] The Boardman collection's greatest advantage at LACMA is the opportunity for serendipitous comparisons, however. Where else might Bischoff's "raunchy existential meditation on potato-ness, decay, and beauty"[64] (his *Pomme de Terre–Pathètique–Tragique* brooch of 2002)[65] be appreciated alongside Claes Oldenburg's "mundane... baked potato [imbued] with sexual innuendo"[66] (his *Baked Potato #1* of 1963)?[67]

Thanks to the generosity of Lois and Bob Boardman, the educational advantages and playful enjoyment of this new and rich resource are also now available anytime to anyone with an internet connection via the museum's website, just waiting for viewers to create their own virtual collections of strange and fantastic objects: perhaps a brooch embedded in a book, a collar made of an enormous red flower, or a tiny party hat trapped in acrylic.

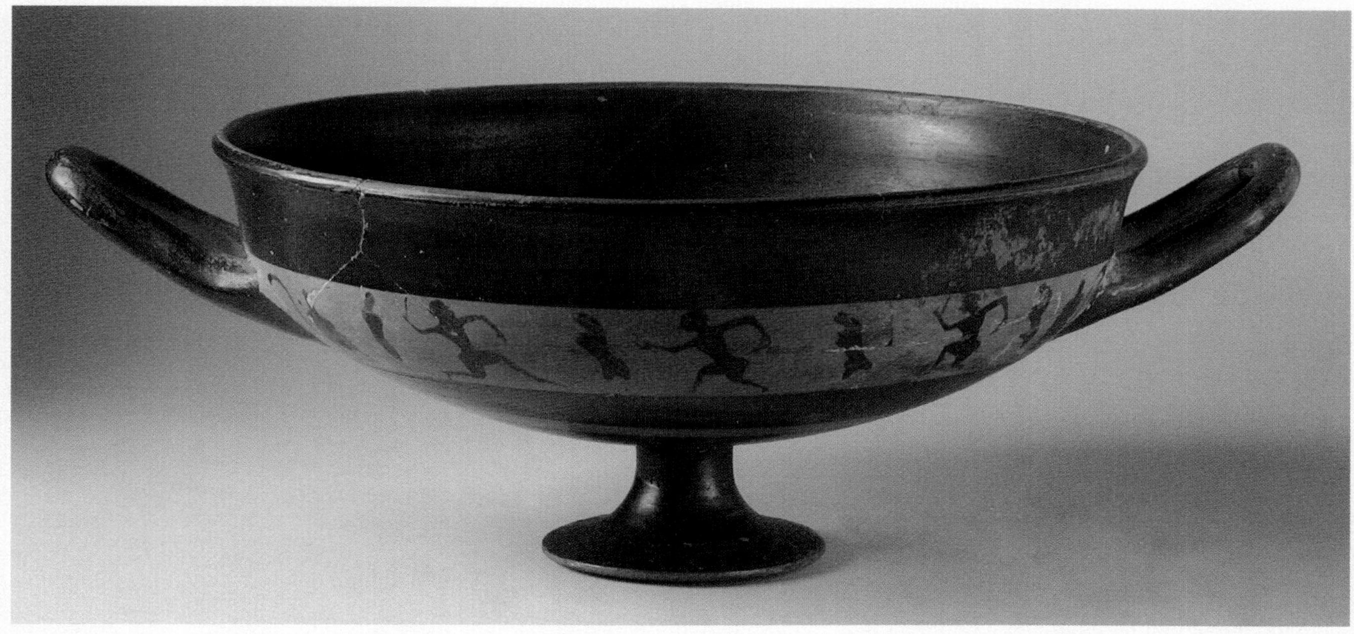

FIG. 28
Black-figure band-cup with Dionysiac revelers, c. 530 BCE, terracotta, 4 ¼ × 12 × 8⅝ in. (10.8 × 30.5 × 22 cm), Los Angeles County Museum of Art, William Randolph Hearst Collection, 50.9.42

Notes

Epigraph: Georg Christoph Stirn diary entry, Bodleian Library, University of Oxford, MS Add, B67, as translated in H. Hager, Appendix II, in review of *Geschichte der Deutschen in England*, by K. H. Schaible, *Englische Studien* 10 (1887): 450. The "robe" mentioned is the most important artifact to have survived from the period of first contact between the Native Americans of Virginia and European settlers.

1. The collection would later form the core of the founding collection of the University of Oxford's Ashmolean Museum (the first purpose-built museum), which opened its doors on Broad Street on May 24, 1683. See Martin Welch, "The Foundation of the Ashmolean Museum," in *Tradescant's Rarities: Essays on the Foundation of the Ashmolean Museum, 1683, with a Catalogue of the Surviving Early Collections*, ed. Arthur MacGregor (Oxford, England: Clarendon Press, 1983), 59–69.

2. As described by the King refuting the 1661 charge brought against Tradescant by the Office of Revells. See State Papers (Domestic) for the reign of Charles II, The National Archives of the UK, SP 29/38/74, as quoted in Arthur MacGregor, "The Tradescants as Collectors of Rarities," in *Tradescant's Rarities: Essays on the Foundation of the Ashmolean Museum, 1683, with a Catalogue of the Surviving Early Collections*, ed. MacGregor (Oxford, England: Clarendon Press, 1983), 23. "The Ark" preceded the Ashmolean Museum by half a century, but the precise date that it first opened its doors is not known. The surviving evidence from visitors suggests it was accessible on a regular basis and that admission depended on a small fee rather than on status or gender.

3. Charles Hoole, *New Discovery of the Old Art of Teaching School: In Four Small Treatises* (London, 1660), as cited in MacGregor, "The Tradescants as Collectors of Rarities," 23.

4. The Protestant Academy at Altdorf near Nuremberg, Germany, became a university on October 3, 1622, through a charter granted by Emperor Ferdinand II. See John Flood, *Poets Laureate in the Holy Roman Empire: A Bio-bibliographical Handbook* (Berlin: Walter de Gruyter, 2006), clii.

5. "1. 'Birds', 2. 'Fourfooted beasts', 3. 'strange Fishes', 4. 'Shell-creatures', 5. 'Insects, terrestriall', 6. 'Mineralls', 7. 'Outlandish Fruits', 8. 'Mechanicks', 9. 'Other variety of Rarities', 10. 'Warlike Instruments', 11. 'Garments, Habits, Vests, Ornaments', 12. Utensils and Household-stuffe', 13. 'Numismata', and 14. 'Medalls'." See April London, "Musaeum Tradescantianum and the Benefactors to the Tradescants' Museum," in *Tradescant's Rarities: Essays on the Foundation of the Ashmolean Museum, 1683, with a Catalogue of the Surviving Early Collections*, ed. Arthur MacGregor (Oxford, England: Clarendon Press, 1983), 24.

6. For the historic role of variety in the appreciation of wonder see Joy Kenseth, "The Age of the Marvelous: An Introduction," in *The Age of the Marvelous*, exh. cat., ed. Kenseth (Hanover, NH: Hood Museum of Art, Dartmouth College, 1991), 44.

7. *The Diary of John Evelyn*, ed. E. S. de Beer, vol. 2 (Oxford, England: Clarendon Press, 1955), 356–57.

8. For a discussion of the phenomenon and notable collections of the period (including the examples mentioned here), see Arthur MacGregor, "Collectors and Collections of Rarities in the Sixteenth and Seventeenth Centuries," in *Tradescant Rarities: Essays on the Foundation of the Ashmolean Museum, 1683, with a Catalogue of the Surviving Early Collections*, ed. MacGregor (Oxford, England: Clarendon Press, 1983), 70–97 esp. 73–75, 80.

9. Variations in the historic terminology result from social and cultural factors such as geography, chronology, social standing, and personality, according to Oliver Impey and Arthur MacGregor, introduction, in *The Origins of Museums: The Cabinet of Curiosities in Sixteenth- and Seventeenth-Century Europe*, ed. Impey and MacGregor (Oxford, England: Clarendon Press, 1985), xix–xx.

10. Swedish father of modern binomial nomenclature Carl Linnaeus (1707–1778) acknowledged the Tradescants' role in introducing many foreign species by naming a perennial flowering plant still popular in English gardens today *Tradescantia virginiana*. See Jennifer Potter, *Strange Blooms: The Curious Lives and Adventures of the John Tradescants*, paperback edition (London: Atlantic Books, 2007), 112.

11. London, "Musaeum Tradescantianum and the Benefactors to the Tradescants' Museum," 26–39.

12. For a list of works included in the exhibition see Brian Dillon and Marina Warner, *Curiosity: Art and the Pleasures of Knowing*, exh. cat. (London: Hayward Publishing, 2013), 225–32.

13. Dora Thornton, *A Rothschild Renaissance: Treasures from the Waddesdon Bequest* (London: British Museum Press, 2015), 65–71.

14. For a definition of "contemporary jewelry" that discusses this independence in terms of the ability to be self-reflexive and consider the histories and social practices of jewelry, see Damian Skinner, "What Is Contemporary Jewelry?," in *Contemporary Jewelry in Perspective*, ed. Skinner (New York: Lark Books, 2013), 7–15, esp. 11–12.

15. Peter Dormer and Ralph Turner, *The New Jewelry: Trends and Traditions* (London: Thames and Hudson, 1985), 7–20. However, in her lecture "Freedom Has Its Limitations: Jewelry Now, Seen from a Dutch Perspective" on March 18, 2012, at the Pinakothek der Moderne in Munich, Marjan Unger cautioned that, despite the enormous contribution to artistic freedom of expression in jewelry made by jewelers exploring alternative materials in this period, it had not been the first challenge to the status of precious stones and metals in the field (alluding to other instances such as the cast-iron jewelry that expressed Prussian resistance to Napoleon I; the use of base metals, semiprecious stone, glass, shell, and enamel in the Aesthetic Movement; and the incorporation of plastics like Bakelite in the early twentieth century). See http://www.die-neue-sammlung.de/blog/wp-content/uploads/2012/03/Marjan-A21.pdf.

16. Marjan Boot and Lex Reitsma, *The Gijs + Emmy Spectacle* (Rotterdam, Netherlands: NAI, 2014), 44–88.

17. Lee Nordness, *Objects: USA*, exh. cat. (New York: Viking Press, 1970), 235.

18 Cindi Strauss and Keelin M. Burrows, chronology, in *Ornament as Art: Avant-Garde Jewelry from the Helen Williams Drutt Collection, the Museum of Fine Arts, Houston*, ed. Strauss (Stuttgart: Arnoldsche Art Publishers, 2007), 455.

19. Arline Fisch, David Revere McFadden, Ida Katherine Rigby, Robert Bell, Denny Stone, and Anna Beatriz Chadour-Sampson, *Elegant Fantasy: The Jewelry of Arline Fisch* (San Diego: San Diego Historical Society; and Stuttgart: Arnoldsche, 2001), 119; Arline M. Fisch, *Textile Techniques in Metal for Jewelers, Sculptors, and Textile Artists* (New York: Van Nostrand Reinhold, 1975). She had been the Craft Board of Australia's first foreign lecturer in 1972, giving workshops in all eight states (oral history interview with Arline M. Fisch, July 29–30, 2001, Archives of American Art, Smithsonian Institution, Washington, DC).

20. William Butler as quoted in Thomas Fuller, *The History of the Worthies of England*, new edition with notes by John Nichols, vol. 2 (London: Rivington, 1811, first published 1662), 340.

21. Victoria and Albert Museum, "Alexander McQueen: Savage Beauty—About the Exhibition, 14 March–2 August 2015," http://www.vam.ac.uk/content/exhibitions/exhibition-alexander-mc-queen-savage-beauty/about-the-exhibition/. A smaller version of the display appeared in a different iteration of the exhibition at the Metropolitan Museum of Art in 2011. See "Alexander McQueen: Savage Beauty—About the Exhibition, May 4–August 7, 2011," http://blog.metmuseum.org/alexandermcqueen/about/.

22. Susan Cummins, "Eveline Holsappel, Museum Arnhem, Arnhem, The Netherlands," *Art Jewelry Forum*, March 1, 2015, http://www.artjewelryforum.org/curators/eveline-holsappel.

23. Auckland Art Gallery Toi O Tāmaki, "Wunderrūma: New Zealand Jewelry," July 18, 2015, http://www.aucklandartgallery.com/whats-on/events/2015/july/wunderruma-new-zealand-jewellery.

24. Warwick Freeman, "Tales of Wonderland," in *Wunderrūma*, exh. cat. (Wellington, New Zealand: Hook and Sinker Publications, 2014), 28.

25. David Bielander, *Dung Beetle* brooch, 2007, p. 24; Otto Künzli, *Gold Macht Blind* bracelet, designed 1980, this example made c. 1986, p. 41; Sebastian Buescher, *Octocoralia* necklace, 2008, p. 30; Arline Fisch, *Bell Frills* necklace, 1985, p. 54; merry renk, *Green Fire* ring, 1974, p. 161; Manfred Bischoff, *Pomme de Terre–Pathètique–Tragique* brooch, 2002, p. 26.

26. Claudia Swan, *Art, Science, and Witchcraft in Early Modern Holland* (Cambridge, England: Cambridge University Press, 2005), 94.

27. Joy Kenseth, ed., *The Age of the Marvelous* (Hanover, NH: Hood Museum of Art, Dartmouth College, 1991), 33–39, 88.

28. Philipp Hainhofer, quoted in Hans-Olof Boström, "Philipp Hainhofer and Gustavus Adolphus's *Kunstschrank* in Uppsala," in *The Origins of Museums: The Cabinet of Curiosities in Sixteenth- and Seventeenth-Century Europe*, ed. Oliver Impey and Arthur MacGregor (Oxford, England: Clarendon Press, 1985), 132.

29. Aristotle, *Physics*, 2.1, 192b9, in *The Complete Works of Aristotle*, revised Oxford translation, vol. 1, ed. Jonathan Barnes (Princeton, NJ: Princeton University Press, 1984), 329.

30. Philippe Tamizey de Larroque, ed., *Boniface de Borilly, Lettres inédits* écrites *à Peiresc (1618–1631)* (Aix-en-Provence, France: Garcin et Didier, 1891), 48, as translated in Lorraine J. Daston and Katherine Park, *Wonders and the Order of Nature, 1150–1750* (New York: Zone Books, 2001), 267.

31. J. B. Charles, *Flowers and Still-Life: An Anthology in Paint* (London: Studio Publications, limited edition, 1938), ix.

32. Bruce Robertson and Mark Meadow, "Microcosm: Objects of Knowledge," *AI and Society: The Journal of Human-Centred and Machine Intelligence* 14, no. 2 (May 2000): 223–29.

33. See collections online at lacma.org: coffin, Egypt, mid-21st Dynasty (about 1000–968 BCE), M.47.3a–c; Joris Laarman, *Bone Chaise Lounge*, 2006, M.2013.109.

34. Dirk Syndram and Claudia Brink, eds., *The Dream of a King: Dresden's Green Vault*, trans. Geraldine Schuckelt (Munich: Hirmer Verlag Munich, 2011), cat. 4.

35. Patricia Harris and David Lyon, "Mystery and Memory: The Jewelry of Sandra Enterline," *Metalsmith* 24, no. 2 (Spring, 2004), 35.

36. Daniel Jocz, "Meaning in Jewelry: Risk and Reverance," *Metalsmith* 15, 1995 Exhibition in Print, supplement, 25.

37. Wolfram Koeppe and Anna Maria Giusti, *Art of the Royal Court: Treasures in Pietre Dure from the Palaces of Europe* (New York: Metropolitan Museum of Art, 2008), 64.

38. JoAnn Goldberg, "Pavel Opočenský," *Ornament* 9, no. 4 (1986), 44–45, 49.

39. Damian Skinner and Kevin Murray, *Place and Adornment: A History of Contemporary Jewellery in Australia and New Zealand* (Honolulu: University of Hawaii Press, 2014), 141–45.

40. Damian Skinner, *Given: Jewelry by Warwick Freeman* (Auckland, New Zealand: Starform, 2004), 26.

41. *Pharmacopoeia Londinensis, or the New London Dispensatory*, 8th ed., corrected and amended by William Salmon (London: J. Dawks, 1716), 366.

42. Corning Museum of Glass, "Gold Ruby Glass," http://www.cmog.org/article/gold-ruby-glass, accessed December 6, 2015.

43. Patti Bleicher, "Moss 'Case Study' Features Barbara Seidenath," *Crafthaus*, May 14, 2011, http://crafthaus.ning.com/profiles/blogs/moss-case-study-features.

44. Oppi Untracht, *Metal Techniques for Craftsmen: A Basic Manual for Craftsmen on the Methods of Forms and Decorating Metals* (Garden City, NY: Doubleday, 1968), 186–91.

45. Corning Museum of Glass, "Gold Ruby Glass."

46. Catherine Hess and Timothy Husband, *European Glass in the J. Paul Getty Museum* (Los Angeles: J. Paul Getty Museum, 1997), 74; David Buckton, Christopher Entwistle, and Rowena Prior, eds., *The Treasury of San Marco Venice* (Milan: Olivetti, 1984), 129–35; Hugh Tait, *The Golden Age of Venetian Glass* (London: British Museum, 1979), 94.

47. Doug Bucci "Portfolio: Islet," http://www.dougbucci.com/index.php/portfolio/category/1-islet, accessed September 18, 2015; Philadelphia Museum of Art "*Islet | White, Neckpiece*," http://www.philamuseum.org/collections/permanent/321683.html?mulR=2080022870|2, accessed September 18, 2015.

48. Daston and Park, *Wonders and the Order of Nature*, 285–86.

49. The term derives from Ernst Kris, "Der Stil 'rustique'. Die Verwendung des Na-turabgusses bei Wenzel Jamnitzer und Bernard Palissy" (The 'rustic' style: the use of life casts in the work of Wenzel Jamnitzer and Bernard Palissy), *Jahrbuch der kunsthistorischen Sammlungen in Wien*, vol. I (1926), 137–208, as cited in Swan, *Art, Science, and Witchcraft in Early Modern Holland*, 93.

50. Gerd Rothmann and Margit Brand, *Gerd Rothmann: Werkverzeichnis, 1967–2008* (Gerd Rothmann: Catalogue of Works, 1967–2008) (Stuttgart: Arnoldsche Art Publishers, 2009).

51. Marjorie Simon, "Marian Hosking—Nature into Culture," *Metalsmith* 30, no. 3 (2010): 34.

52. Leonard N. Amico, *Bernard Palissy: In Search of Earthly Paradise* (New York: Flammarion, 1996), 7.

53. The fifth cupboard at Schloss Ambras contained elaborate clocks and scientific instruments, see Elizabeth Scheicher, "The Collection of Archduke Ferdinand II at Schloss Ambras," in *The Origins of Museums: The Cabinet of Curiosities in Sixteenth- and Seventeenth-Century Europe*, ed. Oliver Impey and Arthur MacGregor, 46.

54. Anne M. Kern, "From One Exquisite Corpse (in)to Another: Influences and Transformations from Early to Late Surrealist Games," in *The Exquisite Corpse: Chance and Collaboration in Surrealism's Parlor Game*, ed. Kanta Kochhar-Lindgren, Davis Schneiderman, and Tom Denlinger (Lincoln: University of Nebraska Press, 2009), 8–17.

55. Helen Williams Drutt, *Brooching It Diplomatically: A Tribute to Madeleine K. Albright*, exh. cat. (Philadelphia: Helen Drutt, 1998), 60–61.

56. T. A. Heslop, "Contemplating Chimera in Medieval Imagination: St. Anselm's Crypt at Canterbury," in *Raising the Eyebrow: John Onians and World Art Studies—An Album Amicorum in His Honor*, ed. Lauren Golden (Oxford, England: Archeopress, 2001), 153–68.

57. See Horst Bredekamp, *The Lure of Antiquity and the Cult of the Machine: The Kunstkammer and the Evolution of Nature, Art, and Technology* (Princeton, NJ: Markus Weiner Publishers, 1995), 63–80.

58. I am grateful to classical archaeologist David Saunders, associate curator at the Getty Villa in Los Angeles, for suggesting the fragment came from an Athenian black-figure band cup, c. 550–525 BCE.

59. For example, compare Albert Paley, fibula, 1968, p. 151, with LACMA's eighth-century fibula (45.23.40) online.

60. Compare Manfred Bischoff, *Night Visitors* ring, 1998, p. 26; with Edward Ruscha, *Double Standard*, 1969, LACMA (M.2005.132.6) online.

61. See Bobbye Tigerman's discussion of the group also in this volume, pp. 77–83.

62. Compare Merrily Tompkins, *Here Comes Trouble* brooch, 1973, p. 79; with Edward Kienholz, *Back Seat Dodge '38*, 1964, LACMA (M.81.248a–e) online.

63. merry renk, *Green Fire* ring, 1974, p. 161; *Folded* hairband (M.2011.78) and *James Love Peacock* crown (M.2012.55); Arline Fisch, *Bell Frills* necklace, 1985, p. 54, and *Long Cuff* bracelet, 1995, p. 55; Peacock Tail necklace, LACMA (M.2010.39) and *Front & Back* body ornament (M.2014.145a–b, p. 87). Find images of LACMA objects on the museum's website, lacma.org.

64. Deborah Weisgall, "A Disturbing Jewelry Artist with the Midas Touch," *New York Times*, July 28, 2002, http://www.nytimes.com/2002/07/28/arts/art-architecture-a-disturbing-jewelry-art-ist-with-the-midas-touch.html?_r=0.

65. Compare illustration on p. 26 with LACMA's object (M.82.283.4d) online.

66. Carol S. Eliel, "John Altoon: Confronting the Void," in *John Altoon* (New York: Los Angeles County Museum of Art, 2014), 112.

67. Readers can search LACMA's collection online at lacma.org to find images of the works cited here.

Breon O'Casey

(1928–2011, England)

Brooch, before 1994
Gold, silver
1½ × 2⅛ × ⅛ in.

Lois brooch, c. 1994
Silver
2¾ × 5¼ × ¼ in.

Necklace, before 1998
Silver
10½ × 11¼ × ½ in.

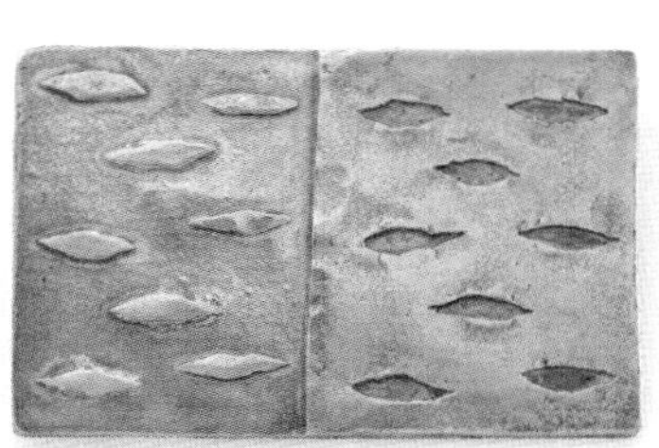

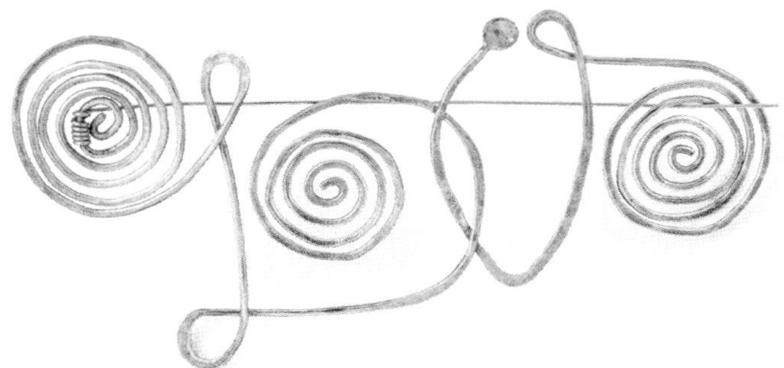

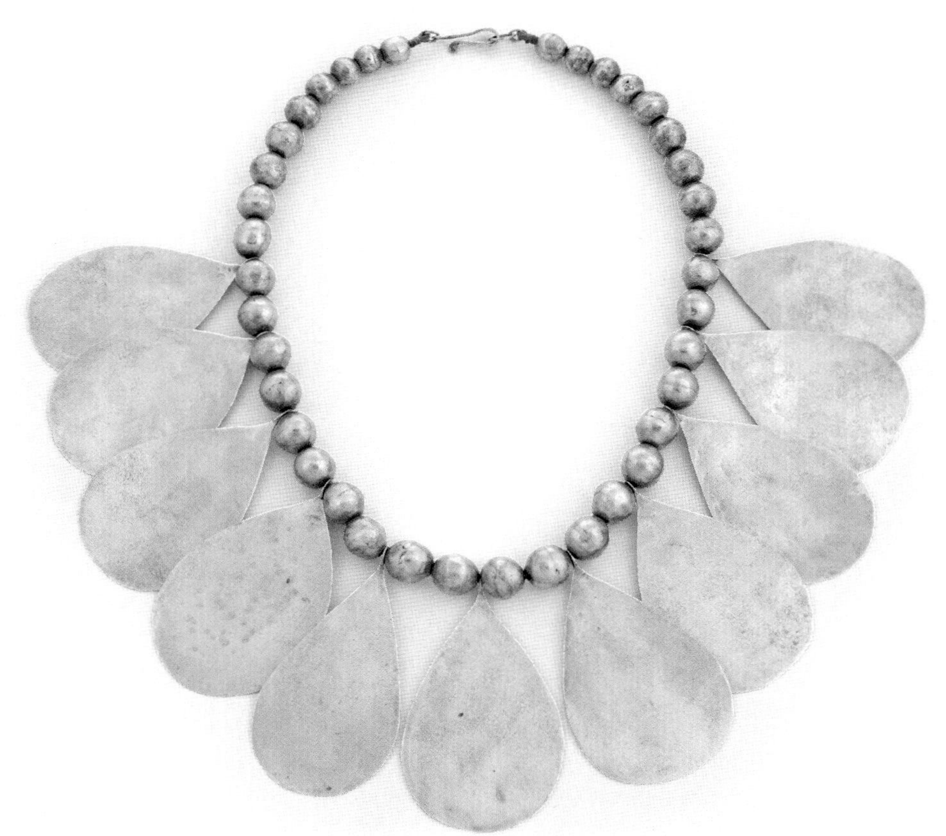

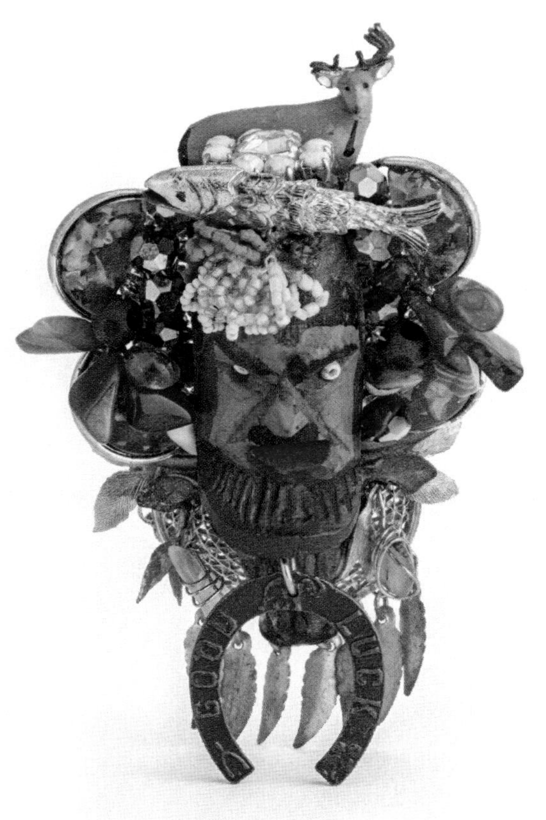

Judy Onofrio

(b. 1939, United States, active Minnesota)

Brooch, 1990
Found objects, beads
5 × 3¼ × 1¾ in.

Pavel Opočenský

(b. 1954, Czechoslovakia [now Czech Republic], active New York)

Brooch, 1986
Ivory, ebony
2⅝ × 4⅛ × ¾ in.

Brooch, 1992–93
ColorCore®
2¼ × 2¼ × ⅞ in.

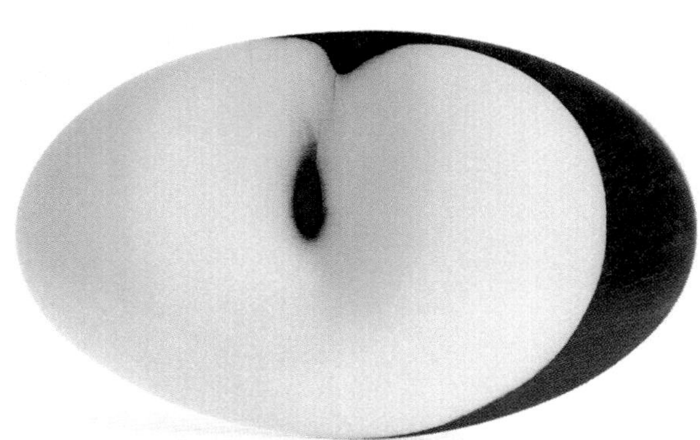

emiko oye

(b. 1974, United States, active California)

Maharajah's 6th **necklace, 2008**
From the series My First Royal Jewels, 2007–09
LEGO® bricks, rubber cord, silver
22¾ × 15⅜ × 2¾ in.

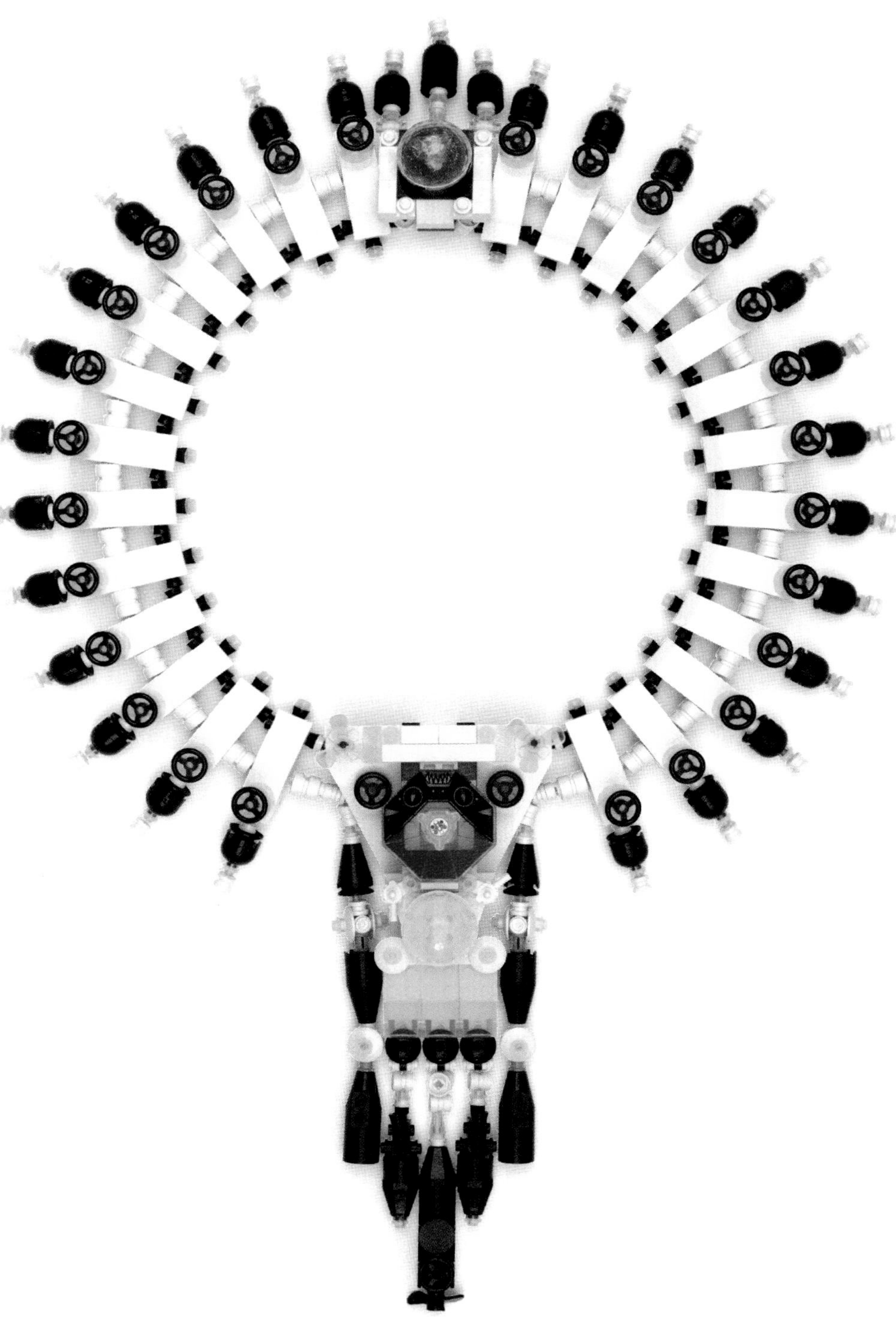

Albert Paley

(b. 1944, United States, active Pennsylvania and New York)

Fibula, 1968
Silver, gilded silver, pearls, labradorite
3 3⁄16 × 4 1⁄8 × 1 3⁄8 in.

Man's ring, 1969
Gold
1 × 3⁄4 × 7⁄16 in.

Pin, 1969
Silver, gold, ivory, pearls, garnet
4 3⁄4 × 6 7⁄8 × 1 in.

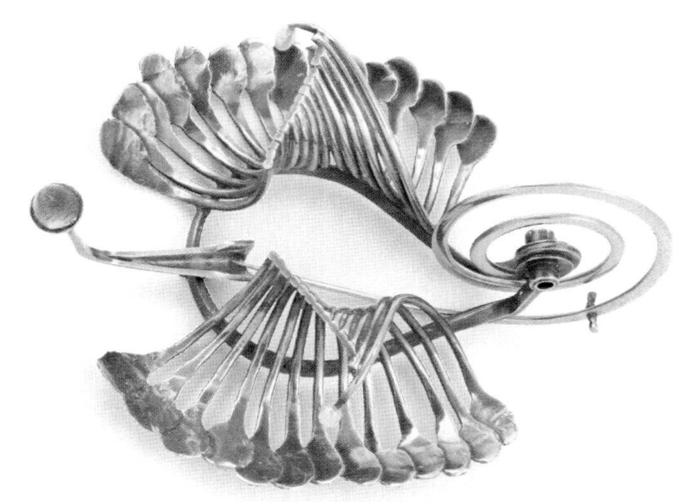

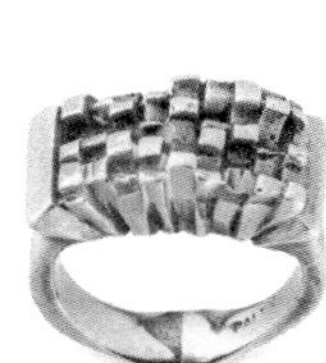

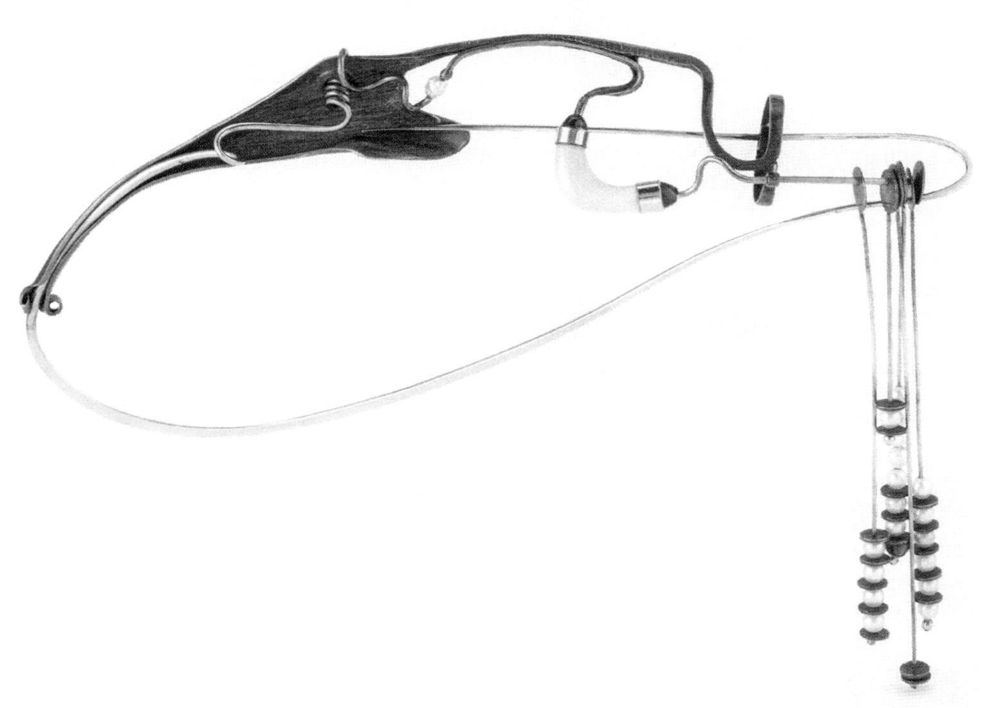

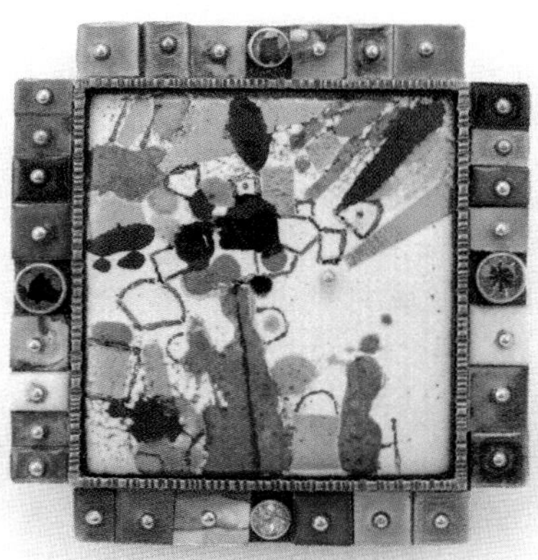

Earl Pardon

(1926–1991, United States, active New York)

Brooch, c. 1990
Enamel on silver, gold, abalone shell, blue topaz, quartz
$1\frac{7}{8} \times 1\frac{13}{16} \times \frac{3}{8}$ in.

Francesco Pavan

(b. 1937, Italy)

Brooch, c. 1985
Gold, silver, copper, copper alloy (nickel silver)
$2\frac{1}{4} \times 2\frac{3}{4} \times \frac{3}{4}$ in.

Ring, 1989
Gold, silver, copper alloys
$2\frac{1}{4} \times 1\frac{3}{4} \times 1\frac{7}{8}$ in.

Brooch, 1998
Gold
$2\frac{1}{8} \times 1\frac{7}{8} \times \frac{3}{4}$ in.

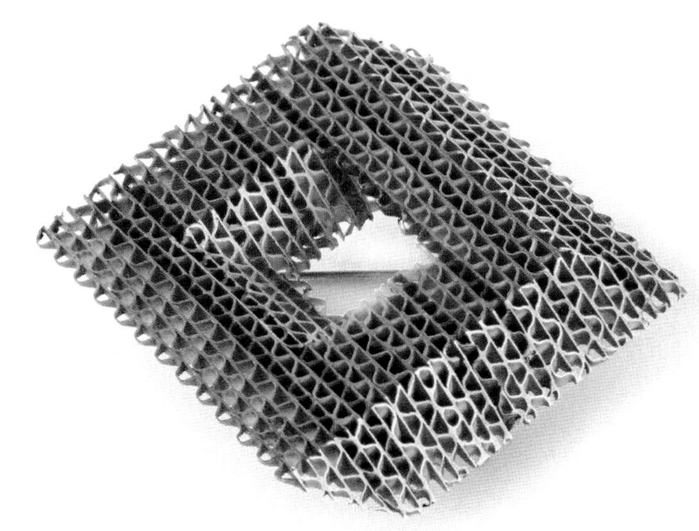

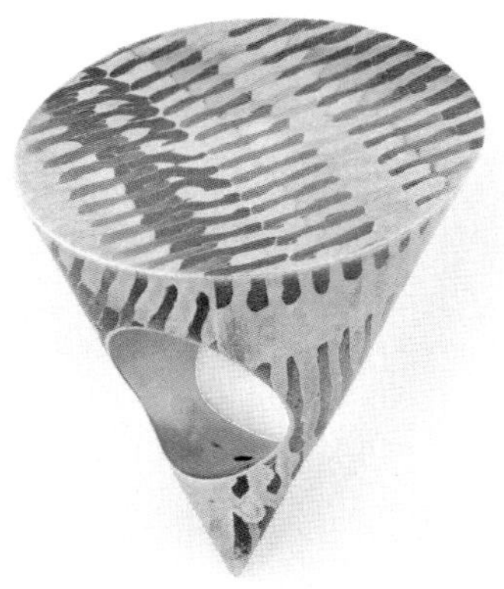

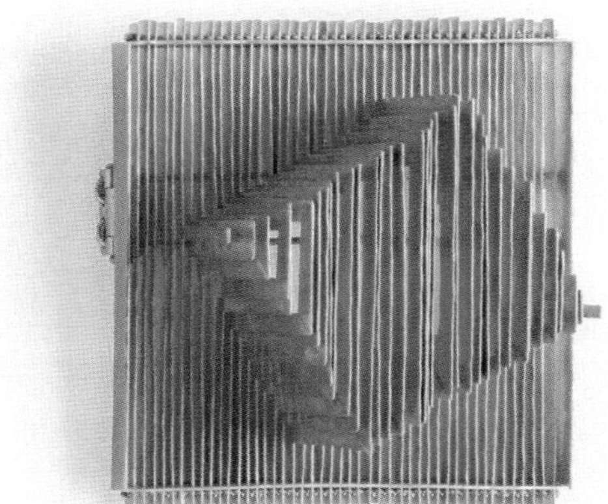

Ruudt Peters

(b. 1950, Netherlands)

Pulmo **brooch, 2011**
From the series Corpus,
2011–12
Polyurethane, silver
5 × 3¼ × 1 in.

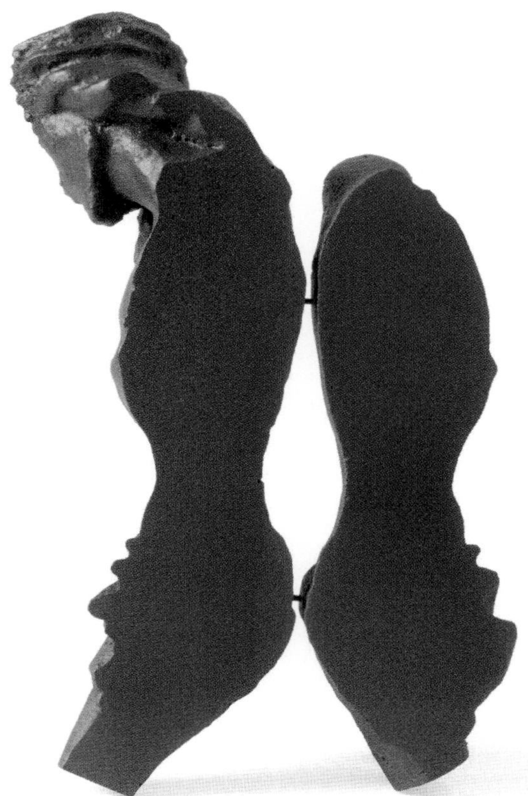

Eugene Pijanowski

(b. 1938, United States, active Michigan, Japan, and Hawaii)

Hiroko Sato-Pijanowski

(b. 1942, Japan, active Michigan)

Oh! I am precious No.5-A
necklace, 1986
Paper cord (*mizuhiki*), canvas
10 × 22 × 9¼ in.

Oh! I am precious No.5-B
bracelet, 1986
Paper cord (*mizuhiki*), canvas
4 × 9½ × 3¼ in.

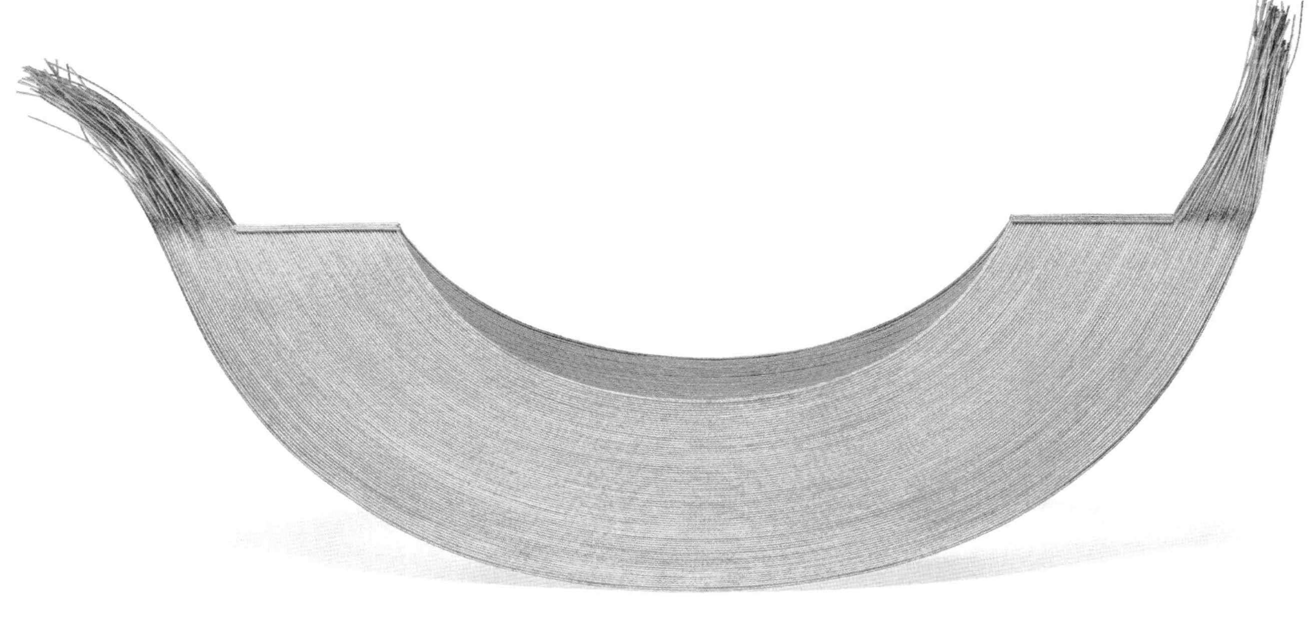

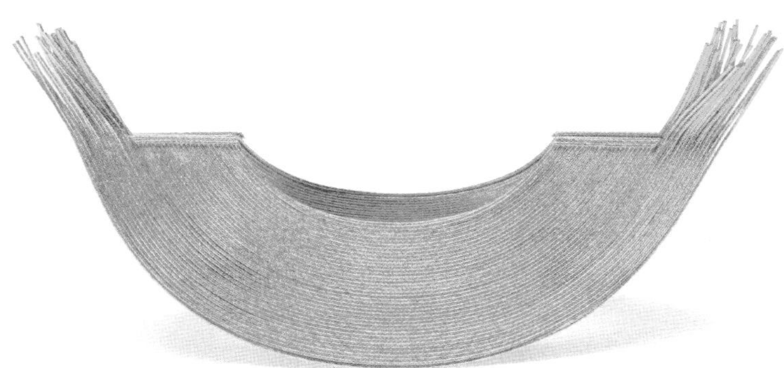

Joseph Pillari

(b. 1985, United States, active Pennsylvania)

***Beachside Humors* brooch, 2011**
Enamel on copper, silver
2 1/8 × 2 13/16 × 1/2 in.

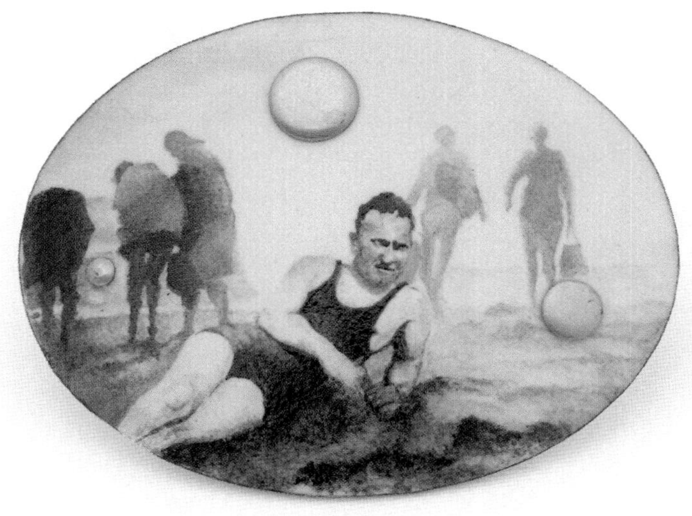

Mario Pinton

(1919–2008, Italy)

Brooch, 1986
Gold, ruby
1 1/2 × 1 1/2 × 1/8 in.

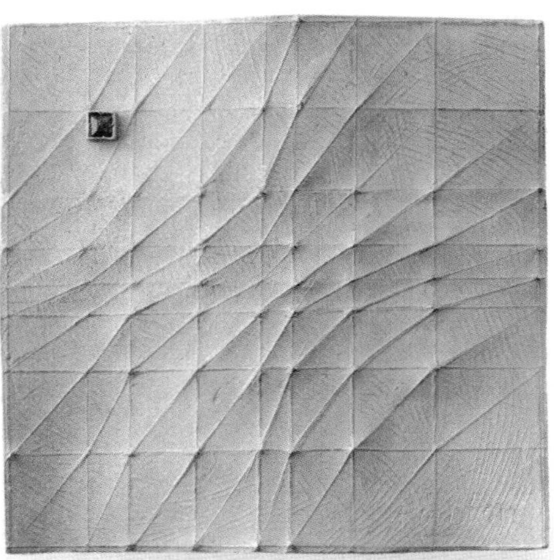

Ramón Puig Cuyàs
(b. 1953, Spain)

***El Rapte de la Sirena* brooch, 1989**
Number 296 from the series Senyors i Senyores (numbers 225–318), 1985–89
Silver, PMMA, acrylic paint
4 ½ × 3 ⅜ × ½ in.

***Invenit Thesaurum* brooch, 2008**
Number 1238 from the series Utopos (numbers 1117–1329), 2007–09
Silver, copper alloy (nickel silver), pearl, marble, bone, paper with epoxy resin
2 ¼ × 3 × ¾ in.

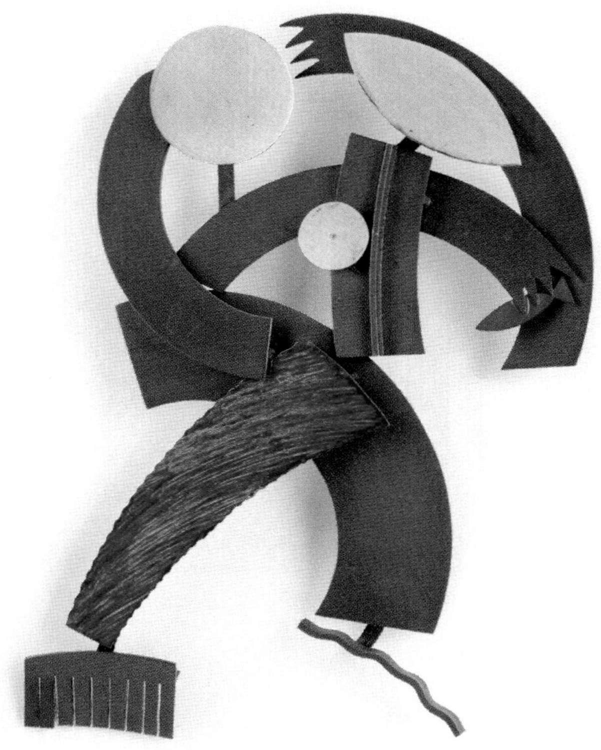

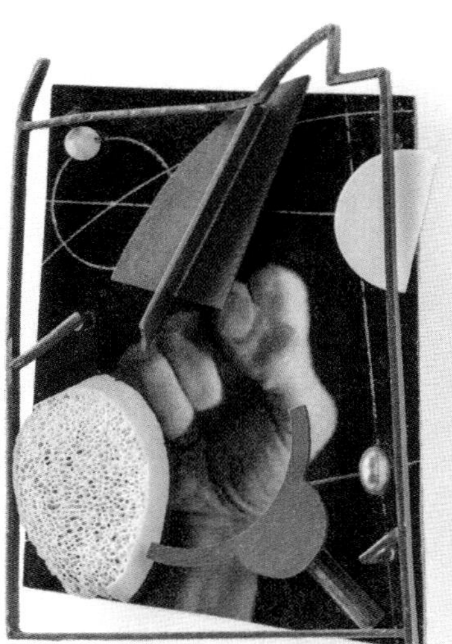

Robin Quigley

(b. 1947, United States, active Rhode Island)

Bracelet, 1981
Epoxy resin, silver
3⅜ × 3⅜ × 1 in.

***Fringe Bracelet*, 1985**
Pewter, epoxy resin, silver
5⅛ × 6⅛ × 1 in.

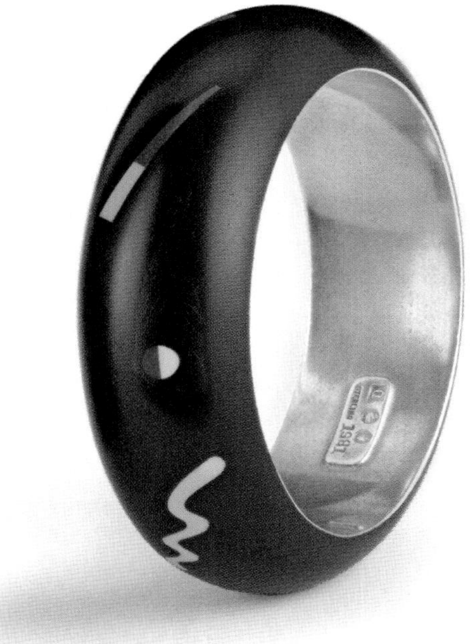

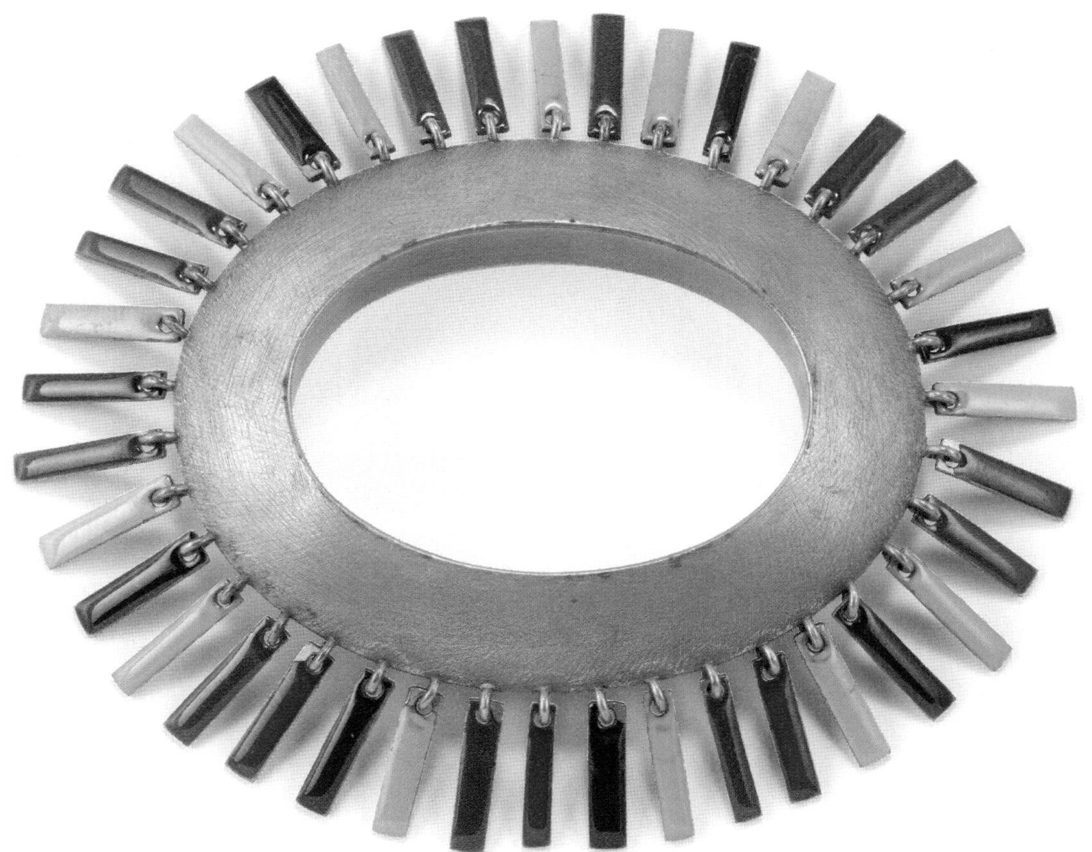

Wendy Ramshaw

(b. 1939, England)

Set of nine rings on stand, 1984
Brass, resin, gold, carnelians, garnets, pink tourmalines, citrine
5 15/16 × 1 1/8 × 1 1/4 in.

Brooch, 1986
Gold, silver, glass
3 1/8 × 5 7/8 × 1 1/4 in.

***Orbit* necklace, 1988–90**
Nickel alloy, resin
10 × 10 × 1 1/4 in.

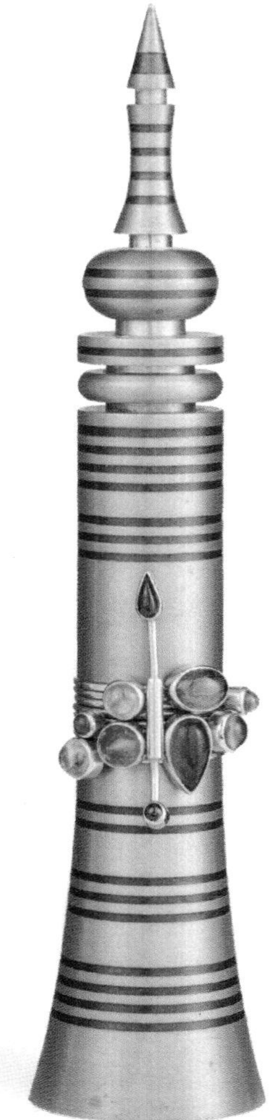

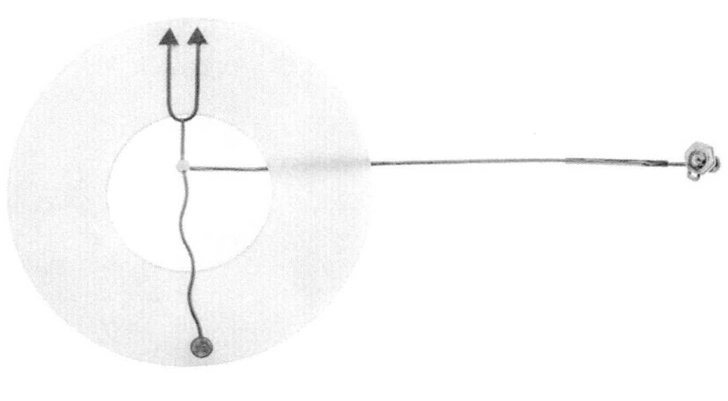

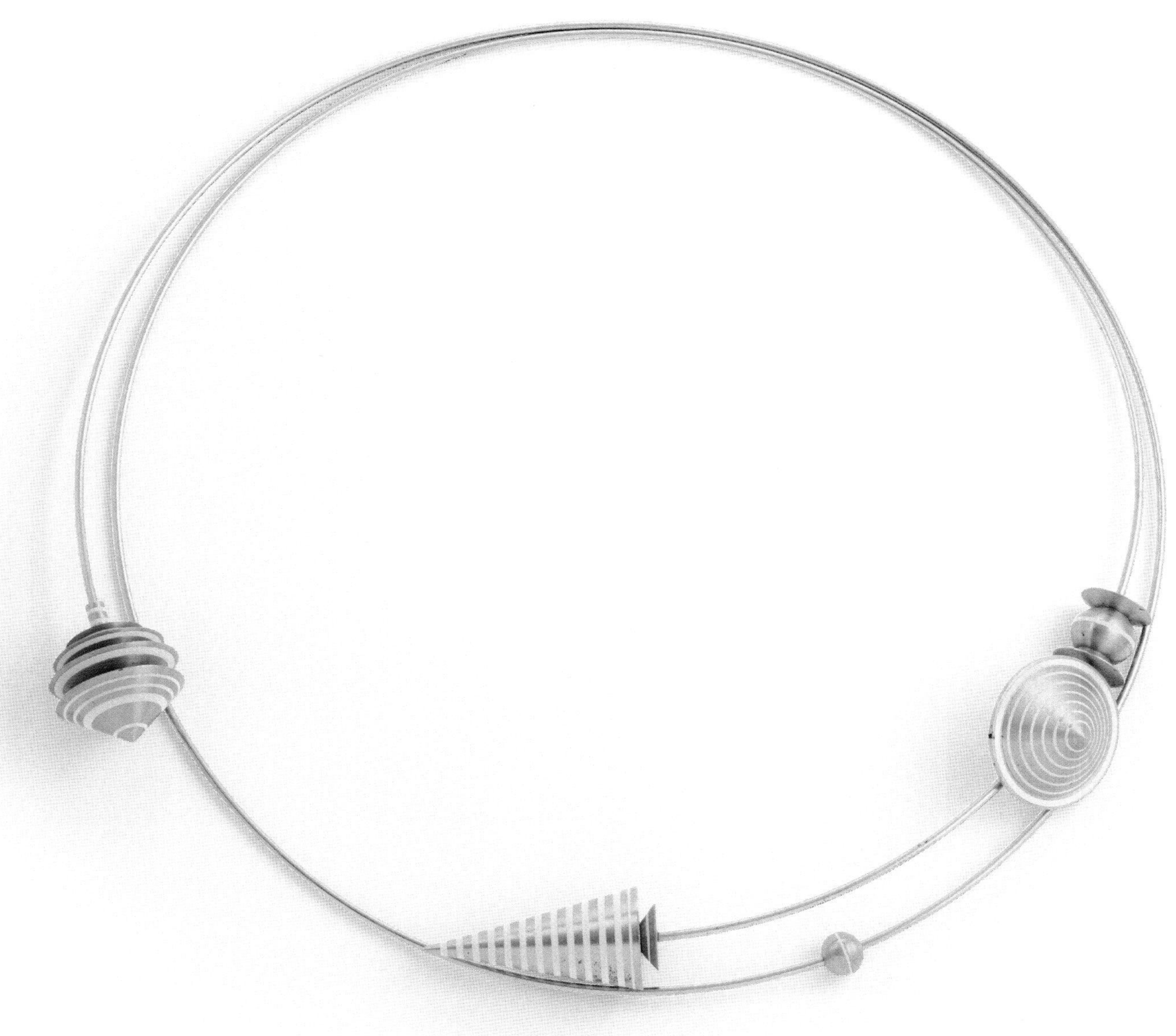

Debra Rapoport

(b. 1945, United States, active California and New York)

Found Metal Neck Piece,
1984
Found metal, plastic-coated wire, acrylic paint, paper cord, waxed linen
12¾ × 8¼ × 1⅛ in.

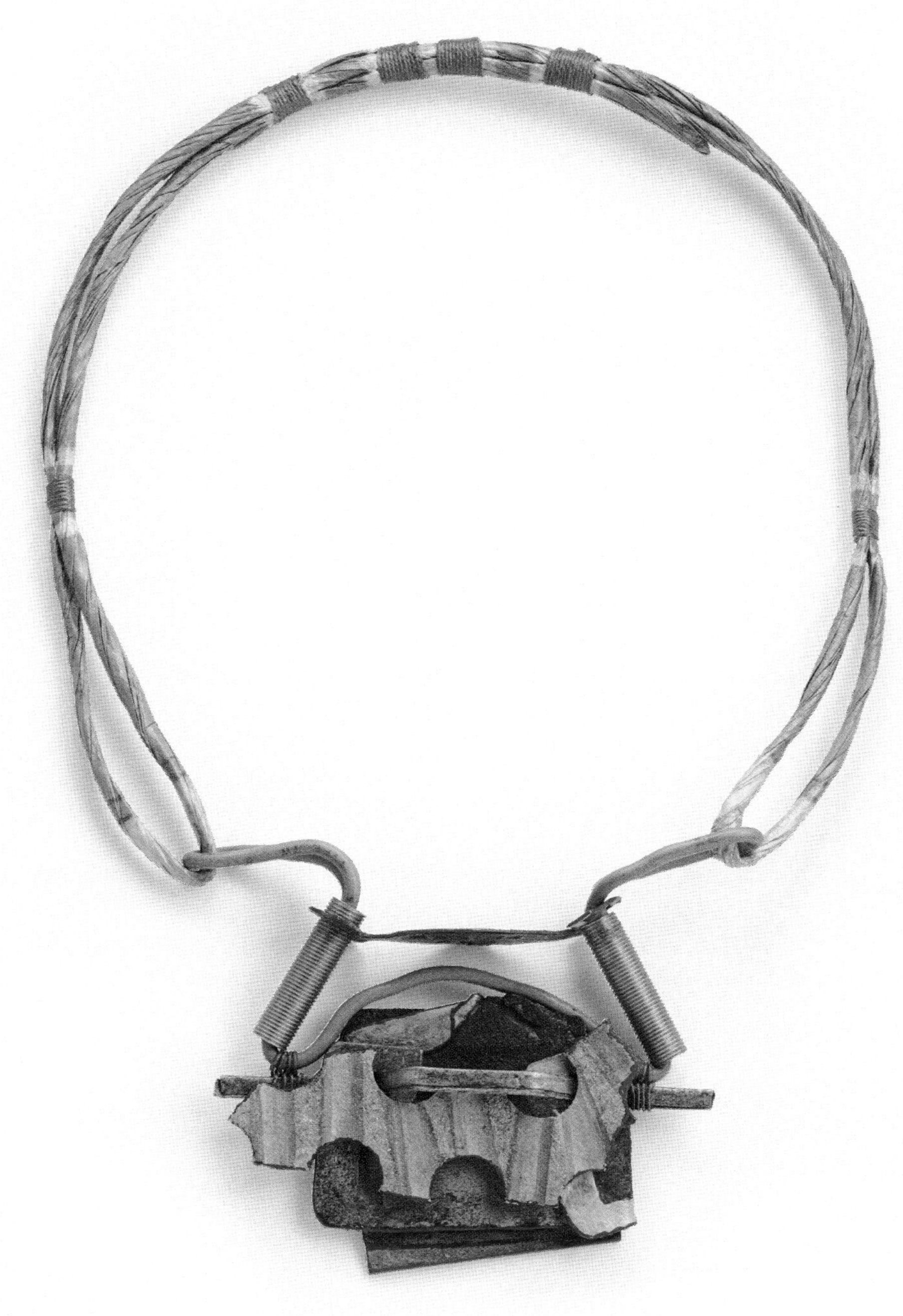

Richard H. Reinhardt

(1921–1998, United States, active Pennsylvania)

Bracelet, 1980
Silver
2⅝ × 2⅞ × 2¾ in.

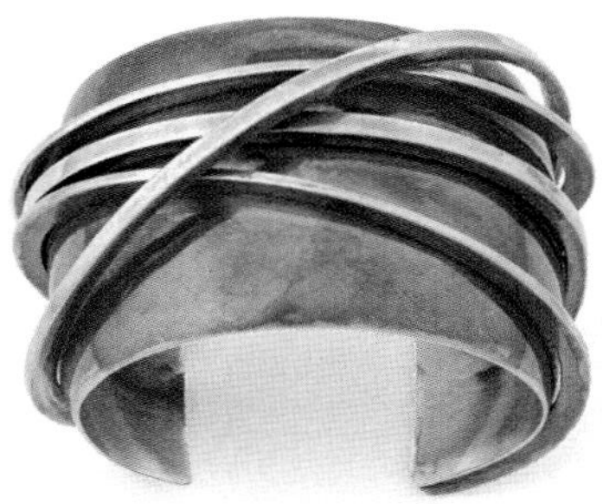

merry renk

(1921–2012, United States, active California)

***Green Fire* ring, 1974**
Gold, rutilated quartz,
tourmaline
1¼ × 1¼ × 1 in.

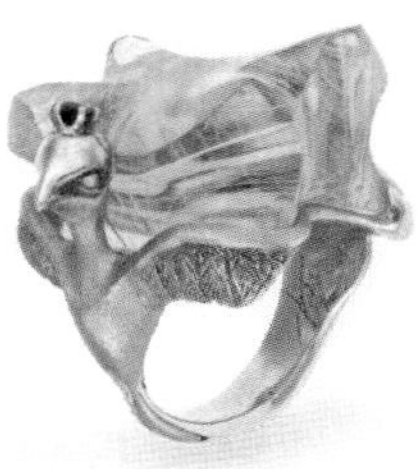

Suzan Rezac

(b. 1958, Czechoslovakia [now Czech Republic],
active Switzerland, New York, and Illinois)

Bracelet, c. 1983
Silver, copper alloys (nickel
silver, *shibuichi*, and *shakudō*)
with gilding
3½ × 3½ × 1 in.

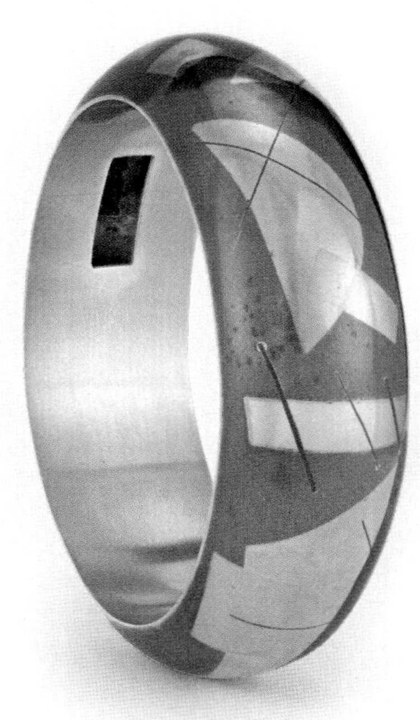

Gerd Rothmann

(b. 1941, Germany)

Zehn Finger am Hals
necklace, 1986
Silver, gilded silver
8¾ × 8¾ × 1⁄16 in.

Die Goldene Nase
nosepiece, 1988
Cast from Lois Boardman's nose
Gold
2¾ × 1⅞ × 1⅜ in.

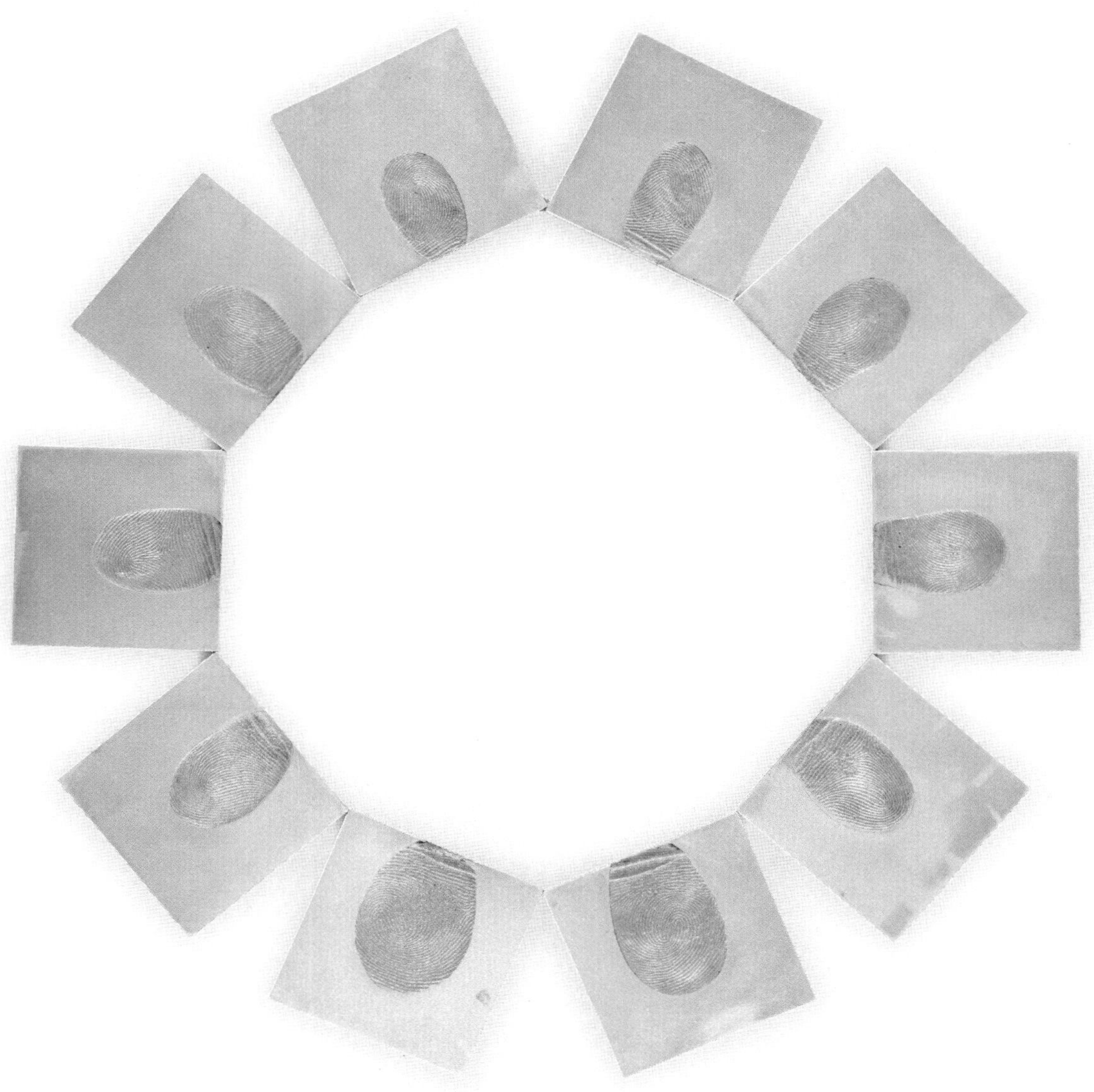

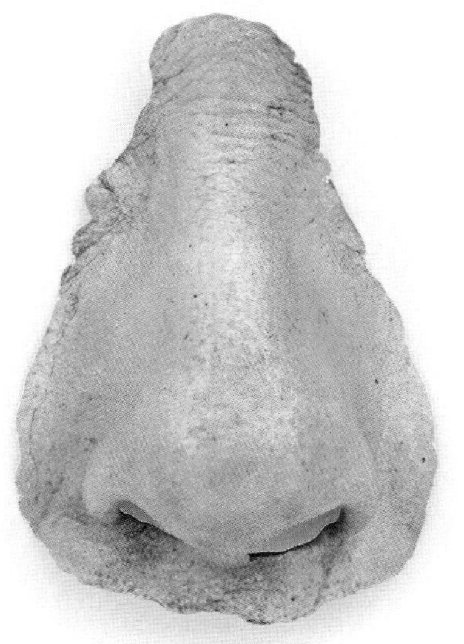

Philip Sajet

(b. 1953, Netherlands)

***Damocles* ring, designed 1987, made 2008**
Gold, jade
2 × 7⁄8 × 1⁄2 in.

***Cactus Quadruple* ring, 2003**
Gold, rusted steel
1¾ × 1¼ × ¼ in.

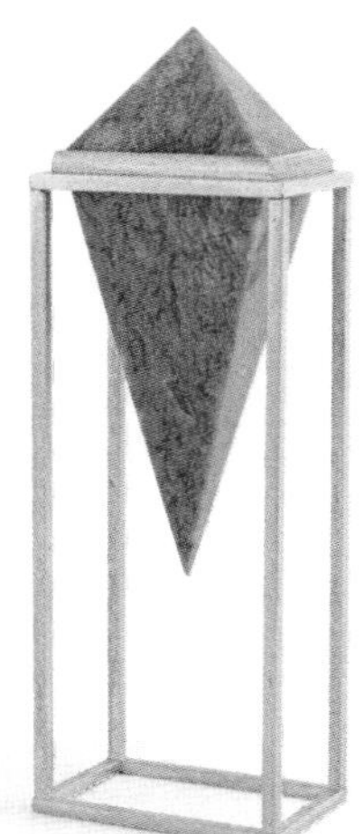

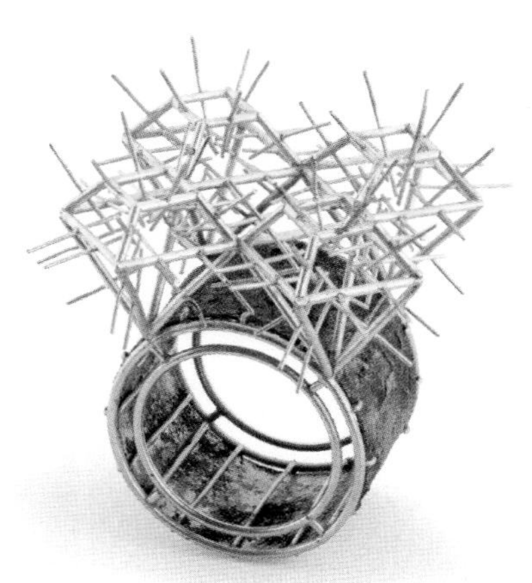

Stephen Saracino

(b. 1948, United States, active New York)

***Airport Terror Ring*, 1984**
Silver, gold, brass
4 × 3¾ × 1½ in.

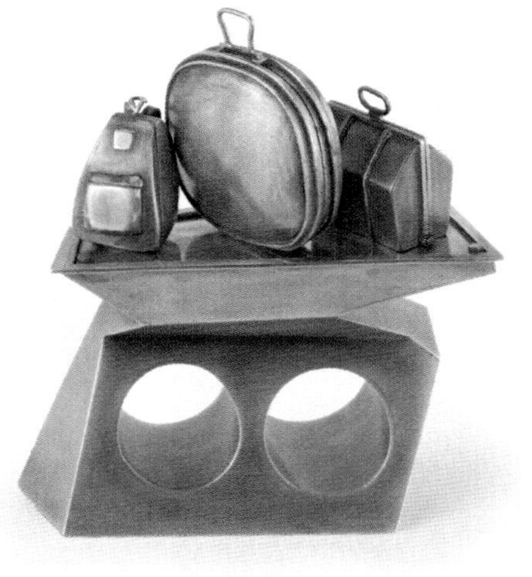

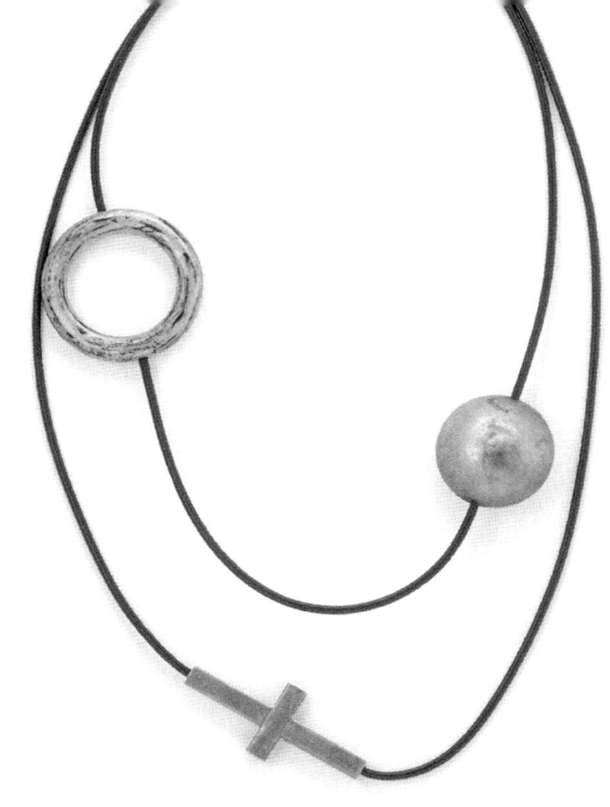

Marjorie Schick

(b. 1941, United States, active Kansas)

Brooch, 1983
Birch dowels, acrylic paint
4¾ × 5¾ × 1½ in.

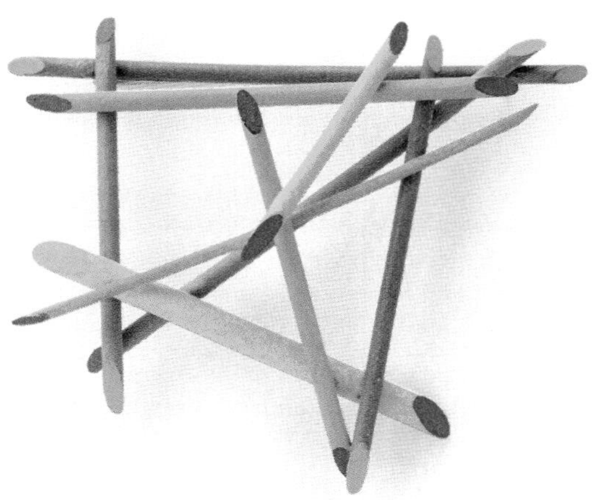

Marianne Schliwinski

(b. 1944, Germany)

***Symbol* necklace, 1986**
Silver, wood with gilding,
rubber cord
56½ in. length

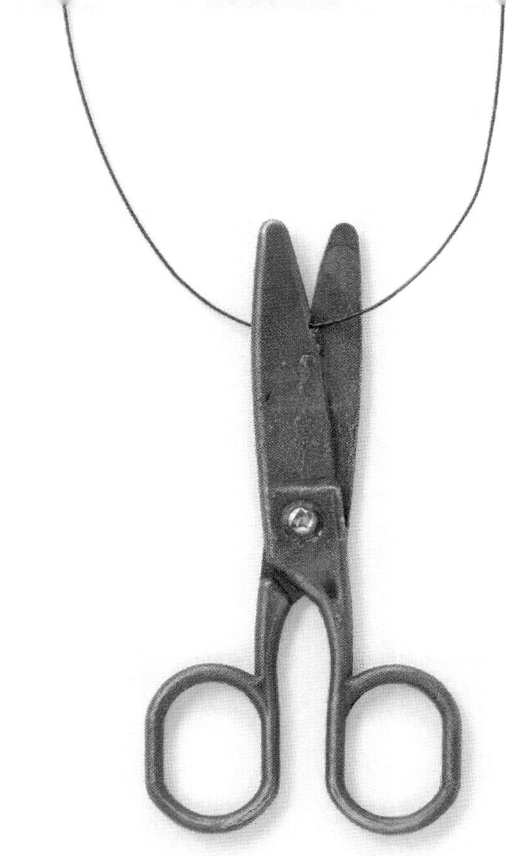

Bernhard Schobinger

(b. 1946, Switzerland)

Hanging Scissors
necklace, 1997
Silver, diamonds, Kevlar®-coated stainless-steel wire, brass
Cord: 38 in. length; pendant: 3 11⁄16 × 1 13⁄16 × 1⁄8 in.

Aufsteigender Rauchquarz
ring, 2001
Enamel on gold, cobalt alloy, diamond splinters, smoky quartz, pearl
1 7⁄8 × 1 3⁄4 × 1 1⁄4 in.

***Smoky Quartz on Countersink Nail* ring, 2010**
Gold, smoky quartz
1 7⁄16 × 1 1⁄4 × 1 1⁄4 in.

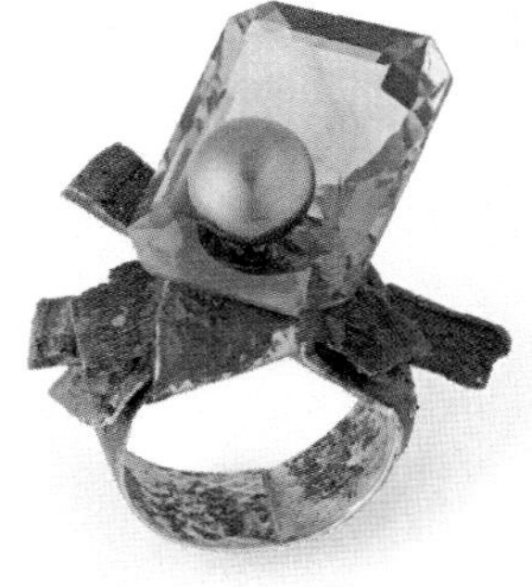

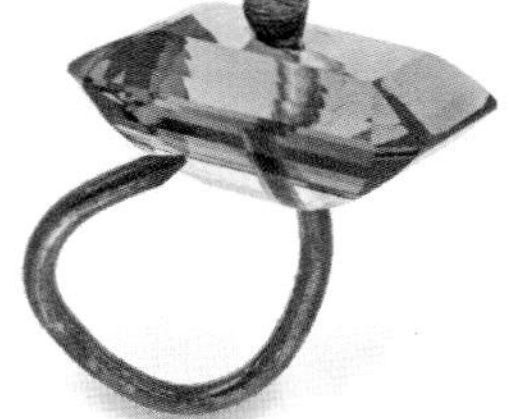

Deganit Stern Schocken

(b. 1947, Israel)

***Necklace #36*, 1983**
From the series Movement in Jewelry, Jewelry in Movement, 1981–c. 1997
Silver, gold, porcelain
Chain: 23 3/16 in. length;
pendant: 2 7/8 × 6 3/8 × 9/16 in.

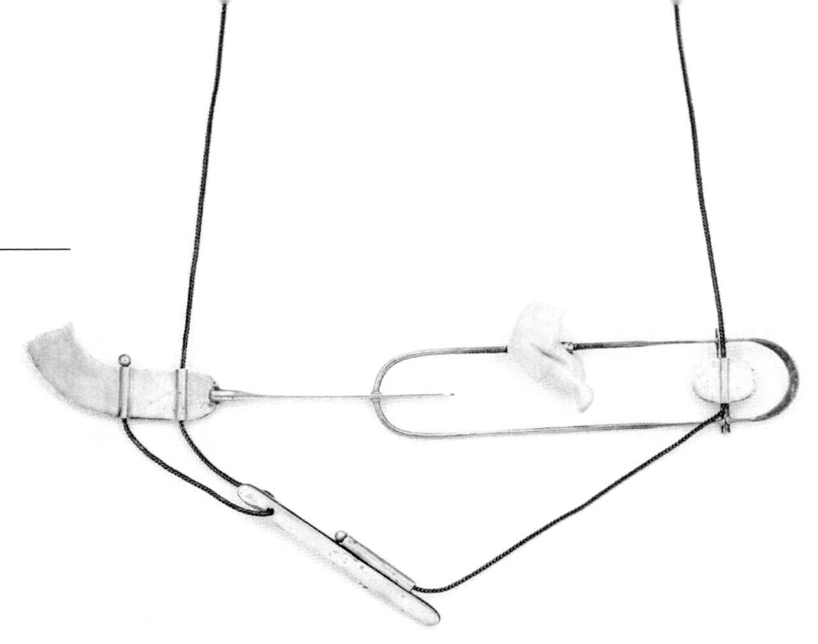

Ann Scott

(b. 1959, United States, active Pennsylvania and Washington)

***Torque*, 1982**
Screenprinted PMMA, copper alloy, silver
10 1/2 × 10 × 2 in.

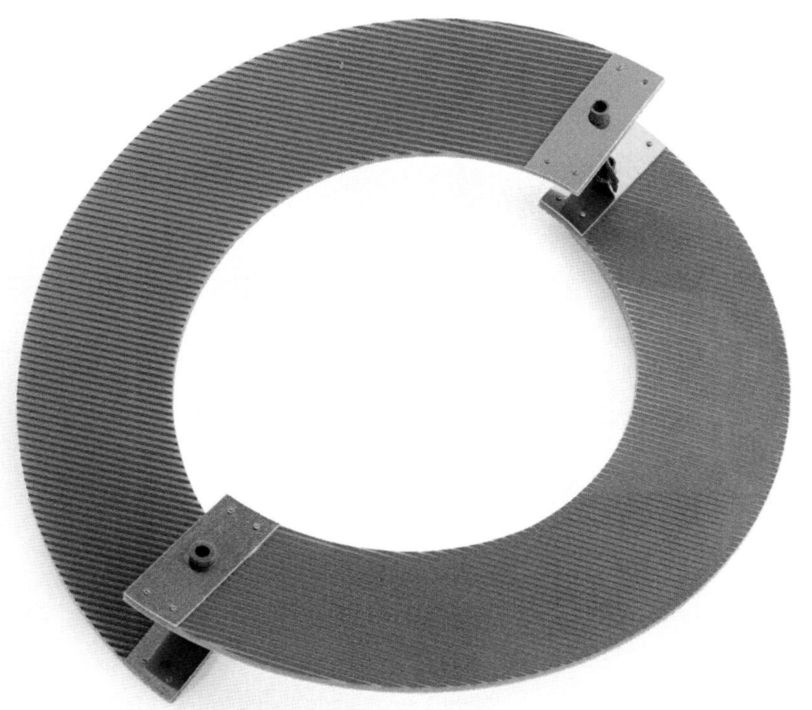

Joyce J. Scott

(b. 1948, United States, active Maryland)

PARTY **necklace, c. 1985**
Glass beads, thread
15 ¼ × 9 ¾ × ⅜ in.

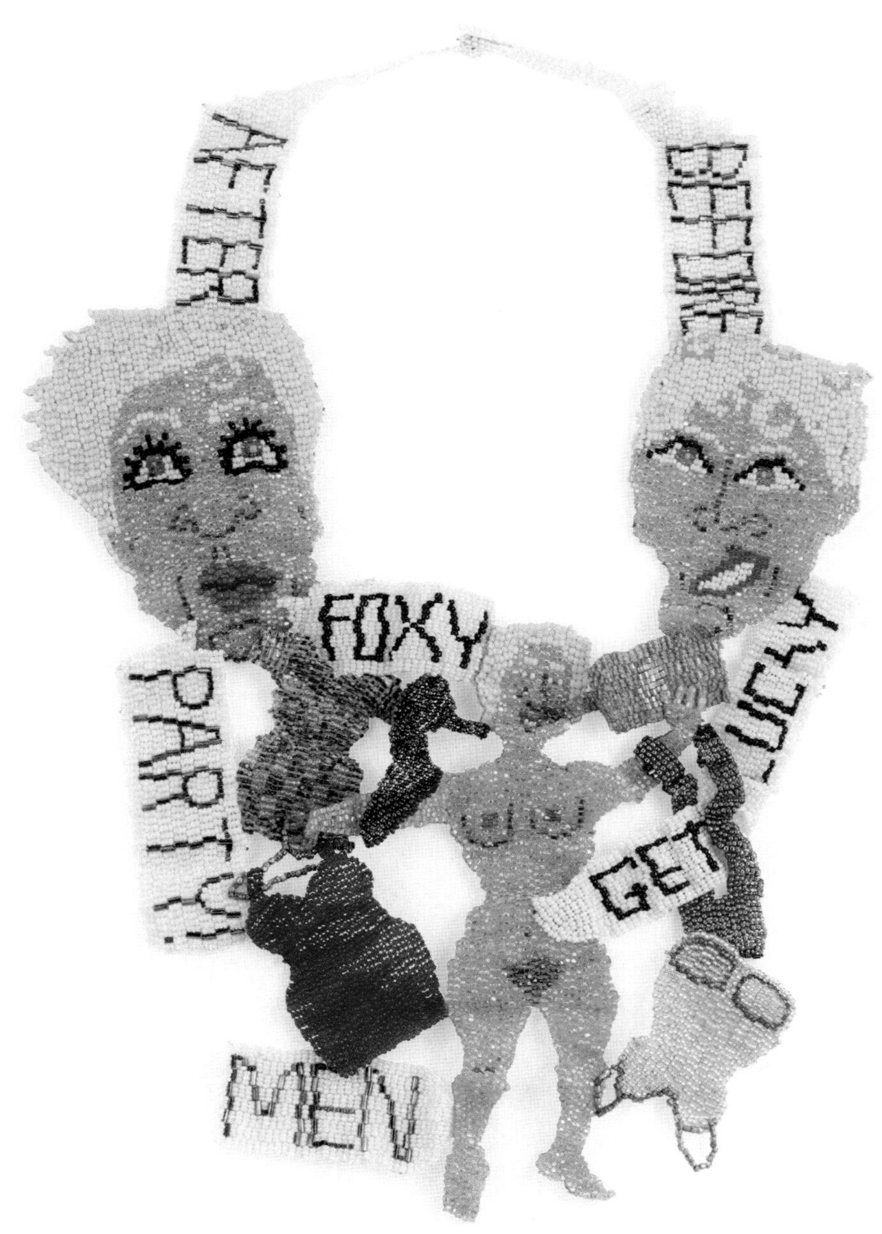

Stephan Seyffert

(b. 1960, Germany)

INVALUABLE **ring, 1992**
Silver, cubic zirconia
1⅛ × 1⅛ × ½ in.

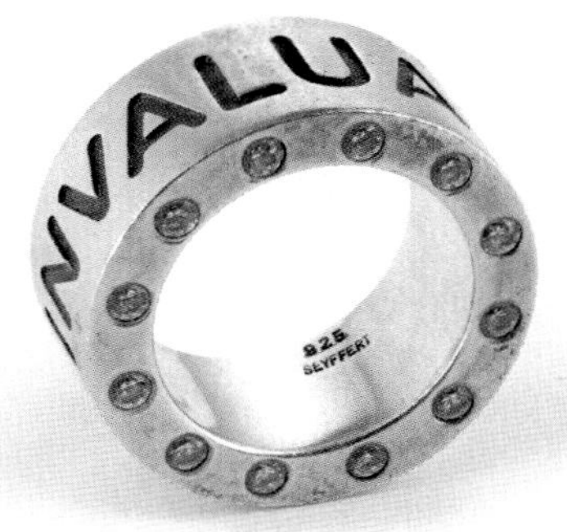

Jiří Šibor

(b. 1966, Czechoslovakia [now Czech Republic])

The United States **brooch, 1997**
Synthetic coral, epoxy resin, stainless steel
Continental US: 1¾ × 2⅞ × ½ in.; Alaska: 1 × 1 × ½ in.; Hawaii: ⅛ × 5⁄16 × ½ in.

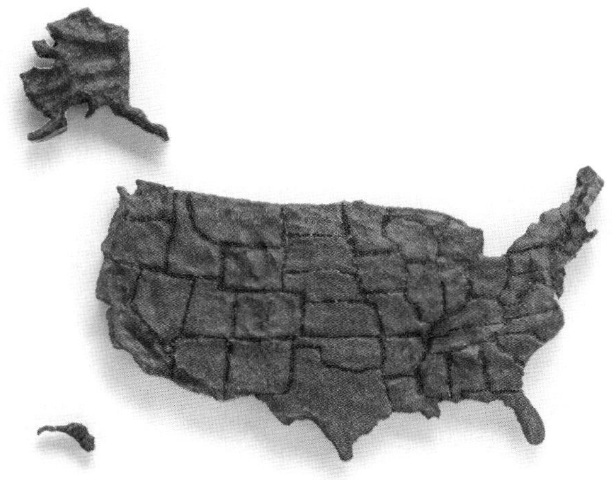

Vera Siemund

(b. 1971, Germany)

Necklace, 2006
Enamel on copper, silver
11¼ × 9¼ × 1⅛ in.

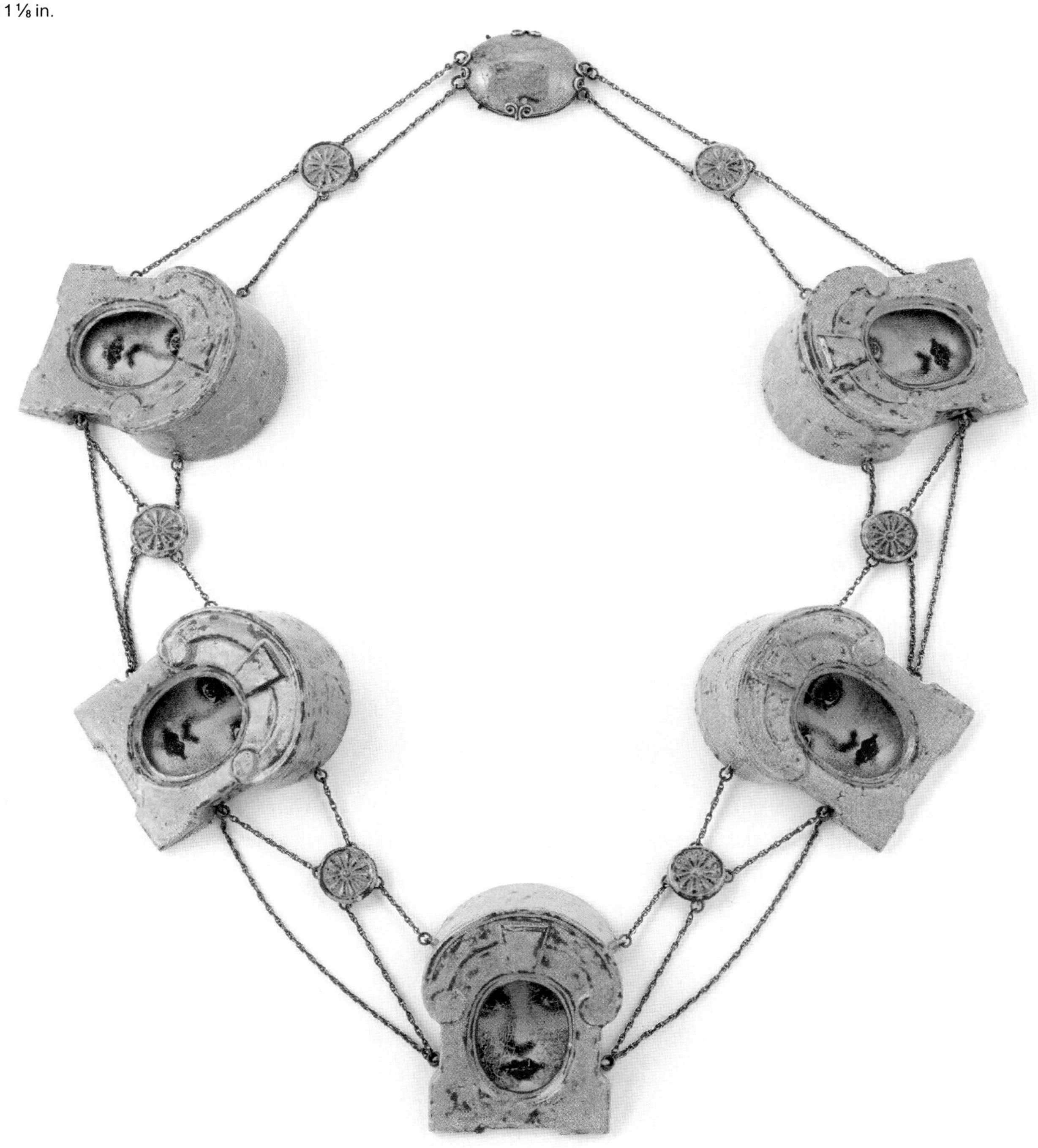

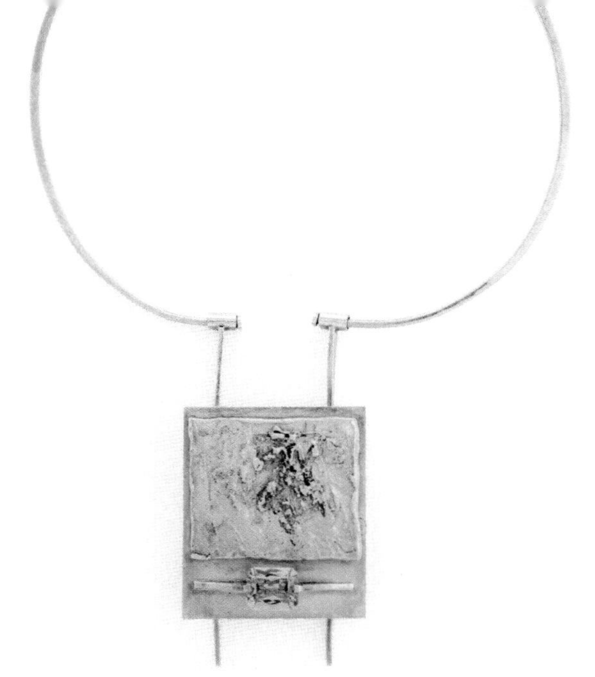

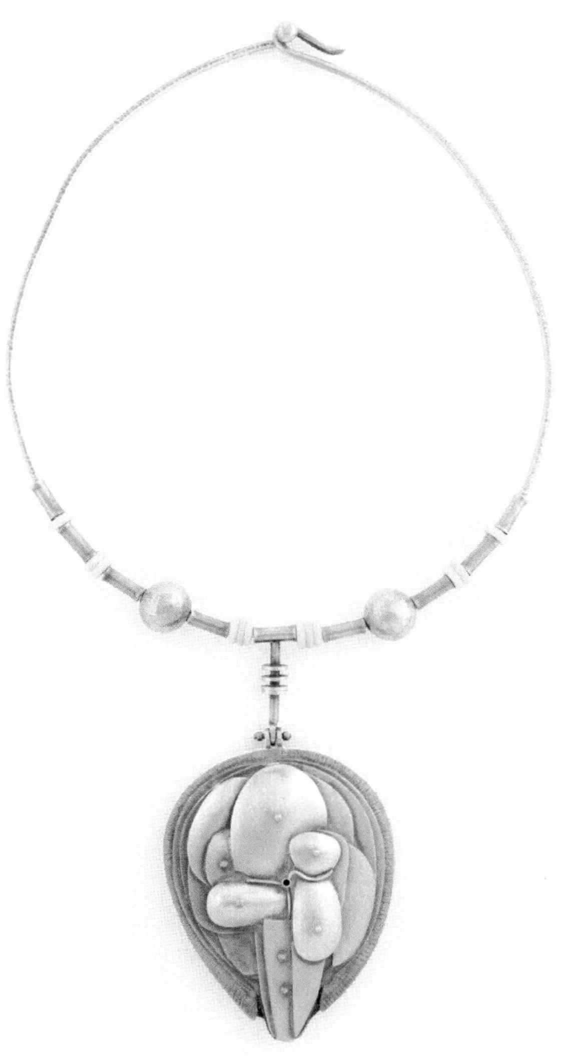

Olaf Skoogfors

(1930–1975, Sweden, active Pennsylvania)

Necklace, 1971
Gilded silver, synthetic gemstone (possibly spinel)
8 ¼ × 5 ¼ × 1 in.

Necklace, 1974
Gilded silver, glass beads
10 × 5 ¼ × ½ in.

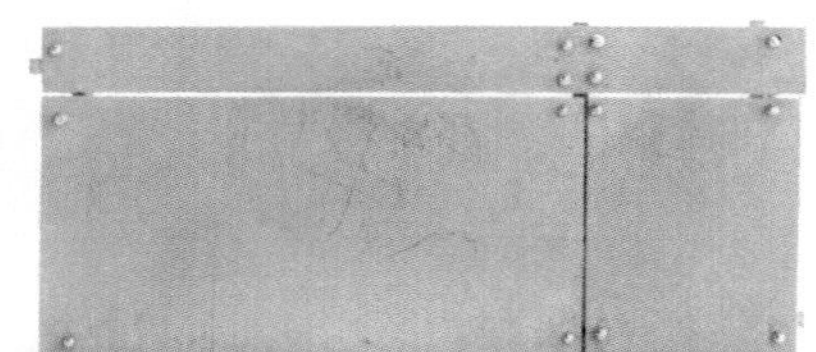

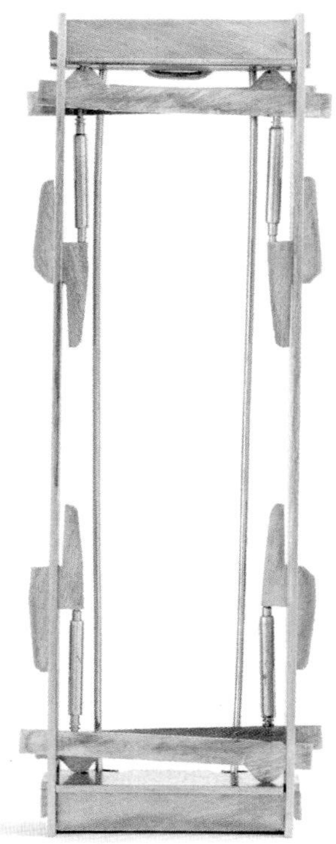

Peter Skubic

(b. 1935, Yugoslavia, active Germany and Austria)

Brooch, 1997
Gold
1 × 2⅛ × ¼ in.

Brooch, 1999
Stainless steel
3⅞ × 1⅜ × 9⁄16 in.

Brooch, 2001
Stainless steel, glass
3¼ × 1¾ × 1⅜ in.

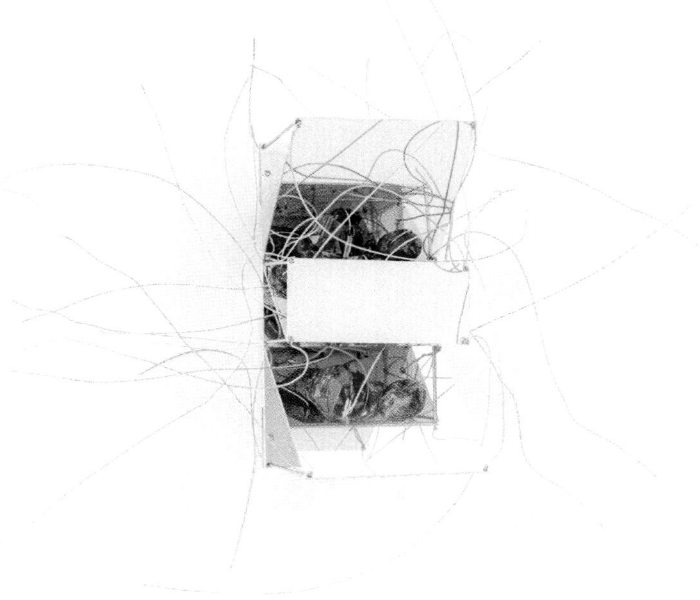

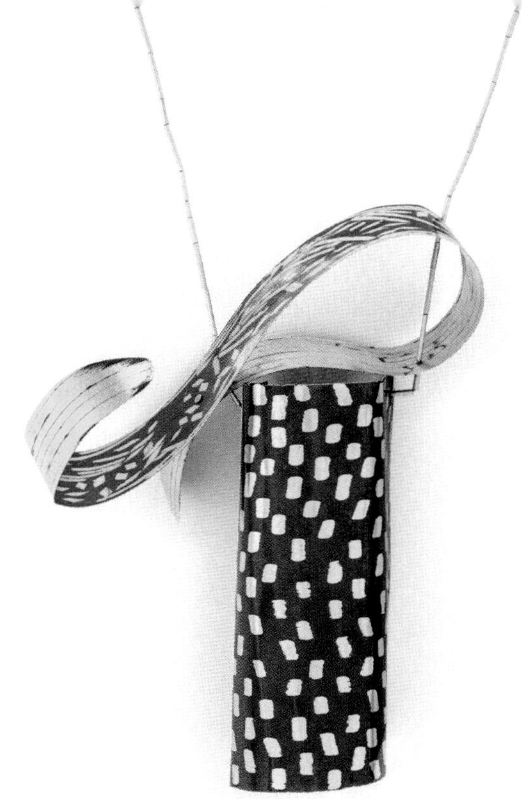

Robert Smit

(b. 1941, Netherlands)

Necklace, 1987
Varicolored gold
Cord: 33½ in. length; pendant: 4½ × 3¾ × 1¼ in.

***Bello's sister* brooch, 1993**
Gold, acrylic paint, painted pearls
5⅜ × 5¼ × ⅞ in.

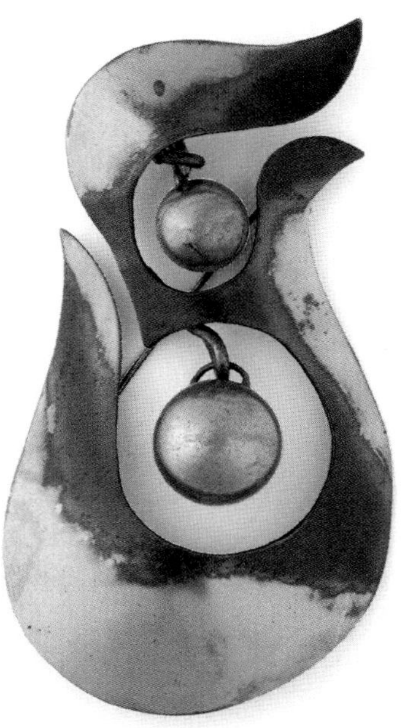

Art Smith

(1917–1982, Cuba, active New York)

Brooch, c. 1955
Copper, brass
3¾ × 2 × ½ in.

Christina Y. Smith

(b. 1951, United States, active California)

Cantaloupe Already Married
brooch, 1989
Silver
2⅝ × 2¼ × ¼ in.

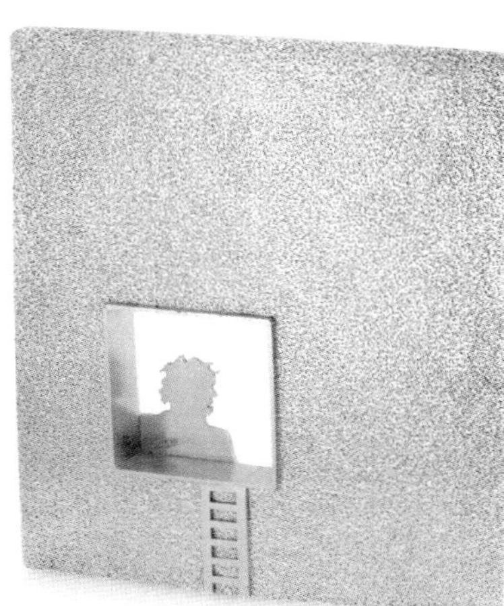

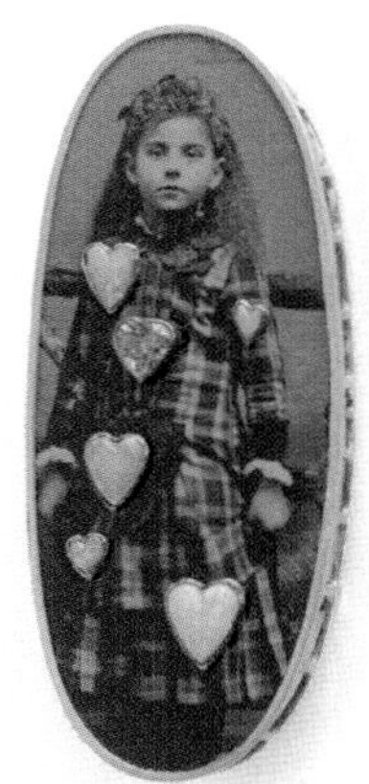

Bettina Speckner

(b. 1962, Germany)

Brooch, 2004
Ferrotype, silver, opals, aquamarine
2 7/16 × 15/16 × 3/8 in.

Brooch, 2007
Heliogravure on zinc, silver, coral
1 1/8 × 3 × 3/8 in.

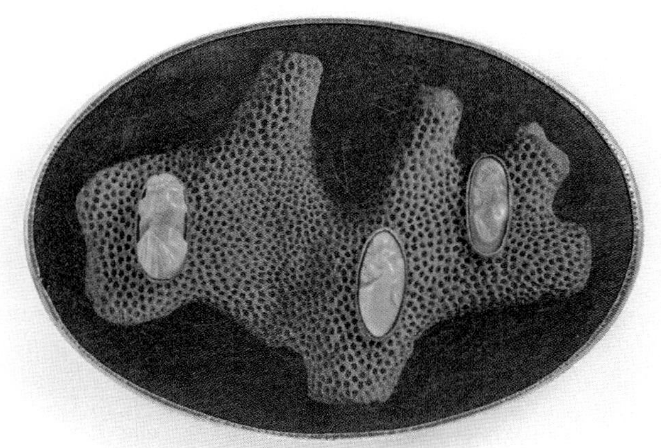

Vaughn Stubbs

(1946–2016, United States, active Pennsylvania)

***Horse and Rider* brooch, 1987**
Plastic toy, archival cardboard, acrylic paint
4 1/4 × 2 1/4 × 1 1/4 in.

***Disney Land* brooch, c. 1989**
PMMA on felt, beads, found objects
2 7/8 × 2 13/16 × 13/16 in.

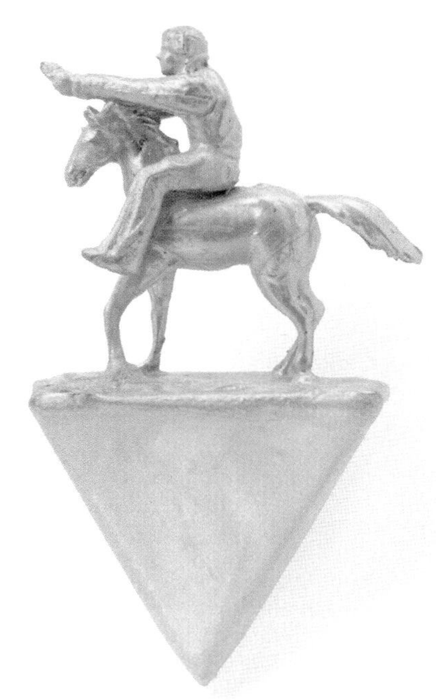

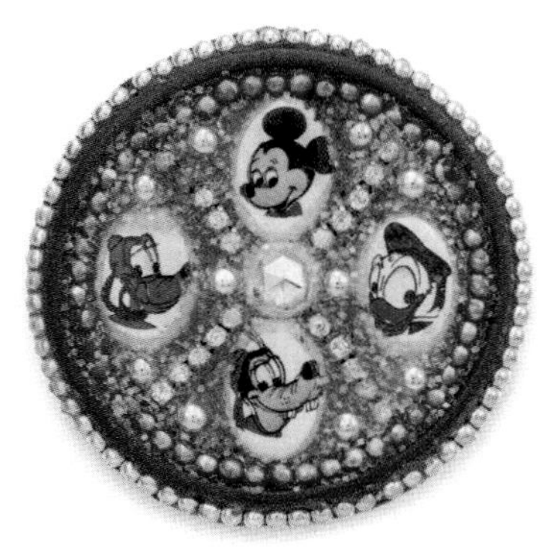

Tore Svensson

(b. 1948, Sweden)

Brooch, 1996
From the series 7 × 7 cm, 1989–99
Steel with gilding
2¾ × 2¾ × 3⁄16 in.

Necklace, 1997
Steel with gilding
12¾ × 9¼ × ¼ in.

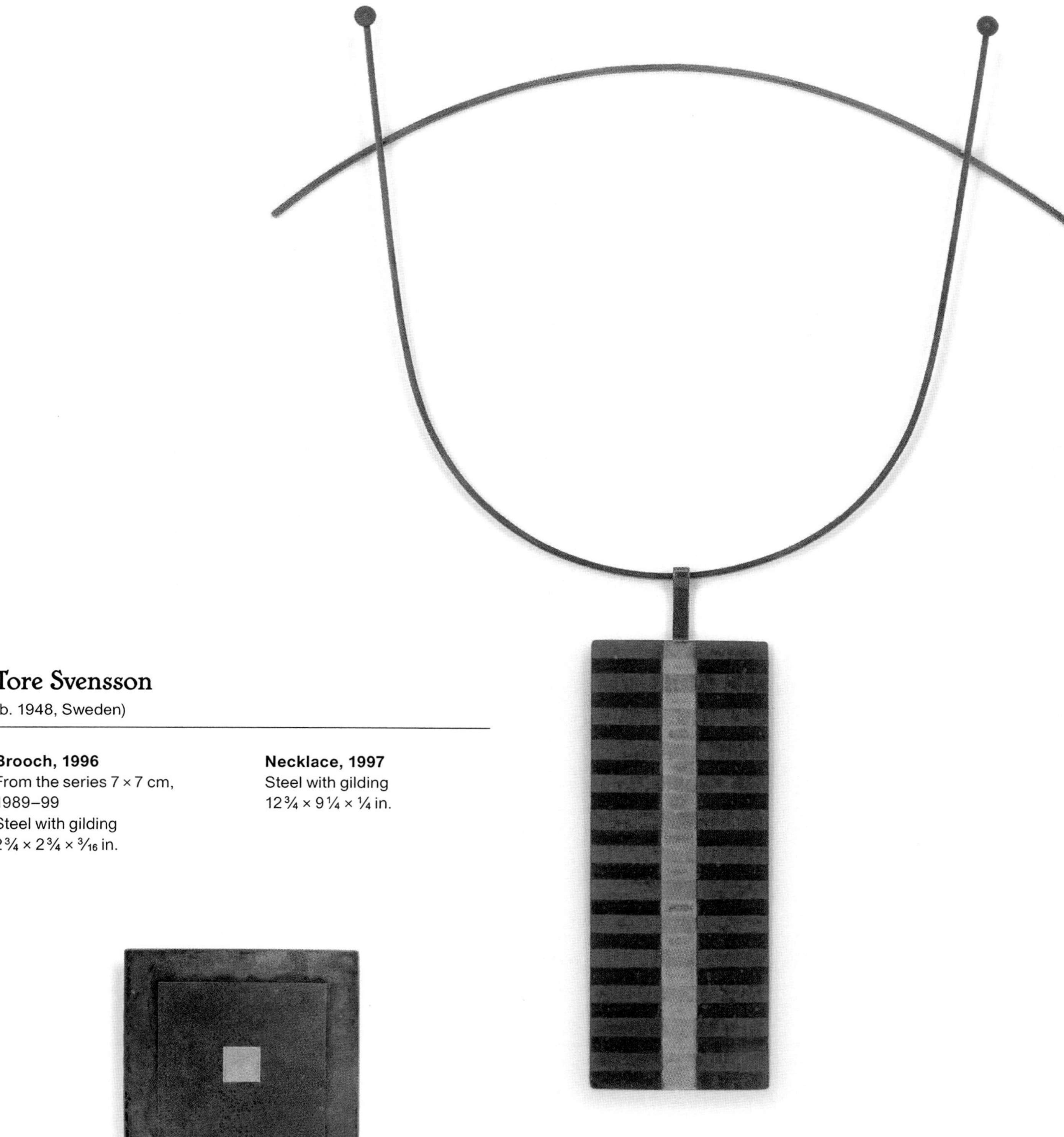

Digital Happy: Contemporary Jewelry in the Internet Age

Benjamin Lignel

Our focus should be not on emerging technologies but on emerging cultural practices.

Henry Jenkins

A growing trend in craft theory suggests that new media is not denaturing craft as much as it is reinforcing craft's existing relational and participatory turn.[1] Craft commentators have been looking at how the functions and ideologies of new media align with the ethos of craft. As a proponent of contemporary jewelry, I, too, am interested in investigating the behaviors these technologies encourage, the narratives they may imply, and the new cultural responsibilities they bring with them. Over the past twenty-five years, new media have transformed nearly all aspects of our lives. The challenge of this essay is to identify how universally accessible technologies and tools that are now part of everyday life have been appropriated by makers and have affected contemporary jewelry specifically.

The emergence and subsequent development of contemporary jewelry from the early 1960s onward overlaps with the rapid transformation of tools that we use to communicate with and about one another. In terms of cultural pollination, this means that the narratives of seminal artists' visits shaping the development of a local community, and the structures of production and transmission of knowledge these stories imply (the studio, the exhibition, the printed catalogue), are losing traction to new media communication. Information is now produced, received, evaluated, and bounced back in a multichannel textual, visual, and audio environment open to all. It does not call for the same mechanisms of physical interaction it once did. This increased capacity for communication is matched by a range of new computer-aided design

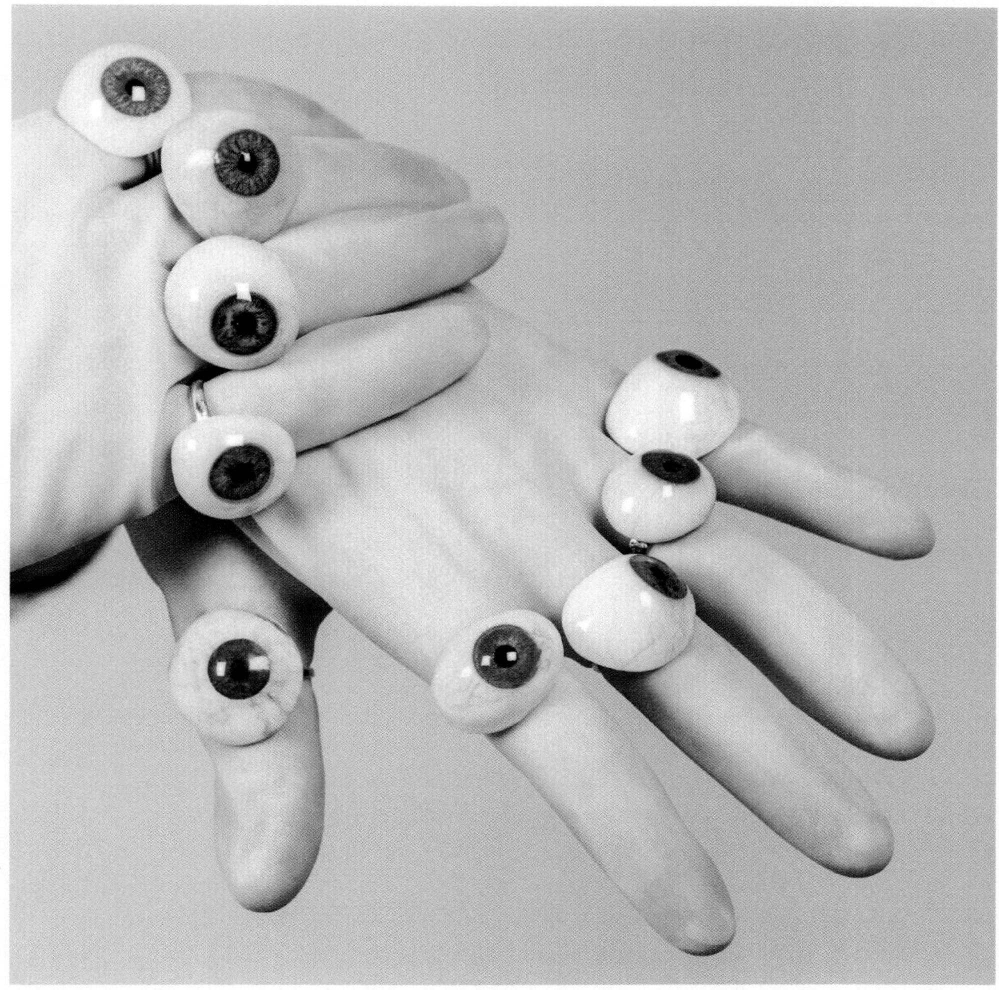

FIG. 1
Remedios Vincent, *Prosthetic* rings, 2013,
resin (antique ocular prosthesis) and bronze

and manufacturing tools. Heralded as the manufacturing equivalent of the personal-computing revolution, these tools have the potential to transform the process of making and have been adopted with some excitement by contemporary jewelers.[2] I therefore use the term "new media" to describe the digital technologies that allow the production, circulation, and transformation of cultural objects, as well as the online platforms that connect data and people.[3] This broad definition is useful because it straddles both fabrication and communication, and like any definition of rapidly changing technologies, it is fluid: "Details may change by the time you read this."[4]

I will focus here on the way jewelers, dealers, educators, and collectors surf, browse, perambulate, search, and otherwise hang out on the web by analyzing the changing nature of their relationships to information. The emergence of 3-D modeling and prototyping, and of the web as a global information resource that creates new opportunities for collaboration, will underlay this discussion. This essay will consider the gap that separates historical cultural practices from the standards that have coalesced around new conventions of data representation, access, and manipulation. I will look specifically at the circulation of information online and at dissemination strategies native to the internet. These processes have reconfigured the relative significance of online and offline activities and signal the growing alliance between the jewelry community and online networks.

To List

What I felt in the 1970s was that contemporary art jewelry was an underground movement. The artists worked separately from the buyers, and there was no contact. Nobody actually knew what was happening.

—Lasse Pahlman

The information paradigm implicitly referred to by collector Lasse Pahlman was one of sketches sent by post, of exhibition catalogues and artist monographs transiting between poles, and of seminars, lectures, and exhibitions far from home that could change a maker's practice. This was a time when the importance of encountering people, objects, or the books about them was premised on the relative insularity of each jewelry center: to exert any influence, jewelers had to travel.

And so they did. During the 1960s and 70s the contemporary jewelry community's vested interest in establishing itself both locally and internationally, and in creating opportunities for professional development, translated into a frenzy of meeting opportunities, including seminal visits later recounted as myths of origin: Vivianna Torun Bülow-Hube's departure from Sweden for France in 1956; Swiss-born Kobi Bosshard's arrival in New Zealand in 1961; or Dutch artists Gijs Bakker and Emmy van Leersum's visit to the United States in the early 1970s under the aegis of the World Crafts Council.

This was the time of snail mail, and the collector's long-distance education model was the catalogue. Primarily conceived as an inventory of formal innovations, the catalogue's classification system and organizing principle reflected the field's ongoing transformation. An early focus on the maker's country of origin and experimentation with materials and processes was reflected in the type of information included in image captions (typically artist name, place of residence, title and date of work, fabrication process and materials). A jeweler's training was invariably framed as genealogical and local—individual expression was assumed to reflect the influence of an identified mentor (typically the apprenticeship master) and of one's direct cultural environment.

Visiting artist's studios was a particular interest of collectors who, like Pahlman and his wife, Helena, started collecting in the pre-internet age and wanted to widen the scope of their holdings beyond their own country's borders. Before the fall of the Berlin Wall, however, the free circulation of goods and people in Europe was still a political dream, not a legal reality, and access could be complicated. Lasse Pahlman remembered: "I drew by hand the forms of the jewelry that I was interested in.... In those days, there were no digital cameras. You could not send a photo. If you put a letter in the post to Estonia, you never knew if it would reach the person."[5]

In 1989 the Wall collapsed. In 1991 the web, as theorized two years earlier by British computer scientist Tim Berners-Lee, became available to the public and permitted the connection and distribution of information across a network of machines (the internet). Then, in 1999, Susan Sarantos, a silversmith based in Newport, Rhode Island, launched a website called Metalcyberspace.[6] It was little more than a hyperlinked list, but to this author living in France, it provided unprecedented access to a global directory of makers and galleries. Sarantos assumed that collectors and makers engaged in the tedious work of gathering information on international jewelry would eventually come across her website. A small drawn portrait of her, reproduced in white on the page's black background, suggested a benevolent, vaguely witchy figure, and heralded, some years before it became mainstream, the web's function as identity-mixer.[7]

To Publish

The computer was my window to the world of jewelry. I am very inquisitive and a visual person. Over many years I slowly learned and developed my eye... I bought pieces solely on the basis of how they looked to me "online." It was great to wander the world in search of objects. From the Western Hemisphere, Europe to Australia to Thailand, I let my fingers do the walking.

—Lois Boardman

Until the 1990s, galleries were the main avenue for learning about current jewelry developments. Catering to collectors, makers, and curators, they also produced modest catalogues extolling the education and exhibition history of the artists they represented. Galleries were, in effect, the sole distributors of objects made in a network of studios more or less local to them. Artists who produced their own printed matter were rare, and galleries shared a form of information monopoly with a few specialized printed periodicals such as *Metalsmith* and *Art Aurea*. But at the end of the decade, two new sites—one American, the other Catalan—signaled the shift from print to semi-independent, professionalized online information sources, and radically changed the way collectors like Lois Boardman would continue to educate themselves.

Art Jewelry Forum (AJF), launched in 1997 by a group of like-minded jewelry collectors in the United States, was primarily conceived as an organization to educate its constituents through direct immersion in local and foreign jewelry centers. It also functioned as a self-aware incubator for the field's cultural stakeholders: curators, historians, and the institutions for which they work. Collectors traveled in small groups to learn about and buy work, and quarterly reports on foreign expeditions were sent to members. The organization soon saw the importance of expanding its mandate, however, and wanted to make the information it gathered available to a wider audience. In 2000 AJF launched its first website, and in 2010 it appointed New Zealand craft historian Damian Skinner as its first editor, thereby recasting itself as a global platform with a mission to "help [its] readership... build knowledge, understanding, and a critical appreciation of contemporary art jewelry."[8] AJF (for which I now serve as editor) currently publishes online an average of sixteen articles, interviews, or reviews per month.

If the art magazine served as AJF's primary model, Catalan platform Klimt02 was initially conceived as a community-wide information board and creative showcase. It was a place to "find information about contemporary jewelry,"[9] as cofounder Leo Caballero explained, and it initially did so by posting captioned images of the work of its members along with a wealth of information about exhibitions, workshops, competitions, and publications happening internationally. Caballero and his fellow cofounder Amador Bertomeu gathered in a single place information about multiple events in the field, achieving what was technically unfeasible for Sarantos's Metalcyberspace: they built a community through connected information. "At the beginning of Klimt02 [in 2002–03], the idea was to create a network, a community, to build it. There wasn't a community, it was more tribal then," Caballero said.[10]

Both organizations can be seen as publishers and they still emulate the "one-to-many" model of legacy media: a sole agent, acting as content commissioner, selects and/or produces content that is then distributed to its readership. Neither platform is without filters, and while both allow users to comment, they act as gatekeepers of the information they publish. Moreover, they categorize that information according to systems that they themselves have created.

Klimt02 and AJF are currently the most visited online platforms to learn about contemporary studio jewelry, whether a user is new to the field or a serious collector. The collectors interviewed for this essay all tended to have built strong relationships with galleries before the founding of the internet and although now less "gallery dependent" for their jewelry education, they continue to use them as respected sources of information on jewelers' creative development and to purchase work.[11] For American collector and AJF chair Susan Cummins, it is out of loyalty toward a business model that she knows is precarious,[12] while Lois Boardman values the decades-long friendship she has forged with someone like gallerist Helen Drutt.[13] Collector Ron Porter prefers to rely on the strong relationships he has built with dealers over the years, and welcomes the counsel and occasional spontaneous suggestions they offer. All of them recognize the internet as an invaluable place for research, however. As Porter explained, "Never has there been such a wealth of information available to anyone who wants it at the touch of a key.... I might start with looking at the use of silk in Korean jewelry and end up with exposure to an exceptional new talent using silk in an entirely new way. It doesn't get much better than this educationally."[14]

To Circulate

Blogging is the way in which we get to complicate the world again.

—David Weinberger

Starting around 2005, a web-surfing culture that was predominantly nomadic started producing tentative forms of cultural real estate: images were harvested and recirculated on Pinterest and Instagram and posted as chatbacks on Facebook. As a result, makers, commentators, and to a lesser extent, collectors, began to respond to new media content in kind, with information gathering and transmission of their own. This evolution is described in media theory as the advent of Web 2.0, and the way it works is at the core of how web users handle information today.

Web 2.0 can be described through the various technical changes that took place at the beginning of this century. The emergence of improved search algorithms, user-generated content, and tagging systems, and the rise of simple, user-friendly blogging templates like WordPress put a much greater share of the distribution and organization of information into the hands of web users. Later in the decade, a number of contemporary jewelry blogs were launched: *Mar de Color Rosa*, under the helm of Montserrat Lacomba (Spain, 2008); followed by Marianne Gassier's *Bijou Contemporain* (France, 2010); Nichka Marobin's *The Morning Bark* (Italy, 2011); and Kellie Riggs's *Greater than or Equal To* (Italy, 2011). These are just a few, and their numbers pale next to the myriad personal Flickr, Tumblr, Pinterest, and Instagram accounts devoted to contemporary studio jewelry.

Putting undue emphasis on technology, however, misses the point of Web 2.0: it was less a technological revolution than what Tim O'Reilly described as a "tipping point."[15] Its importance, according to media specialists Francis Pisani and Dominique Piotet, depended upon the fact that the web was not supported by "major technological innovation.... The technology exists, it is accessible to everyone, and it is cheap."[16] Pisani and Piotet make much of the fact that the "low knowledge barrier"[17] of Web 2.0 was fundamental to the massive appropriation of early platforms such as Myspace by people engaged in creative pursuits. The same argument explains why, ten years later, a large percentage of jewelry makers have their own websites and engage in a variety of online activities through multiple new media platforms.

One example of a maker taking advantage of this user-driven web culture—and of a single artist using multiple platforms for specific purposes—is Remedios Vincent, who started making jewelry as a form of occupational therapy in 2011. Her practice involves the assemblage of antique, often anthropomorphic, found objects (fig. 1) repurposed into jewelry that she describes as "infamous accessories" (tortured, Frankenstein-like collages that are "made to dislike"[18]). Fiercely independent, she does not participate in any public jewelry events and functions largely outside of the contemporary jewelry market. Vincent, a typical "webactor," is a useful example because of the unusual clarity of her investment online: she actively manages five different platforms simultaneously for specific and—very distinct—purposes, which in turn allows her to maintain complete control over the dissemination of her existing work, while building archives of her work in progress. She has a blog and a Tumblr account for posting and commenting on visual arts (both called *Flores en el Ático*); a private Facebook account linked to her jewelry activities; another Tumblr where she inventories parts and supplies used in her work; and an Instagram account to document her jewelry production. (She uses Pinterest infrequently to collect pictures of alternative jewelry and unconventional objects, much like one would a scrapbook.)[19]

Although Vincent is perhaps more active online than most, her multiplatform approach is not rare, and it highlights a few characteristics shared by many of her peers' virtual presences: evidence of hours spent on unpaid work managing one's online presence, a self-selecting readership that engages directly with the jeweler, and a relationship premised on a virtuous circle of exchange embodied in the idea that, as Nichka Marobin explained, "The more you give, the more you get back."[20] Like art historian and fellow blogger Marobin, Vincent channels online her desire to find an audience outside of academic or print media. But this is probably less about being "alternative" than about being self-sufficient.[21] Both Vincent and Marobin use benchmarks of professionalism online that are derived from legacy-media practice; Vincent does not post anything if she can't identify its author, and Marobin provides a bibliography in every post.

Blogs exemplify the way online users are redefining publishing media ("one to many") into circulation media ("many to many"): part of their content is "grabbed" from elsewhere, enriched by their own comments and content, and then reposted on networked platforms that further propel its circulation.[22] Each platform has its codes and readership, and each has a unique way of eliciting meaning from the varied combination of images and text. In general, and in shorthand terms, we could say that it is associative on Pinterest, proclamatory on Facebook, accumulative on Tumblr and Flickr, and discursive on blogs.

This digital environment can divest images of work of the authorial markers that surround and "protect" them in a book, gallery, or museum; images can easily drift away from their source, losing some of their provenance information. They may have neither duration nor origin, and details about authorship, modes of fabrication, or intended function can be lost (although these can often be inferred).

Having fewer coordinates to navigate by does not mean no coordinates exist, however, and one of the most compelling arguments put forward by Pisani and Piotet is that we now consume information that is continuously enriched by the very networks that relay it. Webactors like Vincent or Marobin upload proprietary or aggregated content onto a shared platform. As they tag web objects, they overlay existing classification values with categories of their own. As they share these tags, they participate in an increasingly complex system of circulating information that carries a load of metadata on its back (where the images came from, who liked them, etcetera). This data, Pisani and Piotet note, is "more intelligent thanks to the tools [used by the webactors to assign them value], and more still thanks to the network effect that these tools generate."[23] In its wake, the art-historical notion of cultural objects as genealogical—a perception premised on authorship and artistic influence—is losing ground to a constant recombination of information according to evolving affinities, a perception premised on kinship and viewer endorsement.

To Share

The evolution [toward Web 2.0] invites us to lend more importance to relationships, to flux, to what is being exchanged, to social networks that articulate themselves on a technical network, of which images inspired by plumbing or car travel only give a very imperfect idea.

—Francis Pisani & Dominique Piotet

The rise of blogging is an important, but partial, aspect of our changing online activity: it marks the rise of webactors but does not tell us how networked relationships increasingly govern data management, nor does it say anything about the mutually reinforcing logic of online user participation and information dissemination.[24] In effect, social networking sites are reinventing and spurring how artists' work is shared with other members of the community and the wider world.

In October 2014 someone in the Netherlands chose Donna Greenberg, a Jersey City, New Jersey–based fine artist specializing in polymer clay and metal, as a nominee for #ArtJewelryChallenge, a Facebook dissemination project. The rules of the challenge were simple: post a piece of your own work on your Facebook profile page every day for five consecutive days. Meanwhile, nominate another artist on each of those five days. A nominee then "would also mention the name, or 'tag' the artist/friend that nominated them."[25] Greenberg picked three artists working in metal and mixed media; realizing that polymer clay was absent from the challenge, she selected two polymer artists for her last choices. She recalled that over the next few weeks, "There were dozens, then hundreds, of pieces of jewelry showing up on my timeline daily, all with my name attributed to [them]. At one point I counted over four hundred jewelry posts on my page in one day. By the time the challenge began to die down after January 2015, thousands of pieces of jewelry [had] passed through my page."

One aspect of the challenge was particularly significant: the system of recommendation relied upon an individual's goodwill to post, label, share work, and then nominate five other artists. The beauty of it was that friendly co-optation—as opposed to juried selection—naturally encouraged choosing more, not fewer, people, thus giving lesser-known makers a chance to show their work to, and get feedback from, the community. The great achievement of the "challenge," the initial goal of which was to "fill up Facebook with art jewelry," was to turn selection into an outward-moving, inclusive phenomenon. Ultimately, #ArtJewelryChallenge created connections where before there had been none (in particular between the polymer community and the wider contemporary jewelry world) by leveraging two mutually reinforcing phenomena: jewelers' tendency to think of themselves as a community and social media's ability to channel individual, voluntary contributions into network effects.

To Manufacture

The prognostication of a coming revolution in art jewelry is credible because of the development of new tools capable of creating a similar climate of access in the design, manufacturing, and distribution of objects.

—Gabriel Craig

A brief history of digital fabrication starts with the invention of computing technology; tracks the development of personal computing and the introduction of 3-D modeling tools (computer-aided design or CAD) into design and architecture colleges in the late 1980s; follows the popularization of 3-D prototyping and manufacturing machines between 2005 and 2010; and reaches a high point with the launch of large 3-D models databases such as Thingiverse, and of 3-D modeling software such as SketchUp, Countersketch, Tinkercad, or 123DMake. This story follows roughly the same technical arc as image or graphic-design technologies: the products of an analog technology are mimicked by personal-computer software, resulting in the wider public's participation in an economy hitherto restricted to professionally trained designers using expensive

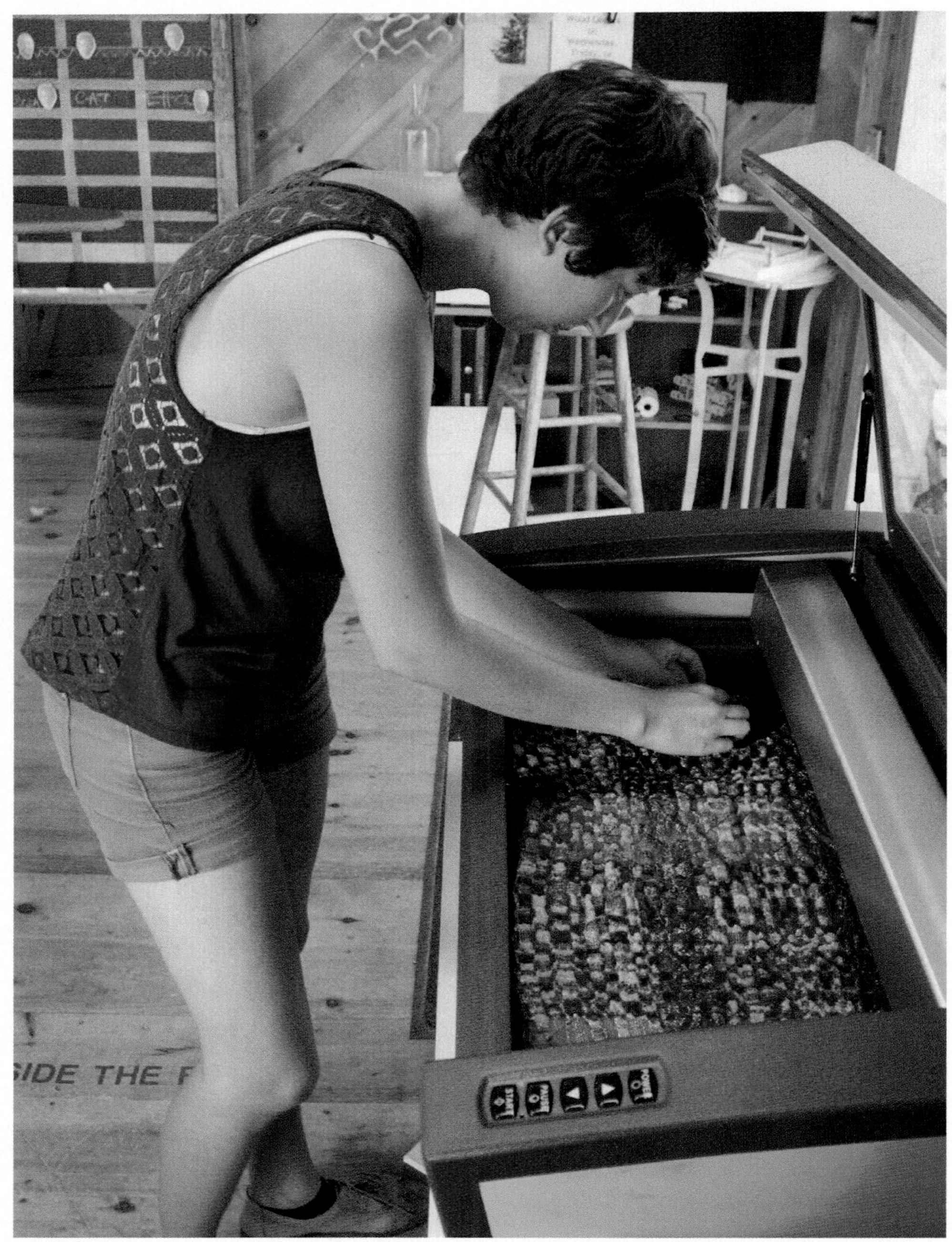

FIG. 2
A student at Haystack Mountain School of Crafts in Deer Isle, Maine, cuts vinyl on a laser cutter in the school's digital fabrication laboratory (fab lab)

machines. And it has the potential to democratize production in the same way that the internet has democratized publishing and the release of music and video content.

Manufacturers of 3-D prototyping machines and modeling software are keen to present their technology as both accessible and revolutionary: computer-aided manufacture (CAM), they say, will usher in an era of personal fabrication and users will cease to rely on outsourced—read "overseas"—manufacturing. Instead, people will just print things at home after modifying them to suit their specific needs and tastes. The market has already anticipated users' reluctance to actually print "at home," and has increased accessibility with a variety of services that make it possible to outsource one-off and batch production and allow on-demand printing. However, those visions of manufacturing self-sufficiency and mechanization of production do not mean quite the same thing for jewelers as for the general public.[26] Jewelers and other craft practitioners have an enormous advantage on the rest of the population in that they do not need to reinvent themselves as makers: for them, digital-manufacturing technology simply offers another set of tools that they may decide to use.

In May 2015 Haystack Mountain School of Crafts then-director Stuart Kestenbaum and Neil Gershenfeld, director of MIT's Center for Bits and Atoms, spoke at the Society of North American Goldsmiths (SNAG) conference in Boston about a miniature fabrication laboratory (fab lab) that they installed at Haystack in Deer Isle, Maine (fig. 2).[27] A fab lab essentially functions as a technological open bar offering various digital modeling and manufacturing tools and providing plenty of opportunities for trial and error. It allows an exploration of multiple techniques that is similar to bench-based iterative experimentation. While Gershenfeld suggested that the fab lab's model and vision hinge on maintaining a "low technological barrier" (like the low knowledge barrier of Web 2.0), craftspeople who have engaged with the technologies insist that mastering digital software—if one is to go beyond the simple tweaking of given parameters—requires time, experimentation, and often a different skill set than that honed for manual making. As digital-manufacturing specialist Arthur Hash (fig. 3) has stressed, learning to use this equipment expertly, "much like mastering a craft, takes years."[28]

If fab labs' promise of personal production as an exciting alternative to industrial manufacture overlaps with craft's own agenda of self-sufficiency, this socioeconomic narrative seems less important to designers than digital manufacture's impact on the process of making itself. Jessica Rosenkrantz and Jesse Louis-Rosenberg, who founded and lead Nervous System, a design studio in Somerville, Massachusetts, describe their work as employing "computer simulation to generate designs and digital fabrication to realize products"[29] (fig. 4). Louis-Rosenberg points out (in reference to projects like Robohand, in which engineers around the world collaborate on open-source designs for prosthetics) that the digital nature of computation data lends itself to collaboration in ways that studio techniques do not: "The nature of the language we use—which is essentially mathematical—means that disparate people with different

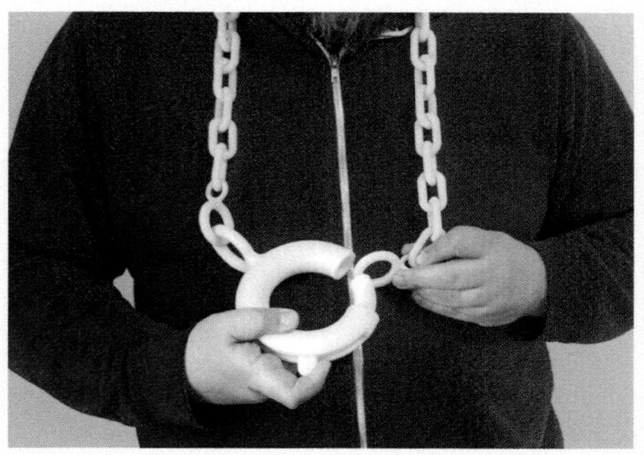

FIG. 3
Arthur Hash, *Clasp* necklace, 2013, ABS plastic and stainless steel, 26 × 12 × 1¼ in. (66 × 30.5 × 3.2 cm), collection of the artist

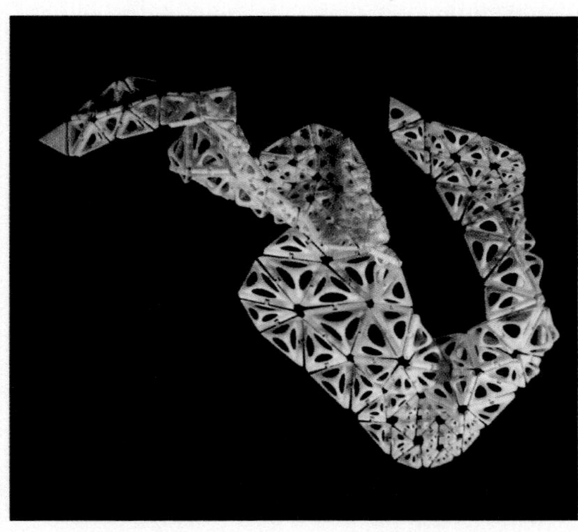

FIG. 4
Jessica Rosenkrantz and Jesse Louis-Rosenberg, Nervous System, *Tetra Kinematics 175-N* necklace, 3-D-printed nylon, 2013, length: 17 in. (43.2 cm), collection of the artists

backgrounds (and often living far apart from one another) can easily work on the same project at the same time. Traditional techniques, by contrast, have a higher access barrier and are sequential: someone fabricates this, then someone else adds to it, etcetera."[30] This statement underscores one of the paradoxes of new media: technology creates distance, in the sense that it mediates direct contact both between people and between people and things, but it also provides platforms and languages that allow far easier transmission, and therefore greater connection, between people.

To Engage

The logic of the art world and the logic of new media are exact opposites. The first is based [on] the romantic idea of authorship which assumes a single author; the notion of a unique... art object; and the control over the distribution of such objects which takes place through a set of exclusive places: galleries, museums, actions. The second privileges the existence of potentially numerous copies, [an] infinitely large number of different states of the same work, author-user symbiosis... the collective, collaborative authorship, and network distribution (which bypasses the art-system distribution channels).

—Lev Manovich

Collaborative and participatory models in craft have surged in the last ten years and encompass an extremely broad array of interactions, both on- and offline. This surge has ideological origins in the Happenings of the 1960s and tends to reframe the craft notion of usership into the fine-art notion of participation.[31] These offline endeavors have since spawned a number of native online projects that similarly embrace the participatory renaissance in craft and tend to use the web to maximize social media's ability to communicate, document, and disseminate projects.[32]

Like their 1960s forebears, these participatory projects are structured as calls for action and usually follow three distinct phases: the circulation of a participation protocol; a form of collective interaction or transaction; and a representation of activity in the social sphere (whether on- or offline). Also like their forebears, participatory actions assume there are disenfranchised communities and aim to enroll these communities in collective acts of creativity, using craft objects

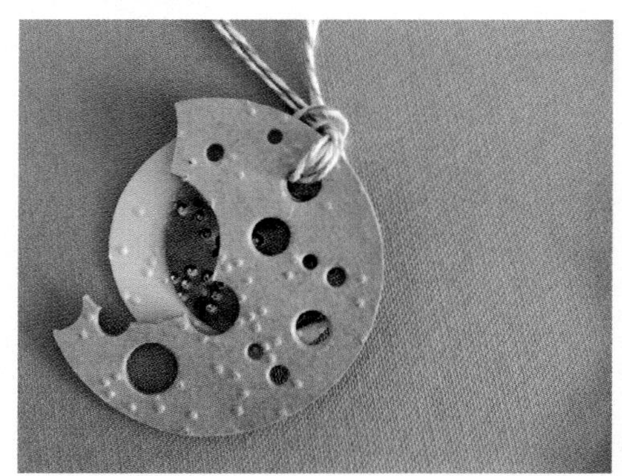

a

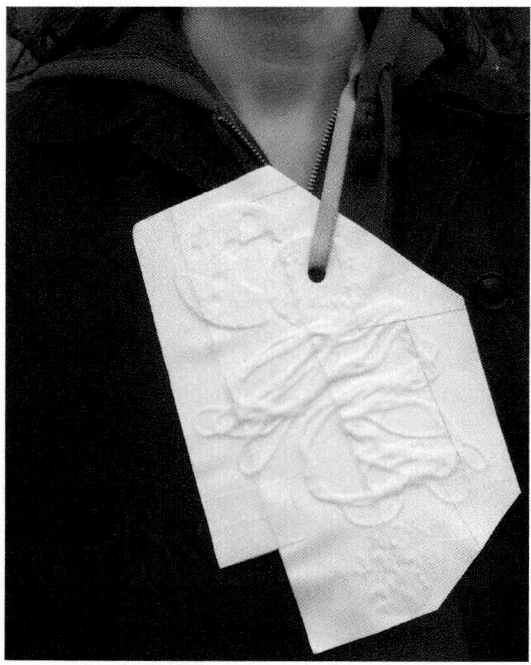

b

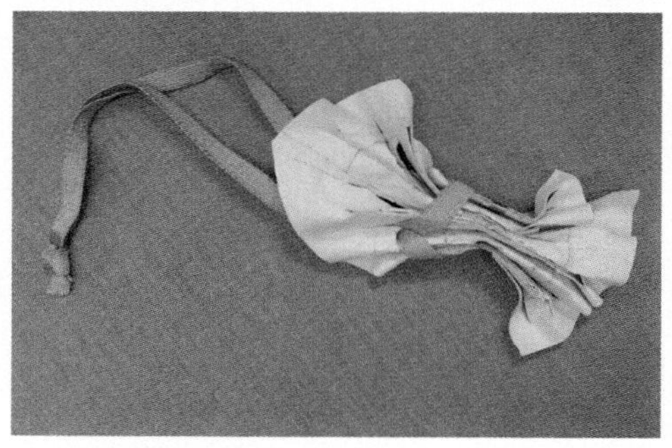

c

FIG. 5a–c
Ojalà Itinerante, *Piece Number 10*. Seed piece made by Alejandra Koreck (a), 2015, paper, cotton string, metal sheet. Koreck handed the piece to Sayumi Yokouchi during the Ojalà Itinerante exhibition at Café Clara during Munich Jewelry Week; first modification by Yokouchi (b), 2015, cotton tape and elastic ribbon. Yokouchi handed the piece to Erin Daily in the Brooklyn Botanic Garden; second modification by Daily (c), 2015, cotton tape, elastic ribbon, copper, elastic cord

or processes as activators. Unlike their predecessors, however, participatory activists today can rely on the serendipitous alignment of their ultimate goal (loosely defined as "outreach efficiency") and some recent technology-driven phenomena, in particular the rise of self-selected online communities that can immediately engage with specific protocols, along with the rise of user-generated content[33] and the attendant renaissance of the amateur.[34]

Ojalà Itinerante, a relatively modest project launched in 2014 by jewelers Patricia Galluci, Sabina Tiemroth, and Alejandra Koreck, illustrates the potential of collaborative authorship in the craft world.[35] Based on the Surrealist concept of the exquisite corpse, the project invites participants to rework, and then pass on for further alteration, a piece of jewelry made by one of the organizers (fig. 5a–c). Participation is free and does not require any special skills. The organizers state that they "emphasize the process, not the result of the finished pieces."[36] The blind faith required to send your work to a relative stranger is represented on Ojalà's Facebook page by a plus sign between the multiple authors of each piece. This project, like many others of its kind, uses social media itself as its primary form of documentation. Images of work in progress, bookended by a list of rules and group pictures of participants in various locations around the world, bear testimony to the global ambition of the project, much as a visual diary would. The organizers function less as artists than as *gamemasters*—a term borrowed from role-playing scenarios and online video gaming—that better describes their dual role as narrators and managers of a short-lived but intense bout of *play*. Participants similarly become *players*, less concerned with individual recognition than with collective action. Like in role-playing, this form of interaction both acknowledges the distinction between master and players and encourages rotation: today's organizers will be tomorrow's players in an endlessly reconfigured list of participants.[37] In this way, new media is providing jewelers with secondary, career-supporting activities as producers, organizers, promoters, commentators, and information aggregators.[38]

To Take Responsibility

We continue to perceive and represent technological innovations much as we did almost 150 years ago: as agents of social change, for better or worse. The climate surrounding 3-D prototyping technology or digital communication is markedly different, however, from that surrounding the introduction of the telephone or automobile: twenty-first-century culture embraces technological innovation, and whatever resistance these technologies may have elicited at first seems to be dissipating in the face of several incontrovertible arguments that underscore the craft field's enthusiastic adoption of new media: the promise of self-sufficiency; the possibility of grassroots diversity through equal access;[39] simple and powerful tools for community building and audience outreach; and the promise of empowerment through participation.

The rise of webactors and the capacity for personal manufacture have begun to challenge the territorial distribution of roles within the field. Physical places once associated with specific activities (the studio, the gallery, the museum, the newsroom) are merging online under the aegis of multitasking individuals such as Marobin, Lacomba, or Vincent, as well as Leonor Hipólito, Zoe Brand, and Mah Rana. It is tempting to think of new media as an extension of existing resources and conditions—the printed page, the photograph, the gallery, the museum, the public square—that carry a stronger sense of "proof." But proof, or legitimacy, may not be this generation's paradigm. Some practices, in fact, do not call for actualization, either because the images they produce have gained some form of autonomy from the objects they refer to, or because online presence (in its rich variety) outperforms and outlives physical existence, or simply because more and more projects are conceived as inseparable from their online existence. This form of digital and cultural penetration implies a shift in the making of craft. Craftspeople are now less dependent on having a gallery, dealers on owning a brick-and-mortar shop, and collectors and curators on visiting either of them. Physical places are less important than the ability to establish connections with others and engage with them using self-managed digital avatars.

This redistribution implies a shift in power, or, perhaps more precisely, a dilution of the authority traditionally held by figures such as the gallerist, journalist, historian, or curator in a sea of unregulated self-expression and personal initiative. The top-down education model, or the figure of the expert, is not annulled, but it must coexist with deliberative forms of discussion, instantaneous commenting, and transversal knowledge sharing. Legitimacy now also takes the form of collective endorsement.

Web 2.0, as described by those who first theorized it, represents an ideal: a form of self-realization in which modes of production and diffusion are in the hands of everyone. It is a democratic dream that abolishes class and boundary, posits mutual support as a principle, and refutes the hegemony of an elite group of decision makers or producers, in favor of nonhierarchical circulation and validation. In the case of craft, this phenomenon prompted the argument that collaborative, open-source paradigms are already part of craft's ethos and of its supposed social mission.[40]

While very seductive, part of the community-powered agency promised by new media begs to be examined. Its promises may confuse global access with equal opportunity and equality of means, and new media may lend token participation a form of political agency that it does not always have.

Pisani has asserted that online communities have not taken power from other institutions as much as they have simply started to exercise their own power. With this comes a responsibility that has not yet been fully envisaged by the networked individuals and webactors that administer today's new media. Most of the online communities or digital work groups discussed in this essay are self-selecting communities very much like the contemporary field itself and based on "opt-in" membership. Opting in means caring enough about that platform's agenda or content to follow or participate in its development. Opting in, in a community whose collective goal is the legitimation of the field of contemporary jewelry, means a willingness to participate. It supposes a form of complicity. Similarly, the social engagement evidenced by new media, as seen in the fab labs, #ArtJewelryChallenge, or various other participatory projects, is always conceived of as functional, positive, friendly. What is at stake here—should we indeed believe that new media is producing new norms of social interaction—is to understand how a culture lobbying for its own cause and buoyed by collective impulses will exceed the limits set by its own agenda and invent the means to encourage and manage debate, dissent, and decision making. Treat participation as something other than political, and it risks becoming a mere cultural—or artistic—motif.

Notes

Acknowledgments: The research for this article was informed by interviews conducted between December 2014 and August 2015. Some are quoted in the text, but a number are not, for lack of space: I would like to express my gratitude to Lois Boardman, Leo Caballero, Susan Cummins, Marion Fulk, Donna Greenberg, Arthur Hash, Nichka Marobin, Kevin Murray, Ron Porter, Jessica Rosenkrantz, Jesse Louis-Rosenberg, Maarten Versteeg, Remedios Vincent, and Namita Gupta Wiggers for so kindly taking the time to answer my questions, shape my understanding of new media, and provide invisible trestles to this essay.

A few conversations have proved invaluable in developing my thoughts on new media: I would like to give special thanks to Fabrice Lanteri, Frédéric F. Martin, and Giulietta Rak. I owe my introduction to the history of Web 2.0 and its main actors to Francis Pisani and Dominique Piotet's *Comment le web change le monde, L'Alchimie des multitudes.* This book exists only in Spanish and French, and whenever I could, I looked up the original source in English. I would like to acknowledge my debt to this book, more than a simple line in the notes will. My final thanks go to Francis Pisani, who kindly agreed to read this essay before publication.

1. For discussion of the participatory turn in craft and contemporary jewelry, see Kevin Murray, "The Change We Can Wear," *Art Jewelry Forum*, May 20, 2010, http://artjewelryforum.org/articles/change-we-can-wear; David Gauntlett, *Making Is Connecting: The Social Meaning of Creativity, from DIY and Knitting to YouTube and Web 2.0* (Cambridge, England: Polity Press, 2011), PDF e-book; and *Build Your Own* (London, Liverpool, Norwich: Crafts Council/FACT/Norwich Museum Service, 2015).

2. Although they were analyzed primarily in relation to jewelers, some of the dynamics discussed in this essay are applicable to other areas of creative expression.

3. Artists are increasingly considering the web as a subject in their work. See Ian Wallace, "What Is Post-Internet Art? Understanding the Revolutionary New Art Movement," *ArtSpace*, March 18, 2014, http://www.artspace.com/magazine/interviews_features/post_internet_art. While I did not find significant examples of jewelers who respond to, critique, examine, or use data from the internet as a fundamental aspect of their work for this essay, it would be a fruitful direction for jewelers to pursue.

4. Lev Manovich, *The Practice of Everyday (Media) Life* (PDF version, 2008), available at http://manovich.net/index.php/projects/the-practice-of-everyday-media-life.

5. Benjamin Lignel, ed., "Helena and Lasse Pahlman," in *AJF Best of Interviews* (Mill Valley, CA: Art Jewelry Forum, 2014), 93.

6. See http://www.metalcyberspace.com.

7. Web platforms have since been used to create multiple discrete projections of oneself, either as avatars (in the gaming industry), as aliases (in online chat rooms), or simply as representations of multiple professional selves.

8. Art Jewelry Forum's editorial mission statement, as repurposed on Klimt02, http://klimt02.net/publications/publishers/ajf-publications.

9. Leo Caballero, email to author, December 15, 2014.

10. Leo Caballero, interview with the author, April 23, 2015, followed by email to author, May 17, 2015.

11. American collector Marion Fulk, email to author, May 27, 2015.

12. Susan Cummins, email to author, June 17, 2015.

13. Lois Boardman, email to author, July 21, 2015.

14. Ron Porter, emails to author, May 27 and June 11, 2015.

15. Early Web 2.0 advocate Tim O'Reilly, as quoted in Francis Pisani and Dominique Piotet, *Comment le web change le monde, L'Alchimie des multitudes* (Paris: Pearson, 2008), 13.

16. Pisani and Piotet, *Comment le web change le monde,* 51 (author's translation).

17. Ibid., 27 (author's translation).

18. See Kim Dhillon, "A Moodboard Moment: Feeas," Not Just a Label (NJAL) website, June 2, 2015, https://www.notjustalabel.com/editorial/a-moodboard-moment-feeas.

19. Remedios Vincent, email to author, June 19, 2015.

20. Nichka Marobin, email to author, May 28, 2015.

21. When asked what inspires her about new media, blogger and artist Remedios Vincent responded, "The possibility of complete self-management." Vincent, email to author, June 19, 2015.

22. For an historical analysis of this transformation, see Pisani and Piotet, *Comment le web change le monde,* 215. For a more detailed discussion on the passage from old media to new media, see in particular Doc Searls, "Giant Zero Journalism, Cont'd," blog, October 22, 2014, https://blogs.law.harvard.edu/doc/2014/10/22/giant-zero-journalism-contd/; and Henry Jenkins, "Eight Traits of the New Media Landscape," *Confessions of an Aca-Fan*, blog, November 6, 2006, http://henryjenkins.org/2006/11/eight_traits_of_the_new_media.html .

23. Pisani and Piotet, *Comment le web change le monde,* 66–67 (author's translation).

24. The textbook examples for describing the phenomenon, which combines network effects and crowdsourcing, are Wikipedia and before it, CDDB (Compact Disc Database). For a complete discussion on the various ways that shared databases are filled, see Dan Bricklin's *The Cornucopia of the Commons: How to Get Volunteer Labor*, website, 2000–2006, http://www.bricklin.com/cornucopia.htm.

25. All quotes by Donna Greenberg are from an email to the author, June 19, 2015.

26. For a detailed account of jewelers' appropriation of personal manufacture and distribution, see Gabriel Craig's excellent "Art Jewelry 2.0," *Art Jewelry Forum*, February 24, 2011, http://www.artjewelryforum.org/articles/art-jewelry-20.

27. Benjamin Lignel, "WTF is M.I.T. Doing at SNAG?," *Art Jewelry Forum*, July 6, 2015, http://www.artjewelryforum.org/articles-series/wtf-is-mit-doing-at-snag.

28. Arthur Hash, email to author, April 28, 2015.

29. See the Nervous System website, http://n-e-r-v-o-u-s.com.

30. All quotes from Jessica Rosenkrantz and Jesse Louis-Rosenberg (Nervous System) come from an interview with the author, May 20, 2015, followed by email to the author, June 24, 2015. Since 2007 Nervous System has been designing "growth algorithms," which are used to develop objects that are manufactured using digital fabrication processes. However, the most appealing (and probably the most radical) aspect of their work is not its technological novelty, or the shift from object making to algorithm design, but in their economic outlook and their ambition, which Jessica Rosenkrantz describes as a desire to create one-offs that compete with mass-produced objects.

31. For a historical overview and critical appraisal of participatory art, see Claire Bishop, *Artificial Hells—Participatory Art and the Politics of Spectatorship* (London and New York: Verso, 2012).

32. See, for example, The Opulent Project discussed by Julia Morris, "Collecting and Social Media," *Art Jewelry Forum*, February 4, 2012, http://www.artjewelryforum.org/articles/collecting-and-social-media.

33. For more on the development of user-generated content, see Lev Manovich, *The Practice of Everyday (Media) Life*; and Jeff Howe, "The Rise of Crowdsourcing," *Wired*, June 2006, http://archive.wired.com/wired/archive/14.06/crowds.html.

34. Howe, "The Rise of Crowdsourcing."

35. To avoid conceptual slippage between two terms that are hard to pin down, I will define "collaborative" as "engaging several people with recognized skill sets in the different stages of a project," and "participatory" as "inviting people with no presupposed skills to contribute/make/participate in an exercise of community empowerment."

36. See Ojalà's Facebook page: https://www.facebook.com/notes/348784821978454/

37. The three most prevalent roles currently being synthesized online are commentator, organizer, and maker, each of which may be realized via a distinct platform. Some characteristics of online identity are quite different from institutional—or for that matter, legal—identification: the images we project of ourselves online are fluid, digressive, multiple. The search for different audiences encourages webactors to cultivate multiple online personas, and it is exciting to think of the performative aspect of online identity as part of a slow pixelization of the singular author in favor of individual projects and the communities that rally around them.

38. Recent sociological research focusing on labor conditions in the arts points to the causal relation between precariousness in the arts and professional polymorphism. See sociologist Pierre-Michel Menger's description of the contemporary artist's economy as one of "multiple job-holding, occupational-role versatility, portfolio diversification of employment ties" in "Artistic Labor Markets: Contingent Work, Excess Supply, and Occupational Risk Management," in *Handbook of the Economics of Art and Culture*, vol. 1 (Paris: École des Hautes Études en Sciences Sociales, 2006), PDF e-book, http://faos.ku.dk/pdf/undervisning_og_arrangementer/2010/ARTISTIC_LABOR_MARKETS_191010.pdf; and Sophie Le Coq, "Le travail artistique: effritement du modèle de l'artiste créateur? (Artistic Work: crumbling of the model of the artist as a creator?)," *Sociologie de l'Art* 3/2004 (OPuS 5): 111–31, www.cairn.info/revue-sociologie-de-l-art-2004-3-page-111.htm.

39. For an interesting link between the participatory tendencies of nineteenth-century folk culture and the "explosion of grassroots expression" online, see Jenkins, "Eight Traits of the New Media Landscape."

40. For a description of craft as "intrinsically democratic" and several examples of participatory projects, see the Crafts Council's (UK), *Build Your Own*.

David Tisdale

(b. 1956, United States, active California, New York, and Connecticut)

Bracelet, 1984
Anodized aluminum, silver, onyx, agate
2 ¼ × 3 ¼ × 1 ¼ in.

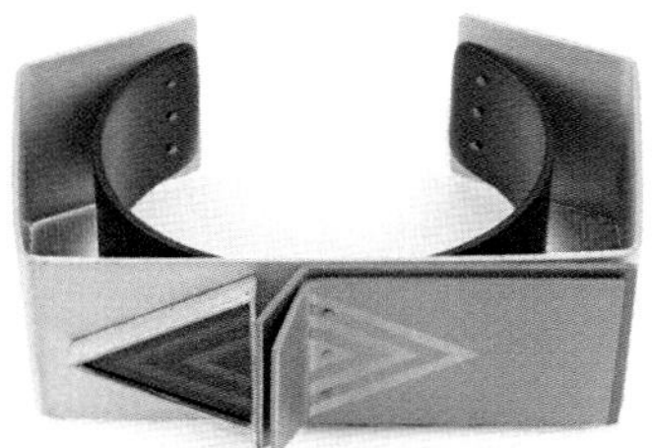

Felieke Van der Leest

(b. 1968, Netherlands, active Norway)

***Spermheart* brooch, designed 1996**
Viscose thread over felt and rubber
3 ¼ × 1 × ½ in.

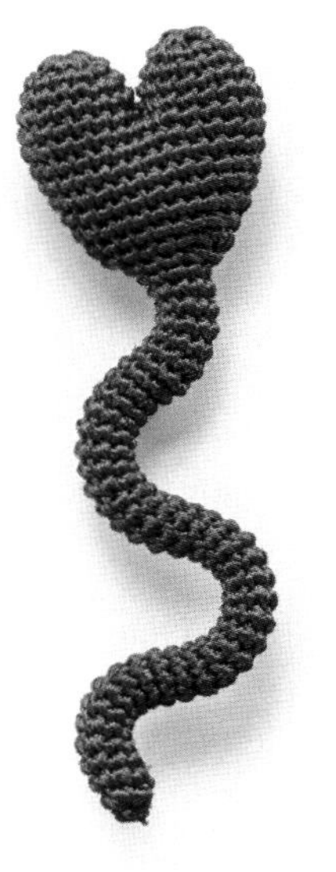

Emmy van Leersum

(1930–1984, active Netherlands)

Armband, 1970–71
Number 29 in the series vouwen en inzagingen, 1970–71
Aluminum
2 ¾ × 2 ¾ × 3 ⅛ in.

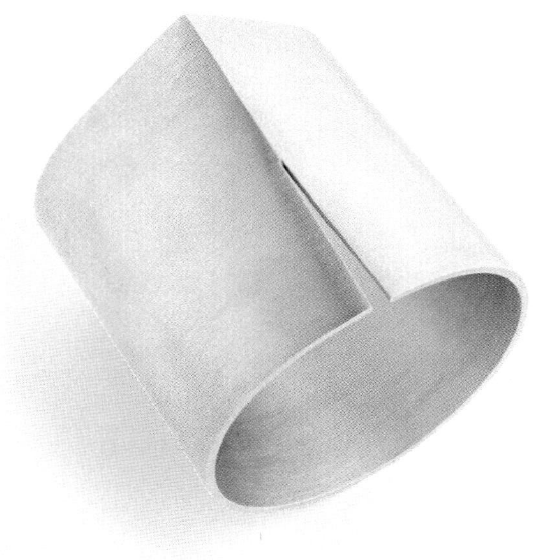

Tone Vigeland

(b. 1938, Norway)

Necklace, 1982
Silver, gold, gilded silver, rutilated quartz, nephrite
7 × 7 × 1 in.

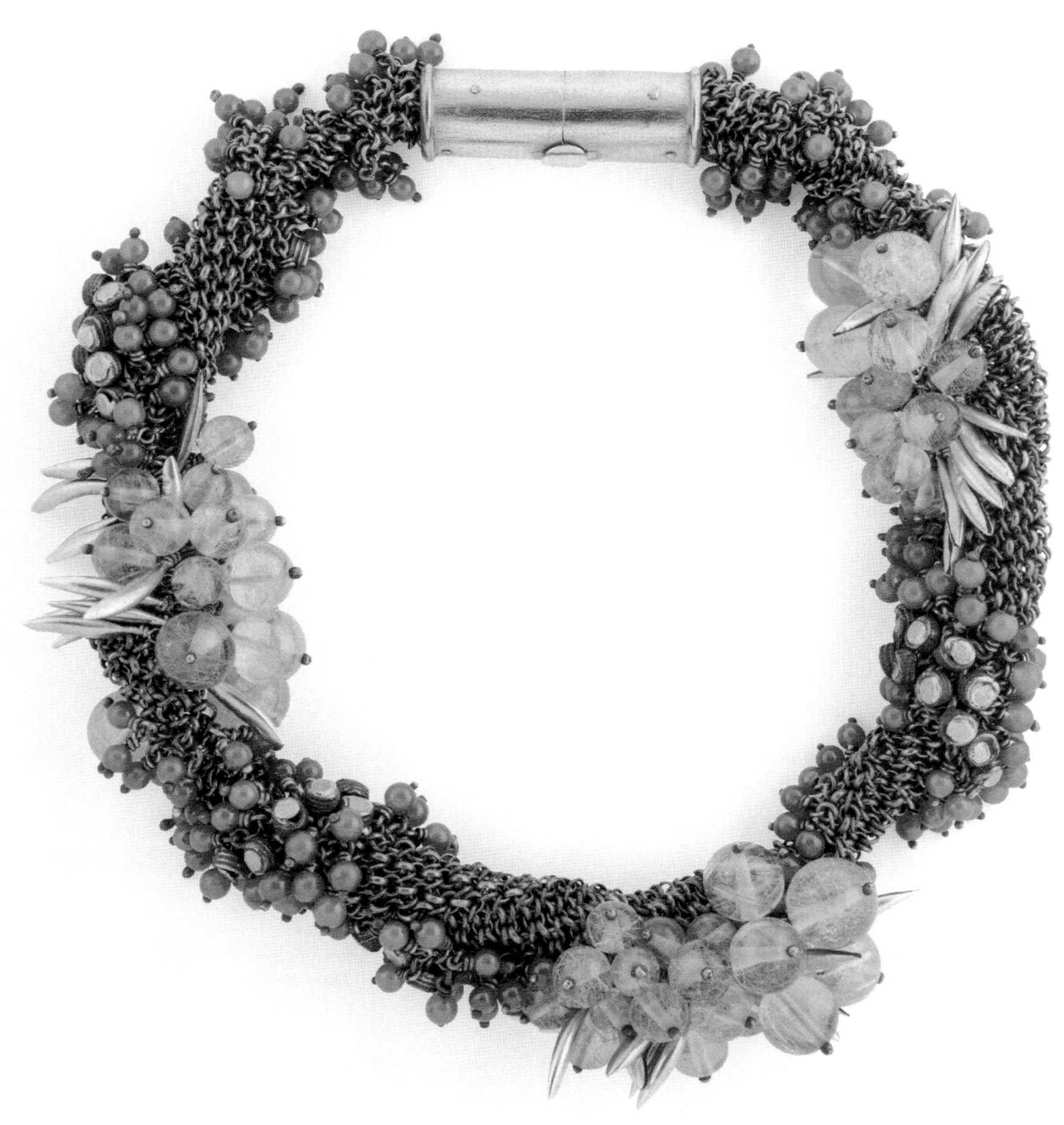

Tone Vigeland

(continued)

Necklace, c. 1985
Nickel-plated brass, steel nails
11 × 8½ × ¾ in.

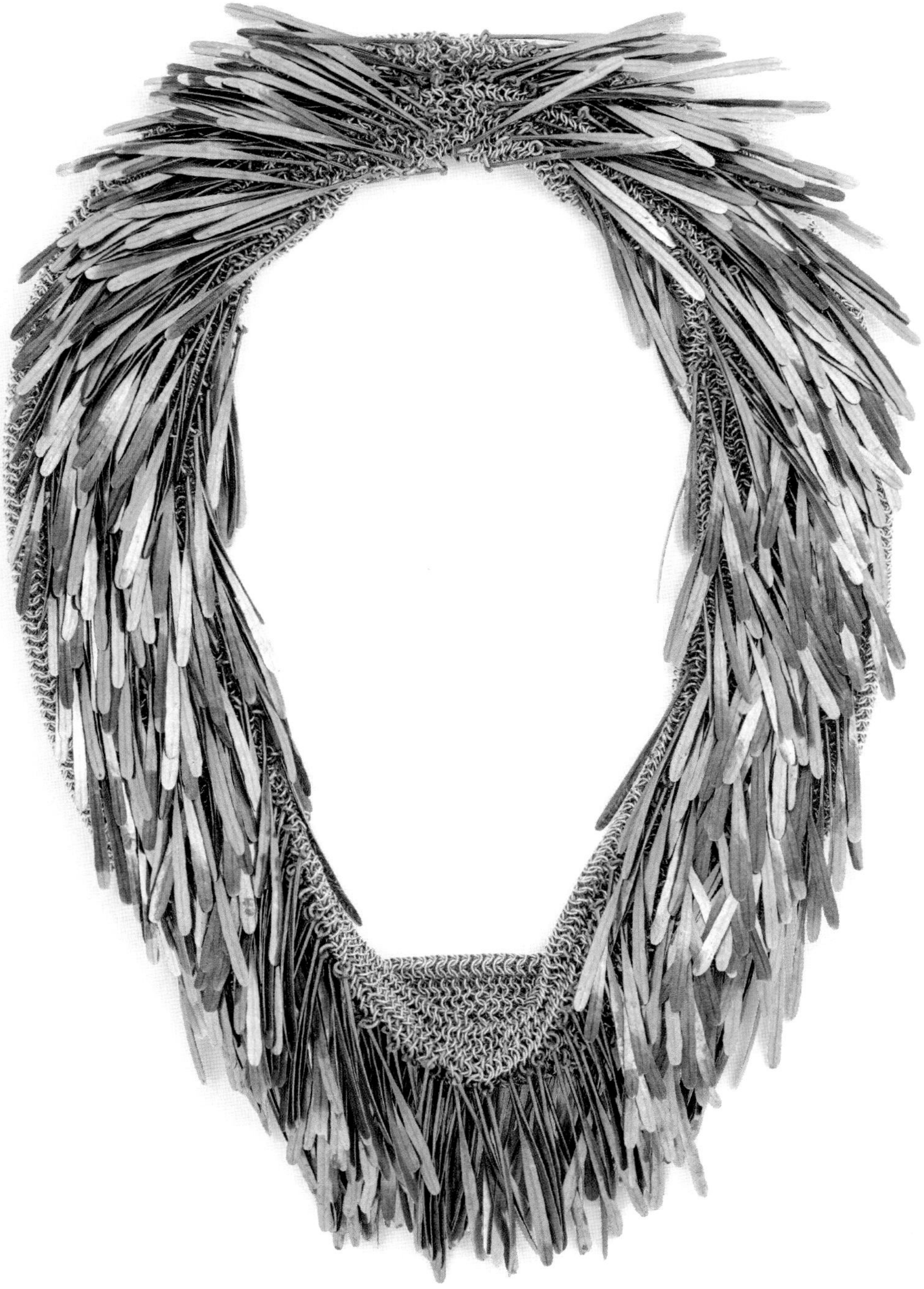

Graziano Visintin

(b. 1954, Italy)

Brooch, 2004
Gold, enamel, gold leaf
2 × 2⅛ × ⅜ in.

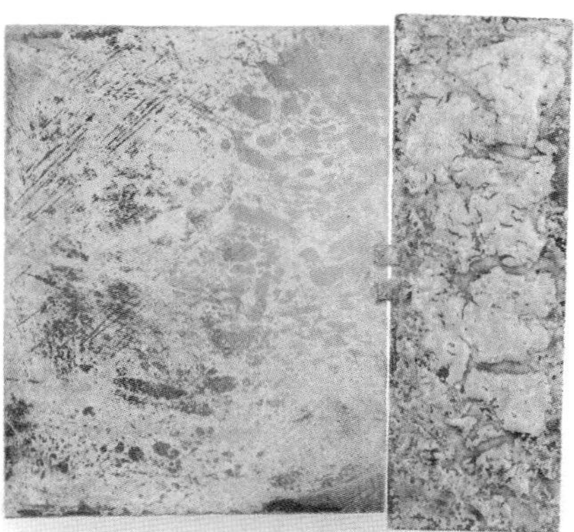

David Watkins

(b. 1940, England)

***Gyro Bangle*, designed 1975, made 1976**
Aluminum
5 × 5 × 3/8 in.

***Wing Wave 3* set of three necklaces, 1983**
Neoprene-coated steel wire, neoprene-coated wood
11 1/2 × 12 3/8 × 1/4 in.

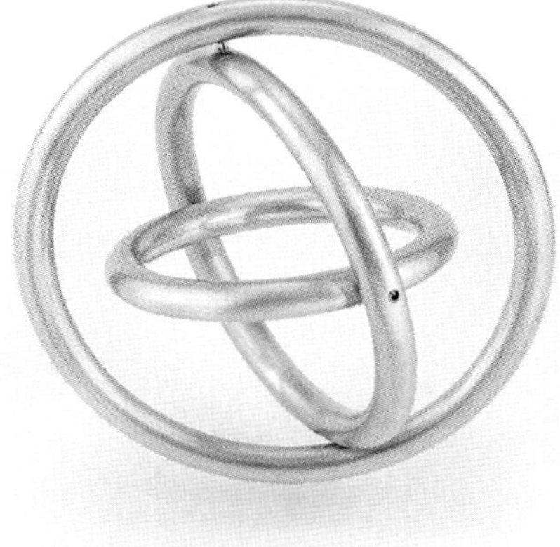

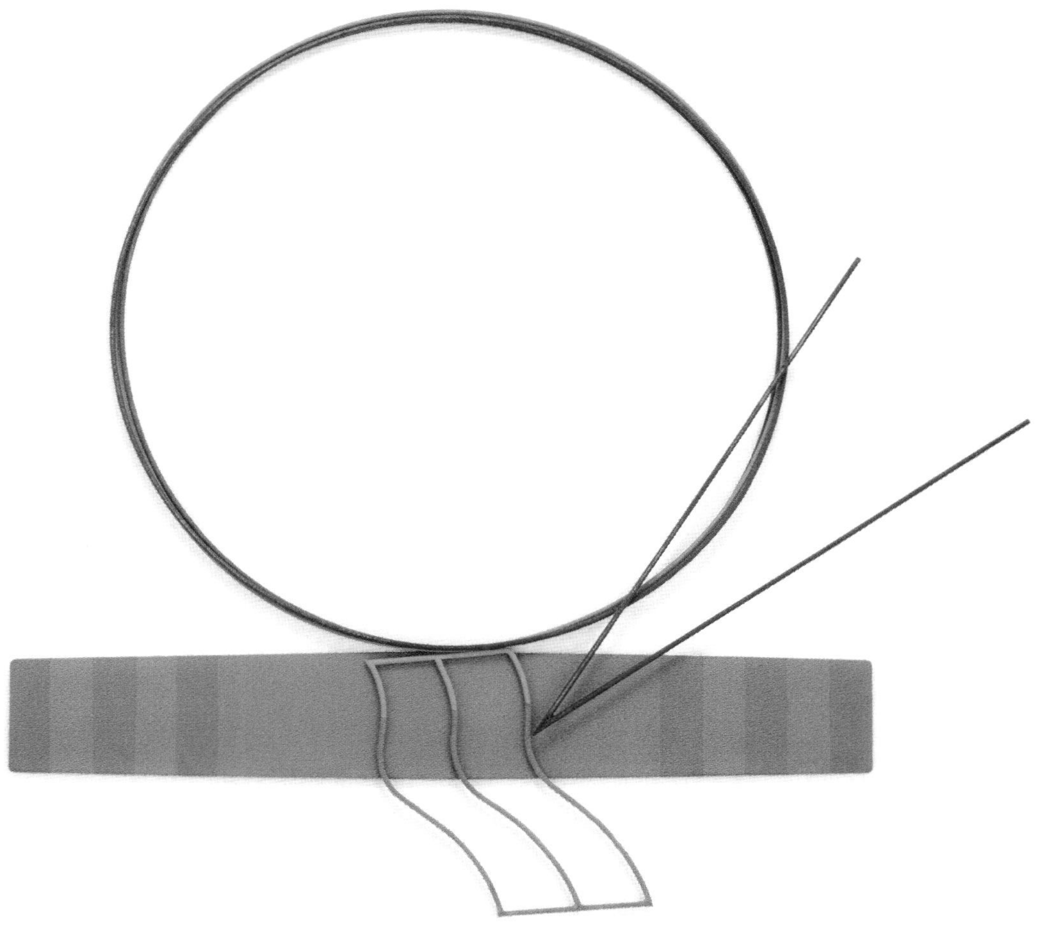

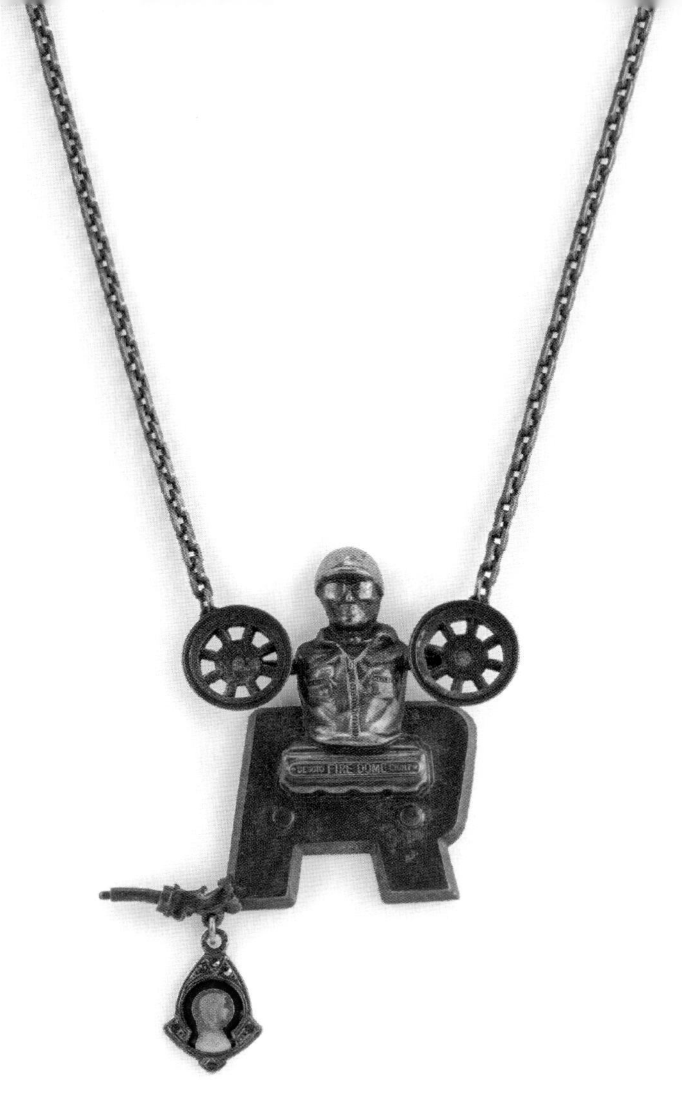

J. Fred Woell

(1934–2015, United States, active Maine)

The Winning **necklace, 1975**
Silver, bronze, brass,
religious medal
Chain: 20½ in. length;
pendant: 3 × 2½ × ⅜ in.

Nancy Worden

(b. 1954, United States, active Washington)

***Grafting* necklace, 2000**
Silver, gold, gilded copper
7 ⅛ × 9 ½ × 3 ½ in.

***Gilding the Past* necklace, 2001**
Gilded copper, Japanese and US currency (including 1964 and 1965 Kennedy half dollars with gilding), coral, turquoise, bone, brass
17 ¼ × 17 ¾ × ¾ in.

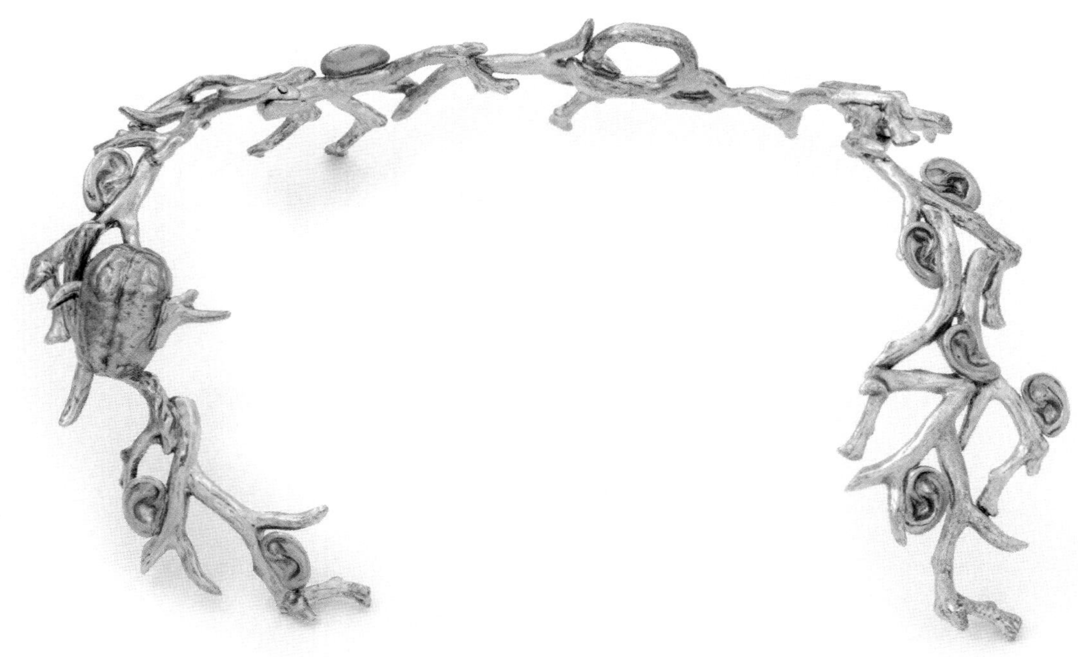

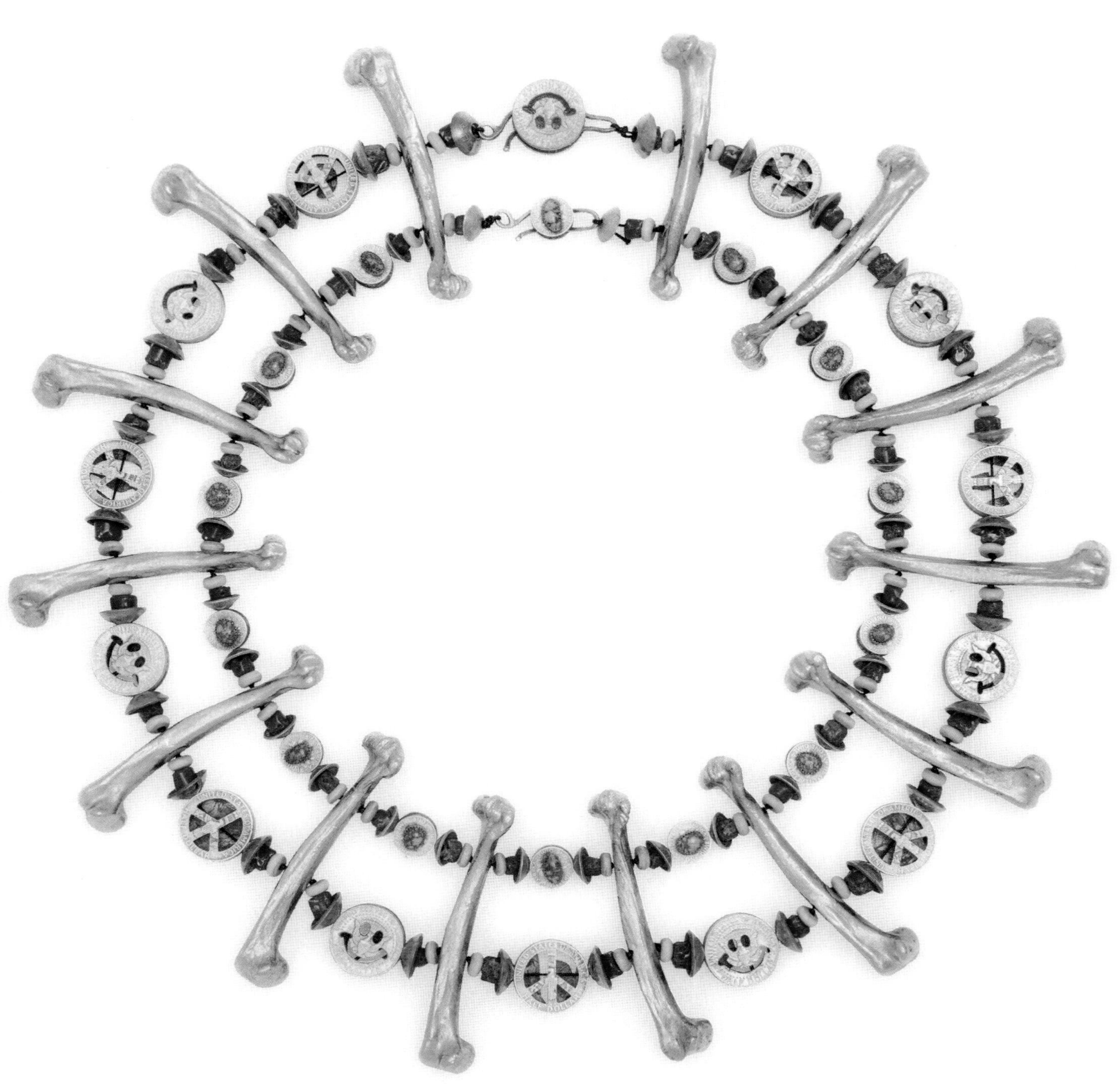

Nancy Worden

(continued)

***The Leash* necklace, 2003**
Mink, US currency, silver, brass, nickel, freshwater pearls, mother of pearl, glass, chrome-plated metal
Necklace: 9 ¼ × 8 ¾ × 2 ¾ in., leash: 19 ¾ in. length

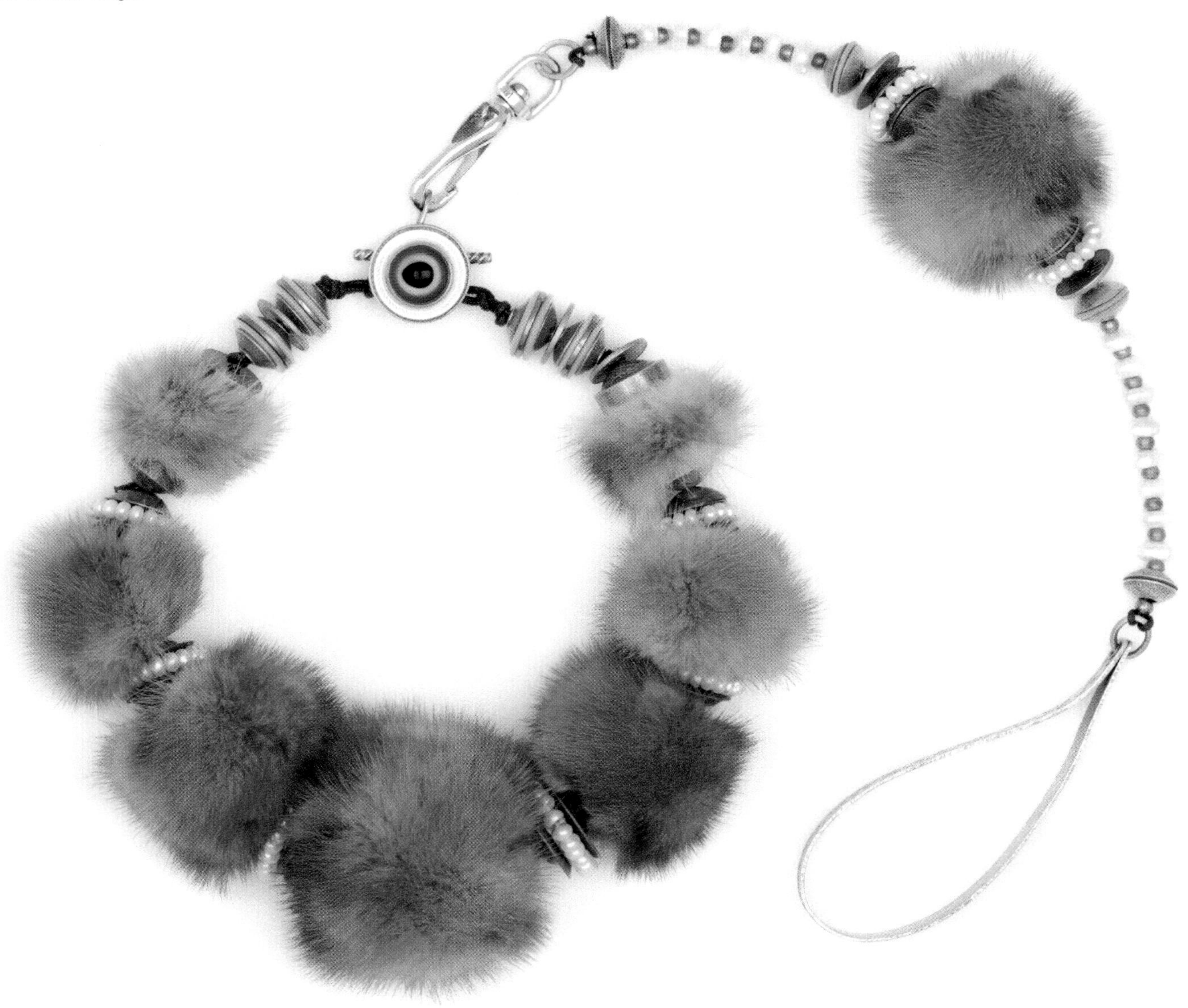

Alberto Zorzi

(b. 1958, Italy)

Brooch, 1986
Stainless steel, gold, lapis lazuli
3½ × 2 × 1 in.

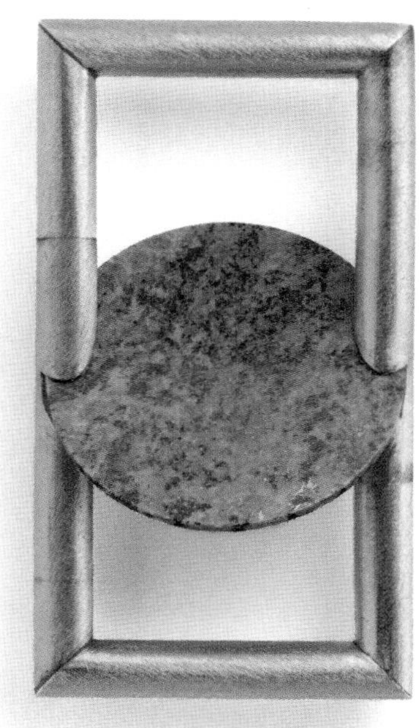

Between Friends

Helen W. Drutt English

It all began when we were born, nine months apart. I, the eldest, entered the world in November 1930, in Winthrop, Massachusetts. After the normal gestation period, Lois followed in August 1931 in Chicago. But it would be half a century before we met and connected so profoundly over our passion for and dedication to contemporary crafts. Who would have thought that our gal Lois, who had immigrated to South Pasadena, California, would find happiness and aesthetic rapport with a roommate from Philadelphia?

"Separated at birth," we were reunited in 1980 at Black Mountain College near Asheville, North Carolina—a holy seat in the history of crafts.[1] James Melchert, the director of the Visual Arts Program of the National Endowment for the Arts, invited Lois's great friend Eudorah Moore, former curator of the *California Design* exhibitions at the Pasadena Art Museum, to serve as the crafts coordinator at the NEA. With project coordinator John McLean, Moore launched the National Crafts Planning Project with a mission to meet craftspeople, hear their needs and aspirations, and make recommendations for action. The task force that they assembled comprised thirty-two individuals dedicated to the resurgence of the craft movement.[2] At Black Mountain we were trained by consultant Michael Doyle to hold town meetings and seminars. Divided into four groups of eight, we would fan out across America, meeting with craftsmen, curators, and collectors to understand their challenges and needs. Lois Boardman was my roommate at Black Mountain and on the road; we were two women with different personalities but similar interests. One (Lois) remained married to her life's partner, Robert Boardman, while the other moved through multiple marriages, strengthened during the separations by a passion for work and the crafts.

For several months, we traveled throughout the northeast states interviewing and gathering testimony from craftspeople. I adorned myself daily with brooches by Stanley Lechtzin, Eleanor Moty, Albert Paley, and Olaf Skoogfors—a visual invitation for inquiries about the field. When the "honeymoon" was over and we returned to our respective homes, we had bonded, joined in laughter and our commitment to the arts, and shared intimate details of our personal lives. Lois was witness to my courtship with Maurice English (whom I married in December 1981), and I developed deep friendships with Fanny, Double, and Trouble, her late beloved poodles, and, of course, Dr. Bob.

Visually and aesthetically seduced by my daily ornamentation, within a year Lois informed me that she wanted to create

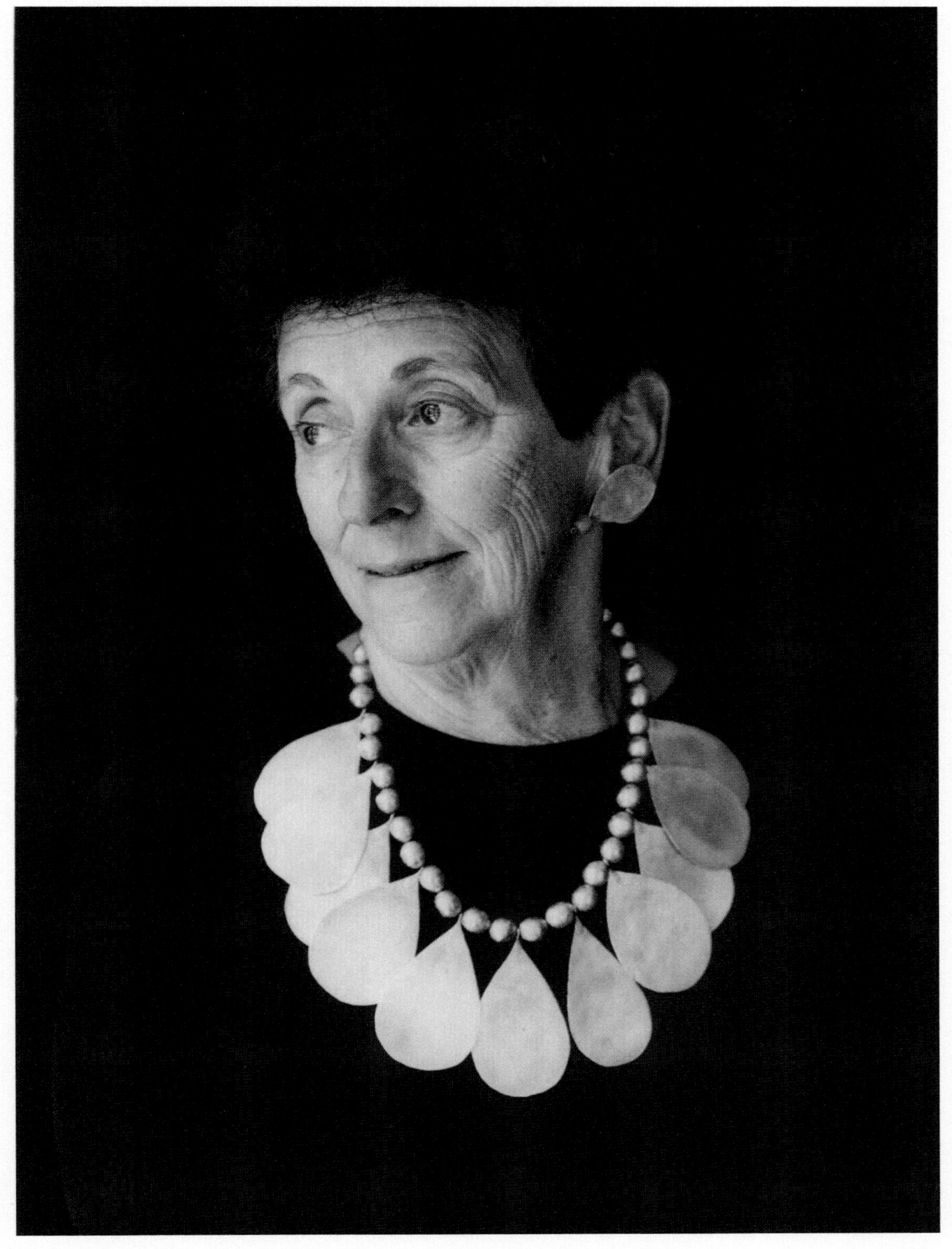

FIG. 1
Lois Boardman wearing a Breon O'Casey necklace (see p. 218) and earrings

a collection of contemporary jewelry. In return, she introduced me to the Southern California ceramists she knew so well, such as Ralph Bacerra, Philip Cornelius, Jun Kaneko, Mineo Mizuno, Adrian Saxe, and Peter Shire.

———— • ————

In late September 2015, after decades of accumulation, I organized our complete correspondence—papers, invoices, faxes, emails, postcards, and letters dating back to 1981—in chronological sequence. As I pored over the years of our friendship, I began to realize how our interactions had changed because of technology and the emergence of the internet.

In the beginning, long before faxes, I was Lois's mentor and introduced her to my artists—Gijs Bakker, Claus Bury, Lechtzin, Bruno Martinazzi, Paley, Wendy Ramshaw, Bernhard Schobinger, Skoogfors—through telegrams and handwritten notes. In 1984, after frequent telephone conversations, typed invoices began to record the formation of the collection. Faxes would soon replace the verbal dialogue. Written passages about artists and drawings of objects began to flood the loose-leaf pages. A unique exchange was under way: I sent my stream-of-consciousness poems to Lois; she sent to me postcards from Canada, Bhutan, China, Jordan, and Turkey. I sent FedEx packages with jewels to South Pasadena for approval or return. She sent snow globes, magnets, fruitcakes, and assorted souvenirs to me in Philadelphia.

A decade later, the faxes ebbed and email messages—shorter, more direct, and almost impersonal—dominated our communications. Lois would ask, "What have you seen lately that has caught your eye?" Or she would send fifty playful images of animals in ludicrous situations. The computer had become Lois's mentor and playmate and sated her curiosity with instant images and information from around the world.

During the 1990s, the professional umbilical cord was really being severed. New technologies were allowing Lois to pursue her interest in jewelry and she began to seek information from various sources. She had graduated "college," earned her visual collector's "master's degree," and now ventured forth independently, making bold choices as her personal aesthetic expanded. She forged her own relationships with national and international galleries—Gallery Funaki in Melbourne; Gallery S.O. in London; Galerie Spektrum in Munich; Ornamentum Gallery in Hudson, New York; Sienna Gallery in Lenox, Massachusetts; Galerie Marzee in Nijmegen, the Netherlands; Fingers Contemporary Jewellery in Auckland—sometimes secretly and occasionally with choices that were alien to my aesthetic. The collection, while rooted in my guidance, increasingly began to reflect Lois Boardman herself.

———— • ————

Memory always shapes our lives as we recall events. Epistolary messages, in addition to conversations, are great links to lost moments and help to revive the past while we remain in the present. What follows is a rough chronology of my friendship and professional relationship with Lois, with excerpts from our correspondence.

November 1983

My husband Maurice English dies suddenly. My friendship with Lois has obviously grown beyond the world of ornamentation. She flies to Philadelphia to spend twenty-four hours with me, consoling me in my grief.

October 8, 1985

Handwritten letter from Lois to Helen

I surely hope that you can become as well known in the West as in the East—among the spending public. Made a list from the book of The New Jewelry *(Peter Dormer) that really appealed to me: Gerd Rothmann—earpieces; Otto Künzli—neckpieces; Bruno Martinazzi—brooches.*[3] *I am really afraid, although I love the use of new materials to base any collection on same (material), unless they figure a surefire way to preserve them. I also love well-designed dramatic figurative pieces; if I do keep this up as a collection, I must start becoming less emotional and more thoughtful altogether.*

Peter Dormer's book, a seminal text in the field, highlights the use of alternative materials. Dormer had lived in my Philadelphia home, where he partially researched his books. Education is primary in developing a collection, and I begin to build Lois's library with books complementing her visual pursuits. Lois carefully selects works in alternative materials by jewelers such as Künzli as well as by traditional goldsmiths such as Martinazzi.

June 8, 1991

I attend the postwedding celebration (fig. 2) of Lois's son Peter Boardman and his wife, Nobuko, in Pasadena. Lois and I share intimate feelings and have long discussions about jewelry; our social and aesthetic pursuits become one. Lois encourages me to appear "decked out" in unique jewelry, so I wear a Peter Chang purple bracelet inlaid with vibrant colors and a Bakker *Bouquet* brooch. Lois wears a Claude Lalanne cast and gilded bronze "lips" necklace, her first independent acquisition. Lois's desire to introduce me to potential West Coast collectors is realized when Mary Coquillard and Katherine Schwarzenbach become interested in the field.

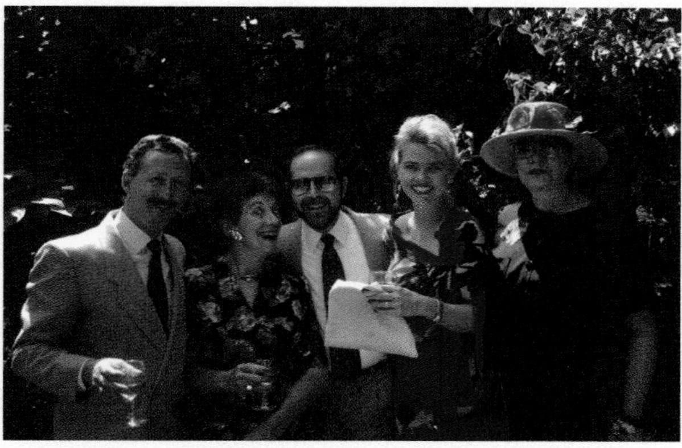

FIG. 2
Paul Alanis, Lois Boardman, Loren Ostrow, Allison Alanis, and Helen W. Drutt English at postwedding celebration of Lois and Bob's son Peter Boardman and Nobuko Fujita, Pasadena, June 8, 1991

August 23, 1992

Fax from Helen to Lois

I will study your files and become as astute as possible in response to the formation of your collection. I consider it a great privilege to work with you. As you know, whenever possible, I will hold works until the moment is economically realistic and comfortable for you. As I grow older, I begin to think—fewer people in depth.

Lois pursues this approach by collecting many examples by Manfred Bischoff, Sharon Church, Georg Dobler, Martinazzi, Falko Marx, and Nancy Worden.

January 30, 1995

Handwritten letter from Lois to Helen (figs. 3–4)

Why I started buying into adornment & metals . . .
1st I had been around crafts for many years thru the Pasadena Museum exhibition program, California Design—
2nd I was thrown into a situation where I was Helen Drutt's roommate for a year, thanks to the federal government—
3rd Or, maybe 1st, I am a woman & love to adorn, even though I don't look the part—a closet adorner—
4th Live in earthquake country—
5th Have granddaughters & daughters that could enjoy these objects as well, give them an interest—as it gave me an interest—outside of the normal humdrum—
6th Not the least—love the material.

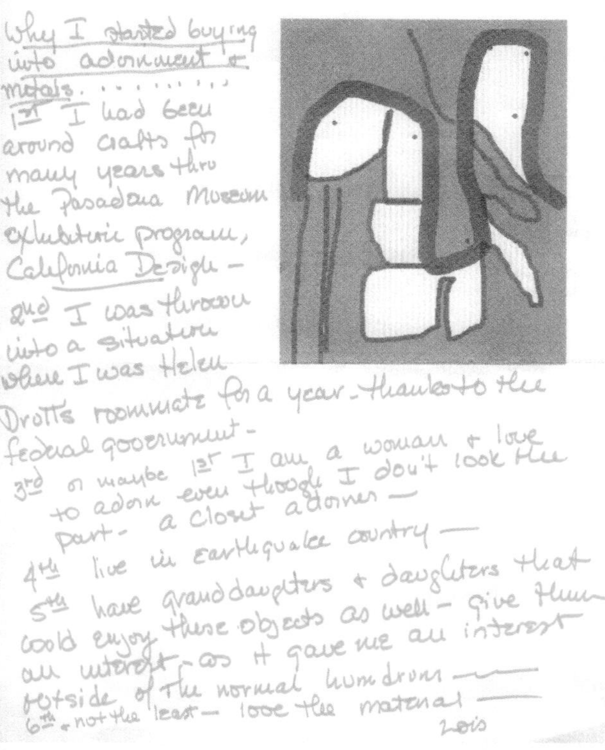

Why I started buying
into adornment &
metals. . . . . . .
1st I had been
around crafts for
many years thru
the Pasadena Museum
exhibition program,
California Design –
2nd I was thrown
into a situation
where I was Helen
Drutt's roommate for a year - thanks to the
federal government -
3rd or maybe 1st I am a woman & love
to adorn even though I don't look the
part - a closet adorner —
4th live in earthquake country —
5th have granddaughters & daughters that
could enjoy these objects as well - give them
an interest - as it gave me an interest
outside of the normal humdrum —
6th - not the least - love the material —
Lois

FIG.3
Handwritten letter from Lois to Helen, January 30, 1995

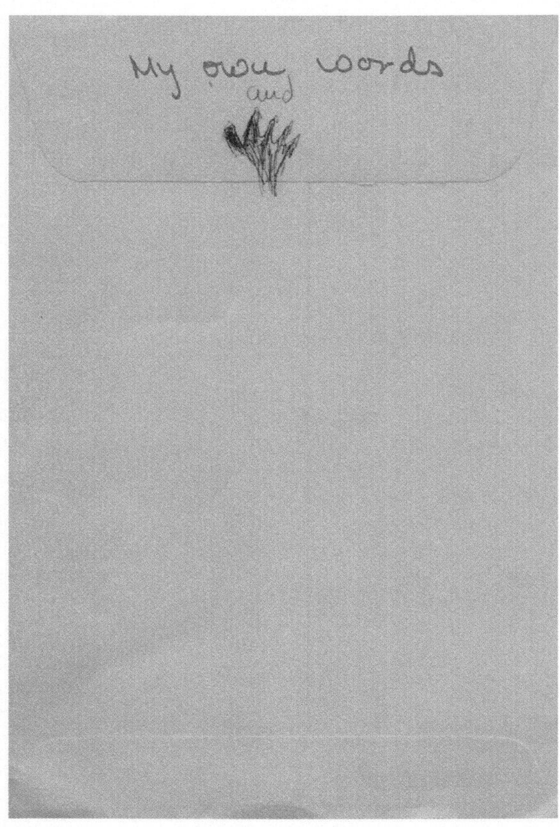

FIG. 4
Boardman inscribed "My own words and" on an envelope above a drawing of a hand

Lois and Bob's decision to give the collection to LACMA in 2013 would come from their great sense of philanthropy and love of the crafts. It would also be inspired by the gift's potential to reinforce the importance of the field, providing the artists with greater visibility. The intention of the gesture would be to educate and enrich the broader public about contemporary jewelry and attract further gifts to the museum.

July 23, 1996

Typed fax from Lois to Helen

Helen, I am confused as to what, or if, I should buy of Bury's. You provide info: the more you provide, the more confusing it gets. What I should buy is from every period, but I do not have the bucks for that, so, what do I do?

Lois and I work together to carefully develop an acquisition plan that can realize her desire, as I search for unique works. Primary artists are listed, knowing that unexpected works may appear as artists offer works previously held by others.

October 3, 1997

Typed fax from Lois to Helen

Would you please fax me a picture of the Dobler chunky amethyst neckpiece, if you think it is something I should have? That sounds dumb. If I am to collect and you are advising me, then what's the game plan? Have a good weekend wherever you'll be.

Lois refers to my peripatetic life, and deep conversations ensue on how to proceed with her collection. A secondary market is beginning to develop that can alter "the game plan." The three *d*'s—death, divorce, debt—enhance the opportunities.

February 4, 1999

Helen lectures at Museum of Contemporary Art, Los Angeles

Betty Duker, the program chair at the Pasadena Art Alliance (PAA) has invited me in a letter on November 8, 1998, to deliver a lecture about Lois Boardman's collection of international contemporary jewelry. The presentation is held at the Museum of Contemporary Art (MOCA) in Los Angeles, courtesy of Betye Burton, a supporter of both the PAA and MOCA. Members of the Los Angeles County Museum of Art's (LACMA's) Costume Council and MOCA's Projects Council are invited. Lois photographed her PAA friends wearing her jewelry, and these images are shown during the lecture, demonstrating how she encouraged the field in Southern California.

February 5, 1999

Email from Lois to Helen

Helen, I can't tell you how much I appreciate this friendship, which has lasted despite two strong personalities.

United in our passion for the work, our friendship triumphs over personality differences. I have learned that silence is a way in which Lois expresses disinterest.

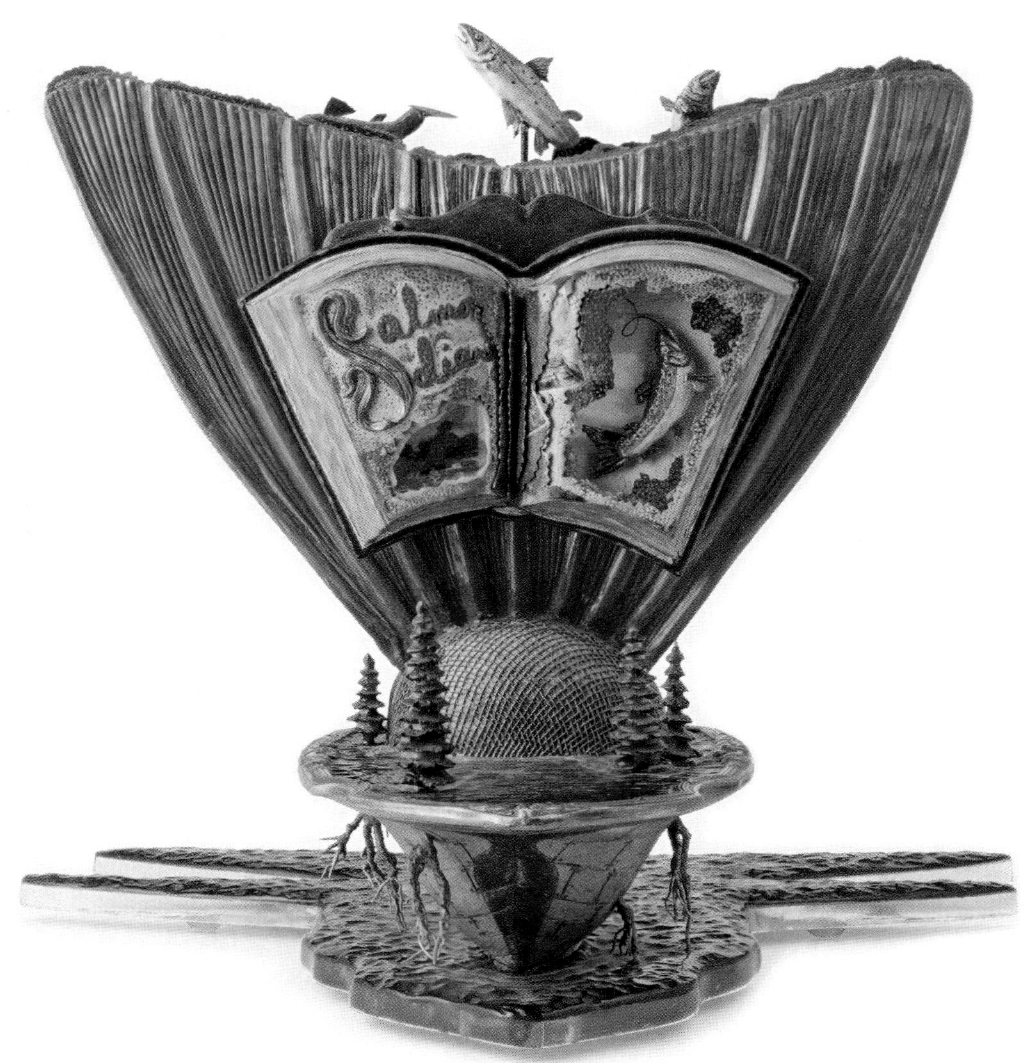

FIG. 5
Robin Kranitzky and Kim Overstreet, *Salmon Dream* brooch and stand (1999), commissioned by Helen Drutt in honor of Lois Boardman's sixty-eighth birthday, August 18, 1999. Removing the brooch reveals an image of Lois wearing a crown. Base supports a rotating wheel of salmon swimming upstream

February 9, 1999

Handwritten letter from Helen to Lois

I was not aware that you wished to renew your interest in building a collection again; I'm pleased that that is so, and I can assist you. Gone are the days when you can work with someone in the European manner, with a real trust in the intellect and eye, and I'm delighted you feel that way.

There has been a hiatus for over a year due to limited funds. One of my role models is Daniel-Henry Kahnweiler, Picasso's dealer, who educated and nurtured his clients in support of his artists with great patience.

October 8, 1999

Letter from Robin Kranitzky and Kim Overstreet to Helen regarding the Salmon Dream brooch and stand (fig. 5, see also p. 141) commissioned for Lois

Hopefully, she will find a bit of humor and understand our sincere hard work as well as the enjoyment that went into making Salmon Dream. *At first, we thought that creating a piece of sculpture that reflected a fishing theme would be like swimming against the current. Much to our surprise, after some research and much discussion, we reeled in what we thought was a really fun idea!*

August 18, 2001

Lois's 70th birthday, Campbell River, British Columbia

Lois's friends honor her by commissioning a hand-carved, heart-shaped brooch set with diamonds by Sharon Church (fig. 6). This is an appropriate symbol for Lois's years of friendship, as well as for her service to the Pasadena Art Alliance. Lois and Bob plan a unique celebration of her seventieth year of life, inviting forty friends to their home in Campbell River to experience Lois's passion for nature and, in particular, salmon fishing. We hear and see eagles soar overhead; we learn that a quiet ripple on the surface of the water may bring a salmon to our hook. We discover a great diversity in Lois's friends, who share an admiration for her commitment to the arts and to Dr. Bob.

December 22, 2006

A card arrives announcing Dr. Robert Boardman's retirement on March 31, 2007. He plans to become part-time adviser to the Lois Boardman collection.

March 10–13, 2010

SNAG conference, Houston

We attend the Society of North American Goldsmiths (SNAG) conference in Houston, where Lois is attracted to the work of San Francisco jeweler emiko oye. We enjoy a continuing dialogue as Lois selects an oye necklace (see p. 150) that will look best on display rather than worn. The prospect of an exhibition is a primary Boardman concern, and her selection over my advice is strong. I recognize that my classical and conceptual taste is sharply contrasted by her attraction to large scale and idiosyncratic imagery. I also discover that she is very interested in European works beginning with the 1960s.

March 17–21, 2011

Munich

For over half a century, Schmuck has been a gathering of a unique "family" united by a passion for art and jewelry.[4] We are joined in friendship and the opportunity to exchange ideas and embrace each other while viewing international jewelry exhibitions.

Lois and Bob Boardman and my husband H. Peter Stern and I have breakfast with Manfred Bischoff and dine with Wendy Ramshaw and David Watkins, who jointly hold a public conversation at the Neue Pinakothek. At Gerd Rothmann's home, Lois and Bob are photographed wearing gold crowns (see p. 12). During her visit Lois acquires an early Tone Vigeland necklace originally exhibited at Electrum Gallery in London circa 1970.

September 20, 2014

Email from Lois to Helen

Thought you might be interested in this piece made of feathers (see p. 115). *It was made by a former Californian now living and working in New Mexico named Nicki Marx. Several years ago she was in a California Design show and was shown in New York by the store Julie's [Julie: Artisans' Gallery]. She went off the radar for many years till a gallery here somehow saw her work and met up with her and is showing it.*[5] *The only reason I mention her is that I felt you needed to know and see her work. It is you!!!!!!!!*

After three decades, our relationship is reversed.

———— • ————

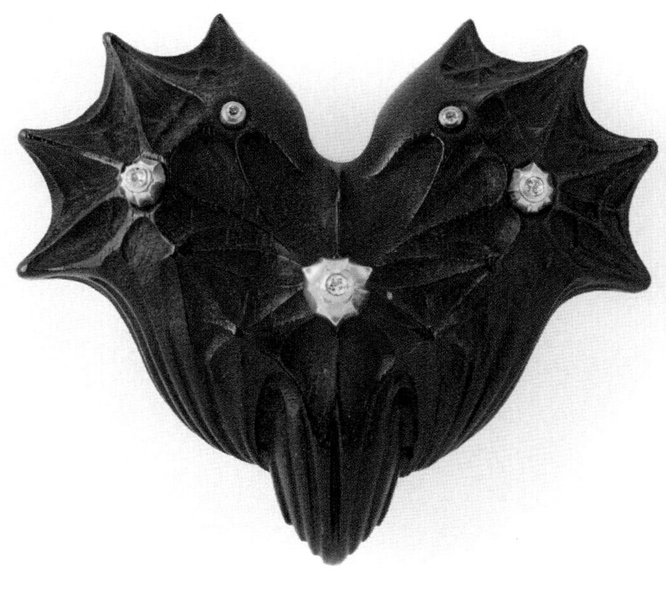

FIG. 6
Sharon Church, *Purple Heart* brooch, 2003

Modern photographic portraits frequently depict subjects as foils of their possessions. Think of Man Ray's portrait of Nancy Cunard (fig. 7): her image becomes the background for a collection of African ivory bracelets. Breon O'Casey was astonished and delighted when I presented him with a photographic book of his patrons wearing his work on the occasion of his seventieth birthday in 1998. From far and near, they came to Philadelphia to be photographed by Andrea Baldeck. Lois Boardman's portrait for the occasion reveals a collector who shares my aesthetic, wearing a classic silver necklace (fig. 1). Years later, a 2015 portrait by Miriam Künzli for *Art Aurea* (fig. 8) captures Lois demonstrating the expanding scope of her independent vision in a neckpiece by Afke Golsteijn made of taxidermied-parakeet wings mounted onto fabric.

A thirty-four-year epistolary friendship has evolved into one of long telephone calls and meetings in New York, Pasadena, Philadelphia, and Munich. Passion for the field and an exchange of serious dialogue mixed with laughter have strengthened both our shared and separate paths in the pursuit of work. The founding of the Lois Boardman collection, begun as a friendship in 1981, was sealed in 1984 with several important acquisitions. In 2016 LACMA will exhibit and publish the mature collection—and become a major new destination for international contemporary jewelry.

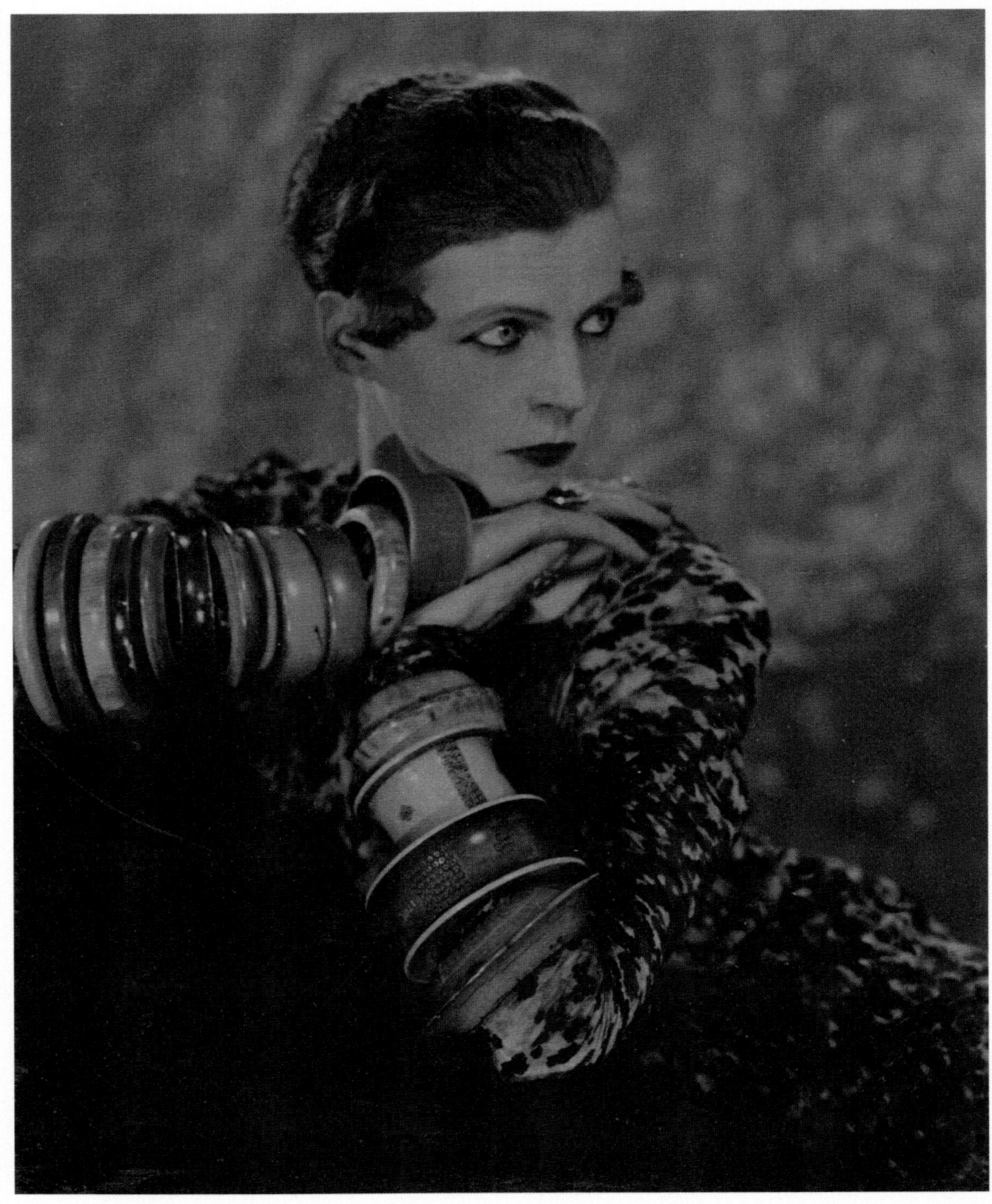

FIG. 7
Man Ray, *Nancy Cunard*, 1926, gelatin silver print, 3⁹⁄₁₆ × 2⅝ in. (9.1 × 6.6 cm), The Metropolitan Museum of Art, New York, Ford Motor Company Collection, gift of Ford Motor Company and John C. Waddell, 1987 (1987.100.131)

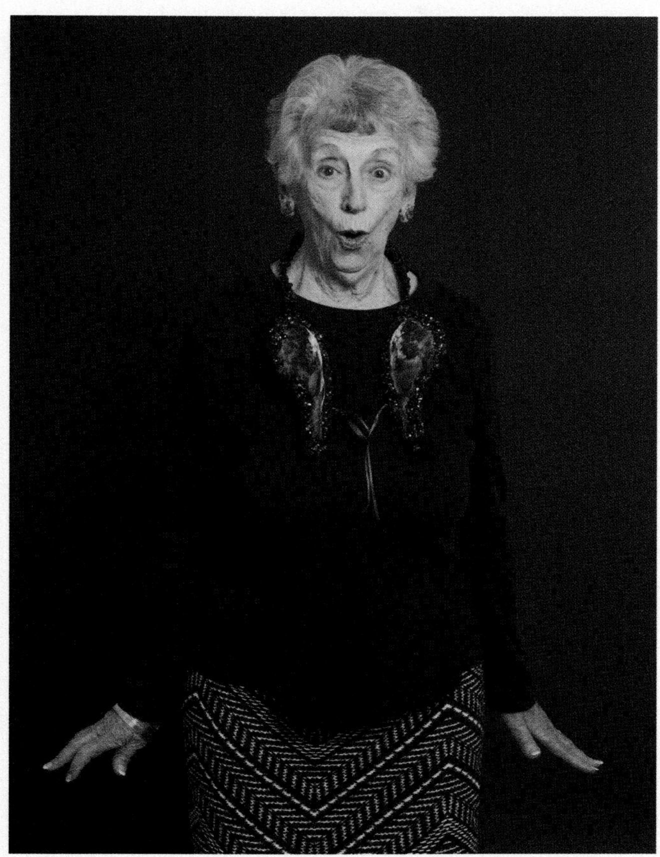

FIG. 8
Lois wearing *I Earned My Wings* necklace
by Afke Golsteijn, 2015

Notes

1. Black Mountain College (1933–57) was an innovative school with an interdisciplinary curriculum founded on the educational principles of John Dewey. Prominent students and faculty who influenced the course of avant-garde art and craft included Josef and Anni Albers, John Cage, Merce Cunningham, Buckminster Fuller, Karen Karnes, and others. See Helen Molesworth with Ruth Erickson, *Leap Before You Look: Black Mountain College, 1933–1957* (Boston: Institute of Contemporary Art/Boston and New Haven, CT: Yale University Press, 2015).

2. Among the participants in the program were Ruth Asawa, Willis Bing Davis, Bernard Kester, Ruth Kohler, John Outterbridge, and Bruce Schnabel (now known as Simon Toparovsky).

3. Editors' note: *The New Jewelry: Trends and Traditions* by Peter Dormer and Ralph Turner was published by Thames and Hudson in 1985 and was one of the first volumes to consider this new field of jewelry. Helen sent a copy to Lois and Bob Boardman on June 20, 1985, and inscribed it: "The new you is setting trends and traditions in Southern California. May this book be simply an introduction of what is to be! Love, Helen."

4. Schmuck (German for "jewelry") is an annual exhibition that occurs within the context of the Internationale Handwerksmesse (an immense craft trade fair) in Munich. A major event for the jewelry field, it is accompanied by many related satellite exhibitions and programs that comprise Munich Jewellery Week.

5. Editors' note: curator Katie Nartonis and gallerist Gerard O'Brien curated an exhibition of Nicki Marx's work at Reform Gallery in Los Angeles in fall 2014.

Checklist of the Collection

Abbey Chamberlain Brach,
Rosie Chambers Mills, and Bobbye Tigerman

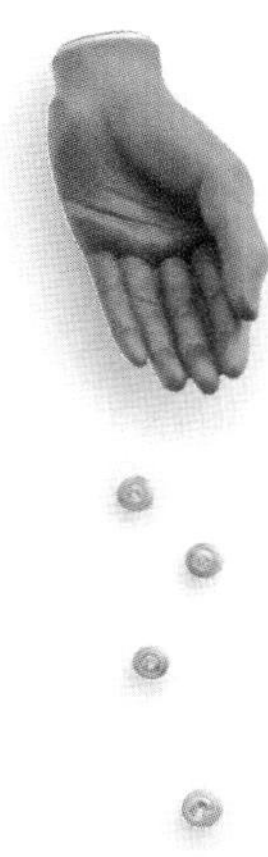

Works are listed alphabetically by artist. For artists with multiple pieces in the collection, those works are listed chronologically. The country of birth is provided for each artist, followed by any additional active locations in chronological order (without repeating places). For jewelers practicing in the United States, those states where the artists spent a substantial period of time making jewelry are included. Correspondingly, for jewelers working outside of the United States, only relevant countries of residence are listed. The term *silver* is used to describe metals that are at least 925/1000 silver and meet the sterling standard. The abbreviation *PMMA* is used for polymethyl methacrylate, also known as acrylic or by trade names Acrylite, Lucite, Perspex, and Plexiglas. Polyvinyl chloride is abbreviated *PVC*. Generally, dimensions are listed for pieces oriented as worn; height precedes width precedes depth. Marks are recorded as they appear on the works. The term *artist's mark* is used in lieu of describing complex artist symbols. Hallmarks are not transcribed but their meanings are described, and legible text appears in parentheses. Page numbers refer to references elsewhere in the book; italicized page numbers signal illustrations. Please consult LACMA's collection online at lacma.org for additional information and detailed photography of marks.

All works are credited Los Angeles County Museum of Art, gift of Lois and Bob Boardman.

Sharon Church, *Scatter Pins*, 1998

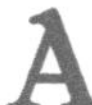

VICKI AMBERY-SMITH
(b. 1955, England)

Tuscan ring, 1988
Silver, varicolored gold
1⅜ × ⅞ × ¾ in. (3.5 × 2.2 × 1.9 cm)
Hallmarks for: artist (VAS); sterling; London; 1988
M.2014.198.1
p. *16*

Renaissance Farmhouse brooch, 1989
Silver, varicolored gold, emerald
11⁄16 × 2½ × ⅜ in. (1.8 × 6.4 × 1 cm)
Hallmarks for: artist (VAS); sterling; London; 1989
M.2014.198.2
p. *16*

KLAUS ARCK
(b. 1956, Germany)

Brooch, 1986
Painted balsa, plastic filament, felt, stainless steel
1¼ × 6¾ × 1⅛ in. (3.2 × 17.2 × 2.9 cm)
Marks: B612-60; K. Arck 86
M.2014.198.3
p. *16*

GIAMPAOLO BABETTO
(b. 1947, Italy)

Cerchio Triangolo necklace, 1983
Gold, alkyd resin
5⅝ × 5⅝ × ⅛ in. (14.3 × 14.3 × .3 cm)
Marks: G. Babetto / 1983 / 750 / 18K · 1
M.2014.198.4
p. *16*

ROBERT BAINES
(b. 1949, Australia)

Brooch No. 122, 1999
From the series Bloodier than Black, 1998–present
Silver
6¾ × 5¾ × 2 in. (17.2 × 14.6 × 5.1 cm)
M.2014.198.5
p. *17*

Neckpiece No. 26, 2010
From the series Redder than Green, 2009–present
Powder-coated silver, gilded silver, styrene plastic
10½ × 7 × 3¼ in. (26.7 × 17.8 × 8.3 cm)
M.2014.198.6
pp. *12*, *17*

GIJS BAKKER
(b. 1942, Netherlands)

Circle in Circle bracelet, designed 1967, this example made 1989
PMMA
2⅝ × 4¾ × 4¾ in. (6.7 × 12.1 × 12.1 cm)
Marks: gijs bakker
M.2013.221.1
p. *18*

Dew Drop necklace, 1982
PVC, print
19½ × 21⅝ × 1⁄16 in. (49.5 × 54.9 × .2 cm)
Marks: "dew drop" 1982 m 33; GBakker
M.2014.198.7
pp. *19*, 42, 132, *133*

Edberg brooch, 1985
From the series Sports Figures, 1985–91
PVC, newspaper, citrine, gold
6½ × 3¾ × ⅜ in. (16.5 × 9.5 × 1 cm)
Marks: Edberg; GBakker '85
M.2014.198.8
p. *20*

The Cry brooch, 2010
Number 1 from an edition of 5
Silver, diamonds
3⅞ × 2½ × ½ in. (9.8 × 6.4 × 1.3 cm)
Marks: GIJS BAKKER; 1/5
M.2014.198.9
p. *20*

RALPH BAKKER
(b. 1958, Germany, active Netherlands)

Necklace, designed 2001, made 2007
Niello on silver, silver, gold
8¾ × 8¾ × ⅛ in. (22.2 × 22.2 × .3 cm)
M.2014.198.10
pp. *21*, *134*, 135–36

RedKrock necklace, 2004
From the series Krock, 2004–08
Enamel on silver, gold
8¾ × 6¼ × ⅝ in. (22.2 × 15.9 × 1.6 cm)
M.2014.198.11

BORIS BALLY
(b. 1961, United States, active Pennsylvania and Rhode Island)

D.P.W. Brooch, 1995
Aluminum traffic sign
1⅞ × 4⅝ × ⅝ in. (4.8 × 11.8 × 1.6 cm)
Marks: BALLY; © 95
M.2014.198.12a–c

MICHAEL BECKER
(b. 1958, Germany)

6 × 5 × 8 brooch, 1990
Gold, synthetic spinel
⅜ × 3¾ × ½ in. (1 × 9.5 × 1.3 cm)
Marks: 6 × 5 × 8; 750; MB; 90
M.2014.198.13
p. *22*

Brooch, 1999
Gold
1½ × 1½ × ⅜ in. (3.8 × 3.8 × 1 cm)
Marks: 750 MB
M.2014.198.14
p. *22*

JAMIE BENNETT
(b. 1948, United States, active New York)

Coloratura II brooch, 1984
Number 2 of 23 in the series Coloratura, 1984–85
Enamel on copper, silver
1½ × 3¾ × ¼ in. (3.8 × 9.5 × .6 cm)
Marks: J Bennett 84
M.2014.198.15
p. *22*

Petrossa Neckpiece 4, 1990
Number 4 of 5 in the series Petrossa, 1989–90
Enamel on copper, gold
13⅛ × 6¼ × ½ in. (33.3 × 15.9 × 1.3 cm)
Marks: Bennett
M.2014.198.16a–b
p. *23*

DAVID BIELANDER
(b. 1968, Switzerland, active Germany)

Dung Beetle brooch, 2007
From an edition of 50
Stainless-steel teaspoon, gold
2¾ × 1⅞ × 1 in. (7 × 4.8 × 2.5 cm)
Marks: artist's mark; 1
M.2014.198.17
pp. *24*, 146

Koi bracelet, 2013
Leather, thumbtacks, silver
5¼ × 5 × 4½ in. (13.3 × 12.7 × 11.4 cm)
Marks: artist's mark
M.2013.221.2
p. *24*

JOAN FRAERMAN BINKLEY
(1927–2000, United States, active Illinois)

Necklace, 1984
Ceramic with luster glazes, brass
10 × 9¼ × 1¼ in. (25.4 × 23.5 × 3.2 cm)
M.2014.198.80

MANFRED BISCHOFF
(1947–2015, Germany, active Italy)

Haus des Philosophischen Zerfalls brooch, 1987
Silver with gilding
2 9/16 × 3 11/16 × 1/2 in. (6.5 × 9.4 × 1.3 cm)
M.2014.198.18

Physikalisches Modellbild brooch, 1987
Silver with gilding, coral
3 1/16 × 3 1/4 × 5/8 in. (7.8 × 8.3 × 1.6 cm)
Marks: artist's mark; 87
M.2014.198.19
p. *25*

The Absent Third brooch, 1989
Gold, silver, copper, rose twig, stone
4 1/2 × 3 1/4 × 1 1/16 in. (11.4 × 8.3 × 2.7 cm)
M.2014.198.20

Ring, 1993
Gold, mirror, coral
1 3/4 × 1 1/2 × 1 1/4 in. (4.5 × 3.8 × 3.2 cm)
Marks: artist's mark; 93
M.2014.198.21
p. *25*

Rinderwahnsinn brooch, 1994
Gold, coral, imitation coral
4 1/8 × 4 × 1 1/4 in. (10.5 × 10.2 × 3.2 cm)
Marks: artist's mark; 94
M.2014.198.22

Night Visitors ring, 1998
Gold, coral
1 1/4 × 1 1/2 × 1 in. (3.2 × 3.8 × 2.5 cm)
Marks: MB 98
M.2013.221.3
pp. *26*, 144, 147

Night Visitors drawing, 1998
Ink and graphite on board
11 1/2 × 8 1/4 in. (29.2 × 21 cm)
Inscription: night visitors
Pierced to attach *Night Visitors* ring
M.2014.198.27
p. *26*

Zoological brooch, 1998
Gold
3 5/8 × 2 3/4 × 1 1/4 in. (9.2 × 7 × 3.2 cm)
Marks: artist's mark; 98
M.2014.198.23
p. *25*

Pomme de Terre–Pathètique–Tragique brooch, 2002
Gold, coral
2 × 2 7/8 × 7/8 in. (5.1 × 7.3 × 2.2 cm)
Marks: artist's mark; II
M.2014.198.24
pp. *26*, 144, 146

Pomme de Terre–Pathètique–Tragique drawing, 2002
Ink and graphite on paper mounted on board
11 1/2 × 8 1/4 in. (29.2 × 21 cm)
Inscription: pomme de terre pathètique tragique
Pierced to attach *Pomme de Terre–Pathètique–Tragique* brooch
M.2014.198.28
p. *26*

LIV BLÅVARP
(b. 1956, Norway)

Necklace, designed 1991, this example made 2001
Birch, alkyd paint, brass, elastic cord
9 1/2 × 8 × 3 in. (24.1 × 20.3 × 7.6 cm)
Marks: LB 01
M.2014.198.29
p. *27*

SERGEI BLUMIN
(b. 1947, Soviet Union [now Russia], active New York)

Declaration of Love brooch, 1986
From the series Nude Pin, 1986
Silver, gold
1 3/4 × 2 3/4 × 1/2 in. (4.5 × 7 × 1.3 cm)
Marks: Sergei Blumin 86
M.2014.198.30

JOSE MARIA BRIBIESCA
(b. 1936, United States, active New Zealand)

Ring, 2013
From the series 77, 2013
Chrome-plated brass, PMMA
1 1/2 × 1 5/8 × 5/8 in. (3.8 × 4.1 × 1.6 cm)
M.2014.198.91

HELEN BRITTON
(b. 1966, Australia, active Germany)

Last Bird brooch, 2006
Silver, onyx, glass, paint
4 × 3 3/4 × 3/4 in. (10.2 × 9.5 × 1.9 cm)
M.2014.198.31
p. *28*

Last Cowboy 3 brooch, 2006
Silver, glass, sapphires, plastic
2 × 2 3/4 × 1 in. (5.1 × 7 × 2.5 cm)
Marks: artist's mark
M.2014.198.33

Strange brooch, 2006
Silver, glass
1 1/2 × 2 1/4 × 5/8 in. (3.8 × 5.7 × 1.6 cm)
Marks: artist's mark
M.2014.198.34
p. *28*

Two Houses earrings, 2010
Silver, paint, diamonds
Each: 1 1/4 × 1 1/4 × 1 in. (3.2 × 3.2 × 2.5 cm)
Marks: artist's mark
M.2014.198.32a–b

DOUG BUCCI
(b. 1971, United States, active Pennsylvania)

Islet | Stainless bracelet, designed 2010, this example made 2012
Number 6 from an edition of 20, plus 2 artist proofs
Bronze-infiltrated stainless steel
4 1/4 × 4 1/4 × 1 in. (10.8 × 10.8 × 2.5 cm)
Marks: artist's mark; 06/20 (on box)
M.2014.198.35
pp. *29*, 136, *137*

SEBASTIAN BUESCHER
(b. 1978, Germany, active England and Netherlands)

Pregnant Tree Boy brooch, 2006
Wood, glass, alcohol, black widow spiders, porcelain, pearl, cotton thread, silver
2 1/4 × 4 3/4 × 1 1/4 in. (5.7 × 12.1 × 3.2 cm)
M.2014.198.37a–b
pp. 142, *143*

Octocoralia necklace, 2008
From the series Hadal Realm, 2008–09
Ceramic, sea urchin spines, wool yarn, synthetic thread
17 × 10 × 1 in. (43.2 × 25.4 × 2.5 cm)
M.2014.198.36
pp. *30*, 146

JITTRAKARN BUNTERNGPIBOON
(b. 1986, Thailand)

Ring, 2009
From the series Build ME, 2009
Rhodium-plated brass
2 1/8 × 2 7/16 × 1 15/16 in. (5.4 × 6.2 × 4.9 cm)
M.2016.161.1

CLAUS BURY
(b. 1946, Germany)

Ring, 1971
Gold, PMMA
1 7/8 × 1 7/16 × 7/8 in. (4.8 × 3.7 × 2.2 cm)
Marks: 750
M.2013.221.4
p. *31*

Brooch, 1973
Varicolored gold
2 5/8 × 2 7/16 × 1/2 in. (6.7 × 6.2 × 1.3 cm)
Marks: artist's mark; BURY; 750
M.2014.198.38
p. *31*

Metallzeichnung brooch, 1977
Gold, silver, copper alloy
2 × 4 1/4 × 1/4 in. (5.1 × 10.8 × .6 cm)
Marks: Bury 77; 9
M.2014.198.39
p. *31*

C

PIERRE CAVALAN
(b. 1954, France, active Australia)

Brooch, c. 1990–95
Silver-plated brass, rhinestones, found objects
6 3/4 × 3 1/2 × 1/2 in. (17.2 × 8.9 × 1.3 cm)
Marks: PIERRE CAVALAN
M.2014.198.41
p. *32*

Semaphore Necklace #1, 1997
Copper alloy, found objects 8 1/2 × 9 1/4 × 1/2 in. (21.6 × 23.5 × 1.3 cm)
Marks: 1997; PIERRE CAVALAN
M.2014.198.40
p. *32*

ANTON CEPKA
(b. 1936, Czechoslovakia [now Slovakia])

Brooch, 1986
Silver, PMMA
1 × 4 1/2 × 1/2 in. (2.5 × 11.4 × 1.3 cm)
Hallmarks for: Slovakia 900 silver guarantee; 900/1000 silver; sponsor
M.2014.198.42
p. *33*

KAI CHAN
(b. 1940, China, active Canada)

Mountains & Seas brooch, 1997
Balsa, watercolor
2 3/4 × 4 3/4 × 3/4 in. (7 × 12.1 × 1.9 cm)
Marks: Mountains & Seas Kai Chan '97
M.2014.198.43

PETER CHANG
(b. 1944, England, active Scotland)

Bracelet, 1989
PMMA and plastic grout on polystyrene foam
6 × 6 × 2 in. (15.2 × 15.2 × 5.1 cm)
M.2014.198.45
p. *34*

Brooch, 1990
PMMA, PVC, and glitter on polystyrene foam
5 1/4 × 2 × 3/4 in. (13.3 × 5.1 × 1.9 cm)
M.2014.198.44

Bracelet, 1995
PMMA and resin on polystyrene foam
6 × 6 × 3 in. (15.2 × 15.2 × 7.6cm)
M.2013.221.5
p. *35*

SHARON CHURCH
(b. 1948, United States, active Pennsylvania)

Long Chain necklace, 1986
Silver, onyx, diamonds
16 1/4 × 11 3/8 × 7/8 in. (41.3 × 28.9 × 2.2 cm)
Marks: CHURCH; STERLING; ©
M.2014.198.46
p. *36*

Foliate Harness necklace, 1997
Silver, leather
6 × 10 × 3/4 in. (15.2 × 25.4 × 1.9 cm)
Marks: STERLING; CHURCH; ©
M.2014.198.51a–b
p. *37*

Necklace, 1998
Silver
9 1/4 × 5 1/2 × 1 in. (23.5 × 14 × 2.5 cm)
Marks: ©; CHURCH; STERLING
Made with Richard H. Reinhardt's hammer
M.2014.198.52

Scatter Pins, 1998
Lemonwood, gold, buffalo horn, diamonds
Hand pin: 2 3/4 × 1 1/4 × 1 in. (7 × 3.2 × 2.5 cm); each diamond pin: 3/8 × 3/8 × 3/8 in. (1 × 1 × 1 cm)
Marks: CHURCH; 14K (on each pin)
M.2014.198.47.1–.5
pp. *38*, *208*

Speak Softly brooch, 1998
Gold, buffalo horn
5 1/2 × 1 1/4 × 1 in. (14 × 3.2 × 2.5 cm)
Marks: ©; CHURCH; 14K
M.2014.198.48a–d

Lion's Head necklace, c. 1999
Silver, boxwood
9 1/2 × 6 1/2 × 1 7/8 in. (24.1 × 16.5 × 4.8 cm)
Marks: CHURCH; STERLING; ©
M.2013.221.6a–b
p. *38*

Earrings, 2002
Silver, diamonds
Each: 1 7/8 × 1 3/8 × 1/2 in. (4.8 × 3.5 × 1.3 cm)
Marks: STERLING; CHURCH; ©
M.2014.198.50a–b

Purple Heart brooch and earrings, 2003
Purpleheart, gold, diamonds
Brooch: 3 × 3 × 1 1/4 in. (7.6 × 7.6 × 3.2 cm); each earring: 2 1/8 × 1 1/8 × 7/8 in. (5.4 × 2.9 × 2.2 cm)
Marks: CHURCH; 14K; © (on brooch and one earring)
M.2014.198.49.1–.2
pp. 204, *205*

SUSAN COHN
(b. 1952, Australia)

3 tooth-saw bracelet, 1985
From the series Saw, 1984–85
Anodized aluminum alloy
6 1/4 × 6 3/4 × 1 1/4 in. (15.9 × 17.2 × 3.2 cm)
Marks: artist's mark
M.2014.198.53
p. *39*

ROS CONWAY
(b. 1951, England)

HUGH O'DONNELL
(b. 1951, England)

At the Snare III brooch, 1984
Enamel on silver, gold
3 × 2 × 1/8 in. (7.6 × 5.1 × .3 cm)
Hallmarks for: artist; sterling; London; 1984
M.2014.198.54
p. *39*

KEN CORY
(1943–1994, United States, active Washington)

How to Fix Your Snake belt buckle, 1976
Enamel on copper, brass
2 7/8 × 2 7/8 × 3/4 in. (7.3 × 7.3 × 1.9 cm)
Marks: KEN CORY 1976
M.2014.198.55
pp. 78, *79*

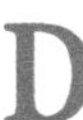

D

JOHANNA DAHM
(formerly Johanna Hess-Dahm, b. 1947, Switzerland)

Rod Brooch, 1983
Silver, stainless-steel wire
12 × 1 1/2 × 1/4 in. (30.5 × 3.8 × .6 cm)
Marks: 925; artist's mark
M.2014.198.57

InbetweenfingerThing hand ornament, 1985
PMMA, polyethylene cord
1 1/4 × 1 3/8 × 1 3/8 in. (3.2 × 3.5 × 3.5 cm); cord from top of ornament: 2 in. (5.1 cm) length
Marks: HESS
M.2014.198.56

PETER DE WIT
(b. 1952, Netherlands, active Sweden)

Necklace, 1983
Silver, anodized aluminum
8 3/4 × 9 3/4 × 1 in. (22.2 × 24.8 × 2.5 cm)
Hallmarks for: artist (PETER DE WIT); Linköping; Sweden; 830/1000 silver; 1983
Marks: METALL
M.2014.198.58
p. *44*

LAM DE WOLF
(b. 1949, Netherlands)

Headdress, 1986
From the series Hommage à la Libre Pensée, 1986
Cotton fabric, kindling sticks, paint
$30 \times 23 \times 14$ in. ($76.2 \times 58.4 \times 35.6$ cm)
Marks: artist's mark
M.2014.198.59
p. *45*

ELISABETH JESUS GUENNAIBIM DEFNER
(formerly Elizabeth Kodré-Defner, b. 1931, Austria)

Rodent Skull necklace, 1984
Gold, steel, silver, opal, emerald, diamond, rubies
$7\frac{13}{16} \times 6\frac{1}{8} \times \frac{1}{2}$ in. ($19.8 \times 15.6 \times 1.3$ cm)
Marks: E. Kodre; E. Kodre-Defner; 1984; E Kodre-D[efner]; artist's mark; 750
M.2013.221.7a–b
p. *46*

AURELIE DELLASANTA
(b. 1980, Switzerland)

Gandhi Brooch, 2002
From the series About Money, 2002–05
Rhinestones, Indian paper money, brass, silver, enamel
$1\frac{1}{2} \times 1\frac{1}{2} \times \frac{3}{8}$ in. ($3.8 \times 3.8 \times 1$ cm)
M.2014.198.60

PAUL DERREZ
(b. 1950, Netherlands)

Wisselring, designed 1975
Silver alloy, PMMA
Ring: $1 \times \frac{13}{16} \times \frac{1}{4}$ in. ($2.5 \times 2.1 \times .6$ cm);
inserts: $\frac{1}{2} \times 1 \times \frac{1}{8}$ in. ($1.3 \times 2.5 \times .3$ cm)
Marks: artist's mark
M.2014.198.61a–e

Fan Brooch, 1982
Anodized aluminum knitting needles, PVC sheet, PMMA
$4\frac{1}{2} \times 2\frac{1}{2} \times \frac{1}{8}$ in. ($11.4 \times 6.4 \times .3$ cm)
M.2014.198.62a–b

Pebble Collar, 1985
Cork with spray paint, cotton cord
$18 \times 14\frac{1}{2} \times 2$ in. ($45.7 \times 36.8 \times 5.1$ cm)
M.2014.198.63
p. *47*

GEORG DOBLER
(b. 1952, Germany)

3-D Illusion brooch, designed 1980, made 1981
Acrylic-coated copper alloy
$3\frac{1}{4} \times 5\frac{3}{8} \times \frac{7}{8}$ in. ($8.3 \times 13.7 \times 2.2$ cm)
M.2013.221.8
p. *48*

Brooch, 1982
Silicon-coated steel
$\frac{7}{8} \times 7\frac{1}{4} \times 1$ in. ($2.2 \times 18.4 \times 2.5$ cm)
M.2014.198.64

Wassily K. brooch, 1986
Silicon-coated stainless steel
$6\frac{1}{2} \times 11 \times 1\frac{1}{4}$ in. ($16.5 \times 27.9 \times 3.2$ cm)
M.2014.198.65
p. *49*

Ring, 1989
Silver, amethyst
$1\frac{1}{2} \times 1\frac{5}{16} \times 1$ in. ($3.8 \times 3.3 \times 2.5$ cm)
Marks: DOBLER 925
M.2014.198.69

Ring, designed 1989, made 1990
Silver, citrine
$1\frac{1}{2} \times \frac{15}{16} \times \frac{13}{16}$ in. ($3.8 \times 2.4 \times 2.1$ cm)
Marks: DOBLER 925
M.2014.198.72

The Aesthetic of Minerals necklace, 1990
Rose quartz, smoky quartz, quartz, citrine, tourmaline, silver
$7\frac{3}{4} \times 7\frac{1}{2} \times 1\frac{3}{8}$ in. ($19.7 \times 19.1 \times 3.5$ cm)
Marks: DOBLER 925
M.2014.198.70

Brooch, designed 1992, made 1994
Gold
$2 \times 6\frac{1}{4} \times \frac{7}{8}$ in. ($5.1 \times 15.9 \times 2.2$ cm)
M.2014.198.67

Brooch, 1998
Gold, silver
$1\frac{15}{16} \times 1\frac{15}{16} \times \frac{3}{16}$ in. ($4.9 \times 4.9 \times .5$ cm)
Marks: DOBLER; 925 • 750
M.2014.198.66
p. *50*

Brooch, 1998
Gold, blue topaz
$1\frac{5}{8} \times 2\frac{7}{8} \times 1\frac{3}{16}$ in. ($4.1 \times 7.3 \times 3$ cm)
Marks: 750 DOBLER
M.2013.221.9
p. *50*

Happiness of Grapes brooch, 1998
Silver, amethyst
$2 \times 4 \times \frac{3}{4}$ in. ($5.1 \times 10.2 \times 1.9$ cm)
M.2014.198.68
p. *50*

Trouble with Beauty necklace and earrings, designed 2004, made 2006
Silver, citrine, rutilated smoky quartz
Necklace: $8\frac{1}{2} \times 7\frac{1}{2} \times 1\frac{3}{16}$ in. ($21.6 \times 19.1 \times 3$ cm);
each earring: $2\frac{7}{8} \times \frac{11}{16} \times \frac{1}{2}$ in. ($7.3 \times 1.8 \times 1.3$ cm)
Marks: 925 (on each earring)
M.2014.198.71.1–.2
p. *51*

GEMMA DRAPER
(b. 1971, Spain)

Brooch, 2012
From the series Strain's rhetoric, 2012
Copper alloy, silver alloy
$5 \times 4\frac{3}{4} \times \frac{1}{4}$ in. ($12.7 \times 12.1 \times .6$ cm)
M.2014.198.73
p. *51*

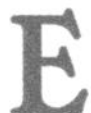

ROBERT EBENDORF
(b. 1938, United States, active Georgia, New York, and North Carolina)

Necklace, designed 1984, made 1984–85
Chinese newspaper on Styrofoam, gold foil, acrylic lacquer, copper, plastic
$12\frac{1}{2} \times 9\frac{1}{2} \times 2$ in. ($31.8 \times 24.1 \times 5.1$ cm)
Marks: R Ebendorf
M.2014.198.74
p. *52*

EVA EISLER
(b. 1952, Czechoslovakia [now Czech Republic], active New York)

Brooch, 1987
Slate
$1\frac{9}{16} \times 4\frac{3}{4} \times \frac{5}{8}$ in. ($4 \times 12.1 \times 1.6$ cm)
Marks: E. EISLER 87
M.2014.198.75a–c
p. *53*

SANDRA ENTERLINE
(b. 1960, United States, active California)

Queen Bee brooch, 1998
Gold, queen yellow jacket, pollen, glass
$1\frac{1}{2} \times 1\frac{1}{2} \times \frac{5}{8}$ in. ($3.8 \times 3.8 \times 1.6$ cm)
Marks: 18K; Sandra Enterline 98.
M.2014.198.76
pp. *53*, 128–29, *128*

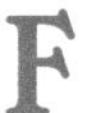

SITA FALKENA
(b. 1957, Curaçao, active Netherlands)

Bracelet, 1988
From the series Nest, 1987–88
Anodized aluminum, stainless steel
$4\frac{1}{4} \times 5\frac{1}{2} \times 1\frac{3}{4}$ in. ($10.8 \times 14 \times 4.5$ cm)
M.2015.252.37

ARLINE FISCH
(b. 1931, United States, active California)

Bell Frills necklace, 1985
Silver, gold
13 × 13 × 2 in. (33 × 33 × 5.1 cm)
Marks: artist's mark; 85; STERLING; HKB29
M.2014.198.77
pp. *54*, 88, 144, 146, 147

Long Cuff bracelet, 1995
Color-coated copper, silver
5¾ × 5¾ × 11 in. (14.6 × 14.6 × 27.9 cm)
Marks: artist's mark; 99
M.2013.221.10
pp. *55*, 144, 147

STEVEN FORD
(b. 1964, United States, active Pennsylvania)

DAVID FORLANO
(b. 1964, United States, active Pennsylvania and New Mexico)

Brooch, 2006
From the series O'Keeffe, 2005–present
Painted polymer clay, silver
2½ × 2½ × 1 in. (6.4 × 6.4 × 2.5 cm)
Marks: forlano ford; • 925
M.2014.198.78

ANNA FRALING
(b. 1955, Germany)

Brooch, 1987
Stainless steel, brass
2 × 3¼ × ½ in. (5.1 × 8.3 × 1.3 cm)
M.2014.198.79
p. *56*

WARWICK FREEMAN
(b. 1953, New Zealand)

Lure brooch, 1984
Pāua shell, pebble, PMMA, fiber
5⅜ × 4⅛ × 1⅜ in. (13.7 × 10.5 × 3.5 cm)
Marks: W • F
M.2013.221.11
pp. 130, *131*

DONALD FRIEDLICH
(b. 1954, United States, active Rhode Island and Wisconsin)

Brooch, 1984
From Erosion Series, 1983–92
Slate, gold, silver
1 3/16 × 1⅝ × ⅜ in. (3 × 4.1 × 1 cm)
Marks: D. Friedlich 1984; 18k, Sterling, 14k
M.2014.198.81

KARL FRITSCH
(b. 1963, Germany, active New Zealand)

Ring, 1999
Silver, ruby, diamonds
1¼ × ¾ × ¾ in. (3.2 × 1.9 × 1.9 cm)
Marks: KF
M.2014.198.82

Ring, c. 2000
Gold, cognac diamonds
⅞ × ⅞ × 9/16 in. (2.2 × 2.2 × 1.4 cm)
Marks: KF
M.2014.198.83

Ring, 2005
Silver, glass
2 × 1¼ × 1 in. (5.1 × 3.2 × 2.5 cm)
Marks: KF
M.2013.221.12
pp. *2* (title page), *42*

MAX FRÖHLICH
(1908–1997, Switzerland)

Ring, 1985
Silver
1⅛ × 2 × 1⅝ in. (2.9 × 5.1 × 4.1 cm)
Marks: MF; 925
M.2014.198.85

Ring, 1985
Silver
1⅛ × 2 × ⅞ in. (2.9 × 5.1 × 2.2 cm)
Marks: artist's mark; 925
M.2014.198.86
p. *56*

Brooch, 1997
Gold
2⅛ × 2⅛ × ¼ in. (5.4 × 5.4 × .6 cm)
Marks: artist's mark; 750; artist's mark; 750
M.2014.198.84
p. *56*

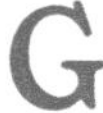

SUSIE GANCH
(b. 1970, United States, active Virginia)

Static Orbital Model #3 (Menorah), 1999
From the series About Space, 1997–2003
Silver, stainless steel
15½ × 19½ × 14½ in. (39.4 × 49.5 × 36.8 cm)
Marks: SG; STERLING
M.2013.221.13
p. *57*

ELIZABETH GARRISON
(b. 1952, United States, active Florida and New York)

Under the Fish brooch, 1982
Silver, brass, enamel, found object, agate, bone
2 × 3 × ⅜ in. (5.1 × 7.6 × 1 cm)
Marks: Elizabeth Garrison 1982
M.2015.252.1
p. *58*

Moon #2 brooch, 1985
Number 2 of 7 from the series Moon, 1985–87
Silver, copper, enamel, bone, gold
3¼ × 2¾ × ⅜ in. (8.3 × 7 × 1 cm)
Marks: Elizabeth Garrison 1985
M.2015.252.2

Nightshrine brooch, 1987
Number 1 of 3 from the series Nightshrine, 1987
Silver, copper, enamel, mother of pearl, gold
2½ × 1½ × ¼ in. (6.5 × 3.8 × .6 cm)
Marks: Elizabeth Garrison 1987
M.2015.252.3
p. *58*

THOMAS GENTILLE
(b. 1936, United States, active New York)

Pin in three parts, c. 1968
Copper, alabaster epoxy resin, ebony epoxy resin, ostrich eggshell, gold
Each: 2¼ × 2½ × ¼ in. (5.7 × 6.4 × .6 cm)
Marks: T. Gentille (on each)
M.2014.198.88a–c
p. *58*

TONI GOESSLER-SNYDER
(1942–1982, b. Germany, active Pennsylvania)

Brooch, after 1971
Silver, ivory
2½ × 2¼ × 7/16 in. (6.4 × 5.7 × 1.1 cm)
M.2014.282.1

Brooch/pendant, 1975
Silver with gilding, enamel
2⅝ × 3 13/16 × 11/16 in. (6.7 × 9.7 × 1.8 cm)
Marks: TONI; artist's mark; 24k; STERLING
M.2015.252.4
p. *59*

LISA GRALNICK
(b. 1956, United States, active New York and Wisconsin)

Brooch, 2000
Gold
1½ × 2¼ × ½ in. (3.8 × 5.7 × 1.3 cm)
Marks: Gralnick; 2000; 18K Gold
M.2014.198.89
p. *59*

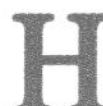

GÉSINE HACKENBERG
(b. 1972, Germany, active Netherlands)

Delft Blue "Plooischotel" Necklace, 2012
1943 Royal Delft earthenware dish, nylon cord, gold
Necklace: 47½ in. (120.7 cm) length;
dish: 14¼ × 14¼ × 2¾ in. (36.2 × 36.2 × 7 cm)
Marks: artist's mark; '12
M.2014.198.90a–b
p. *60*

LAURIE J. HALL
(b. 1944, United States, active Washington and Oregon)

Wheelbarrow brooch, 2004
Silver, yew
2¼ × 5⅝ × 1⅞ in. (5.7 × 14.3 × 4.8 cm)
Marks: Laurie Hall; L. HALL; 2004
M.2015.252.6
pp. 74, *76*

Bubble-Tea necklace, 2005
Silver, coral, paper tea label, PMMA, styrene plastic, glass beads
14½ × 7 × ½ in. (36.8 × 17.8 × 1.3 cm)
Marks: L. HALL; 925
M.2015.252.5
p. *61*

ANDREA MAXA HALMSCHLAGER
(b. 1961, Austria, active Germany)

Great Spiral bracelet, 1986
From the series Paperwork, 1986
Silk paper, brass, copper, stainless steel
8 × 8 × 5 in. (20.3 × 20.3 × 12.7 cm)
Marks: A. Halmschlager MAX 86 6/6
M.2015.252.7
p. *62*

SUSAN H. HAMLET
(b. 1954, United States, active New York and Massachusetts)

Shim Bracelet #1, 1983
Stainless steel, polyethylene tubing, silver, PMMA, electrical wire insulation
3⅝ × 3⅝ × ½ in. (9.2 × 9.2 × 1.3 cm)
Marks: HAMLET
M.2015.252.8
p. *63*

WILLIAM HARPER
(b. 1944, United States, active Ohio and Florida)

Barbarian Bracelet #1, 1980
Silver with gilding, enamel on copper, gold
4¾ × 4¾ × 13⁄16 in. (12.1 × 12.1 × 2.1 cm)
Marks: William HARPER 1980; BARBARIAN BRACELET #
M.2015.252.9
p. *64*

Brooch, 1983
Silver, gold, enamel on copper, pearl, moonstone
4¼ × 1½ × 5⁄16 in. (10.8 × 3.8 × .8 cm)
M.2015.252.10
p. *64*

JUHANI HEIKKILÄ
(b. 1956, Finland)

Homo Communicans brooch, 1997
Brass, rosewood, ebony
4⅛ × 3⅜ × ⅝ in. (10.5 × 8.6 × 1.6 cm)
M.2015.252.11
pp. 139, 142, *142*

THOMAS HERMAN
(b. 1957, United States, active Iowa, California, New Mexico, and New York)

Slate & Gold Leaf Brooch, 1999
Slate with gilding
⅞ × 7¼ × ⅜ in. (2.2 × 18.4 × 1 cm)
Marks: Tom Herman; 99
M.2015.252.12

MIRJAM HILLER
(b. 1974, Germany)

Syspera brooch, 2011
Powder-coated stainless steel
4½ × 5 × 2½ in. (11.4 × 12.7 × 6.4 cm)
M.2015.252.13
p. *65*

Loperenias brooch, 2012
Powder-coated stainless steel
8¼ × 7 × 2½ in. (21 × 17.8 × 6.4 cm)
M.2013.221.14

HIRAMATSU YASUKI
(1926–2012, Japan)

Ring, n.d.
Gold
1¼ × ¾ × ⅜ in. (3.2 × 1.9 × 1 cm)
Marks: artist's mark; 保城 (artist's name); K20; JAPAN
M.2015.252.14
p. *66*

RON HO
(b. 1936, United States, active Washington)

Tibetan Reliquary necklace, 2012
Silver, stone beads, Tibetan iron keys, stone earplug
14½ × 7¾ × ⅞ in. (36.8 × 19.7 × 2.2 cm)
Marks: RON HO
M.2013.221.15
pp. *66*, 74, *75*

TINA FUNG HOLDER
(b. 1946, British Guiana [now Guyana], active Illinois and Wisconsin)

Goddess Supra Necklace, 1979–85
From an edition of 10 in the series Goddess, 1979–present
Safety pins, cotton thread, glass beads
Bib: 7½ × 7 × ⅜ in. (19.1 × 17.8 × 1 cm);
each cord: 12 in. (30.5 cm) length
Marks: artist's mark
M.2014.198.87

MARIAN HOSKING
(b. 1948, Australia)

Moveable Seaweed brooch, 2006
Silver
5½ × 5½ × ¼ in. (14 × 14 × .6 cm)
M.2015.252.16

Leaf litter WA brooch, 2009
Silver
3¼ × 3¼ × 1 in. (8.3 × 8.3 × 2.5 cm)
M.2015.252.15
pp. *67*, 138, *138*

MARY LEE HU
(b. 1943, United States, active Washington)

Bracelet #20, 1983
Silver, gold
3¾ × 3 × ½ in. (9.5 × 7.6 × 1.3 cm)
Marks: HU
M.2015.252.17
pp. *67*, 86

JOHN IVERSEN
(b. 1953, Germany, active New York)

Circle Pin, 1988
Enamel, gilded copper alloy
4½ × 4½ × ¼ in. (11.4 × 11.4 × .6 cm)
Marks: John Iversen; 1988
M.2015.252.18
p. *67*

J

HERMANN JÜNGER
(1928–2005, Germany)

Brooch, c. 1970
Gold, opals, enamel
1 7/8 × 1 1/2 × 3/8 in. (4.8 × 3.8 × 1 cm)
Marks: artist's mark
M.2015.252.19
p. *94*

Necklace, 1993
Silver, gold, hematite, granite, wood box for storage
Wire: 19 1/2 in. (49.5 cm) length; box: 5 3/4 × 5 3/4 × 7/8 in. (14.6 × 14.6 × 2.2 cm)
Marks on wire: NIESSING; manufacturer's mark; 750
Marks on box: 75; artist's mark; 93
M.2015.252.21a–e
p. 94

Brooch, 1997
Gold, semiprecious stones, possibly resin
2 1/4 × 2 1/16 × 1/2 in. (5.7 × 5.2 × 1.3 cm)
Marks: Jünger 97, artist's mark
M.2013.221.16
p. *95*

Brooch, 1999
Silver
2 3/8 × 2 3/8 × 1/4 in. (6 × 6 × .6 cm)
Marks: Jünger 99, artist's mark
M.2015.252.20

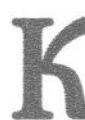

JUDITH KAUFMAN
(b. 1955, United States, active Connecticut)

Point of Woods brooch, 2002
Gold, tourmaline, onyx, silver, pearls, spinels, shell
5 11/16 × 2 1/8 × 1/2 in. (14.5 × 5.4 × 1.3 cm)
Marks: KAUFMAN
M.2015.252.22
p. *95*

Abstract Track brooch, 2003
Gold, aquamarine
2 × 2 1/4 × 1/2 in. (5.1 × 5.7 × 1.3 cm)
M.2015.252.23

BETSY KING
(b. 1953, United States, active Virginia and New Jersey)

Just a Peek necklace, 1980
Silver, brass, leather, print, PMMA, garnets, silk thread, snakeskin
Chain: 21 1/2 in. (54.6 cm) length;
pendant: 3 3/8 × 2 1/2 × 3/4 in. (8.6 × 6.4 × 1.9 cm)
Marks: STERL[ING]
M.2015.252.24

Chicago City Bolo, 1988
Silver, copper, brass, plastics, postcard, synthetic spinel
Cord: 36 1/2 in. (92.7 cm) length;
slide: 6 1/4 × 2 13/16 × 7/8 in. (15.9 × 7.1 × 2.2 cm)
M.2015.252.25
p. *96*

Earth Angel brooch, 1994
Silver, copper, brass, paper, polycarbonate sheet, foil, ivory
3 11/16 × 4 1/16 × 3/8 in. (9.4 × 10.3 × 1 cm)
Marks: BK 94
M.2014.282.2
p. *96*

ALICE H. KLEIN
(b. 1956, United States, active Pennsylvania, Wisconsin, and Delaware)

Necklace, 1982
PMMA, Cratex wheels, copper alloy (nickel silver), silver
9 1/8 × 6 3/4 × 3/4 in. (23.2 × 17.2 × 1.9 cm)
Marks: ALICE H. KLEIN; © 1982; PROTOTYPE; EDITION OF 12
M.2015.252.26
p. *97*

Bracelet, 1983
Silver, PMMA
2 1/2 × 3 × 1 3/4 in. (6.4 × 7.6 × 4.5 cm)
Marks: ALICE H. KLEIN · P·1·A·BRACELET · FEB. 1983 ©
M.2015.252.27

ESTHER KNOBEL
(b. 1949, Poland, active Israel)

Brooch, mid-1980s
From the series Warrior, 1982–87
Steel can, alkyd paint, elastic cord, stainless steel
4 1/2 × 6 1/2 × 1/4 in. (11.4 × 16.5 × .6 cm)
M.2015.252.28
p. *97*

A Kit for Mending Thoughts pin set, 2005
Gold, silver, paper-lined tin box for storage
Square piece: 2 5/16 × 2 3/8 × 1/16 in. (5.9 × 6 × .2 cm);
box (closed): 3 × 7 1/8 × 3/4 in. (7.6 × 18.1 × 1.9 cm)
M.2015.252.29a–f
p. *97*

FRIEDRICH KNUPPER
(1947–1987, Germany)

Necklace, 1984
Silver, iron, cellulose nitrate on brass and silver
12 × 8 1/16 × 1/2 in. (30.5 × 20.5 × 1.3 cm);
Marks: F Knupper; 1984
M.2015.252.30
p. *98*

RENA KOOPMAN
(b. 1945, United States, active Massachusetts)

Earrings, 1990
Varicolored gold
Round earring: 1 5/16 × 1 5/16 × 1/2 in. (3.3 × 3.3 × 1.3 cm);
square earring: 1 3/16 × 1 3/16 × 3/8 in. (3 × 3 × 1 cm)
Marks: ©; RENA; 18K
M.2015.252.32a–b
pp. *15*, *99*

Donut Pin, 1992
Varicolored gold
2 × 2 × 1/4 in. (5.1 × 5.1 × .6 cm)
Marks: © RENA; 18K; 22K
M.2015.252.31

Earrings, 1994
Varicolored gold, copper alloy (*shakudō*)
Each: 1 1/2 × 1 1/2 × 1/4 in. (3.8 × 3.8 × .6 cm)
Marks: © RENA; 18K; 22K
M.2015.252.33a–b

ROBIN KRANITZKY
(b. 1956, United States, active Virginia)

KIM OVERSTREET
(b. 1955, United States, active Virginia)

Night Garden brooch, 1990
Balsa, silver, brass, copper, PMMA, Micarta™, printed paper, glass beads, found objects
3 3/4 × 2 3/4 × 1 1/2 in. (9.5 × 7 × 3.8 cm)
Marks: Kim Overstreet . . . #1537 . . . 1990 . . . Robin Kranitzky
M.2015.252.34
pp. 132, *132*, 135

Salmon Dream brooch and stand, 1999
Wood, PMMA, brass, silver, copper, polymer clay, printed paper, acetate, Micarta™, found objects
Brooch: 2 3/4 × 4 1/2 × 3/4 in. (7 × 11.4 × 1.9 cm);
stand: 8 × 9 × 8 1/2 in. (20.3 × 22.9 × 21.6 cm)
Inscription: Created in Honor of Lois Boardman's 68th Birthday August 18 1999
Marks on brooch: "Salmon Dream"; #1702 – 1999; · Kim Overstreet · Robin Kranitzky ·
Marks on stand: "Salmon Dream"; #1702 – 1999; · Robin Kranitzky · Kim Overstreet ·
M.2015.252.35a–b
pp. 139, *141*, *203*, 204

CHARON KRANSEN
(b. 1950, Netherlands)

Necklace, 1985
Number 36 from an edition of 50
Elastic cord, gilded brass
7 × 6 3/8 × 1/8 in. (17.8 × 16.2 ×.3 cm)
M.2015.252.36

CAROLYN KRIEGMAN
(1933–1999, United States, active New Jersey)

Necklace, 1969
PMMA, metal rings
19 3/4 × 13 3/4 × 10 1/2 in. (50.2 × 34.9 × 26.7 cm)
Marks: C Kriegman '69
M.2015.31
p. *100*

Necklace, 1969
Silver, smoky citrine
13 × 5 1/8 × 5/8 in. (33 × 13 × 1.6 cm)
Marks: artist's mark; STERLING
M.2015.253
p. *101*

DANIEL KRUGER
(b. 1951, South Africa, active Germany)

Necklace, 1984
Silver, silk cord
Cord: 24 1/2 in. (62.2 cm) length;
pendant: 1 1/2 × 4 1/2 × 1 1/2 in. (3.8 × 11.4 × 3.8 cm)
M.2015.252.38
p. *102*

Necklace, 1987
Gold, mirror and glass fragments
8 1/2 × 8 1/2 × 1/2 in. (21.6 × 21.6 × 1.3 cm)
Marks: 750; artist's mark
M.2015.252.39
p. *102*

ELKE KUHN
(formerly Elke Kuhn Moore, b. 1942, United States, active New York)

Liberty Celebration necklace, designed 1986, made 1986–2000
Ribbons, PVC novelty erasers, painted paper clips, nylon buttons, brass beads, copper wire
Cord: 39 in. (99.1 cm) length; pendant:
8 × 11 1/2 × 2 in. (20.3 × 29.2 × 5.1 cm)
M.2015.252.74

Valentine Neckpiece, designed 1992, made 2000
Ribbons, polymer clay, thread bobbins, copper wire
12 × 15 × 2 in. (30.5 × 38.1 × 5.1 cm)
M.2015.252.73

OTTO KÜNZLI
(b. 1948, Switzerland, active Germany)

Gold Macht Blind bracelet, designed 1980, this example made c. 1986
Rubber, gold
3 1/16 × 3 × 1/2 in. (7.8 × 7.6 × 1.3 cm)
M.2013.221.17
pp. *41*, 42, 146

Centifolia brooch, 1983
From the series Wallpaper Brooches, 1982–85
Wallpaper on polymethacrylimide foam
5 1/8 × 3 1/2 × 2 1/2 in. (13 × 8.9 × 6.4 cm)
M.2013.221.19
p. *103*

Heart brooch, 1985
Number 4 from an edition of 10
Acrylic lacquer on polymethacrylimide foam
3 3/4 × 3 1/2 × 1 3/4 in. (9.5 × 8.9 × 4.5 cm)
M.2013.221.18
p. *103*

Fragment necklace, 1986
From the series Fragments, 1986–88
Wooden frame, stainless-steel wire
15 3/4 × 6 × 1 1/4 in. (40 × 15.2 × 3.2 cm)
M.2015.252.40
p. *104*

Fragment necklace, 1986
From the series Fragments, 1986–88
Wooden frame, stainless-steel wire
17 3/4 × 10 1/4 × 7/8 in. (45.1 × 26 × 2.2 cm)
Marks: Otto Künzli 1986
M.2016.161.2

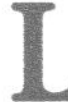

SOFIE LACHAERT
(b. 1958, Belgium)

Circles bracelet/necklace (chp20), designed 1984
Produced by chp . . . ? (established as Chi ha paura . . . ?) Amsterdam, founded 1996
Silver
11 1/2 × 10 × 1/4 in. (29.2 × 25.4 × .6 cm)
M.2015.252.41

REBEKAH LASKIN
(b. 1955, United States, active New York)

Brooch, 1984
Enamel on copper, silver
1 3/4 × 1 3/4 × 1/4 in. (4.5 × 4.5 × .6 cm)
Marks: LASKIN
M.2015.252.42
p. *104*

STANLEY LECHTZIN
(b. 1936, United States, active Pennsylvania)

Ring #18 C-5, designed 1968, made 1981
Gold, watermelon tourmaline
1 5/16 × 15/16 × 9/16 in. (3.3 × 2.4 × 1.4 cm)
Marks: LECHTZIN; 14K
M.2015.252.43
p. *105*

Brooch #70 C, 1970
Gilded silver, hessonite grossular garnet
2 × 6 1/2 × 3/4 in. (5.1 × 16.5 × 1.9 cm)
Marks: artist's mark; STERLING; LECHTZIN
M.2015.252.44
p. *105*

Torque #40 D, 1973
Gilded silver, polyester resin, freshwater pearls
19 × 7 1/4 × 2 in. (48.3 × 18.4 × 5.1 cm)
Marks: S. LECHTZIN; STERLING; 1973
M.2013.221.20a–b
p. *106*

SHERRY LEEDY
(b. 1949, United States, active Missouri)

Bracelet, 1998
Glass beads, quartz beads, shell beads, thread
5 × 5 × 1 1/2 in. (12.7 × 12.7 × 3.8 cm)
M.2015.252.83

KEITH LEWIS
(b. 1959, United States, active Washington)

"Charm" (Sexual Self-Portrait) bracelet, 2002
From the series Bawdy Baubles, 2001–09
Gilded silver, enamel, horn, bone
5 1/4 × 5 1/4 × 1/4 in. (13.3 × 13.3 × .6 cm)
M.2015.252.45
pp. 82, *82*, 92

Maritimus cunnum lingit assibus IIII brooch, 2002
Gilded silver, enamel, pearls, diamonds
4 × 2 3/8 × 5/8 in. (10.2 × 6 × 1.6 cm)
Marks: KAL; 2002; Maritimus cunnum lingit assibus IIII
M.2015.252.46
p. *107*

PAUL LOBEL
(1899–1983, Romania, active New York)

Stradivarius brooch, c. 1945
Silver
3 × 1 × 1/2 in. (7.6 × 2.5 × 1.3 cm)
Marks: LOBEL; STERLING
M.2015.252.47
p. *108*

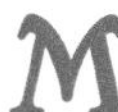

LINDA MacNEIL
(b. 1954, United States, active Massachusetts)

Elements Necklace (26–84), 1984
Number 26 from the series Elements, 1979–present
Glass, Vitrolite glass, gold
9¾ × 7½ × ⅝ in. (24.8 × 19.1 × 1.6 cm)
Marks: macneil
M.2015.252.49
p. *108*

Neck Collar (2–88), 1988
Number 2 from the series Neck Collars, 1986–present
Gilded brass, glass
7½ × 5⁵⁄₁₆ × 1½ (19.1 × 13.5 × 3.8)
Marks: macneil
M.2015.252.48

FRITZ MAIERHOFER
(b. 1941, Austria)

Crumblestone Farm brooch, 1976
PMMA, aluminum printing foil, silver, gold
3³⁄₁₆ × 2³⁄₁₆ × ½ in. (8.1 × 5.6 × 1.3 cm)
Marks: artist's mark; 20/20; Maierhofer 1976
M.2015.252.50

Brooch, 1977
Silver, gold
2¼ × 2¼ × ½ in. (5.7 × 5.7 × 1.3 cm)
Marks: artist's mark
M.2015.252.51
p. *109*

Ring, 2009
Silver
3 × 2¼ × 1¾ in. (7.6 × 5.7 × 4.5 cm)
Marks: 925; artist's mark; Maierhofer 09
M.2015.252.52
p. *109*

CARLIER MAKIGAWA
(b. 1952, Australia)

Shrine for Kanzaburo brooch, 1987
Stainless steel, silver, papier-mâché with gilding
3¼ × 2¾ × ¾ in. (8.3 × 7 × 1.9 cm)
Marks: SHRINE FOR KANZABURO; Carlier Makigawa 1987
M.2015.252.54
p. *109*

Brooches, n.d.
Steel, coated copper wire, painted wood, stones
a: 1⅜ × 1¾ × ½ in. (3.5 × 4.5 × 1.3 cm);
b: 1⅜ × 2 × ½ in. (3.5 × 5.1 × 1.3 cm)
M.2015.252.53a–b

KADRI MÄLK
(b. 1958, Estonia)

Black Box brooch, 2011
Jet, spinels, rhodium-plated gold
1¾ × 2¹⁄₁₆ × ⅝ in. (4.4 × 5.2 × 1.6 cm)
M.2016.161.3

K. LEE MANUEL
(1936–2003, United States, active California)

Necklace, c. 1977
Feathers, acrylic and fabric paint, leather, nylon
15 × 17½ × ½ in. (38.1 × 44.5 × 1.3 cm)
Marks: k. lee manuel
M.2015.252.55
pp. 83, *84*, *110*

STEFANO MARCHETTI
(b. 1970, Italy)

Brooch, 2004
Gold, silver
2⅝ × 2½ × 1 in. (6.7 × 6.4 × 2.5 cm)
Marks: SM 2004
M.2015.252.56
p. *111*

CHARLES MARKS
(b. 1937, New Zealand, active Netherlands)

Triadic bracelet (chp11b), designed 1982
Produced by chp...? (established as Chi ha paura...?) Amsterdam, founded 1996
Gilded steel
3 × 3¼ × 1¾ in. (7.6 × 8.3 × 4.5 cm)
M.2015.252.57

BRUNO MARTINAZZI
(b. 1923, Italy)

Goldfinger bracelet, designed 1969, made 1970
Number 9 of 12 left-hand *Goldfinger* bracelets
Varicolored gold
2⅞ × 2⅜ × 2⅛ in. (7.3 × 6 × 5.4 cm)
Marks: MARTINAZZI; IX/XII
M.2015.252.58
p. *112*

Venus brooch, 1980
Gold
2 × 2 × ¾ in. (5.1 × 5.1 × 1.9 cm)
Marks: MARTINAZZI
M.2013.221.21
p. *112*

Mito/Logos brooch, 1989
Varicolored gold
1⁷⁄₁₆ × 2⁵⁄₁₆ × ½ in. (3.7 × 5.9 × 1.3 cm)
Marks: MARTINAZZI
M.2015.252.62
p. *113*

Dike/Themis ring, 1990
Varicolored gold
1⅜ × 1¼ × 1¼ (3.5 × 3.2 × 3.2)
Marks: MARTINAZZI
M.2015.252.60

Le Ore Dell' Amore ring, 1995
Gold
1½ × 1⅛ × 1¼ in. (3.8 × 2.9 × 3.2 cm)
Marks: MARTINAZZI
M.2015.252.59

Narciso earring, 1997
Gold
2¼ × 1 × ½ in. (5.7 × 2.5 × 1.3 cm)
Marks: MARTINAZZI
M.2015.252.63

E se, rivolto, inver' di lei si piega, quel piegare è amor necklace, 1999
Gold
8 × 5¼ × ¾ in. (20.3 × 13.3 × 1.9 cm)
Marks: MARTINAZZI
M.2015.252.6 1
p. *113*

FALKO MARX
(1941–2013, Germany)

Brooch, 1989
Athenian pottery fragment, gold, diamond
1½ × 2¾ × ⅝ in. (3.8 × 7 × 1.6 cm)
Marks: 750; M
M.2015.252.64
pp. *114*, 144, *144*, 147

Brooch, 1989
Gold, plastic-coated steel, emeralds, diamonds, ruby
1¾ × 2¾ × ¼ in. (4.5 × 7 × .6 cm)
Marks: FM
M.2015.252.65
p. *114*

Ring, 1989
Gold, porcelain, metal filings, liquid, glass
1¾ × 1¼ × 1 in. (4.5 × 3.2 × 2.5 cm)
Marks: Falko Marx; KÖLN 89; 750; 900
M.2013.221.22
p. *114*

Earrings, 1990
Gold, steel wires, glass
Each: 1¼ × 1 × ⅜ in. (3.2 × 2.5 × 1 cm)
Marks: FM 90 (on each)
M.2015.252.66a–b

Ring, n.d.
Gold, liquid, glass
1½ × 1⅛ × 1⅛ in. (3.8 × 2.9 × 2.9 cm)
M.2015.252.67

NICKI MARX
(b. 1943, United States, active California and New Mexico)

Royal Raiment necklace, 1973
Peacock feathers, suede
27½ × 17 × ⅛ in. (69.9 × 43.2 × .3 cm)
Marks: ROYAL RAIMENT; Marx; '73
M.2014.198.93
pp. 84, *85*, *115*, 204

RICHARD MAWDSLEY
(b. 1945, United States, active Kansas and Illinois)

Wonder Woman in Her Bicentennial Finery necklace, 1975
Silver, pearls, smoky quartz
13¾ × 5½ × ¾ in. (34.9 × 14 × 1.9 cm)
Marks: STERLING; RM
M.2015.252.69
p. *116*

Albatross Boston Tea Medal necklace, 1999–2000
Silver with gilding
13¾ × 5½ × ⅞ in. (34.9 × 14 × 2.2 cm)
Marks: RM; STERLING
M.2015.252.48
p. *117*

PETER MCKAY
(b. 1951, New Zealand)

Dark Plain set of ten brooches, 2006
Silver with gilding
Largest brooch (VI): 1 11/16 × 1⅜ × ¼ in. (4.3 × 3.5 × .6 cm)
Marks: I–X (respectively); artist's mark (except X); STG (except X); 24CT (III & VII only)
M.2015.252.70a–j
p. *118*

BRUCE METCALF
(b. 1949, United States, active Pennsylvania and Ohio)

Swimming Blind in a Sea of Moons brooch, 1986
Silver with paint, brass, PMMA, colored pencil on Mylar®
3½ × 4⅝ × ⅝ in. (8.9 × 11.8 × 1.6 cm)
Marks: Bruce Metcalf; 86
M.2015.252.71
p. *118*

Think Too Much brooch, 1986
Silver, brass
2⅞ × 3⅛ × ½ in. (7.3 × 7.9 × 1.3 cm)
Marks: Bruce Metcalf; '86
M.2014.198.92
p. *118*

Wood Pin #115, 1995
Number 115 of 160 from the series Wood Pins and Figure Pins, 1986–97
Gilded maple, gilded copper, copper
4⅝ × 2⅞ × 1 in. (11.8 × 7.3 × 2.5 cm)
Marks: METCALF 95
M.2015.252.72

Handwork Necklace, 1999
Beech, holly, mahogany, cork, brass, silver, gold
14½ × 9½ × 2 in. (36.8 × 24.1 × 5.1 cm)
Mark: METCALF '99
M.2013.221.23
p. *119*

LOUIS MUELLER
(b. 1943, United States, active California, Rhode Island, and New York)

Crossword 3 brooch, 1986
Number 3 of 7 from the series Crossword, 1986
Gilded silver, onyx, lapis lazuli, amethyst, agate
2 3/16 × 2 3/16 × 5/16 in. (5.6 × 5.6 × .8 cm)
M.2015.252.75
p. *120*

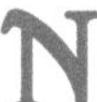

TED NOTEN
(b. 1956, Netherlands)

Crown-Ring, 1997
Number 2 from an edition of 2
PMMA, gold
1⅝ × 1 9/16 × 11/16 in. (4.1 × 4 × 1.8 cm)
Marks: T.N.; 2/2
M.2015.252.76
pp. *120*, 136, *136*

Fashionista Golden Girl necklace, 2010
From the series Fasionista Golden Girl, 2010
Glass-infiltrated nylon, gold
15 × 15 × 1 in. (38.1 × 38.1 × 2.5 cm)
M.2013.221.24
p. *121*

O

BREON O'CASEY
(1928–2011, England)

Brooch, before 1994
Gold, silver
1½ × 2⅛ × ⅛ in. (3.8 × 5.4 × .3 cm)
Inscription: FOR – Lois; FROM – Breon
M.2015.252.77
p. *148*

Lois brooch, c. 1994
Silver
2¾ × 5¼ × ¼ in. (13.3 × 7 × .6 cm)
M.2015.252.79
p. *148*

Necklace, before 1998
Silver
10½ × 11¼ × ½ in. (26.7 × 28.6 × 1.3 cm)
M.2015.252.78
pp. *148*, *199*, 205

OGURA RITSUKO
(b. 1951, Japan)

Brooch, 2001
Corrugated cardboard, acrylic paint, silver
3 × 3¼ × 1¾ in. (7.6 × 8.3 × 4.5 cm)
Marks: artist's mark; SILVER; JAPAN
M.2015.252.80

JUDY ONOFRIO
(b. 1939, United States, active Minnesota)

Brooch, 1989
Found objects, beads, thread
6½ × 3¼ × 1½ in. (16.5 × 8.3 × 3.8 cm)
M.2015.252.84

Brooch, 1990
Found objects, beads, thread
5 × 3¼ × 1¾ in. (12.7 × 8.3 × 4.5 cm)
M.2015.252.81
p. *149*

Bracelet, 1994
Glass beads, thread
4⅜ × 4½ × 1⅝ in. (11.1 × 11.4 × 4.1 cm)
M.2015.252.82

PAVEL OPOČENSKÝ
(b. 1954, Czechoslovakia [now Czech Republic], active New York)

Brooch, 1986
Ivory, ebony
2⅝ × 4⅛ × ¾ in. (6.7 × 10.5 × 1.9 cm)
Marks: artist's mark
M.2014.282.3a–c
pp. 130, *130*, *149*

Brooch, 1992–93
ColorCore®
2¼ × 2¼ × ⅞ in. (5.7 × 5.7 × 2.2 cm)
M.2016.21.1a–c
p. *149*

EMIKO OYE
(b. 1974, United States, active California)

Maharajah's 6th necklace, 2008
From the series My First Royal Jewels, 2007–09
LEGO® bricks, rubber cord, silver
22 3/4 × 15 3/8 × 2 3/4 in. (57.8 × 39.1 × 7 cm)
Marks: eo 2008; 1 – 06
M.2016.21.2
pp. *150*, 204, *back cover*

Aegean 1x4 bracelet, 2010
LEGO® bricks, rubber cord, silver
3 × 3 × 1 1/4 in. (7.6 × 7.6 × 3.2 cm)
M.2016.21.3

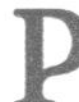

BARBARA PAGANIN
(b. 1961, Italy)

Microftalmo ring, 1993
Gold, silver, jade, diamonds
1 3/8 × 1 1/2 × 3/4 in. (3.5 × 3.8 × 1.9 cm)
M.2016.21.4
p. *232* (colophon)

Brooch, 1999
Number 6 of 9 from the series Nove Baccelli, 1999
Silver, gold, glass beads, freshwater pearls
3/4 × 3 3/4 × 1/2 in. (1.9 × 9.5 × 1.3 cm)
Marks: B. Paganin 1999 6/9 Special Edition for Galerie Sofie Lachaert
M.2016.21.5

ALBERT PALEY
(b. 1944, United States, active Pennsylvania and New York)

Fibula, 1968
Silver, gilded silver, pearls, labradorite
3 3/16 × 4 1/8 × 1 3/8 in. (8.1 × 10.5 × 3.5 cm)
Marks: [PA]LEY 68; STERLING
M.2013.221.25
pp. 144, 147, *151*

Man's ring, 1969
Gold
1 × 3/4 × 7/16 in. (2.5 × 1.9 × 1.1 cm)
Marks: PALEY
M.2016.21.6
p. *151*

Pin, 1969
Silver, gold, ivory, pearls, garnet
4 3/4 × 6 7/8 × 1 in. (12.1 × 17.5 × 2.5 cm)
Marks: PALEY; 69; artist's mark; STERLING; 14K
M.2014.282.4
p. *151*

EARL PARDON
(1926–1991, United States, active New York)

Brooch, c. 1990
Enamel on silver, gold, abalone shell, blue topaz, quartz
1 7/8 × 1 13/16 × 3/8 in. (4.8 × 4.6 × 1 cm)
Marks: STERLING; 14K; Pardon; 1717
M.2016.21.7
p. *152*

FRANCESCO PAVAN
(b. 1937, Italy)

Brooch, c. 1985
Gold, silver, copper, copper alloy (nickel silver)
2 1/4 × 2 3/4 × 3/4 in. (5.7 × 7 × 1.9 cm)
M.2016.21.9
p. *152*

Ring, 1989
Gold, silver, copper alloys
2 1/4 × 1 3/4 × 1 7/8 in. (5.7 × 4.5 × 4.8 cm)
Marks: Pavan
M.2016.21.8
p. *153*

Brooch, 1998
Gold
2 1/8 × 17/8 × 3/4 in. (5.4 × 4.8 × 1.9 cm) Marks: Pavan
M.2016.21.10
p. *153*

RUUDT PETERS
(b. 1950, Netherlands)

Capital bracelet, 1983
Screenprinted Formica®
4 1/4 × 4 1/4 × 1/8 in. (10.8 × 10.8 × .3 cm)
M.2016.21.12

Capital brooch, 1983
Screenprinted Formica®, stainless steel
9 1/2 × 1 7/8 × 1/8 in. (24.1 × 4.8 × .3 cm)
M.2016.21.11a-d

Pulmo brooch, 2011
From the series Corpus, 2011–12
Polyurethane, silver
5 × 3 1/4 × 1 in. (12.7 × 8.3 × 2.5 cm)
M.2013.221.26
p. *153*

EUGENE PIJANOWSKI
(b. 1938, United States, active Michigan, Japan, and Hawaii)

HIROKO SATO-PIJANOWSKI
(b. 1942, Japan, active Michigan)

Oh! I am precious No.5-A necklace, 1986
Paper cord (*mizuhiki*), canvas
10 × 22 × 9 1/4 in. (25.4 × 55.9 × 23.5 cm)
M.2016.21.13
p. *154*

Oh! I am precious No.5-B bracelet, 1986
Paper cord (*mizuhiki*), canvas
4 × 9 1/2 × 3 1/4 in. (10.2 × 24.1 × 8.3 cm)
M.2016.21.14
p. *154*

JOSEPH PILLARI
(b. 1985, United States, active Pennsylvania)

Beachside Humors brooch, 2011
Enamel on copper, silver
2 1/8 × 2 13/16 × 1/2 in. (5.4 × 7.1 × 1.3 cm)
Marks: pillari
M.2016.21.15
p. *155*

MARIO PINTON
(1919–2008, Italy)

Brooch, 1986
Gold, ruby
1 1/2 × 1 1/2 × 1/8 in. (3.8 × 3.8 × .3 cm)
Marks: 1.86 Pinton K18
M.2016.21.16
p. *155*

RAMÓN PUIG CUYÀS
(b. 1953, Spain)

El Rapte de la Sirena brooch, 1989
Number 296 from the series Senyors i Senyores (numbers 225–318), 1985–89
Silver, PMMA, acrylic paint
4 1/2 × 3 3/8 × 1/2 in. (11.4 × 8.6 × 1.3 cm)
Marks: PUIG; CUYAS
M.2016.21.17
p. *156*

Fruere Album brooch, 2008
Number 1229 from the series Utopos (numbers 1177–1329), 2007–09
Silver, copper alloy (nickel silver), enamel, pearls, onyx, paper with epoxy resin
2 1/8 × 2 1/8 × 1/2 in. (5.4 × 5.4 × 1.3 cm)
Marks: PUIG; CUYAS; 1229; 2008; FRUERE ALBUM
M.2016.21.18

Invenit Thesaurum brooch, 2008
Number 1238 from the series Utopos (numbers 1117–1329), 2007–09
Silver, copper alloy (nickel silver), pearl, marble, bone, paper with epoxy resin
2 1/4 × 3 × 3/4 in. (5.7 × 7.6 × 1.9 cm)
Marks: PUIG; CUYAS; 1238; 2008; INVENIT THESAURUM
M.2016.21.19
p. *156*

ROBIN QUIGLEY
(b. 1947, United States, active Rhode Island)

Bracelet, 1981
Epoxy resin, silver
3⅜ × 3⅜ × 1 in. (8.6 × 8.6 × 2.5 cm)
Marks: artist's marks; STERLING; 1981
M.2016.21.20
p. *157*

Multi-Color Necklace, 1984
Pewter, epoxy resin
14 × 7¾ × ⅜ in. (35.6 × 19.7 × 1 cm)
Marks: artist's marks; PEWTER; 84
M.2016.21.21

Fringe Bracelet, 1985
Pewter, epoxy resin, silver
5⅛ × 6⅛ × 1 in. (13 × 15.6 × 2.5 cm)
Marks: artist's marks; PEWTER; 85
M.2016.21.22
p. *157*

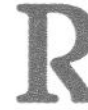

WENDY RAMSHAW
(b. 1939, England)

Set of nine rings on stand, 1984
Brass, resin, gold, carnelians, garnets, pink tourmalines, citrine
5 15/16 × 1⅛ × 1¼ in. (15.1 × 2.9 × 3.2 cm)
Hallmarks for: artist (WR); gold; 18 karat; London; 1984
M.2016.21.25.1–.2
p. *158*

Brooch, 1986
Gold, silver, glass
3⅛ × 5⅞ × 1¼ in. (7.9 × 14.9 × 3.2 cm)
Hallmarks for: artist (WR); sterling; London; 1986
M.2016.21.25.24
p. *158*

Orbit necklace, 1988–90
Nickel alloy, resin
10 × 10 × 1¼ in. (25.4 × 25.4 × 3.2 cm)
M.2016.21.23
p. *159*

Set of seven rings on stand, 1995
PMMA, gold, blue indicolite tourmaline, iolite, amethysts, sapphire
5⅞ × 1 × 1 3/16 in. (14.9 × 2.5 × 3 cm)
Hallmarks for: artist (WR); gold; 18 karat; London; 1995
M.2013.221.27.1–.2

DEBRA RAPOPORT
(b. 1945, United States, active California and New York)

Found Metal Neck Piece, 1984
Found metal, plastic-coated wire, acrylic paint, paper cord, waxed linen
12¾ × 8¼ × 1⅛ in. (32.4 × 21 × 2.9 cm)
Marks: D Rapoport 1984
M.2016.21.26
p. *160*

VERNON REED
(b. 1948, United States, active Texas)

Visage Mnemonique necklace, 1987
Anodized titanium, liquid-crystal display, gilded brass, PVC, PMMA, microcomputer, software
8½ × 6¼ × ½ in. (21.6 × 15.9 × 1.3 cm)
Marks: © 1987; VERNON REED
M.2016.21.27
pp. 139, *140*

RICHARD H. REINHARDT
(1921–1998, United States, active Pennsylvania)

Bracelet, 1980
Silver
2⅝ × 2⅞ × 2¾ in. (6.7 × 7.3 × 7 cm)
Marks: REINHARDT; HANDWROUGHT; STERLING; ©; 7 · 19 · 80
M.2016.21.28
p. *161*

MERRY RENK
(1921–2012, United States, active California)

Green Fire ring, 1974
Gold, rutilated quartz, tourmaline
1¼ × 1¼ × 1 in. (3.2 × 3.2 × 2.5 cm)
Marks: renk
M.2016.21.29
pp. 144, 146, 147, *161*

SUZAN REZAC
(b. 1958, Czechoslovakia [now Czech Republic], active Switzerland, New York, and Illinois)

Bracelet, c. 1983
Silver, copper alloys (nickel silver, *shibuichi*, and *shakudō*) with gilding
3½ × 3½ × 1 in. (8.9 × 8.9 × 2.5 cm)
Marks: Suzan Rezac
M.2016.21.30
p. *161*

Bracelet, c. 1983
Silver
5¾ × 5¾ × 1 in. (14.6 × 14.6 × 2.5 cm)
M.2016.21.31

Brooch, 1983
Silver
2¼ × 2¼ × ¼ in. (5.7 × 5.7 × 0.6 cm)
M.2016.21.81

GERD ROTHMANN
(b. 1941, Germany)

Zehn Finger am Hals necklace, 1986
Silver, gilded silver
8¾ × 8¾ × 1/16 in. (22.2 × 22.2 × .2 cm)
M.2016.21.32
p. 138, *162*

Die Goldene Nase nosepiece, 1988
Cast from Lois Boardman's nose
Gold
2¾ × 1⅞ × 1⅜ in. (7 × 4.8 × 3.5 cm)
M.2013.221.28
pp. *4* (table of contents), 8, *9*, 138, *163*

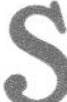

PHILIP SAJET
(b. 1953, Netherlands)

Damocles ring, designed 1987, made 2008
Gold, jade
2 × ⅞ × ½ in. (5.1 × 2.2 × 1.3 cm)
M.2016.21.33
pp. *14*, *163*

Cactus Quadruple ring, 2003
Gold, rusted steel
1¾ × 1¼ × 1¼ in. (4.5 × 3.2 × 3.2 cm)
M.2013.221.29
front cover, p. *163*

STEPHEN SARACINO
(b. 1948, United States, active New York)

Airport Terror Ring, 1984
Silver, gold, brass
4 × 3¾ × 1½ in. (10.2 × 9.5 × 3.8 cm)
Marks: Saracino '85; STERLING, 14KY
M.2013.221.30
p. *164*

MARJORIE SCHICK
(b. 1941, United States, active Kansas)

Brooch, 1983
Birch dowels, acrylic paint
4¾ × 5¾ × 1½ in. (12.1 × 14.6 × 3.8 cm)
M.2016.21.34
p. *164*

MARIANNE SCHLIWINSKI
(b. 1944, Germany)

Symbol necklace, 1986
Silver, wood with gilding, rubber cord
56½ in. (143.5 cm) length
M.2016.21.35
p. *164*

BERNHARD SCHOBINGER
(b. 1946, Switzerland)

Hanging Scissors necklace, 1997
Silver, diamonds, Kevlar®-coated stainless-steel wire, brass
Cord: 38 in. (96.5 cm) length; pendant: 3 11/16 × 1 13/16 × 1/8 in. (9.4 × 4.6 × .3 cm)
Marks: B/S, 19[...]/97
M.2016.21.36
p. *165*

Aufsteigender Rauchquarz ring, 2001
Enamel on gold, cobalt alloy, diamond splinters, smoky quartz, pearl
1 7/8 × 1 3/4 × 1 1/4 in. (4.8 × 4.4 × 3.2 cm)
Marks: B.S. 2001.; 750
M.2016.21.37
p. *165*

Smoky Quartz on Countersink Nail ring, 2010
Gold, smoky quartz
1 7/16 × 1 1/4 × 1 1/4 in. (3.7 × 3.2 × 3.2 cm)
M.2013.221.31
p. *165*

DEGANIT STERN SCHOCKEN
(b. 1947, Israel)

Necklace #36, 1983
From the series Movement in Jewelry, Jewelry in Movement, 1981–c. 1997
Silver, gold, porcelain
Chain: 23 3/16 in. (58.9 cm) length; pendant: 2 7/8 × 6 3/8 × 9/16 in. (7.3 × 16.2 × 1.4 cm)
M.2016.21.38
p. *166*

ANN SCOTT
(b. 1959, United States, active Pennsylvania and Washington)

Torque, 1982
Screenprinted PMMA, copper alloy, silver
10½ × 10 × 2 in. (26.7 × 25.4 × 5.1 cm)
Marks: Ann Scott © 1982; Ann Scott © 1982
M.2016.21.39
p. *166*

JOYCE J. SCOTT
(b. 1948, United States, active Maryland)

PARTY necklace, c. 1985
Glass beads, thread
15 1/4 × 9 3/4 × 3/8 in. (38.7 × 24.8 × 1 cm)
M.2016.21.40
p. *167*

BARBARA SEIDENATH
(b. 1960, Germany, active Rhode Island)

Hand ornament, 2003
Silver, quartz, enamel
1 3/4 × 2 × 1 3/16 in. (4.5 × 5.1 × 3 cm)
Marks: BS '03 925
M.2016.21.41
pp. 135–36, *135*

STEPHAN SEYFFERT
(b. 1960, Germany)

INVALUABLE ring, 1992
Silver, cubic zirconia
1 1/8 × 1 1/8 × 1/2 in. (2.9 × 2.9 × 1.3 cm)
Inscription: INVALUABLE
Marks: 925; SEYFFERT
M.2016.21.42
p. *168*

Kreuz ring, 1992
Silver, synthetic rubies
1 1/4 × 1 3/8 × 1 3/8 in. (3.2 × 3.5 × 3.5 cm)
Marks: 925; SEYFFERT
M.2016.21.43

SONDRA SHERMAN
(b. 1958, United States, active Germany, Rhode Island, and California)

Flowers and Still Life brooch, box, and display table, 2010
From the series Found Objects, 2010–present
Silver, book, painted birch
Brooch: 3 1/4 × 3 1/4 × 3/8 in. (8.3 × 8.3 × 1 cm); box: 10 × 7 1/2 × 7/8 in. (25.4 × 19.1 × 2.2 cm); table: 40 3/8 × 16 × 12 in. (102.6 × 40.6 × 30.5 cm)
M.2013.221.32a–b, M.2013.222a–f
pp. 126, *127*

HELEN SHIRK
(b. 1942, United States, active California)

Pendant with Phantom Quartz, 1974
Silver, phantom quartz
14 1/4 × 9 × 1 in. (36.2 × 22.9 × 2.5 cm)
Marks: H·Shirk; STERLING; 1974
M.2013.221.33
pp. 88, *89*

Bracelet with Agate, 1975
Silver, copper, brass, agate
3 1/2 × 4 1/2 × 1 1/2 in. (8.9 × 11.4 × 3.8 cm)
M.2016.21.44
p. *13*

Bracelet TR8, 1982
Silver, anodized titanium
2 1/2 × 3 1/2 × 1 1/2 in. (6.4 × 8.9 × 3.8 cm)
Marks: H·Shirk
M.2016.21.45

Brooch AS9, 1994
Silver, gold
5 1/4 × 2 × 1 in. (13.3 × 5.1 × 2.5 cm)
Marks: H·Shirk; STERLING; 14K
M.2016.21.46

JIŘÍ ŠIBOR
(b. 1966, Czechoslovakia [now Czech Republic])

The United States brooch, 1997
Synthetic coral, epoxy resin, stainless steel
Continental US: 1 3/4 × 2 7/8 × 1/2 in. (4.5 × 7.3 × 1.3 cm); Alaska: 1 × 1 × 1/2 in. (2.5 × 2.5 × 1.3 cm); Hawaii: 1/8 × 5/16 × 1/2 in. (.3 × .8 × 1.3 cm)
Marks: DCC; DCC
M.2016.21.47a–c
p. *168*

VERA SIEMUND
(b. 1971, Germany)

Necklace, 2006
Enamel on copper, silver
11 1/4 × 9 1/4 × 1 1/8 in. (28.6 × 23.5 × 2.9 cm)
Inscription: Lina
Marks: 925
M.2016.21.48
p. *169*

OLAF SKOOGFORS
(1930–1975, Sweden, active Pennsylvania)

Necklace, 1971
Gilded silver, synthetic gemstone (possibly spinel)
8 1/4 × 5 1/4 × 1 in. (21 × 13.3 × 2.5 cm)
Marks: OLAF SKOOGFORS; STERLING
M.2016.21.50
p. *170*

Necklace, 1974
Gilded silver, glass beads
10 × 5 1/4 × 1/2 in. (25.4 × 13.3 × 1.3 cm)
Marks: OLAF SKOOGFORS; STERLING; 1974
M.2016.21.49
p. *170*

PETER SKUBIC
(b. 1935, Yugoslavia, active Germany and Austria)

Brooch, 1997
Gold
1 × 2⅛ × ¼ in. (2.5 × 5.4 × .6 cm)
Marks: SKUBIC 97
M.2016.21.51
p. *171*

Brooch, 1999
Stainless steel
3⅞ × 1⅜ × 9/16 in. (9.8 × 3.5 × 1.4 cm)
Marks: SKUBIC 99
M.2016.21.52
p. *171*

Brooch, 2001
Stainless steel, glass
3¼ × 1¾ × 1⅜ in. (8.3 × 4.4 × 3.5 cm)
Marks: SKUBIC 01
M.2016.21.53
p. *171*

ROBERT SMIT
(b. 1941, Netherlands)

Necklace, 1987
Varicolored gold
Cord: 33½ in. (85.1 cm) length;
pendant: 4½ × 3¾ × 1¼ in. (11.4 × 9.5 × 3.2 cm)
Marks: artist's mark
M.2016.21.54
p. *172*

Bello's sister brooch, 1993
Gold, acrylic paint, painted pearls
5⅜ × 5¼ × ⅞ in. (13.7 × 13.3 × 2.2 cm)
Marks: Robert Smit '93
M.2016.21.55
p. *172*

ART SMITH
(1917–1982, Cuba, active New York)

Brooch, c. 1955
Copper, brass
3¾ × 2 × ½ in. (9.5 × 5.1 × 1.3 cm)
Marks: Art Smith
M.2013.221.34
p. *173*

CHRISTINA Y. SMITH
(b. 1951, United States, active California)

Work, Work, Work bracelet, c. 1986
Silver, PMMA
2 × 4½ × 3 in. (5.1 × 11.4 × 7.6 cm)
M.2016.21.57
p. 90, *90*

Cantaloupe Already Married brooch, 1989
Silver
2⅝ × 2¼ × ¼ in. (6.7 × 5.7 × .6 cm)
M.2016.21.56
p. *173*

BETTINA SPECKNER
(b. 1962, Germany)

Brooch, 2004
Ferrotype, silver, opals, aquamarine
2 7/16 × 15/16 × ⅜ in. (6.2 × 2.4 × 1 cm)
Marks: artist's mark
M.2016.21.58
p. *174*

Brooch, 2007
Heliogravure on zinc, silver, coral
1⅛ × 3 × ⅜ in. (2.9 × 7.6 × 1 cm)
Marks: artist's mark
M.2016.21.59
p. *174*

VAUGHN STUBBS
(1946–2016, United States, active Pennsylvania)

Bracelet, 1984
Papier-mâché on archival cardboard, acrylic paint, Mylar®
3⅞ × 3½ × 2⅞ in. (9.8 × 8.9 × 7.3 cm)
Marks: VAUGHN STUBBS '84
M.2016.21.64

Bronto brooch, 1987
Plastic toy, archival cardboard, acrylic paint
4¼ × 2½ × ½ in. (10.8 × 6.4 × 1.3 cm)
Inscription: Bronto
Marks: VAUGHN STUBBS '87
M.2016.21.61

Brooch, 1987
PMMA on felt, found objects
2½ × 2⅜ × 1 in. (6.4 × 6 × 2.5 cm)
Marks: V. STUBBS '87
M.2016.21.62

Dove of Peace brooch, 1987
PMMA on felt, found objects
2 11/16 × 2¾ × ¾ in. (6.8 × 7 × 1.9 cm)
Marks: VAUGHN STUBBS 8/15/87
M.2016.21.65

Horse and Rider brooch, 1987
Plastic toy, archival cardboard, acrylic paint
4¼ × 2¼ × 1¼ in. (10.8 × 5.7 × 3.2 cm)
Marks: VAUGHN STUBBS 87
M.2016.21.60
pp. *7*, *174*

Disney Land brooch, c. 1989
PMMA on felt, beads, found objects
2⅞ × 2 13/16 × 13/16 in. (7.3 × 7.1 × 2.1 cm)
M.2016.21.63
p. *174*

TORE SVENSSON
(b. 1948, Sweden)

Brooch, 1996
From the series 7 × 7 cm, 1989–99
Steel with gilding
2¾ × 2¾ × 3/16 in. (7 × 7 × .5 cm)
Hallmarks for: company (HTS); Göteborg; 1996; artist (tore)
M.2016.21.66
p. *175*

Necklace, 1997
Steel with gilding
12¾ × 9¼ × ¼ in. (32.4 × 23.5 × .6 cm)
Hallmarks for: company (HTS); Göteborg; 1997; artist (tore)
M.2016.21.67
p. *175*

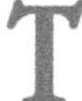

DAVID TISDALE
(b. 1956, United States, active California, New York, and Connecticut)

Bracelet, 1984
Anodized aluminum, silver, onyx, agate
2¼ × 3¼ × 1¼ in. (5.7 × 8.3 × 3.2 cm)
Marks: David Tisdale ©1984
M.2016.21.68
p. *188*

MERRILY TOMPKINS
(b. 1947, United States, active Washington)

Here Comes Trouble brooch, 1973
Copper, silver, enamel, plastic eyes, photographs, PMMA, sawdust
2¾ × 3¼ × ¾ in. (7 × 8.3 × 1.9 cm)
Marks: Merrily Tompkins; 8/73
M.2016.21.69
p. 79, *79*

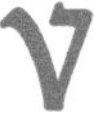

JACOMIJN VAN DER DONK
(b. 1963, Netherlands)

Necklace, 2006
From the series Winterdracht, 2006
Epoxy resin on beech, leather, gold
43 in. (109.2 cm) length
M.2016.21.70

FELIEKE VAN DER LEEST
(b. 1968, Netherlands, active Norway)

Spermheart brooch, designed 1996
Viscose thread over felt and rubber
3 1/4 × 1 × 1/2 in. (8.3 × 2.5 × 1.3 cm)
M.2016.21.71
p. *188*

EMMY VAN LEERSUM
(1930–1984, active Netherlands)

Armband, 1970–71
Number 29 in the series vouwen en inzagingen, 1970–71
Aluminum
2 3/4 × 2 3/4 × 3 1/8 in. (7 × 7 × 7.9 cm)
Marks: EMMY v. LEERSUM
M.2014.120
p. *188*

FRANS VAN NIEUWENBORG
(b. 1945, Netherlands, active Denmark)

MARTIJN WEGMAN
(b. 1955, Netherlands)

Closed necklace, designed 1973
Aluminum, elastic cord, polyacetal plastic
7 × 7 × 3/4 in. (17.8 × 17.8 × 1.9 cm)
Marks: FRANS VAN NIEUWENBORG/MARTIJN WEGMAN
M.2016.21.73

Zipper necklace, designed 1973
Zinc and cotton zipper, PVC
Cord: 28 1/2 (72.4 cm) length;
zipper clasp: 3/8 × 7/16 × 1/8 in. (1 × 1.1 × .3 cm)
M.2016.21.72

TONE VIGELAND
(b. 1938, Norway)

Necklace, 1982
Silver, gold, gilded silver, rutilated quartz, nephrite
7 × 7 × 1 in. (17.8 × 17.8 × 2.5 cm)
Marks: Tone Vigeland 82
M.2016.21.74
p. *189*

Necklace, c. 1985
Nickel-plated brass, steel nails
11 × 8 1/2 × 3/4 in. (27.9 × 21.6 × 1.9 cm)
M.2016.21.75
p. *190*

GRAZIANO VISINTIN
(b. 1954, Italy)

Brooch, 2004
Gold, enamel, gold leaf
2 × 2 1/8 × 3/8 in. (5.1 × 5.4 × 1 cm)
Marks: ·VISINTIN·; 2004
M.2016.21.76
p. *191*

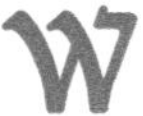

DAVID WATKINS
(b. 1940, England)

Gyro Bangle, designed 1975, made 1976
Aluminum
5 × 5 × 3/8 in. (12.7 × 12.7 × 1 cm)
M.2016.21.77
p. *192*

Wing Wave 3 set of three necklaces, 1983
Neoprene-coated steel wire, neoprene-coated wood
11 1/2 × 12 3/8 × 1/4 in. (29.2 × 31.4 × .6 cm)
M.2013.221.35a–c
p. *192*

J. FRED WOELL
(1934–2015, United States, active Maine)

The Winning necklace, 1975
Silver, bronze, brass, religious medal
Chain: 20 1/2 in. (52.1 cm) length;
pendant: 3 × 2 1/2 × 3/8 in. (7.6 × 6.4 × 1 cm)
Marks: STERLING; J FRED WOELL 1975
M.2016.21.78
p. *193*

Arctic Setdown brooch, 1990
Silver, quartz
1 1/2 × 2 3/8 × 7/8 in. (3.8 × 6 × 2.2 cm)
Marks: © J. FRED WOELL 1990; 925
M.2016.21.79
pp. 128–29, *128*

NANCY WORDEN
(b. 1954, United States, active Washington)

Armed and Dangerous necklace, 1998
US currency, brass rifle shells, onyx, malachite, silver, acrylic, gold
14 1/8 × 9 7/8 × 3/4 in. (35.9 × 25.1 × 1.9 cm)
Inscription: THEY PREACH THE GOSPEL OF LOVE THEY PRACTICE THE GOSPEL OF HATE
Marks: STERLING; WORDEN
M.2013.221.40
pp. 80, *81*

Balancing Right and Left necklace, 2000
Silver, US and Japanese currency, copper, brass, onyx, polyester brushes
10 1/2 × 11 × 1 1/2 in. (26.7 × 27.9 × 3.8 cm)
Marks: WORDEN; STERLING; 2000
M.2013.221.36

Grafting necklace, 2000
Silver, gold, gilded copper
7 1/8 × 9 1/2 × 3 1/2 in. (18.1 × 24.1 × 8.9 cm)
Marks: WORDEN; 2000
M.2013.221.38
p. *194*

Gilding the Past necklace, 2001
Gilded copper, Japanese and US currency (including 1964 and 1965 Kennedy half dollars with gilding), coral, turquoise, bone, brass
Necklace: 17 1/4 × 17 3/4 × 3/4 in. (43.8 × 45.1 × 1.9 cm) Inscription: GOOD OLD DAYS
Marks: WORDEN; 2001
M.2013.221.37
pp. *1* (frontispiece), *15*, *195*

The Leash necklace, 2003
Mink, US currency, silver, brass, nickel, freshwater pearls, mother of pearl, glass, chrome-plated metal
Necklace: 9 1/4 × 8 3/4 × 2 3/4 in. (23.5 × 22.2 × 7 cm);
leash: 19 3/4 in. (50.2) length
Marks: WORDEN
M.2013.221.39
p. *196*

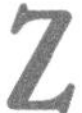

ALBERTO ZORZI
(b. 1958, Italy)

Brooch, 1986
Stainless steel, gold, lapis lazuli
3 1/2 × 2 × 1 in. (5.1 × 8.9 × 2.5 cm)
Marks: A. Zorzi '86
M.2016.21.80
p. *197*

Acknowledgments

Bobbye Tigerman

Marilyn B. and Calvin B. Gross Associate Curator
Los Angeles County Museum of Art

Rosie Chambers Mills

The Rosalinde and Arthur Gilbert Foundation Associate Curator
Los Angeles County Museum of Art

First and foremost, we thank benefactors Lois and Bob Boardman, who entrusted us with their cherished collection of contemporary studio jewelry. We continue to be impressed by the Boardmans' foresight and are humbled by their generosity in allowing the Los Angeles County Museum of Art (LACMA) to preserve and interpret their exceptional collection, astutely amassed over decades. (Our sincere thanks go as well to Beau and Guy Noir, whose warm canine company we enjoyed on each trip to South Pasadena to study the collection.)

Receiving a collection into a large museum like LACMA requires the expertise of a broad cross section of its staff, and we sincerely appreciate the Registrar's Office and the Art Preparation and Installation Department for facilitating this process. Collections Managers Samantha Forsko and Alyssa Morasco ensured the safe transport and storage of each piece. Conservators Natasha Cochran, Jena Hirschbein, and Silviu Boariu exercised extraordinary skill and judgment in preserving both the intended appearance of the objects as well as the signs of their use. Conservation Scientists Charlotte Eng, Laura Maccarelli, Karen Bishop, and Frank Preusser identified the wide range of materials in this collection through testing and close physical inspection. Conservators John Hirx and Elizabeth Schaeffer also helped, and independent gemology consultant Brittany Bednash determined the composition of many of the stones. Supervising Photographer Peter Brenner captured sensational images of the work, dedicating many hours to complete the task on time. His colleague Jonathan Urban documented artist's marks, and Imaging Coordinator Laura Cherry facilitated the entire process. We are grateful as well to Wayne Shimabukuro for taking wonderful photographs of Lois wearing her jewelry for this catalogue. Lacy Simkowitz, former curatorial administrator, coordinated the initial accession of the gift and managed the Boardmans' invaluable donation of jewelry books to LACMA's Balch Art Research Library. Our thanks to the librarians, particularly Kristi Yuzuki, for processing this additional resource, which is now available to scholars by appointment.

Exhibition Designer Martin Sztyk and Assistant Director of Exhibition Design and Production Victoria Turkel Behner took our complex requirements and created an elegant installation. Graphic Designers Carrie Kawamura and David Karwan created a fitting and beautiful visual identity for the show, and mount makers Holly Rittenhouse and David Armendariz fashioned ingenious and very discrete object supports to ensure all pieces could be photographed and displayed at their best. Vice President of Technology and Digital Media Amy McCabe Heibel and Digital Media Product Developer Tomas Garcia helped us conceive and realize the augmented-reality feature in the gallery, allowing visitors to photographically superimpose images from the collection on themselves. We also thank the Exhibition Programs Department, Sabrina Lovett and Zoë Kahr in particular, for shepherding the project to completion. Amber Smith, Jane Burrell, and Karen Satzman in Education were crucial in developing and executing several public programs that reached the jewelry community and those beyond it. Our colleagues in Communications and Marketing helped promote the exhibition to the widest possible audience as well.

Beyond Bling would not have come to fruition without the support of important funders who recognized the significance of the project and the impact it would have on the jewelry field. We are deeply grateful to the Rotasa Foundation, the John and Robyn Horn Foundation, the Pasadena Art Alliance, and LACMA's Decorative Arts and Design Council for helping us realize both the exhibition and the publication. In addition to their support through the Rotasa Foundation, Susan Cummins and Rose Roven proved to be wise counselors and staunch advocates. We also appreciate the Society of North American Goldsmiths (SNAG) for its sponsorship and in-kind promotion of the exhibition. We extend profound gratitude to D. Harry Montgomery of Typecraft for printing a beautiful book and generously underwriting its cost. We also thank David Mayes and the entire Typecraft staff for their dedication to this collaboration. And we value the vital assistance of LACMA's Development Department—notably Melissa Bomes, Kris Lewis, Chi-Young Kim, and M. Consuelo Gugol—in securing funding to support both the book and exhibition.

LACMA Publisher Lisa Gabrielle Mark championed this catalogue from the start, and we thank her for her steadfast support and guidance through the entire process, from concept to bound book. We also commend Graphic Designers Lorraine Wild of Green Dragon Office and David Karwan, LACMA's art director, who immersed themselves in the material to design an intelligent book that sensitively reflects its subject matter. By the same token, we appreciate our editor, Jennifer MacNair Stitt, who perceptively enhanced the clarity of the text; and Senior Rights and Reproductions Associate Piper Severance, along with Administrative Assistant Carly Rustebakke, who capably obtained important images and permissions. We gratefully acknowledge contributing authors Helen W. Drutt English, Blake Gopnik, and Benjamin Lignel and thank them for their thoughtful and incisive essays. We owe a special debt of gratitude to Helen, who combed through her archives to provide extensive information about the history and provenance of the collection and located many documents that helped us understand its formation and growth. At the beginning of the project, we sent out a research survey to every collection artist we could find. We are immensely grateful to all of them for their responsiveness and attention to our queries; indeed, one of the most rewarding aspects of the project has been getting to know so many jewelers. We also thank several jewelry and craft scholars, including Liesbeth den Besten, Ulysses Grant Dietz, Elizabeth Essner, Julie Ewington, Toni Greenbaum, Tanya Harrod, Damian Skinner, Davira Taragin, Namita Gupta Wiggers, and most of all Cindi Strauss, for their insights and wisdom as we researched the collection.

We are exceptionally grateful to Exhibitions Associate Abbey Chamberlain Brach, who was instrumental in all aspects of the accession of the collection and organization of the book and exhibition. Abbey performed extensive research on artists in the collection and led the writing of the checklist with her keen eye, extraordinary attention to detail, and remarkable organizational skills. Curatorial Administrator Minyoung Park, with her customary grace and good spirit, coordinated the myriad administrative aspects of bringing the collection to LACMA and mounting the exhibition. She played a crucial role in the photography of hundreds of pieces on a very tight deadline, for which we are truly indebted. We give heartfelt thanks as well to a dedicated team of interns and volunteers in the Decorative Arts and Design Department, including Brooke Devenney, Joan Seidl, Joseph Valencia, and Jocelyn Wong, who conducted research on the artists and objects in the collection. We also thank veteran volunteer Marilyn Gross for her more than thirty-five years of loyal service; she provided administrative support at this busy time. We are especially appreciative of curator Wendy Kaplan, our department head, who at every turn unstintingly supported our efforts to produce a publication and exhibition worthy of the Boardman collection. Finally, we thank CEO and Wallis Annenberg Director Michael Govan for his unwavering encouragement and visionary belief that the Boardmans' jewelry collection is an essential addition to the encyclopedic holdings of the Los Angeles County Museum of Art.

Index

Page references for Boardman collection objects may be found in the Checklist of the Collection (pp. 208–23). Non-Boardman works are listed below by artist. Page numbers in italics indicate illustrations.

D

E

F

G

H

I

J

Photo Credits

Photos © Museum Associates / LACMA, unless otherwise noted.

Front cover, 14, 163 top right, 163 bottom right: © Philip Sajet; **1:** detail © Nancy L. Worden; **2, 42:** © Karl Fritsch; **4, 162, 163 left:** © Gerd Rothmann; **7, 174 top right, 174 bottom right:** © Vaughn Stubbs; **9:** photo © Wayne Shimabukuro; **11:** photo by Scott Gries/Getty Images; **12 left:** photo © Gerd Rothmann; **12 right:** photo by Peter Loughrey, courtesy of Los Angeles Modern Auctions (LAMA); **13, 89:** © Helen Shirk; **15:** artwork in background © Michael Heizer, photo © Wayne Shimabukuro; **16 top left, 16 bottom left:** © Vicki Ambery-Smith; **16 top right:** © Klaus Arck; **16 bottom right:** © Giampaolo Babetto; **17:** © Robert Baines; **18, 19, 20:** © Gijs Bakker; **21:** © Ralph Bakker; **22 top left, 22 bottom left:** © Michael Becker; **22 right, 23:** © Jamie Bennett; **24:** © David Bielander; **25, 26:** © Manfred Bischoff Estate; **27:** © Liv Blåvarp, Kampenvegen 8, 2850 Lena, Norway; **28:** © Helen Britton; **29:** © Doug Bucci; **30:** detail © Sebastian Buescher; **31:** © Claus Bury; **32:** © Pierre Cavalan; **33:** © Anton Cepka; **34, 35:** © Peter Chang; **36, 37, 38, 205, 208:** © Sharon Church; **39 top:** © Susan Cohn; **39 bottom:** © Ros Conway and Hugh O'Donnell; **41, 103, 104 left:** © Otto Künzli/Artists Rights Society (ARS) New York/VG Bild-Kunst, Bonn; **43:** © Johanna Dahm, photo by Johanna Dahm; **44:** © Peter de Wit; **45:** © Lam de Wolf; **46:** © Elisabeth Jesus Guennaibim Defner; **47:** © Paul Derrez; **48, 49, 50, 51 top:** © Georg Dobler; **51 bottom:** © Gemma Draper; **52:** © Robert Ebendorf; **53 top:** © Eva Eisler; **53 bottom, 128 bottom:** © Sandra Enterline; **54, 55, 87:** © Arline Fisch; **56 left:** © Anna Fraling; **56 top right, 56 bottom right:** © Estate of Max Fröhlich; **57:** © Susie Ganch; **58 top left, 58 top right:** © Elizabeth Garrison; **59 top:** © Estate of Toni Goessler-Snyder; **59 bottom:** © Lisa Gralnick; **60:** © Gésine Hackenberg; **61, 76 left:** © L. Hall; **62:** © Andrea MAXA Halmschlager; **64:** © William Harper; **65:** © Mirjam Hiller; **66 top:** detail © Ron Ho; **66 bottom:** © Estate of Hiramatsu Yasuki; **67 top left:** © Marian Hosking; **67 top right:** © Mary Lee Hu; **67 bottom:** © John Iversen; **69:** © Estate of Margaret De Patta, photo © M. Lee Fatherree; **71:** © Estate of Ruth Penington, photo © Doug Yaple; **72:** © Estate of Donald Paul Tompkins, photo © The Museum of Fine Arts Houston; **73:** © Estate of Ramona Solberg; **75:** © Ron Ho; **76 right:** © Kiff Slemmons, photo © Doug Yaple; **77, 79 left:** © Beverly Cory for the Estate of Ken Cory; **79 right:** © Merrily Tompkins; **80, 81, 194, 195, 196:** © Nancy L. Worden; **82:** © Keith Lewis; **84:** detail © Family of K. Lee Manuel; **85:** © Marx 1973; **86:** © William Clark Estate, photographed for the University of California, Berkeley Art Museum and Pacific Film Archive by Colin McRae; **90, 173 right:** © Christina Y. Smith; **94, 95 left:** © Eva & Ike Jünger; **95 right:** © Judith Kaufman; **96:** © Betsy King; **97 left:** © TKO Designs Inc.; **97 top right, 97 bottom right:** © Esther Knobel; **98:** © Estate of Friedrich Knupper; **99:** © RENA; **100, 101:** © Carolyn Kriegman Estate; **102:** © Daniel Kruger, South Africa/Germany; **104 right:** © Rebekah Laskin; **105, 106:** © Stanley Lechtzin; **107:** © Keith A. Lewis; **108 left:** © Estate of Paul Lobel; **108 right:** © Linda MacNeil; **109 top left, 109 top right:** © Fritz Maierhofer; **109 bottom:** © Carlier Makigawa; **110:** © Family of K. Lee Manuel; **111:** © Stefano Marchetti; **112, 113:** © Bruno Martinazzi; **114, 144:** © Estate of Falko Marx; **115:** detail © Marx 1973; **116, 117:** © Richard Mawdsley; **118 left:** © Peter McKay; **118 top right, 118 bottom right, 119:** © Bruce Metcalf; **120 left:** © Louis Mueller; **120 right, 121, 136 bottom:** © Ted Noten; **123:** Digital image courtesy of the Getty's Open Content Program; **125:** © Alexander McQueen/ Victoria and Albert Museum, London; **127:** © Sondra Sherman; **128 middle, 193:** © J. Fred Woell Estate; **130:** detail © Pavel Opočenský; **132 right, 203:** © Kranitzky & Overstreet; **133:** detail © Gijs Bakker; **134:** detail © Ralph Bakker; **135 right:** © Barbara Seidenath; **137:** detail © Doug Bucci; **138 bottom:** detail © Marian Hosking; **140:** © 1987, Vernon Reed; **141:** detail © Kranitzky & Overstreet; **142:** © Juhani Heikkilä; **143:** © Sebastian Buescher; **148:** © Estate of Breon O'Casey; **149 left:** © Judy Onofrio; **149 top right, 149 bottom right:** © Pavel Opočenský; **150, back cover:** © emiko oye; **151:** © Paley Studios Archive; **152 left:** © Estate of Earl Pardon; **152 right, 153 top left, 153 bottom left:** © Francesco Pavan; **153 right:** © Ruudt Peters; **154:** © Eugene Pijanowski and Hiroko Sato Pijanowski; **155 top:** © Joseph Pillari; **155 bottom:** © Mario Pinton Estate; **156:** © Ramón Puig Cuyàs; **157:** © Robin Quigley; **158, 159:** © Wendy Ramshaw; **160:** © Debra Rapoport; **161 top left:** © Richard H. Reinhardt Estate; **161 top right:** © Estate of Merry Renk; **161 bottom:** © 2016 Suzan Rezac. All rights reserved.; **164 top left:** © Stephen Saracino; **164 bottom left:** © Marjorie Schick; **164 right:** © Marianne Schliwinski; info@marianne-schliwinski.de; **165:** © Bernhard Schobinger; **166 top:** © Deganit Stern Schocken; **166 bottom:** © Ann Scott; **167:** © Joyce J. Scott; **168 top:** © Stephan Seyffert; **168 bottom:** © Jiří Šibor; **169:** © Vera Siemund; **170:** © Estate of Olaf Skoogfors; **171:** © Peter Skubic; **172:** © Robert Smit; **173 left:** © Art Smith Estate; **174 top left, 174 bottom left:** © Bettina Speckner; **175:** © Tore Svensson; **177:** © Remedios Vincent, photo © Gosia Janik and Fernando Ocaña; **182:** photo courtesy of Haystack Mountain School of Crafts, Deer Isle, Maine; **183 top:** © Arthur Hash, photo courtesy of Arthur Hash; **183 bottom:** © Nervous System, Inc., photo courtesy of Nervous System, Inc.; **184:** photo courtesy of Proyecto Ojalá; **188 top left:** © 1984 David Tisdale; **188 top right:** © Felieke Van der Leest; **188 bottom:** © Emmy van Leersum Estate; **189, 190:** © Tone Vigeland; **191:** © Graziano Visintin; **192:** © David Watkins; **197:** © Alberto Zorzi; **199:** photo © Andrea Baldeck; **201 left:** photo courtesy of Helen W. Drutt English; **201 right:** © Helen W. Drutt English; **206:** © Man Ray Trust/Artists Rights Society (ARS), NY/ADAGP, Paris 2016, image © The Metropolitan Museum of Art/Art Resource, NY; **207:** photo by Miriam Künzli for Art Aurea; **232:** © Barbara Paganin

Los Angeles County Museum of Art
Board of Trustees, 2016

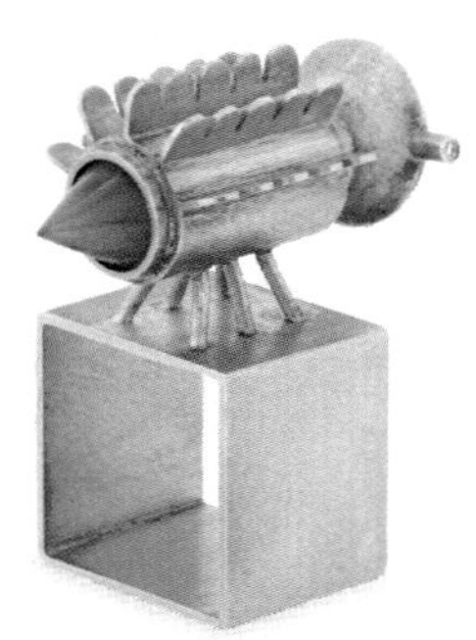

Published in conjunction with the exhibition *Beyond Bling: Jewelry from the Lois Boardman Collection* at the Los Angeles County Museum of Art, Los Angeles, California (October 2, 2016–February 5, 2017)

This exhibition was organized by the Los Angeles County Museum of Art. Support was provided in part by the Pasadena Art Alliance and the Society of North American Goldsmiths (SNAG).

The catalogue was made possible by the Rotasa Foundation, Typecraft, the John and Robyn Horn Foundation, and the Decorative Arts and Design Council of LACMA.

Publisher: **Lisa Gabrielle Mark**

Editor: **Jennifer MacNair Stitt**

Designers: **Lorraine Wild & David Karwan**

Photographers: **Peter Brenner & Jonathan Urban**

Rights and Reproductions:
Piper Severance & Carly Rustebakke

Indexer: **Christy Stroud**

Printer: **Typecraft, Pasadena, California**

5905 Wilshire Boulevard
Los Angeles, California 90036
(323) 857-6000
www.lacma.org

This book is typeset in Chesterfield, Caponi, and Union.

Copublished by Los Angeles County Museum of Art and DelMonico Books, an imprint of Prestel, a member of Verlagsgruppe Random House GmbH

Prestel Verlag
Neumarkter Strasse 28,
81673 Munich

Prestel Publishing Ltd.
14–17 Wells Street
London W1T 3PD

Prestel Publishing
900 Broadway, Suite 603
New York, NY 10003

www.prestel.com

ISBN 978-3-7913-5562-7

Library of Congress Cataloging-in-Publication Data

Names: Los Angeles County Museum of Art, author. | Mills, Rosie Chambers. | Tigerman, Bobbye, 1978-
Title: Beyond bling : contemporary jewelry from the Lois Boardman collection / Rosie Chambers Mills & Bobbye Tigerman ; with essays by Helen W. Drutt English, Blake Gopnik, Benjamin Lignel, Rosie Chambers Mills, Bobbye Tigerman.
Description: Los Angeles : Los Angeles County Museum of Art ; New York : DelMonico Books/ Prestel, 2016.
Identifiers: LCCN 2016032913 | ISBN 9783791355627 (hardback)
Subjects: LCSH: Jewelry--History--21st century--Exhibitions. | Art metal-work--History--21st century--Exhibitions. | Boardman, Lois--Art collections--Exhibitions. | Jewelry--Private collections--California--Los Angeles--Exhibitions. | Los Angeles County Museum of Art--Exhibitions. | BISAC: ART / Collections, Catalogs, Exhibitions / General. | ANTIQUES & COLLECTIBLES / Jewelry.
Classification: LCC NK7310.5 .L67 2016 | DDC 739.270740794/93--dc23
LC record available at https://lccn.loc.gov/2016032913

Front cover: Philip Sajet, *Cactus Quadruple* ring, 2003; **Back cover:** emiko oye, *Maharajah's 6th* necklace, 2008; **p. 1 (frontispiece):** Nancy Worden, *Gilding the Past* necklace (detail), 2001; **p. 2 (title page):** Karl Fritsch, ring, 2005; **p. 4 (table of contents):** Gerd Rothmann, *Die Goldene Nase* nosepiece, 1988; **p. 232 (colophon):** Barbara Paganin, *Microftalmo* ring, 1993

Printed and bound in the United States